Holocaust and Memory

Holocaust and Memory

The Experience of the Holocaust and Its Consequences:
An Investigation Based on Personal Narratives

BARBARA ENGELKING

Edited by GUNNAR S. PAULSSON

Translated by EMMA HARRIS

Leicester University Press
London and New York
in association with the European Jewish Publication Society

Leicester University Press
A Continuum imprint
The Tower Building, 11 York Road, London SE1 7NX
370 Lexington Avenue, New York, NY 10017-6503

in association with
The European Jewish Publication Society (EJPS)
PO Box 19948
London N3 3ZJ
www.ejps.org.uk

First published 2001

Originally published in Polish as *Zagłada i pamięć* © Barbara Engelking and
Wydawnictwo IFiS PAN, Warsaw, 1994

Support for this translation gratefully received from the Stanley Burton Centre for
Holocaust Studies, University of Leicester

Introduction and editorial apparatus © Gunnar S. Paulsson 2001

British Library Cataloguing-in-Publication Data
A catalogue record for this book is available from the British Library.

ISBN 0-7185-0159-4 (hardback)

Library of Congress Cataloging-in-Publication Data
Engelking, Barbara, 1962-
    [Zagłada i pamięć. English.]
    Holocaust and memory : the experience of the Holocaust and its
consequences : an investigation based on personal narratives / by Barbara Engelking;
edited by Gunnar S. Paulsson; translated by Emma Harris.
        p. cm.
    Includes bibliographical references and index.
    ISBN 0-7185-0159-4
        1. Holocaust, Jewish (1939-1945)—Poland—Sources. 2. Jews—Poland—
Interviews. 3. Holocaust survivors—Poland. 4. Poland—Ethnic relations.
    I. Paulsson, Gunnar S. II. Title.

    DS135.P6 E5713 2001
    940.53'18'09438—dc21   00-069637

Typeset by BookEns Ltd, Royston, Herts
Printed and bound in Great Britain by Creative Print & Design, Wales

The European Jewish Publication Society is a registered charity which gives grants to
assist in the publication and distribution of books relevant to Jewish literature, history,
religion, philosophy, politics and culture.

Contents

Foreword, *Zygmunt Bauman*   vii

Editor's Introduction, *Gunnar S. Paulsson*   xi

Introduction, *Barbara Engelking*   1

1. The Ghetto, the 'Ayran Side', Concentration
    Camps: Wartime Experiences of Poles and Jews
    Compared   20

2. Daily Life in the Ghetto   81

3. Why Did It Happen?   215

4. The Psychological Consequences of Holocaust
    Experiences   243

5. The Legacy of the Holocaust   304

Bibliography   331

Index   341

Foreword

Zygmunt Bauman

There are many books which try to keep the consciences of the living alert and vigilant by familiarizing them with the sufferings of the Holocaust victims, the cruelty of their persecutors and the callousness of many witnesses to the crime. There are many books which attempt to assure that the perpetrators of the crime and their inhumanity are not forgotten and do not go unpunished or escape condemnation. And there is also a fast-growing volume of books that monitor the success and failure, chances and limitations of both attempts, trying to find out how memory and forgiveness work and how, if at all, events that escape both logic and the expressive capacity of human language may be remembered, told and absorbed. This book does all three things, but it is unlike any book of any of the three categories. This book is, first and foremost, a Herculean effort to reforge the subjective, utterly personal experience of the victims into the joint memory of humanity and so to make the memorializing both feasible and viable, as well as aesthetically potent; a relentless search for a way to express the unshared experience in a form in which it can be shared; an effort to spell out the ineffable, to open the mind and emotions of the readers to an experience which defies reason and transcends the capacity of ordinary pity and commiseration.

The author is a young person born long after the last furnace in Auschwitz had been extinguished. She was not herself marked for extermination, nor was she a child or a relative of the Holocaust victims and so she seeks neither vengeance nor compensation for the sufferings inflicted. No one in her family co-operated with the executioners or their henchmen, and if she feels the need to comprehend that past which was not hers, this is not in order to put the shame for the guilt to rest and to live with the unliveable. She was not a witness to the crime; not a bystander, scarred with the singeing memory of impotence or cowardice. In short, Barbara Engelking has no personal accounts to settle and no axe to grind – just the ordinary, all-too-human urge to take the side of the oppressed, the degraded, humiliated and hunted down, to see the world through their eyes and condemn what they saw for what seeing it had done to them. And her message is directed to people like her. So addressed, the message acquires crucial significance at a time when the executioners are too old to be brought to trial and the victims too old to testify.

The author had set herself a truly daunting task. There is hardly a more formidable challenge to human skills and wits than the need to verbalize a throughly personal, lived-through experience in a way that allowed it to be lived through, vicariously, by those who did not experience it. One of the reasons the author undertook such a harrowing and excruciatingly difficult task might have been her wish to repay the moral debt which all of us, by the very fact of escaping the slaughter, knowingly or unknowingly bear to the victims of the horrifying crime and its incurably wounded survivors. There was, though, another reason as well, and one that seems to loom particularly large among the author's intentions: the recognition that without the understanding of the awesome potential of inhumanity which the experience of the Holocaust threw wide open, our life – the life of all those lucky not to have been ever earmarked for extinction and unscathed by its perpetration, would be both unsafe and ethically flawed. Barbara Engelking speaks on behalf of the victims; but – let me repeat – she speaks to her contemporaries, to people whom the experience of the Holocaust may disclose itself only in the form of other people's memory; and she speaks to them so that these alien memories might become their own.

The book is the product of protracted, laborious and scrupulous research and draws on a most extensive and varied assembly of documents. But the archival evidence, factual accounts and even personal narratives would have remained remote, dry and cold if not for the author's remarkable gift of empathy. Barbara Engelking gives the witnesses of the Holocaust a voice which readers of this book will understand; but also a kind of voice which will make them feel the pain and the torments and the humiliation of the struggle for survival waged by people denied their human dignity. Under her pen, memories come alive again. This book is one long and deep insight into the darkness unrelieved by moral impulse and compassion, and into the horrors of abandonment and of the loneliness that stems from the neighbours' indifference. For that reason, this is a profoundly moral book; and a powerful warning that has lost little if any of its urgency and topicality.

Many a reader would probably regret the spiritual comfort lost in the course of the reading. But that comfort is the last thing which any of us, concerned with making our world hospitable to dignified social life, can afford. Barbara Engelking understood that; and we must be grateful to her for helping us to do the same.

Editor's Introduction

Gunnar S. Paulsson

English speakers with some knowledge of the subject who encounter a book about the Holocaust by a Polish author may tend to suspect the author's motives: is this another shot in the Polish-Jewish polemic of the past fifty years, another attempt to whitewash the Polish record and defend Polish honour against alleged calumnies from abroad? Such suspicions should at once be set aside. Barbara Engelking is not interested in polemics: her intention is not to attack or defend anyone, but to write a serious book about the Holocaust. She is a Polish author writing for a Polish readership, to be sure, and her work is interesting as an example of the new scholarship of post-Communist Poland; but her work also has universal interest and significance.

Universality makes translation possible and worthwhile; but translation is also transplantation, in this case from the Polish discourse to the very different discourse within which these matters are discussed in the English-speaking world. The nature of this Polish discourse will not be familiar to many readers, who will therefore at times be puzzled by the direction that the argument takes. Readers are urged to be patient: they will ultimately see that there is a point to seeing the Holocaust through unfamiliar eyes. But a few introductory remarks may be in order to help understand the nature of Dr Engelking's project.

Polish readers will have been brought up to think of the Second World War above all as a tragedy that befell the Polish nation, with the fate of the Jews in the background. From the point of view of the average Pole the Jews were a national minority, and their fate was exotic, outside the Polish experience, vaguely troubling but of secondary concern. The Holocaust is studied in Polish schools, but in a rather superficial way. This was especially so during the Communist era, when it was characterized as an aspect of the 'anti-fascist' struggle; but the treatment of the subject in contemporary school texts remains far from satisfactory. Engelking's first task, therefore, is to explain to her Polish readers, patiently, how the Jewish experience of the war differed from that of the Poles – not in abstract terms ('Poles were killed in large numbers, but the Nazis intended the complete extinction of the Jews'), but in terms of personal experience and subjective perception. She explains how the Jewish experience was different from that of the Poles, through the eyes of those who underwent that experience rather than from the perspective of the postwar analyst or theorist. As an explanatory device, she hits upon the happy analogy drawn by Roger Caillois between war and feasts in ancient times, both extraordinary periods and experienced as time-out-of-time. (Here a small problem of translation intrudes: the Polish word for feast-day, *'święto',* has the connotation of a 'holy' (*święty*) time, in a way that the English word 'holiday' has lost. A feast-time here means also a holy time.) For Poles the Second World War, a feast-time or holy time in this sense, is recalled as a time of exceptional solidarity, of extraordinary, memorable, historically meaningful events, and also as sacred, a time sanctified by an enormous sacrifice of blood, spilt to defend Poland from her enemies. For the Jews, on the other hand, the war was not a holy but a cursed time, having none of these positive aspects: Jewish blood was spilt, not in defence of the Jewish community, but in the course of its almost complete destruction. Even the acts of armed resistance that took place could not, in the nature of things, have been more than symbolic, in defence perhaps of honour, but without hope of preserving or defending anything else. The Jewish-German war was a one-sided war, a war of the Nazis upon the Jews, whereas the Polish-German war, however unequal, was a war between nations that allowed the Poles to mount a real defence and emerge from it with pride.

All this needs to be explained, not to that dedicated minority of Polish academics who have taken up Jewish history and the Holocaust as their life's work, but to a general readership with limited knowledge and characteristic misconceptions. An English-speaking reader encountering these passages of Dr Engelking's book might be bemused by them, like a spectator to a foreign rite of some kind. But the English-speaker also has much to learn from this comparison of experiences. First, where Poles tend to know little about the Jewish catastrophe, most Westerners know equally little about what befell the Poles during that time. Too often, Western writing about the Holocaust in Poland treats the subject in a vacuum, seemingly assuming that the Poles, on the other side of the ghetto wall, were enjoying a normal, peacetime existence. If relatively few of them extended a helping hand to the Jews, it follows, the reasons must be antisemitism, malice and indifference, rather than terror and the limited possibilities available in a country undergoing a particularly severe form of Nazi occupation. A balanced understanding of what happened in Poland must, without apologetics, take the country's overall conditions into account. Polish readers will do so automatically, and it is instructive to see in what terms Dr Engelking addresses them: this is surely the direction that reasoned discussion will have to take, if the objective is to be mutual understanding rather than confrontation for its own sake.

Unlike the apologists who habitually leap to the defence of Polish honour at any sign of criticism, Dr Engelking does not deny or minimize the extent of the prejudice, ill-will and outright criminality that Jews encountered. She transmits and amplifies, sympathetically and in a matter-of-fact way, the accusations of the survivors whom she interviews. As a Pole speaking to Poles, she does not arouse the defensive reaction inevitable when such accusations are flung at Poland from abroad: her words are received as food for thought, an opportunity to reflect, to rue, to regret. With the end of Communism, Poland has come also the end of the distorted rhetoric, both Communist and anti-Communist, that disfigured the debate over Polish-Jewish relations for so many years. Poland is now free. This means, on the one hand, that antisemites can raise their ugly voices once again – and this is the aspect of freedom that tends to find the headlines in the West – but on the other, that Poland is able to reflect freely on the historical record, revealing of deep flaws as well as heroism, and begin to come at last to a mature rather than a polemical and propagandistic understanding of the past. Though this form of dialogue is still far from universal in Poland, it is surely a step forward.

It is important for the intelligent Western reader to get behind the headlines and understand the nature of the dialogue now going on in Poland: to understand that serious scholarship, free of ideological burdens, is well developed, and that Polish scholars are now both willing and able to make a unique and important contribution to our understanding of the Holocaust and its implications. Engelking is only incidentally interested in Polish-Jewish relations, and not at all interested in defending Polish honour; she is above all a serious, knowledgeable, and sensitive scholar of her subject, whose nationality is irrelevant. It is my privilege, as the editor of this translation, to help bring her work – and with it, current Polish scholarship – to the attention of the English-speaking public.

Dr Engelking contributes many new and original insights into her subject, 'the experience of the Holocaust and its consequences in the light of autobiographical relations'. Not least, she introduces to Western readers a group of Holocaust survivors whose existence is barely suspected in the West – those who, after the war, did not emigrate to Israel or America, but who stayed in Poland, think of themselves as Poles, and have played a full part in the postwar history of the Polish nation. Their perspectives are very different from those of survivors who sought their destiny abroad. They are perspectives well worth the effort of acquaintance.

There were four main streams of Jewish life in prewar Poland: first, the Zionists, who thought of the Jews as a nation deserving, like other nations, of its own homeland; second, the diasporists (Bundists and Folkists), to whom the Jews were a nation of a new, transcendent kind, which should not emigrate but defend its rights in the countries where Jews lived; third, the traditionalists, whose sense of identity centred upon religion and to whom nationalism of any kind was anathema; and finally the assimilationists, 'Poles of the Mosaic faith', to whom the way forward was to emulate their Western coreligionist by adopting the language, culture, and sense of national identity of the country in which they lived, while continuing to adhere to the Jewish faith.

These four streams met with different fates during and after the Holocaust. The traditionalists fared worst: otherworldly and having few contacts with Polish society, they were unable either to escape from the ghettos and survive 'on the Aryan side', or to formulate a coherent response to the atrocious realities with which they were faced. Their response was most often fatalistic, in the spirit of *Kiddush Hashem* (holy martyrdom), and few of them survived. The assimilationists, on the other hand, fared the best, because they had the best prospects of escape and survival outside the Jewish world, and also because they tended to be drawn from the prosperous classes and so to have the economic resources and social contacts needed in any milieu to survive during that time. The non-assimilated Jews who survived the Nazi occupation were mainly those who were lucky enough to survive the camps; smaller numbers survived as partisans, in 'family camps' in the forests, or hiding in strict seclusion.

After the war 300,000 Jews remained in Poland, but most of them were not Holocaust survivors. They had fled to the Soviet Union in 1939–40 and spent the war years there; among them were to be found Jews of all kinds. Therefore all four streams of Polish Jewry came together again after the war; but another sorting-out soon took place. Zionists for the most part went to Israel between 1948 and 1950. Diasporists and traditionalists, on the other hand, tried to form new Jewish communities in the lands which Poland acquired from Germany in the postwar territorial settlement. When these attempts failed, they largely emigrated, either to Israel or to America. Only the assimilationists stayed behind.

It is not surprising, then, that the view of Poland which has become prevalent in the west is the view of Jewish nationalists, whether diasporist or Zionist, and that the voice of those who, after all, followed the same assimilationist course that Jews in Britain or the USA have followed has been drowned out. Yet these are the Jews who know Poland best, not only Poland as it was then, but through all the postwar developments as well. Their voice – certainly critical, passionately and yet dispassionately recording everything bad as well as good in the Jewish experience of those years – is heard in this book, and for the first time is now made available to the English-speaking world. Dr Engelking freely admits that the survivors whom she interviews are not a representative sample of the wartime Jewish community; but they are much more nearly representative of those who survived 'on the soil of Poland', since they are precisely those whom conditions favoured. Theirs is therefore an authentic voice of Jews and Holocaust survivors, the missing middle voice between the accusatory and defensive notes struck by nationalists on both sides. It is these Jews who have the best chance of explaining to a Polish audience the pain, the isolation and the contempt they experienced from their Polish fellow-citizens during that time, and at the same time to a Western audience, which knows little about these things, the friendship, the self-sacrifice, the solidarity of those who extended a hand to help. The Jews who stayed in Poland know Poland well, and they also know the Jewish experience of the Holocaust well: it is they, therefore, who are best placed to act as interpreters, with credibility on both sides, and who can help to end the dialogue of the deaf of the past fifty years.

This is therefore a translation of many kinds: first, of the Jewish experience into terms that a Polish readership can understand; second, a linguistic translation; third, a cultural translation, from the Polish to the English-speaking context. The translation has been ably carried out by Emma Harris, who lectures in English Literature at the University of Warsaw. My own role as editor has mainly been limited to technical and historical matters. I have added some footnotes to explain historical contexts that will be familiar to Poles but perhaps not to English speakers, and here and there I have commented on differences between subjective perceptions and historical reality. It must always be kept in mind that this is not an historical account, but one which explores the psychological and social dimensions of the Holocaust – not the Holocaust 'as it really was', in Ranke's phrase, but as it affected those who lived through it. For example the issue of passivity has been much debated by historians, and readers familiar with this debate may be struck by the seemingly unquestioning acceptance by many (not all) of Dr Engelking's eyewitnesses of the belief that the Jews did not resist. But the question raised in this book has nothing to do with the extent of Jewish passivity or resistance in reality, but rather with the belief, perhaps the self-accusation, of many of the survivors that they did not do enough to oppose the Nazis. This belief coexists with an awareness of the reality of resistance in its many forms, particularly the 'heroism of everyday life', which Dr Engelking has been at pains to document. To forestall possible criticism based on a misunderstanding of the author's intentions, I have, in the appropriate footnote, given a brief history of Jewish resistance during the

Holocaust, and tried to make it clear that self-accusation is unjustified. Nevertheless it is real.

Some technical problems may be noted here. There is much poetry in this book – 'that which is lost in translation' – which Mrs Harris has beautifully rendered into idiomatic English. But some nuances are of course impossible to capture. This is true not only of translation from Polish into English, but also of translation into Polish of many of the sources that Dr Engelking has consulted. A case in point is Emily Dickinson's verse 'After a great pain', a few lines of which, in translation, headed Chapter 4 of the Polish edition. Rendered literally back into English it would go something like this:

> Great pain is replaced by the routine of suffering
> As grass the Grave, so Nerves overgrow convention
> The numbed Heart knows not if it was into him
> that these spikes really stuck. When – Yesterday?
> Or an Age ago?

which serves the purpose at hand. But the original is quite different:

> After a great pain, a formal feeling comes –
> The Nerves sit ceremonious, like Tombs –
> The stiff Heart questions was it He, that bore,
> And Yesterday, or Centuries before?

This is obviously better poetry, but it does not convey the desired meaning; and besides, it is loaded with a Christian allusion (He that bore … Centuries before), lost in the Polish version, that would be inappropriate to the context.

In some cases, nuances have been gained rather than lost in translation. A case in point is Caillois' word *fête*, which as pointed out above has in Polish the connotation of 'holy day'. It is precisely this connotation, impossible to render concisely in English, which has inspired Dr Engelking. The contrast between 'feast time' and 'cursed time' is in Polish, as it were through an enharmonic change, also the contrast between the sacred and the cursed, and is a metaphor that precisely explains the difference between the Polish and Jewish perceptions of war. There are other felicities of this kind.

In editing this translation, I tried at first to find the originals of all the works to which Dr Engelking has referred in Polish translation, so as to avoid double-translation and hence drift of meaning. It is an academic's instinct to get as close to the sources as possible. But in getting closer to the cited originals, as in the examples just cited, we would be getting farther from the material with which Dr Engelking worked. To stay as close as possible to her intentions, it was necessary to stay as close as possible to the sources, not in their original incarnation, but as she had read them. It was obviously not desirable to 'improve' on Emily Dickinson through re-translation, so that in that particular case her verse was replaced, with the author's consent, by a suitable biblical quotation; but in other cases, translation from the Polish versions of cited texts proved to be the best course.

Where standard English translations of foreign language originals are available, these are also often less satisfactory for the present purpose than the available Polish translations. For example, the standard English translation of Chaim Kaplan's diary (Kaplan 1999; originally in Hebrew) omits numerous passages which appear in the Polish translation. In these cases, again, translation from the Polish proved to be a better procedure than trying to refer to the more accessible English versions. This will make it somewhat more difficult, though certainly not impossible, for interested readers to find their way to the *Urtext*; but then it is not really the purpose of this book to serve as a gateway into an existing literature: it is too original for that.

Among the problems in translating the cultural context for the western reader is the apparent exoticism of Polish names. Unfamiliar with Polish orthographic conventions, many readers will for example be baffled by such street names as 'ulica Świętokrzyska', 'ulica Świętojerska' or 'Plac Trzech Krzyży'. In fact they mean, respectively, Holy Cross Street, St George Street and Three Crosses Square. The main intersection in central Warsaw is the meeting of Marszałkowska and Aleje Jerozolimskie – Marshal Street and Jerusalem Avenue (the latter so called because it used to lead to the Jewish quarter, across the Vistula in Praga). The well-guarded boundary between the main ghetto and the Jewish cemetery was, appropriately enough, Trench Street (Okopowa). There are other resonances of this kind. Standing guard just to the east of the ghetto is Iron Gate Square (Plac Żelaznej Bramy), from which Border Street (Graniczna) ran to one of the ghetto gates. The headquarters of the Warsaw Ghetto Uprising was, as many readers will know, at Miła 18; but the irony of this address – 18 Pleasant Street – will be lost on those who do not know Polish.

At first the idea occurred of translating all these names, but this would confuse the many readers who know some of them in their Polish form. Giving translations as footnotes proved unwieldy. The best solution is perhaps to provide a table of a few of these translations for the interested reader, to show their homely character. Here are some of the well-known streets in the Warsaw ghetto:

Ceglana	–	Brick Street
Chłodna	–	Cool Street
Ciepła	–	Warm Street
Dzielna	–	Brave Street
Dzika	–	Wild Street
Gęsia	–	Goose Street
Krochmalna	–	Starch Street
Nalewki	–	Cordials Street
Niska	–	Low Street
Nowolipki	–	New Linden Street
Ogrodowa	–	Garden Street
Pawia	–	Peacock Street
Smocza	–	Dragon Street
Solna	–	Salt Street
Żelazna	–	Iron Street

Other streets are named after persons (Zamenhofa, after Ludwik Zamenhof, the Polish-Jewish inventor of Esperanto), places (Leszno, a nearby town), or local institutions (Bonifraterska, after the monastery of the 'Good Brothers'; Karmelicka, after a Carmelite convent).

Holocaust and Memory consists of an introduction and five chapters. The introduction lays the theoretical framework and introduces Dr Engelking's methodology. The first chapter examines the differences between the Polish and Jewish experiences of the Second World War; the second explores the varieties of Jewish experience, in the three environments in which it was played out: the ghetto, the camps and the 'Aryan side'. The third chapter looks at how the 22 survivors whom Dr Engelking interviewed interpreted their experiences. Chapter 4 is concerned with the psychological consequences of having gone through the experience of the Holocaust, for the survivors and for subsequent generations. The final chapter deals with the social and cultural heritage of that experience. Throughout, the focus is less on historical facts than on subjective experience, as it was played out in the theatre of the mind and the emotions rather than in the real world.

Subjective experience has its limits, but they are limits which humanize and render comprehensible. What was objectively an incomparably worse fate – the complete destruction of the Jewish community in Poland – was for survivors, subjectively, somewhat comparable. Suffering could be compared to suffering, death to death. The Jew on the Aryan side had to maintain a more complicated façade than an ordinary Pole, but the Pole, too, had to live 'by pretence'. The Jew in a concentration camp suffered worse conditions than the 'Aryan' prisoner – but all prisoners suffered starvation, brutality, the threat of death. The one aspect of the Jewish experience that cannot be compared to that of non-Jews was that experience which left no survivors to tell about: the extermination camps and the gas chambers, the murder squads that killed Jews in their millions. Here we are left to imagine. As a subjective experience, to be shot as a Jew by an *Einsatzkommando* or as a Pole by a firing squad was probably much the same thing, and to die from inhaling poison gas was no less terrifying but perhaps less painful than to die of starvation or a beating. It is not in the area of individual, subjective experience that the Holocaust is incomparable to other events, but in the horrible yet objective historical fact of the destruction of an entire people. That people's customs, language and future are gone for ever. Poland was reborn after the war; a new Jewish world was born in Israel, but the thousand-year-old culture of the European *Ashkenazim* died at Treblinka and Auschwitz. Nevertheless not all writing on the Holocaust need be overwhelmed by that fact. Barbara Engelking gives us a book that is scholarly and analytical, allowing for reflection suitable to the magnitude and enormity of the events; yet it is a book which is human in scale, the work of a good and sympathetic listener. It deserves to find a wide readership.

Oxford, January 2001

The poetry of Wladyslaw Szlengel is reprinted by kind permission of the Ringelblum Archive, Poland.

Introduction

Barbara Engelking

> ... nothing more can be attempted than to establish the
> beginning and direction of an infinitely long road. Pretending
> to any systematic and definitive completeness would be, at least,
> a self-illusion. Perfection can here be obtained by the individual
> student only in the subjective sense that he communicates
> everything he has been able to see.
>
> George Simmel

The subtitle of this book is *The Experience of the Holocaust
and Its Consequences: An Investigation Based on Personal
Narratives.*

Why, first, *the experience of the Holocaust?*

I have chosen this subject because of my absolute conviction
that in the twentieth century we have witnessed here in Poland
something unique – something unprecedented in the history
of the world. A feeling of a common responsibility in the
historical sense, and a common heritage in the moral sense, can
be expressed only through attempting to understand what
happened. My book is an attempt of this kind.

Why, secondly, *the consequences of the experience?*

There is no point in locking up the experience of the Holocaust
in the past. In any case, that would be impossible. The events
present too great an ethical and moral challenge for us to ignore
them. The loneliness and suffering of the survivors are too evident
for us to remain indifferent. The Polish national conscience is too
greatly burdened by sins against solidarity, against the common
brotherhood of man, to allow us to remain silent.

Why, thirdly, *on the basis of personal narratives?*

How else can one try to share in other people's suffering
except through the experience of an encounter, an encounter

with the Other in Emmanuel Levinas's sense? This kind of encounter seems to me the only possible way to arrive at an understanding, all the more since the experience of the Holocaust touches on Infinity.

*

Poland has an extensive literature dealing with the war and the concentration camps. Many films and television serials have been made, many books, memoirs, and academic studies written, about the Second World War. Knowledge about wartime experiences is 'a kind of folklore of national memory for us Poles' (Werner 1971, p. 13). In literature and the arts, the dominant mode of portraying the experiences of war is what Andrzej Werner has called 'the martyrological trend'

> by which I mean a certain type of thinking about the events of the last war, and particularly the concentration camps, which is represented in the literature of martyrology. It is also however reflected on a much wider scale – in journalism, through the mass media of radio and television, in hundreds and thousands of lectures and speeches, in the activities of particular socio-political institutions (ZBoWiD),[1] and so on. It forms an integral part of our culture, a model with by no means an insignificant range of influence.

The martyrological formula is emotional, based on value judgements, moralistic: it leaves no doubt about what is good and what is evil. The heroes are mainly crystal-pure, the victims are saintly and the Germans are without exception wicked. As Werner (1971, p. 11) has noted, there is an absence in Poland of serious, non-stereotyped, critical analyses not only of the form of communication of wartime experiences, but also and above all of the wartime experiences themselves. To date, with only a few exceptions, the martyrological formula has obtained – apparently for fear that 'any attempt at dialogue might be seen as sacrilege'.

Without entirely denying the value of, and need for, the martyrological trend in writing and thinking about the events of the last war, perhaps I might be allowed to opt for a less well-represented approach, marked by the names of Tadeusz Borowski, Miron Białoszewski, Primo Levi and others: that of 'moral concern'. This does not portray the experiences of war in black and white terms, does not evaluate and does not pass judgments. It poses questions that are uncomfortable for all of us: questions about obedience leading to participation, about passivity in the face of the annihilation of the innocent, about moral responsibility. All – executioners, victims, witnesses, whose roles can after all be interchangeable – are drawn into the circle of responsibility, for their actions, for the world, for the future of mankind.

Out of this feeling of responsibility that arises from the cognitive perspective of 'moral concern' is born a need to understand the experiences of people who went through the horrors of the war. But to understand in what way? Through the emotions – by empathy, putting ourselves in the other person's position? I fear the imagination cannot stretch so far. Through the intellect, then – by abstracting from individual human stories some essence of wartime experience, by constructing something like Weber's 'ideal type'? I fear this would lead to over-simplification and superficiality. Or perhaps by dissecting the experience of the war into its essential components, so that we could describe the rules that governed the world in those days? But a description of this kind would have to be given in today's language, which is not always adequate, and would in itself constitute some sort of impropriety. And yet, if we want to understand the experiences of the war and their meaning, we have to choose some way forward.

My book is about an exceptional kind of experience of war: the experience of the Holocaust. This experience was the common lot of six million Jews who were killed by the Nazis during the Second World War. Only a few escaped this attempt at annihilation: those who were lucky enough to survive the concentration camps, or those who managed to live under cover 'on the Aryan side'. How many of them were there? Ringelblum estimated that about 30,000 Jews escaped from the ghettos, of whom about half went into hiding in Warsaw (Ringelblum 1988b, p. 9). Postwar estimates by the Jewish Historical Institute suggest that between 50,000 and 60,000 Jews were saved in Poland as a whole. About 300,000 Jews escaped to Russia, and some of them were repatriated to Poland after the war. The majority of these survivors emigrated from Poland, if not immediately after the liberation, then after 1968. At the moment, there are between 4,000 and 5,000 Jews living in Poland. How many of them survived the war in this country? There are about

1,250 members of the Association of Jewish Second World War Ex-Combatants and War Victims, although not all of them fall into the category which is of interest to me here since some of them went through the war in the Soviet Union. Some indication of the size of the group of 'Holocaust survivors' may be gained from the numbers applying for compensation from the Polish-German Reconciliation Foundation. About 800 people have made these applications on the grounds of persecution 'because of race' in camps or ghettos.[2] We have to remember that, for various reasons, not everyone has applied for compensation of this kind, but nonetheless we might take the figure of 800 people as the estimated number of Holocaust survivors currently living in Poland.

I interviewed 22 people who met the criteria which I had established for 'survivors', that is, they considered themselves to be Jews, or Poles of Jewish origin, and for this reason had suffered persecution by the Nazis during the Second World War, which they had experienced as adults or teenagers; and they continued to live in Poland to the present day. This group was fairly specific: it was restricted both territorially and socially.

The territorial restrictions stemmed from the fact that for many reasons I conducted most of the interviews with survivors who lived in Warsaw. It was easiest for me to make contact with these people, and to meet them more than once for conversations that lasted for several hours. I conducted two interviews outside Warsaw: one in Łódź (Mariusz, Interview 18) and one in Gdańsk (Edward, Interview 26). But the fact that most of the conversations took place in Warsaw does not mean that all the people I talked to had been through the Warsaw ghetto. They had survived the war in different places:

- one person had been in the Białystok ghetto (Edward, Interview 26);
- one person had been in the Kraków ghetto, and then Auschwitz (Józef, Interview 36);
- one person had been in the Lublin ghetto and then lived under cover in Warsaw (Iza, Interview 32)
- three people had been in the Łódź ghetto, and then in concentration camps (Arnold, Interview 9; Barbara, Interview 10; Ewa, Interview 17);

- three people had been initially in Russia, and then after Germany invaded Russia they had been in the Warsaw ghetto, later living under cover 'on the Aryan side' (Anna, Interview 27; Irena, Interview 28; Alina, Interview 33);
- ten people had been in the Warsaw ghetto from the time when it was set up, of whom:

    two were deported during the ghetto uprising and survived concentration camps (Rysiek, Interview 11; Marek, Interview 37);

    the remaining eight left the ghetto at varying points and lived under cover 'on the Aryan side' (Adina, Interview 13; Mariusz, Interview 18; Irka, Interview 20; Władysław, Interview 25; Stefan, Interview 29; Helena, Interview 30; Ryszard, Interview 34; Jerzy, Interview 35).

- three people were not in the ghetto: they survived the whole war in more or less intensive hiding in Warsaw or other towns (Andrzej, Interview 22; Tomasz, Interview 31; Anka, Interview 38).

The social limitations of the sample consist in the fact that the majority of the survivors (18 people) that I talked to were people with higher education. This constitutes a diagnostic flaw in my interpretation. In a certain sense, my description of the experiences of the Holocaust and the interpretation proposed by the survivors apply only to the intelligentsia. For many reasons, which I will discuss in Chapter 1, it was easiest for the polonized Jewish intelligentsia to survive. Jews who did not speak Polish, the poor with no financial resources, and the Orthodox Jews who had no Polish friends or acquaintances were in a much worse situation. The only one of the people I talked to whose first language was Yiddish rather than Polish said:

> Very few ordinary people, people of my type, survived. It was easiest for the assimilated Jews to survive. And for the most part they were the ones who wrote the memoirs after the war. I was from a different class – Jewish Jews, not in the religious sense, but the Jewish proletariat. (Edward, Interview 26)

His observation about survivors' memoirs is accurate. Most of these memoirs were written by educated people, who were used to reflecting on their experiences and to an intellectual analysis of the world. Their wartime experiences are the best-known and best-documented, from numerous postwar publications. Why, then, did I not decide on a reinterpretation of the Holocaust on the basis of memoirs? Mainly because they do not answer the questions which I was asking myself and to which I wanted to hear answers from the people I interviewed. A published memoir is a closed entity, subject to the rules of telling history – that is, the rules of the succession of events in time, ordered narrative themes, etc. Most of the memoirs deal only with the period of the ghetto and the war, ending immediately after the liberation. I was however interested both in what happened before that – what was the survivors' background, what views they held, what plans they had had for their future – and what happened afterwards: how they interpreted their experiences, how they lived with them, and how their later lives were affected by them.

From my point of view, spoken testimony has in many ways greater value than the written. It forces the person listening into the role of an active participant in an encounter rather than that of a passive reader. The person who tells the story and the person who listens make a common effort towards mutual understanding, and become participants in a process of establishing meanings. They are able to observe one another's reactions, and where necessary to explain things that are not clear to one or the other of them. The narrator does not have to respect the chronology of events, and often relates them in a different order which suits him better: for example, according to the emotional charge that they carry. The story is not closed and ended, and one can ask the questions to which one is seeking answers, questions that are often fairly personal, and difficult for the person speaking.

Above all, however, direct contact with the person telling the story can be, as it was for me, an exceptionally rewarding experience. I, too, was sometimes overcome by the frequently painful emotions of the people I was talking to, and the suffering they relived as a result of recounting the dramatic events of their story.

Through empathy, which only direct contact could make possible, I was better able to understand the experiences of Holocaust survivors. Although we are often moved to tears or made angry by reading memoirs from the ghetto, that is a completely different kind of identification with the narrator: it is much more anonymous. In direct contact, the quality of identification with the narrator is more profound, and leaves a more lasting impression.

The wish to arrive at a profound understanding of the experiences of the survivors, and my conviction that it was possible to get through to their experiences by an Encounter, dictated the only possible methodology for this study: the biographical method. 'Society is nothing more than a partly ordered synthesis of many individual lives, and every individual attitude and aspiration is a real social force', wrote Florian Znaniecki, the precursor of the biographical method in sociology.[3]

The experience of the Holocaust, which is so difficult and painful to talk about, requires a careful and empathetic listener whose goodwill, assistance and desire to understand ought to make it easier for the narrator to cope with her or his own emotions. This was why my conversations took the form of narrative interviews, and sometimes, when necessary, of clinical or therapeutic interviews.

I accepted the definition of the 'narrative interview' proposed by Norman Denzin (1990, p. 53): that biography presents the experience and definitions of a given individual, a given group of people or a given organization in the way that these individuals, groups or organizations view their experience; that human behaviour must be examined and understood from the viewpoint of those that it concerns. According to Denzin (1990, p. 55), the aim of biographical analysis is to find meaning in the experience of ordinary people. The life stories that we examine bear the hallmark of the historical moment, and therefore meaning takes priority over method in biographical analysis.

Therapeutic intervention was necessary in some interviews because of my assumption that meaning took priority over method. This was an obvious result of the subject matter of the interview: many people, when they recall their sufferings, relive them; it would not be ethical in this situation to create a barrier and leave the narrator alone with revived memories of the past. Confronted by the other person's suffering, the listener must at least attempt to participate in it, and must provide support, creating an atmosphere of trust and understanding. For these reasons, I believe that the only possible way of conducting the conversation is participation and involvement on the part of the researcher; to apply inflexible rules of research to auto-narration would be absurd and immoral, and would moreover make it impossible to obtain credible material.

This kind of interview, which assumes that in order to understand other people's experience it is necessary to establish a good relationship with the subject, also has certain negative consequences. It is, for example, impossible to establish an equally good relationship with everyone. Many factors contribute to this. It might be merely how one feels physically and mentally on a particular day, but there is also that instinctive sympathy or antipathy towards a particular person which constitutes the essence of all inter-personal contact. I do not therefore consider all the interviews to have been equally successful, using as a subjective measure of success the level of profundity and openness of contact between myself and the person I was talking to. In two interviews, I did not really manage to establish a good relationship with the subjects at all. In the remaining twenty, the level and quality of the contact varied, and sometimes also varied from meeting to meeting. This is why the interviews are quoted in the book with varying frequency; the most frequently cited are interviews where I managed to establish a good, or very good, relationship, where during the conversation a kind of bond was forged and a feeling of mutual understanding developed.

How did I find the people I interviewed? I used the method of snowball sampling applied in some sociological research (e.g. Biernacki and Waldorf 1981). In this method, the people investigated create a 'chain of contacts' – that is, every person interviewed arranges contact with the next one, often with someone they know, and so on. This was how I conducted my research. The first people I talked to gave me the addresses or telephone numbers of further people, and these later did the same. Some of the people I talked to were 'public figures', in the sense that they had published their memoirs about the war years, and it was therefore easy to find them. In all, I interviewed 22 Holocaust survivors; six people refused to talk to me.

My contact with the people I interviewed usually took place in three stages. The first stage was when I telephoned (or wrote), introducing myself and explaining that I was working on the question of the Holocaust, and asking to meet them. If they agreed, I arranged the first interview. The second stage was personal contact, and carrying out the interview. Only two interviews were completed during one meeting, while for the rest, there were two, three, four, or even five sessions. I taped the conversations. In two cases, when the person being interviewed did not agree to being taped, I made notes as we went along. The third stage was transcribing the conversation from the tape, and asking the people I had interviewed to expand on or explain certain things (for example, in the case of a poor-quality recording, or surnames or proper names).

The conversation itself took the form of an unstructured narrative interview. I usually first asked my subjects about pleasant childhood memories. They then talked about their parents, grandparents, brothers and sisters, friendships – about the whole of their life up to the outbreak of the war. This extremely interesting material has not, unfortunately, been analysed in the present study, although I intend to make use of it elsewhere.

The second part of the conversation consisted of accounts of events from the period of the war. I tried not to ask too many questions, not to apply pressure and not to force them to give detailed accounts of tragedies. Basically they said as much about their wartime experiences as they themselves wanted, and I did not press them for details.

The third part of the conversation dealt with their postwar lives, work, marriage, their relationships with their children, and also an attempt to interpret and sum up the experiences of their lives. In this part of the conversation, I asked more questions. They were not drawn up as a questionnaire but were spontaneous, and stemmed from the subject matter of the conversation and the problems that the people I was talking to had themselves raised.

Many of the contacts that I made during the research project grew into interesting acquaintanceships, or perhaps I might even dare to say, friendships, which still continue and have given me a great deal of pleasure.

*

My interests in the subject of the experience of the Holocaust evolved considerably during the four years that I was carrying out the research. At first, I intended to talk to the children of survivors and concentrate on the inter-generational communication of these experiences. I carried out sixteen interviews with the second generation (this is why the numbering of my interviews with survivors begins at nine and is not consecutive) before I decided to concentrate exclusively on the experiences of their parents. There were several reasons why I came to this decision.

Firstly, presenting the problems of intra-family transmission would have required deeper case studies, since I observed many examples which did not conform to an established model.

Secondly, for many Poles of Jewish descent born after the war, the year 1968 was the key year in establishing their identity, rather than the family heritage of wartime experiences.[4] To analyse these problems it would have been necessary to conduct many interviews outside Poland, which I was not able to do. Apart from this, a great deal has been written about the problems of the '1968 generation' by Julian Ilicki (1988a) in Uppsala and Małgorzata Melchior (1990) in Warsaw.

Thirdly, because of the advanced age of the majority of Holocaust survivors, interviewing them is a matter of more urgency, for soon there simply will not be any of them left.

I think now that one of my motivations for wishing to talk first to the children of survivors was my fear of dealing directly with such a difficult and painful question. I had a great many reservations of an ethical nature: was it permissible to trouble people who had suffered so greatly in life simply to satisfy my own need to understand? Could one ask them questions which would make them once more remember and relive their suffering? I believe that at first I was afraid of talking directly to the survivors and therefore wanted to arrive at their experiences indirectly – through the accounts of their children. It was only when I found that their children often knew practically nothing about their parents' wartime experiences that I decided to talk to the survivors themselves. I think that many of the people who had not told their children about their own experiences found it easier to talk to someone anonymous, an outsider. The first interviews that I conducted with survivors, and their willingness, indeed sometimes their need, to tell someone about their experiences, broke down my resistance and encouraged me to undertake further conversations. Because my many hours of conversation with survivors produced so much material (the transcripts of these conversations amount to 2,500 pages of typescript) I decided to concentrate exclusively on their experiences.

*

This book has five chapters. Chapter 1 deals with the differences between the war-time experiences of Poles and Jews:[5] in the ghetto, on the 'Aryan side' and in the concentration camps. I have discussed objective differences (legal regulations resulting from decrees of the occupying power) and subjective differences, stemming from the dissimilarity of the wartime experiences of the two nations. On the basis of my material I put forward the hypothesis that at the level of the collective psyche, the situation of the occupation was for Poles dyadic: it was a problem of the relationship between Germans and Poles. The war was – and still is to the present day – seen as a matter between the Poles and the Germans; for the Poles, the problem of the Jews was marginal. From the viewpoint of the Jews, the situation was different. For them, the war was not a dyadic but a triadic experience – a situation of conflict involving themselves, the Poles and the Germans. The Poles, in conducting their war against the Germans, did not need the Jews. The Jews, however, if they wanted to avoid certain death at the hands of the Germans, could not manage without the Poles. They were condemned to suffer their neighbours' charity, pity, decency, hatred, contempt or greed. The relationship was therefore asymmetrical.

In Chapter 1 I also describe the problems that Jews experienced in being 'on the Aryan side': I analyse the catalogue of dangers that they faced and present the verification repertoire, or in other words the store of knowledge and behaviour (like knowledge of the rosary, documents, a 'good' appearance) that was required if they were to exist outside the ghetto. I present the questions of the 'greasy-palmers',[6] of help given to Jews, and the indifference of Poles to their fate.

Chapter 2 is an attempt to reconstruct daily life in the ghetto. Research into everyday life, the most fundamental social experience, is beginning to play an increasingly important role in contemporary sociology. It gives the researcher

> an opportunity to carry out a sociological and therefore academic analysis, which is methodologically and theoretically substantiated, of everything that goes on around us, the world that surrounds us – irrespective of whether the conceptual categories which we intend to use to describe it are reflected in the traditionally accepted categories of what is known as conventional sociology. ... The sociology of everyday life does not constitute a cohesive theoretical standpoint, but consists in bringing together many themes taken from multifarious sources of inspiration. (Zakrzewska 1988, p. 8)

The most frequent sources of inspiration for the sociology of everyday life are symbolic interactionism and ethno-methodology. Disputing the genesis of symbols and meaning, the reality or conventionality of the existence of the social world, both of these approaches inspire multi-thematic and fruitful interpretations of everyday life. I myself find the standpoint expressed by the ethno-methodologists more interesting. This was set out by Alfred Schütz in his essay 'The Enlightened Citizen' (1985), in which he distinguishes three types of knowledge: that of the man in the street, that of the expert, and that of the enlightened citizen. The man in the street lives

> naively, within the internal realities of his own group. ... He treats these as given and does not try to understand their sources or their structure. ... For this reason, among others, his opinions are influenced more by feelings than by information. ... The domain of the expert is a system of imposed realities, imposed by the problem-structure of his field. ... The expert's point of view is not only that the set of problems particular to his field is real, but that it is the only reality. All his knowledge is relative to that frame of reference, established once and for all. ... The domain of the enlightened citizen is an infinite number of frames of reference. In it there are no received and ready goals, no fixed boundary-walls that might offer shelter. The enlightened citizen has to choose his frame of reference according to what interests him; he must investigate areas significant for his interest. ... His posture differs both from that of the expert, whose knowledge is limited by a single system of reality, and from that of the man in the street, who is altogether unconcerned with the

structure of reality. For that reason he must set about constructing rationally-grounded opinions and constantly seek information.

Without attempting to evaluate other people's types of knowledge, but at the same time attempting to see the world with the eyes of an 'enlightened citizen', I try to describe everyday life in the ghetto. The type of material that I have collected dictates a certain type of analysis. The subject matter is mainly the memory of the people I talked to. I have also made use of contemporary material, that is, mainly of memoirs written in the ghetto, or sometimes in a later period. The conceptual categories that I propose in Chapter 2 for describing everyday life in the ghetto are drawn from various trends in sociological and psychological thinking as tools for interpreting as adequately as possible the problems that arise from my analysis of the interviews. I propose fifteen categories in this chapter, which I think enable life in the ghetto to be described. These are: the place; crowding; time; hunger; illness and death; switched-off morality; adaptation; information; mood: between hope and fear; work; study; social and cultural life; social gradations; and the 'Final Solution of the Jewish Question'.

Because the world of the ghetto was entirely different from our own world, it is – in line with the postulates of ethnomethodology and my own convictions – impossible to use the language and categories of peacetime to describe it. I have therefore tried to use contemporary categories in my description of the everyday life of the ghetto.

In Chapter 3 I discuss the interpretations of the Holocaust put forward by the people I talked to. I have sought answers to the questions, 'Why did it happen?' or 'Why was the Holocaust possible?' through breaking them down into questions on the following:

- the causes of Nazism and Fascism;
- the history of the idea of murdering all the Jews, inspired by antisemitism and totalitarianism;
- the obedience of those who carried out the Holocaust, or in the words of Hannah Arendt, the 'banality of evil'; the substitution of executive responsibility for moral responsibility, and inability to place oneself in the situation of the Other;

- the passivity of the victims, interpreted by the people I talked to in categories of the Jewish historical tradition, inability to believe in the Germans' plans, and consequently rational behaviour in an irrational world.[7]

In Chapter 4 I discuss the psychological consequences of wartime experiences, described as 'the experience of mass psychic trauma', 'experience at the limits' or 'extreme trauma'. I present Polish and international research on the subject of Holocaust survivors and former concentration camp prisoners. I attempt to correct certain current stereotypes of the survivor. I discuss questions connected with the specifics of the situation in Poland: the reasons for staying in Poland after the war, for adopting new surnames, and the experience of antisemitism in 1968.

I raise three objections to the image of the survivor portrayed in the literature.

My first objection concerns the non-representative nature of the sample. I am thinking here of the fact that it is mainly 'volunteers' who have been examined, and those who because of their problems have sought professional help. The experience of those who do not want to talk, or who voice no problems, has been entirely ignored by the researchers. Did they experience something different, something more profound and dramatic, do they suffer more? Or quite the opposite – have they cut themselves off entirely from the past, not wanting to speak about it since it no longer holds any significance for them?

My second objection stems from underestimation of cultural differences, resulting probably from the fact that American society did not have direct experience of the war. Perhaps this is why American and international studies have produced an entrenched vision of survivors as victims, which is a research artefact. An important element in this objection is also the underestimation of linguistic differences. In my view, the language of communication is exceptionally important. In what language should accounts of wartime experiences be told? The literature on the subject was written on the basis of communications in various languages. The survivors often had to tell of their experiences in languages which they had learnt only after the war (e.g. English). Could they find the right words in these languages to describe events of which they thought in another language? Were they able to communicate emotions and nuances of meaning, as well as elements of wartime life, in languages which had no words which could precisely convey these meanings? Every language determines an appropriate area of meaning and emotions; it determines ways of naming and communicating the world. It is worth noting that the majority of camp and war memoirs retain German terms and proper names.

I am convinced that it is easier to relate wartime experiences in the language which was used at that time, in which that world was named. For this reason I believe that accounts given by Polish survivors in Polish are more valid, nearer to the inner truth, than accounts given in other languages.[8]

My third objection is that wartime experiences are not differentiated, or in other words that excessively superficial categories are applied: prisoners in ghettos or in the camps and people living under cover 'on the Aryan side' are all described as survivors, without taking into account the fact that such different experiences can have different consequences.

In Chapter 4, I present three short case studies dealing with inter-generational communication of wartime experiences.

In the last chapter, Chapter 5, I consider – in line with the interpretations offered by the people I interviewed – the cultural and social heritage of the Holocaust. I discuss the reasons why these people, often for many years, did not want to talk about their experiences, and the motivations which led them now to decide to do so. I present the problems connected with communicating their experiences: the difficulties of both the narrator and the listener.

At the end of Chapter 5, I describe the Holocaust as a personal experience, an intimate experience which, unfortunately, has changed nothing in the way that mankind thinks and acts, has become neither a lesson nor an obligation. I present Polish attempts to register this experience in the canon of our cultural heritage (for example, the celebrated article, 'A Poor Pole Looks at the Ghetto' by Jan Błoński, and the book *Umschlagplatz* by Jarosław Marek Rymkiewicz), finding that for the time being a choice of this kind can be only an individual choice.

*

In this research I have not tried to achieve the position of a disinterested observer which is postulated by the paradigm of naturalistic sociology. I have been closer to the humanist perspective, which allows the barriers of academic impartiality towards the object of investigation to be broken down. The specific nature of the material that I have been investigating precludes the possibility of keeping one's distance. Research ethics and humility in the face of the enormous suffering of another human being are here at variance with the directive of disinterested observation. Academic distance does not seem to me to be either a necessary or effective route to understanding wartime experiences.

Since, as we know, intellect is not the only channel of arriving at an understanding of reality, it is sometimes desirable to use other means available to us: imagination, intuition, empathy. As I travelled along this route, which was for me the way 'of the heart', I began to observe in myself symptoms of identification with the people I was talking to. At the time when I was conducting the interviews I began to have nightmares about the war. In these, I experienced, often in symbolic form, some of the dramatic experiences of the people I had talked to. I think that these experiences helped me better to understand what – years later – the Holocaust survivors feel, and why they therefore often do not want to talk about their experiences.

*

For five years, I have tried to understand the phenomenon of the Holocaust. At times I have the impression that – for my own personal purposes – I have managed to understand the experiences of the people I talked to. Increasingly often I believe that I am able to imagine what they went through and what they feel now – even though it is impossible to understand their experiences completely. Have I managed to clothe this conviction in words and communicate it? I do not know. This book is an attempt to pass on my inner knowledge.

Notes

1. 'Union of Fighters for Freedom and Democracy', an organization of veterans of Polish regular and underground armed forces in the Second World War, founded in 1949.
2. This information was made available to me by Mr Arnold Mostowicz.
3. J. Chałasiński, *Młode pokolenie chłopów* [The younger generation of peasants] vol. I (Warsaw 1938), introduction by Florian Znaniecki, p. xi. (Editor's note) Znaniecki, regarded as the founder of the school of 'Polish memoir Sociology', is best known in the West for his classic study *The Polish Peasant in Europe and America* (with W.I. Thomas, 1913–18, 3 vols; 4th ed., New York 1974, 2 vols; abridged edition, Champaign-Urbana: University of Illinois Press, 1984).
4. (Editor's note) In 1968, the Communist government in Poland instigated an 'anti-Zionist' campaign, which resulted in the great majority of the Jews still remaining in Poland being deprived of their posts and forced to emigrate.
5. (Editor's note) Persons unfamiliar with the conventions of Polish-Jewish discourse may be surprised by the disjunction between 'Poles' and 'Jews'. Dr Engelking has to this point scrupulously referred to 'Poles of Jewish origin' in order to avoid the appearance of excluding Jews from the national community. But in truth this noble intention cannot be maintained for long, certainly not in the historical context of the Holocaust. Religion, and culture based on religion, has been so much a part of the national self-definition of both groups that neither has ever really felt comfortable with such locutions as 'Poles of Jewish origin' or 'Poles of the Mosaic faith'. Apart from the awkwardness of both phrases, the first implies apostasy and assimilation while the second is inappropriate to secular Jews. The Polish language lacks a blanket term such as 'British' (as distinct from 'English'), or hyphenated expressions such as 'Jewish-American', that might allow ethnic sub-groups to be distinguished while still including them under the national umbrella. It is a sore lack.
6. (Editor's note) People who blackmailed Jews in hiding on the 'Aryan side'; in Polish *szmalcownicy* (singular: *szmalcownik*). As is often the case with slang terms, its origins and precise connotations are uncertain. 'Szmalec' means 'lard', from the German *Schmaltz*. It has been conjectured that they were so called because they 'lived off the fat' of their victims, or were 'greasy types', or could enjoy a fat life because of their unsavoury trade. Ms Harris's translation 'greasy-palmer' is suitably colourful, and as good a guess as any.
7. (Editor's note) As with the other phenomena which Dr Engelking discusses, 'passivity' has to be understood as a psychological construct rather than a historical reality. That Jewish passivity in the face of the Holocaust is accepted as a fact, or perhaps a self-accusation, by her interlocutors should not be taken as implying that it is an accurate historical representation. The belief that victims remained passive or went 'like sheep to the slaughter' has been strongly challenged by historians, and

to the extent that Jews did behave passively it cannot be shown that this was a distinctively Jewish trait. Other victim groups – for example, Soviet prisoners of war and non-Jewish prisoners in concentration camps – were also mistreated and massacred in large numbers with very little sign of resistance, and the entire civilian population of left-bank Warsaw was deported after the defeat of the Warsaw Uprising in 1944 without (for example) any mass attempt to escape. Fortunately, in this case German intentions turned out to be relatively benign.

On the other hand, armed and unarmed resistance in its many forms existed among Jews to at least the same extent as among the Polish population: political parties, newspapers, education, and cultural activities flourished underground in the ghettos, a Jewish partisan movement developed, and armed uprisings took place in more than a dozen ghettos as well as in Auschwitz, Treblinka, Sobibór, and Bełżec death camps. In addition, tens of thousands of Jews managed to escape from the ghettos, deportation trains, and even concentration camps. These Jews lived in hiding 'on the Aryan side', or in 'family camps' in the forests. Many took part in Jewish and non-Jewish partisan movements, joined in the fighting in Warsaw in 1944, and fought with the Polish First Army as it liberated the country in 1944–5.

The accusation of passivity originated with ghetto activists promoting armed resistance; it is found, for example, in the call to arms issued by the Jewish Combat Organization (ŻOB) in Warsaw in January 1943: 'Jews in your masses, the hour is near: you must be prepared to resist, not to give yourselves up like sheep to the slaughter' (AŻIH ARII/333). Ringelblum wrote in anguish, on 15 October 1942:

> Why? Why was there no opposition when the deportation of 300,000 Jews from Warsaw began? Why did they let themselves be led like sheep to the slaughter? Why did it go so easily, so smoothly for the enemy? Why did the perpetrators not suffer even one casualty? Why were 50 SS-men (some say even fewer), with the help of 200-odd Ukrainians and the same number of Letts, able to achieve it so smoothly? (1988a, p.409)

Regrettably, this accusation was also repeated as an anti-Semitic taunt by some Polish sources. Thus the right-wing extremist newspaper *Szaniec*, in a widely-reprinted article, wrote that '[i]f the great majority of the Jews of Europe remained entirely passive when they were killed, so the remnant, in their racially-based materialism, have remained without any motivation to resist' (7 May 1943).

The thesis that the alleged passivity of the Jews was rooted in historical and cultural factors specific to the Jewish community was, however, also put forward by Jewish writers after the war, notably by the dean of Holocaust historians, Raul Hilberg.

As Dr Engelking's interviewee Ryszard notes (Interview 34, cited in Chapter 1, below), resistance in an active sense was limited to a small group while the majority of Jews were preoccupied with staying alive. This was true to a degree among Poles as well, but the problems of survival were much greater and more all-absorbing for the Jews. Since the author's avowed intention is to explore the subjective experience of her interlocutors rather than to document historical reality, the passivity that she discusses is the self-accusation of her subjects, which must be accepted as a social and psychological fact.

8. (Editor's note) The author means, of course, that her subjects and other assimilated Polish Jews can express themselves most comfortably in Polish; this is not necessarily true of Jews who left Poland after the war. The native language of the great majority of Polish Jews was not Polish but Yiddish, in which there is a considerable postwar memoir literature. However, as Dr Engelking has noted, Yiddish-speaking Jews had distinctly poorer chances of survival than the more assimilated Polish speakers. Also by 1939, after twenty years in an independent Polish state, the majority of Polish Jews were bilingual and could speak fluent Polish.

1

The Ghetto, the 'Aryan Side', Concentration Camps

Wartime Experiences of Poles and Jews Compared

[You had to] get used to normal people, simply walking along the street and not creeping along by the walls; get used to not running away at the sight of a German, but to hiding when you saw a face you'd known earlier. Because you never knew who that 'acquaintance' – that person you might have chatted with in prehistoric times in the street or in a café just like one human being with another – might be now. He might still be a human being who was willing to extend a helping hand: there were some like that. He might be human enough to let his eyes slide without recognition over your once-familiar face, and that meant: I don't know you, I don't want to know that you are here, and I won't tell anyone. But he could also be someone who would walk up to you and say, 'Come here, Yid', and hand you straight over to the Germans, or someone who would say, 'Pay me to hold my tongue' and then have the very shirt off your back. All of these things happened. And so there was fear everywhere.

Adina Blady-Szwajger, *Wspomnienia lekarki*
(*A Doctor's Memoirs*)

On 28 September 1939 Warsaw capitulated. On Sunday, 1 October, the Nazi armies entered the city; at 3 o'clock in the afternoon they took over the guard at the City Military Headquarters, after which there was a military parade in Piłsudski Square.

The occupation authorities introduced a whole series of regulations and orders to govern the everyday life of the civilian population. A curfew was imposed, and in December 1939 food rationing was brought in.

In accordance with plans laid even before the capitulation, the Jewish community was ordered to form a Council of Elders, its members to be responsible 'in the literal sense' for carrying out German orders. The engineer Adam Czerniaków was made its Chairman.

On 28 October the Jewish Council of Elders was ordered to draw up lists of all the Jews living in Warsaw; all Jewish bank accounts and deposit accounts were blocked in October, and Jews were forbidden to have more than 2,000 złotys[1] in cash. In November the district commander, Ludwig Fischer, issued a decree on 'the disposal and leasing of Jewish enterprises' and on the 30 November the Nazi-controlled 'reptile' newspaper, *Nowy Kurjer Warszawski*, published the following announcement:

Decree of the Governor of the Warsaw District
on the Jewish Question

From tomorrow, Jews in the Warsaw district will wear distinguishing marks: a white armband with the Star of David.

I decree that from 1 December 1939, all Jews in the Warsaw district over twelve years old must wear a visible mark when outside their homes. For the duration of their visit, this decree also applies to Jews who are only temporarily in Warsaw. For the purposes of this decree, a Jew is:

1) everyone who belongs, or has belonged, to a Jewish religious community organization;

2) everyone whose father or mother belongs, or has belonged, to a Jewish religious community organization.

The mark is to be worn on the right sleeve of outer clothing in the form of an armband, on the outside of which is a blue Star of David on a white background. The white background is to be of the following dimensions: the opposite corners must be at least 8 cm. apart The lines [forming the Star of David] must be 1 cm wide. Failure by Jews to comply with these orders will be severely punished.[2]

On 30 November an order was also issued that Jewish shops had to be marked, and on 18 December that Jewish property was to be registered. In October synagogues had been closed and gathering for prayer in private homes forbidden; on 7 December primary schools for Jewish children were closed. On 26 January

1940, Jews were forbidden to travel by rail, on 27 February it was forbidden to employ Jews in cafés and restaurants, and in March they were barred from entering cafés or restaurants.

In July, Jews were banned from public parks, from sitting down on benches and from walking along the 'better' streets. In mid-1940 Jewish doctors were forbidden to treat 'Aryan' patients, Jews were deprived of the right to practise law and were barred from borrowing books from libraries. In September 1940, they were barred from entering Piłsudski Square, which had been renamed Adolf Hitler Platz.

On 29 September 1940, a 'Jews only' segregated space was introduced on trams; on 31 October Jews were banned from purchasing new stamp series issued for philatelists; on 12 October it was announced that by 15 November all Jews were to move into the area of the newly created ghetto. On 16 November, the ghetto was sealed off from the 'Aryan' side of the city.

From as early as February 1940, Jews had received smaller rations of sugar than Poles, and no rations at all of meat or rye flour (of which the Poles received only small rations). From April 1940, an earlier curfew was imposed for Jews;[3] already, since December 1939, all Jewish men between 14 and 60 had been liable to forced labour.

From this outline summary of the anti-Jewish decrees issued by the occupying authorities we can get some picture of the difference between the legal regulations governing the everyday life of Poles and of Jews. I wish, however, to concentrate not on the objective differences (which is the task of the historian) but on the subjective differences that the people I interviewed talked about. I will try to reconstruct their wartime experiences, the picture of the war and occupation that comes out of their accounts, and is different from the picture of the occupation given by Poles. It is exactly these subjective differences between the two pictures that seem to me the most interesting and worth reflecting on. It was these that, according to the people I talked to, determined their fate during the war, influenced their behaviour at the time, and remained in their memory to the present day.

In order to describe these differences, we have to present models of wartime experience which singled out the Jews from the rest of the population of wartime Poland. I think three such models evolved during the German occupation in Poland: the ghetto, the 'Aryan side', and the concentration camp.

These three model situations cover the full spectrum of differences between Poles and Jews during the Second World War. I will discuss each in turn in this chapter, considering them from the viewpoint of the Jews, in the context of the differences between their experiences and those of the Poles. I have based the account mainly on the interviews that I conducted.

In the discussion I also refer to certain fixed ideas and stereotypes that are widespread in Poland: these are sometimes difficult to put into words, even though they are very common. My interpretations and re-interpretations deal mainly with the Warsaw ghetto, which I treat as a 'model' ghetto; I see it as a place that can provide a representative description of ghettos in general, and of their relationship with the outside world. If some accounts deal with another ghetto, this will be clearly pointed out.

Above all, however, as we begin to consider differences in the way in which the war was experienced and remembered by Poles and Jews, we need to make certain generalizations.

For the Poles, at the level of the collective psyche, the situation of the occupation was dyadic: it was a problem between Poles and Germans.

The Germans were a negative point of reference for the behaviour of Poles during the war, and for the way in which it was later interpreted. This attitude to the Germans – an attitude recreated again and again in Polish history to an invader and occupying power – laid down the canons of morality, patriotism, decency, the rules of the game.

The history of the Second World War is in Poland even now a history that concerns Poles and Germans. This perception of the war has been the logical consequence of centuries of being Germany's neighbour, of the partitions of Poland, and of the very firmly rooted stereotype of the Germans as enemies. The wartime experiences of the Poles during the Second World War were yet another stage in this old conflict. It was something well known, more or less 'accepted', a culturally rooted model of the struggle to survive and retain national identity; it was yet another trial of patriotism, which fitted ideally into the traditional vision of Polish history. From this point of view – which saw the war as a matter between the Poles and the Germans – the problem of the Jews was marginal for the Poles. Absorbed in fighting their own war with the Germans, they experienced it as a test of strength and interpreted it in categories of historic actuality.

Today, with the benefit of 60 years' hindsight, it is clear that what was most new and interesting in this particular war does not fit into the categories used to analyse historic conflicts; new categories have to be found for description and interpretation.

From the point of view of the Jews, the situation looked different. For them, the experience of the war was not dyadic, but triadic: a situation of conflict amongst themselves, the Poles and the Germans. Why? Because already before the war it was a specific characteristic of this particular national minority that, apart from those who had been assimilated into Polish society, the Jews as a whole were outside the framework of the Polish-German conflict (in the same way that they stood outside other conflicts, for example that between the Poles and the Russians). The Jews lived a separate life, closed within the circle of their own tradition, or else torn by the conflict of whether to assimilate (in other words, to renounce their own identity), or to emigrate and look for a friendlier native land, where they would have to construct their identity over again. The role of the 'outsider', whether he is a guest or an enemy, is always different from the role of the host. Jews were to a much greater degree dependent on the Poles – affected by their acceptance or hatred – than were the Poles on the Jews. The relationship was therefore asymmetrical.

The lack of symmetry in this relationship increased dramatically during the war. The Poles did not need the Jews in order to wage their war against the Germans. Meanwhile, the Jews – if they wished to avoid certain death at the hands of the Germans – could not manage without the Poles. They were condemned to suffer the consequences of their neighbours' charity, pity, decency, hatred, indifference or greed. It is because of this asymmetrical dependence on the Poles that I have called the wartime situation of the Jews triadic. Their wartime situation had two points of reference – the Poles and the Germans – while that of the Poles had only one: the Germans.

The differences between the wartime experiences of Poles and Jews resulted not only from differences in their point of reference: there were also differences in the experience of, and sense of, time. Roger Caillois compares war in a contemporary society to feast times in a primitive society. He says that a time of feasting was

> a time of excess, when stocks which had sometimes been saved up for years were squandered, and the most sacred laws, which seemed to be the foundation of life in society, were violated. What was a crime the day before became the rule. New bans replaced the usual ones, and a new discipline came into force, which did not seem designed to remove or tone down intense emotions, but quite the contrary, to provoke them and bring about a state of the highest possible tension. (1973, p. 60)

Caillois later writes of war as a paroxysm in contemporary society, as a threat and disaster, a freeing of the element of death, just as a feast day is a freeing of the element of life and joy. War and feast days are opposed in every detail, and are clearly contradictory in all respects. The point here is not the contradiction in their meaning, but in their dimensions and the function that they perform in the life of the community, the picture that they leave behind in the soul of the individual – in a word, the place that they occupy and not the way in which it comes about. War destroys and completely transforms society, cutting itself off from peacetime by a terrible contrast. It nullifies both anxiety and self-satisfaction; no individual matter can survive it – neither artistic activity, nor happiness, nor even fear. No one can remain on the sidelines and occupy themselves with something else, because war will find employment for everyone. War needs all powers and all energies. The analogy between war and feast days is here total: both feast days and war constitute a break in time in which individuals, each on their own initiative, busy themselves with the most varied undertakings.

War is therefore an experience similar to the experience of the sacrum, an exceptional period. As a kind of time, it is comparable with feasts.

Like feast days, war is also the opposite of the everyday. The continuity of ordinary time is broken, and a new quality of time appears: a mythical, sacral time in which other rules of behaviour apply. One lives in a denser reality; various things take place more quickly; the conventions, manners and social patterns that are essential in peacetime become redundant.

Apart from anything else, war is a time when emotions are experienced more intensely: love, or lasting friendships based on comradeship in arms, are cemented more strongly than any experiences of 'peacetime'. We have to remember that the category of feast time applies to the situation of war, of fighting.

The experience of the occupation is another kind of time. It retains a similar structure – non-continuous, quality time, measured in events, but it does not contain the exaltation and excitement characteristic of periods of fighting. It is time which might be called quasi-feast time, which has certain potential as feast time, and can change into it easily as a result of the external situation (for example, the approaching front, the outbreak of the uprising). The problem of time was noticed and felt already during the war. We can find comments on the specific nature of wartime time in many memoirs. The occupation was a kind of hole in time; it took the life of the individual and of society out of its normal course. Jan Strzelecki wrote about wartime time:

> We experienced time as an area of existence which could soon come to an end. All our lives took place along its edge; every moment, someone fell off. They fell off not only into death – a swift death was one of the nicest of the possible fates –; they fell into torture, into a slow death divided into stages of recurrent torture; they fell into a system of hells, in which great care was taken to deprive death of its normal character. The time we were given, the time that was left to us, was time in which we had not yet fallen into the circle of hells, in which we were still going round the edge, in which we could still bear witness to our choice and our fidelity to it. We were concentrated on this bearing of witness, we had the spontaneity of the asceticism which always accompanies fidelity. Time was given to us not for life, but to bear witness to what we valued more highly. Our attitude to values was permeated by the final nature of the choice.[4]

The necessary pre-condition for certain positive features of wartime experiences is the existence of some group integrated by a common enemy or a common goal. It is this strong feeling of community which is created by war that constitutes its positive social effect, the thing that lives on in the memories of those who took part in it. To a much greater degree than Poles,

Jews were deprived of the opportunities for choice and for bearing witness that Strzelecki writes about. They lived in 'the circle of hells' and experienced daily the torture of dying slowly.

During the war, the Poles undoubtedly experienced a sense of community and brotherhood. Naturally not the whole of society, but certainly the more aware and more patriotically inclined sections of society. And after the war, these experiences – which began with the active resistance groups, the wartime elite – were absorbed by society in general.

The stereotypical image of the wartime experience of Poles is a picture of active struggle against the Germans which was supported and assisted by everyone. This common martyrology, and also the fact that the Germans treated Polish society as a cohesive, hostile monolith, disguised the existence of divisions within the society. The war was for Poles another incarnation of the Roman motto *dulce et decorum est pro Patria mori*.

The stereotypical image of the wartime experience of the Jews is a picture of passivity, isolation, lack of resistance. One of the men I talked to said:

> You know, people often recall the war as something good. War in general. You'll find in literature that war creates certain friendships that would not have been formed in other circumstances. Comradeship at the front, friendships, all mates together. Years later, this is recalled as something good. I think this is true in normal wars. But in that war, there wasn't even that much good.
>
> [On the Polish side there was ...]
>
> Well, yes, on the Polish side. ... There was some of it in the fighting groups, but was there any in society as a whole? Maybe Marek Edelman[5] has some experiences like that from the war. They rescued people from that hospital, hid them, helped. But the people I lived among were different. They weren't people who cared about anything except staying alive. (Ryszard, Interview 34)

For the Jews, the war was not – generally – a time when they experienced a positive sense of community. Their war was not a sacred but a cursed time. Jewish society during the war became unbelievably atomized, fragmented into individuals or individual families, who were concentrated on one, individual goal: to survive. Isolation, hunger and many other factors (which I shall discuss in more detail in the next chapter) led to the shaping of a new quality of war. The Jews did not die for their native land, because it was not a good enough Fatherland (even if they wanted it to be).[6] And so what did they give their lives for? In fact, they did not give their lives: their lives were taken from them.

The German-Jewish war was the first war of a new type, which was not 'a paroxysm of contemporary society' as Caillois would have it. While a 'normal' war is – at the same time as constituting a break in the continuity of ordinary time and a change in its quality – a cleansing experience, catharsis, and also the forming of a *sui generis* positive quality, a 'cursed' war contains no positive elements. The ghetto – making reference to models which had been forgotten, but which had once existed in Western civilization – was a new kind of human experience. It was a raising to the macroscale of the experience of being in the absolute power of one's instincts and the power of another human being.

*

Before I go on to discuss the main theme of this chapter – the subjective differences between Poles' and Jews' experiences of the war – I would like to make two further comments.

Firstly, that an attempt to present some kind of logical pattern in such complex and complicated matters leads unavoidably to generalizations. Neither Polish, nor Jewish (nor German) society was uniform. They were torn by inner conflicts, divided by the past and the present (if at least in the dimensions of activity and passivity or living conditions), and by views of the future: they were differentiated in a simply unprecedented way. In wishing to understand and describe wartime experiences, I have to carry out on the one hand certain simplifications, and on the other, generalizations. They are not to the least extent intended as evaluation or judgement.

Secondly, an enormous polarization of attitudes took place during the war. The mythical quality of time, different from the everyday, was reflected in views of the world, and thereby influenced the behaviour of individuals. The world became much less ambivalent than in peacetime – that is, the divisions between good and evil were clearer, the categories of morality and decency became more perceptible. Poles and Jews – like all communities in a similar situation – behaved nobly, basely, or simply tried to survive. Experiences of this kind, which force an individual to make difficult choices, in some sense re-create him. The past, together with its standards and canons of decency, is suspended. No one knows whether someone who has been decent to date will be decent in war time. Human behaviour during the war followed normal patterns: there were many heroes and many despicable characters, but the majority were indifferent. This was also pointed out by some of the people I talked to:

> War, with its denser reality, in a way placed too high a value on moral behaviour. But the breakdown of human behaviour was normal – a few bastards, a few heroes, the majority terrorized. People reacted differently to the fact that they had become witnesses to the Holocaust. This was not true only of Jews, but also of Poles. Some people said, 'Thank God that I was only an accidental witness, that I didn't get into it'. Others said, 'Since I saw it, I have to draw some sort of conclusion, undertake some kind of obligation, for myself'. (Jerzy, Interview 35)

In the ghetto

> I don't know how it happened that in the ghetto someone brought me a bunch of violets; I carried them in my hand, and a little urchin, who would normally have snatched bread from people – nobody of course carried bread where it could be seen, if they had any – snatched them from me, chewed them and swallowed them.
>
> Adina Blady-Szwajger, *A Doctor's Memoirs*

The first decrees of the German authorities showed that the situation of the Jews in occupied Poland would be worse than the situation of the Poles. From the very beginning, it was clear that there was a division of the population in occupied Poland into second-class (Polish) and third-class (Jewish) citizens.

The Nazi plans for the Jews – plans for their 'final extermination' – were, it would seem, carried out in three main stages:[7] identification, marking and deprivation of rights; concentration and isolation; extermination.

The first two stages, with growing German terror and cruelty, were a preparation for the next stage, and constituted at the same time an opportunity for testing out the possibilities of the Nazis' own efficiency and effectiveness in action as well as the reactions of the world to procedures of this kind. The world's silence made possible the next step in the direction of the 'Final Solution'.

I have discussed briefly the process of marking (by armbands)[8] and deprivation of rights at the beginning of this chapter. I would like now to concentrate on the second and third stages of the German plans for dealing with the Jews, and on describing these stages in categories of the differences between Poles and Jews in their experiences of the occupation. I have distinguished three model situations which characterize these experiences: the ghetto, 'the Aryan side' and the concentration camp. I will begin by presenting the subjective experiencing of the first of these situations: the ghetto.

While the everyday terror of the occupation was at the beginning the common lot of Poles and Jews, the extremum of that terror – the ghetto – was an exclusively Jewish experience. The isolation of the Jews in the ghetto had, especially at the beginning, aspects which were subjectively felt to be positive.

> The scattering of the Jews about the world made Hitler's task easier. And he carried it out by using the weapon of fear. That's the basic instrument of totalitarianism. You can do anything in an atmosphere of fear. In the ghetto, in a certain way, there was some kind of comfort in this context. …

> Yes, really – you could be yourself. There wasn't, after all, a German with a rifle standing over everyone. All around there were only Jews, there was a Jewish administration. There wasn't that inner fear of a possible spy. People who were in hiding were much more susceptible to denunciation. (Ewa, Interview 17)

It would seem that German terror in the ghetto functioned differently from that on 'the Aryan side'. The Germans did not bother to search out individuals who were particularly active or dangerous from their point of view. From the outset they had decided to destroy all the Jews, even though it was only the Wannsee conference on 20 January 1942 that determined the time-scale and methods of their physical destruction. However, before the decisions were taken on how to carry out the extermination, the methods of treating the Jews were much less 'sublimated' than those used on the Poles.

Terror in the ghetto was less selective than on 'the Aryan side'. Paradoxically, thanks to this, political parties (obviously, clandestine ones) functioned freely, and underground newspapers were distributed.

> In mid-1940, underground newspapers began to appear in the ghetto. People looked out for them, it seems to me, firstly because of curiosity, and secondly because this was some kind of germ, or perhaps even form, of resistance. (Jerzy, Interview 35)

> The Germans in general carried out those extermination actions on a mass scale. For example, I know amazingly little about surveillance of people who were working in the underground movement. They were going for mass destruction, they didn't put themselves out terribly much. After all, it is all the same how someone like that dies. In the ghetto, underground newspapers were printed, and I was one of those involved in distributing them. ... There was really a great deal of it going on. And it has to be said, for there were so many things to be afraid of, that my parents for example – when I brought them home, they read them. The fear looked different then. (Irena, Interview 28)

The Germans' treatment of the Jews was ruthless, but not always consistent. Regulations were introduced to isolate the Jewish population and to distress it, but nonetheless, the Germans' behaviour sometimes seems illogical. For example, unlike Poles, Jews were not seized for forced labour in Germany.[9] As Adam Czerniaków noted in his diary (Czerniaków 1983, p. 100; entry for 8 May 1940), at one time Poles who wanted to evade compulsory transportation to forced labour wore Jewish armbands. Another example of inconsistency is the fact that almost to the end of its existence telephones were not disconnected in the ghetto, which seems a serious omission in the Nazi policy of isolating and cutting off the ghetto from 'the Aryan side'. Why was this the case? The people I talked to considered this question:

> Apparently it wasn't possible. ... There were telephones for the whole time, through the whole final liquidation action you could talk on the telephone. Maybe it was technically impossible for them, I don't know. After all, they had their own command post in the ghetto and they had that Judenrat. ... I don't know, evidently it didn't enter their

heads, or else. ... These were people condemned to death, let them say what they liked – I think that was the point. (Anna, Interview 27)

Not only did they not disconnect the telephones, but Poles from the 'Aryan' side came in to repair telephone switch boxes. It was a consistency full of holes. ... There were holes of all kinds. [Immediately after the Action] there was water, electricity, gas. Oh, here's an example of the inconsistency that surprised you – the empty half-city had electricity and gas. And for example, I really can't understand why we attended various courses in the ghetto.

[To keep up appearances ...]

After the deportations? After all that, keeping up appearances? It was all very strange. Sometimes they gave a bit more food, sometimes a bit less, they put on one or another kind of show. For example, the SS drove their cars along the pavements, knocking people over or running them over – that kind of game. ... (Ryszard, Interview 34)

Another of the people I talked to spoke about further examples of German inconsistency:

None of us will ever understand that combination of wonderful organization with nonsense. Do you know that hunger in the ghetto really came to an end with the first liquidation action? Why? Because officially the Warsaw authorities did not know that the population of the ghetto had fallen from four hundred thousand to forty thousand. Do you understand? And they went on giving out ration cards for, maybe not four hundred, but perhaps three hundred thousand. Can you imagine? (Adina, Interview 13)[10]

The Germans, by shutting up the Jews in the ghetto, isolating them from Polish society, created for them an illusory sense of safety. Janina Bauman confirms this in her memoirs:

Nazi propaganda [claimed] that Jews carried lice and disease. Thanks to that, the Germans were afraid of us, and rarely made an appearance in the ghetto, unless maybe in armoured cars. This meant that from the beginning we felt safer in the ghetto than before it was set up. And moreover, life in a closed world among people who were uniformly threatened by an external enemy, and the awareness that nobody was alone in his misery, gave the illusory feeling of relative safety.

The specific nature of terror in the ghetto meant that clandestine political parties operated there more freely than on the other side of the wall (some parties from 'the Aryan side', for example, the Polish Workers' Party – PPR – had their printing presses in the ghetto) (Bauman 1989, p. 57). In 1941, the Germans allowed secondary schools to be opened (including separate ones for Catholic converts); clandestine schools had operated even earlier, in which university courses had been taught, including the university medical course; highly varied courses were also organized officially.

The regulations covering cultural and public life were more liberal in the ghetto than on the 'Aryan side'.[11] This both offered the appearance of normal life and maintained an illusory Jewish hope, deceptive but necessary to the Germans in achieving their goals.

The Germans permitted various self-help and voluntary organizations to function fairly freely in the ghetto. Various artistic events took place openly: theatre performances, concerts. A Jewish Symphony Orchestra was formed, whose members included many outstanding musicians of Jewish origin, prewar citizens of Poland and other countries of Europe, who had ended up in the ghetto.

In the repertoire of this orchestra one can find the works of Beethoven, Bach and Mozart (Fuks 1989). The Germans officially gave permission for performance only of 'Jewish music', but they did not specify precisely what this term was supposed to mean. In any event, the programmes of concerts in the ghetto seem to provide yet another example of Nazi inconsistency. Perhaps this inconsistency was also part of the German plan: it served as camouflage, which by creating the appearances of normal life made it more difficult for the Jews to understand their real position and the annihilation with which they were threatened.

The Jews closed up in the ghetto also got some kind of feeling of safety by being isolated from the experience of Polish antisemitism. Some of them, at least at the beginning, accepted the formation of the ghetto with a certain relief. As Ringelblum (1988a) noted, 'The constant uncertainty, the continual threat of being turned out of our homes, has made some people think: it's better to be in a ghetto as long as that lot can't come in' (entry for 9 September 1940).

It seemed at that time that the Jews would be safer if they were isolated from the aggression and excesses were indulged in with impunity not only by the Germans, but also by Poles. One of the men I talked to told the following story about these excesses:

> On the part of the Poles, you met with contempt, jeers. One day, in Rymarska [Saddlers'] Street, I saw how a couple of Jews who'd been commandeered to sweep up the snow were beaten up by some Poles, by some scum. But a man without an armband, with an 'Aryan' face, began to lecture them – that in the name of Christ you shouldn't beat these poor Jews, and so on. I recognized him; it was a doctor I knew from the hospital. A Jew.

> I walked about the streets with an armband and noted the careful looks that certain people gave me. Some of them would help one day, perhaps even save you, others would be greasy-palmers. Some of them were sorry, others had a sense of satisfaction. A lot of them just weren't interested. In the ghetto, you didn't come into contact with Polish antisemitism, and so you weren't afraid of the Poles. It's paradoxical, but that gave you a certain kind of feeling of safety. After leaving the ghetto, fear of Poles flared up again. (Jerzy, Interview 35)

Another of the people I talked to said:

> September came to an end, and the business with the Jews started. A madwoman wandered about in Marszałkowska Street attacking Jews, hitting them and spitting on them. Teenagers as well ... hooliganism. The Germans couldn't tell who was a Jew, but the Poles could tell. And of course you had to wear armbands. Humiliation, being put down, the first bitter experience of our difference, the 'shameful' Star of David. A year later we were shut up in the ghetto. (Helena, Interview 30)

Chaim Kaplan wrote in his diary about the situation of the Jews at the time before the ghetto was set up:

> They hide away in their homes, sitting with closed shutters, and where there are no curtains, they dim the lights. But even then, they are not sure of being safe. Groups of hooligans and petty criminals roam the streets, force their way into houses, and beat people up and loot. Nazi soldiers with their *Volksdeutch*[12] allies honour us with visits in the evenings. Usually one of them threatens us with a revolver and the others carry out a search. ... Friends have stopped calling on one another. Everyone sits in their own closed and unheated flats, buried in depressing thoughts. We sit in penance through the long, sad winter evenings. Death breathes out at you from every dark nook and cranny.[13]

Israel Gutman in his classic study, *The Jews of Warsaw* (1993), writes:

Let us concentrate on events that took place in the streets of Warsaw for many long months. I am speaking here of attacks by groups of Poles on Jewish passers-by or on Jewish flats. The escalation of brutal anti-Semitic excesses in late 1939 and early 1940 was so great that we can without hesitation speak of a wave of pogroms. (p. 52)

The fact that these excesses were inspired by the Germans was obvious, although it was sad that they so readily found people willing to carry them out.

Ludwik Landau,[14] a sharp-eyed observer and chronicler of the occupation, noted on 27 March 1940 (1962 vol. I, p. 368):

Anti-Semitism today is not a natural development – it is quite clearly imposed on us by the Germans, who are trying to blow up the antagonisms between the Christian and Jewish population. Society's guilt, however, if one can talk about guilt at all in matters like this, lies in the fact that it lets itself be too easily drawn into currents of this kind, doesn't stand up to them enough, and the main responsibility for this lies with the *Sanacja*[15] government, which stirred up antisemitism for reasons similar to those of the Nazis.

All the legal restrictions introduced by the Germans were accompanied by the unpunished plundering of Jewish property. The occupying forces went from Jewish home to Jewish home, simply taking what they liked. One of the people I interviewed spoke of this:

The Nazis sometimes came to the flat to steal something or other. At first we sometimes managed to scare them off, but afterwards it became a procedure euphemistically known as requisitioning. And later even this smokescreen was abandoned. (Jerzy, Interview 35)

Stanisław Sznapman wrote in his diary about the treatment of the Jews in the first period of the occupation:

The gendarmes stopped Jews in the street in broad daylight and took everything that they had with them, I mean parcels and money, to the last farthing. ... Then it was the turn of furniture and other Jewish property. Planned and systematic rounds of Jewish homes began, and the stealing of furniture, ornaments, linen. Some of them completely stripped people's flats, others only partly stripped them. The owners of the flats were forced, by threat of a beating, to carry everything out to the cars themselves.[16]

Chaim Kaplan's diary tells of the atmosphere of danger and

worry in the early phase of the occupation when the German anti-Jewish decrees were being issued.

> The repressions are stepped up from day to day, and even from hour to hour. In the current war, there is now a curious lull. Both sides are preparing for the decisive, unprecedented struggle. ... But the war against the Jews is being waged ceaselessly. It is being fought on two fronts. The first takes the shape of legal restrictions imposed on Jews. Every day there is some new anti-Jewish decree or other. ... The second front of attack against the Jews, and this is even more painfully felt than the first, is robbery and plunder and the terror that accompanies it; these robberies are not, admittedly 'legally justified', but they take place with the tacit approval of the authorities. They daily ruin dozens of Jewish families. The shops have already long ago been stripped bare. ... The Nazis burst into houses with revolvers in one hand and riding-crops in the other. At first they came on the pretext of searching for weapons, but later they abandoned all pretence, and now simply come into flats and steal not only jewels and other valuables, but everything that they find: linen, clothes, furs and even furniture.[17]

All these repressive measures, and the anti-Semitic outbursts that accompanied them, were for many a humiliating and painful experience:

> It was a strange feeling for someone who had always walked with his head held high and had felt that he was a citizen with the same rights as anybody else. There was an all-pervading feeling of humiliation, of being debased, which never left you. Every German could hit you, beat you, drive you brutally to forced labour, and you could not make any reply, absolutely no reply at all. This gives rise to the mentality of enslavement – the first and worst effect of German rule.[18]

The above quotations not only show the difficult situation of the Jews even from the beginning of the occupation, but also confirm my interpretation, offered in the first part of this chapter, that for the Jews the Poles as well as the Germans constituted an important point of reference. The growing antisemitism in prewar Poland, the anti-Jewish excesses inspired by the Germans from the beginning of the occupation and in which Poles took part – all this meant that, paradoxically, the Jews could feel safer when they were isolated in the ghetto.

It would seem that aggression by Poles could be in a certain sense more painful for the Jews than the German terror. The relationship between themselves and the Germans was clear – it was a relationship between two enemies: victor and vanquished, the occupying power and the subjected community. Jews expected nothing from the Germans but persecution, trouble and terror. But they wanted to see Poles as comrades, fellow-citizens, united with them against shared oppression. They thought that they were on the same side of the barricades as the Poles, and they expected from them empathy and solidarity. Manifestations of aggression and antisemitism, which clearly demonstrated that there could be no community of fate between Poles and Jews, must therefore have been all the more painful to them.

In discussing the question of isolation, we should mention the Łódź ghetto, which had certain specific characteristics. Łódź was made part of the Reich,[19] and almost all the Poles were deported from the city and re-settled; in their place Germans from the Baltic region were brought in, and the ghetto was therefore more strictly isolated from 'the Aryan side' than elsewhere. Perhaps for this reason, certain developments, including the utopian, 'positive' aspects of isolation, were more evident there than in other ghettos. This was the only ghetto which had its own currency, which was the apogee of the semblance of independent functioning. This, and also the fact that it was in existence for the longest period of time of all the ghettos – until August 1944 – fostered a stronger psychosis of hope than elsewhere. The people I interviewed who had been in the Łódź ghetto talked about this, and one of them dealt with it in exceptional detail. Perhaps I could at this point quote a long extract from this conversation:

> The Łódź ghetto constituted an exception in the whole German ghetto system. It was in existence from December 1939 to August 1944, or in other words for four and a half years. In the early days, it had a measure of autonomy, but in September 1942, it was turned into a slave labour camp. Łódź, which before the war was an exceptional, tri-national, Polish-German-Jewish city, was incorporated during the war into the territory of the Reich. The Poles from Łódź were mainly resettled. Germans were brought in from Volhynia, Estonia and Latvia. They took over all the Jewish flats in Łódź. The absence of any of the pre-war inhabitants of those districts, and the death penalty for leaving the ghetto, meant that it was, practically speaking, isolated from the

rest of the city. As we know, the ghetto had its own currency – 'Rumkies'[20] – which had no value at all outside its boundaries, and therefore could play no role in motivating trade with the ghetto, smuggling. When the 'Rumkies' were introduced, the Jews had to sell all their valuables and money to the ghetto finance office.

In April 1940, Rumkowski made a proposal that production workshops should be set up in the ghetto, and that these would earn the money to provide food for the ghetto. His philosophy of survival was based on the idea that the Jews should make themselves necessary to some extent to the Germans. Various workshops were set up, known as 'resorts': tailoring, shoemaking, metal working, furriery, carpentry, haberdashery, underwear. The German supervisor of the ghetto was a merchant from Bremen, Hans Biebow.[21] He took decisions about everything connected with work in the ghetto – laid down production levels, working hours, provided raw materials and sold the finished goods, and on the whole made a good profit out of it. He also sold food to the ghetto. The value of the foodstuffs bought per head of the ghetto population daily was 30 pfennigs, and the value of production per head daily was 5 marks. It's easy to reckon that the daily profit from the ghetto was two hundred thousand marks! Especially at the beginning of being shut up in the ghetto, there was the illusion of being able to take the initiative oneself. People with some survival skills managed to operate in tune with the rhythm of the ghetto machine. You could try to get an extra ration of soup here, or to get a food coupon, or easier work, there.

People looked desperately for various ways of escape from the threats of everyday life. Rumkowski understood this need and created various illusions of 'normality'. A symphony orchestra was formed, which had a few quite talented soloists. The concerts were enormously popular. The prestige of the orchestra rose further when they got reinforcements in the shape of excellent Western musicians [when German Jews were resettled in Łódź in 1941].

The framework of something like a Resistance Movement took shape, making it possible to meet the need for action and the illusion of offering opposition to the occupying power. Various slogans were coined, for example 'PP' or *'pracuj powoli'* ('work slowly'). People listened to the radio and passed on information. The real or legendary privileges of the ghetto administration were attacked. And apart from that, young people studied, they read a lot.

But it is worth emphasizing that it is to Rumkowski's credit that the Germans really were in a way external to everything that was happening. Rumkowski did not inform the Germans about all this, because if he had done so, things might have ended badly for the leaders, whose names were after all generally known. (Arnold, Interview 9)

It is of course obvious that the positive sides of isolation were illusory, subjective and short-lived. On the night of 17 to 18 April 1942, 52 people were shot in the Warsaw ghetto – mainly political or social activists. This first great act of terror against a particular target showed that the Germans were well aware of what was happening in the ghetto, and that if they wanted they could take effective action. This was also a pre-announcement of the end of the existence of the ghetto, a prelude to the deportations of July to September 1942. But before that happened the Jews had many real experiences that showed that their situation was considerably worse than that of the Poles.

A forceful experience of the difference in their situation had come with the very opening of the ghetto and the order that Jews must move there. The Germans fairly consistently chose to announce decisions at moments that were of fundamental importance to the Jews: usually on religious holidays.[22] The decision to set up the ghetto was announced on Yom Kippur (the Day of Judgement) in the year 5701, or in other words on 12 October 1940. On that day, Chaim Kaplan noted in his diary:

> The Jewish community in Warsaw, numbering almost half a million, did not subtract anything from its prayers and appealed to their Father in Heaven according to the tradition of Israel. But to our great sorrow, when this holy day was drawing to an end and when the gates of tears were still open, we discovered that our prayers had not been answered, because a new decree has been issued, a barbaric decree whose importance and effects go beyond any of the previous repressive measures to which we have already become accustomed. Finally, the decree on setting up a ghetto has been issued. Admittedly, for the time being it is to be an open ghetto, but there can be no doubt that it will soon be closed.[23]

For many of those who felt that they were Polish, or Jews who were assimilated into Polish society, the experience of having an identity imposed on them was a real shock. Only to a few was it obvious from the beginning that they would not go to the ghetto. The typical wartime biography of Warsaw Jews was

either heeding Umiastowski's appeal[24] and going to the East
with the civilian population, and some time later – at the latest
after the outbreak of the German-Soviet war – returning to
Warsaw, to the ghetto; or entering the ghetto immediately, and
later seeking ways of getting out of it. In other towns also the
Jewish population fled to the East in fear of the Germans, later
returning to their homes and then being sequestered in ghettos.
for those who found themselves in Soviet-occupied areas, the
experience of Nazi occupation was delayed until the German
invasion of 1941, when those who survived the accompanying
massacres were forced into ghettos such as those of Vilna or
Lvov. Those Jews who ended up under Soviet rather than
German occupation were treated as Polish citizens – and so
were transported by the Russians along with everyone else to
Siberia or Kazakhstan.[25] From there, some of them got into
Anders's army, and others joined the Polish Army First Corps.[26]
Their fates were, in a manner of speaking, 'typically Polish', since
the Russians in their persecution of Polish citizens made no
distinction between Poles and Jews. The experience of Soviet
camps – unlike that of German concentration camps – was
common to both Poles and Jews.

Meanwhile, under the German occupation, many Jews who
felt themselves to be Poles of Jewish origin, loyal citizens of the
Polish state, Polish patriots were suddenly deprived of membership of this community. They were condemned instead to be
members of another community which for many was alien.
Nothing, for example, linked them with the groups of religious
or Orthodox Jews, while a great deal united them with the Polish
intelligentsia, with Polish culture and literature. They thought,
spoke and often wrote, in Polish; many of them knew no
Yiddish or Hebrew.

> I knew that I was Polish, at home we spoke Polish, I didn't know
> Yiddish. During the occupation, I actually missed knowing Yiddish,
> because when I worked in Centos[27] during the occupation, I needed
> to speak to some parents and children in Yiddish. My colleagues had
> to help me. (Helena, Interview 30)

Some became aware for the first time in the ghetto of being part
of the Jewish community – a community cemented by a tragic
common fate and dramatic experiences.

You see, I don't regret a single day spent in the ghetto. Everything should have happened to me that happened to everyone who lived there. (Helena, Interview 30)

Others, despite the experience of this common lot, or, rather common destiny, did not and still do not feel that they belong to the community. One of the people I interviewed put it as follows:

No, I very definitely don't feel anything like that. As things turned out, we shared a common fate, but what was the community supposed to consist of? Do two pigeons sitting on the same roof form a community? The word ought to have some kind of precise meaning; it isn't a concept that I use. What do we mean by a community of the living and the dead? I don't know. I'm not saying that it doesn't exist, just that I simply don't know. How can one feel communion with half a million people in the ghetto? (Ryszard, Interview 34)

I do not want at this point to enter into a discussion which is to be the subject of another chapter, but merely to indicate that the subjective differences between the wartime experiences of Poles and Jews undoubtedly influenced their sense of identity and affiliation. By German order, the Jews were deprived of the right to make a voluntary declaration of their sense of identity and affiliation, to identify with Polishness.

The frontier between 'the Aryan side' and the ghetto seemed to be a frontier between two different worlds. The people I interviewed spoke about this:

In the evening I went with Szczęsny to Biała Street. This was where the wall of the ghetto stood, but part of it was made of planks. The 'blue' (Polish) police were on duty there, and every now and again – about every ten minutes – a German came up on a motor cycle. I didn't know that inside the ghetto there were Jewish policemen on duty. Szczęsny didn't know either – after all, he had never been in the ghetto. After the German had been, and we knew that he wouldn't come back for ten minutes, we went up to a 'blue' policeman, and Szczęsny said, 'Let this lady go in, her parents are in there!' And the policeman, without asking for any payment, held back a plank and I entered the ghetto.

I can still remember that I had the impression that I was entering hell. It was completely dark, and terribly crowded. I didn't know where I was, what was happening, why people were tugging at my sleeve –

but people simply couldn't see one another. It was a human ant-heap, and completely dark. Thanks to all this, I somehow got past the Jewish policemen and went off. I only asked the way to Leszno Street – it was fairly close by. It was dreadful, that first contact with the ghetto; I've still got the impression in my head. An impression of an inferno, hell, terror. ... being one step from death, something of that kind. (Anna, Interview 27)

A man from Białystok added:

What did the ghetto look like? My God, what a question. ... The Germans didn't set up the ghetto in the district where most Jews lived before the war. They moved Poles out. The Jews had to fence off the area themselves. Even before they opened the ghetto, Jews were ordered to wear emblems on their left breast and on the back of the right shoulder: a yellow star of David. There was an exodus to the ghetto. I was a young man then, amazed that people went voluntarily. Polish hooligans jeered at those people, pulled their beards, pushed them about, kicked their handcarts, so that their few miserable possessions were scattered. ... Living conditions were macabre. Two and a half or three square metres per person. We had the servant's quarters in a shared flat – for six people. My grandfather was already dead, so there was myself, with my mother, my stepfather, my brother, granny and my aunt. (Edward, Interview 26)

The shock of the compulsory move into the ghetto covered a great many matters. First of all, as I have already noted, the compulsion itself, and consequently, isolation from the community of Polish citizens and being forced to live in a new community, of which they had not necessarily earlier felt themselves part. To this were added a great many more shocks in the area of psychological and living conditions, housing, the sudden and radical fall in their standard of living, hunger, and so on.[28]

I will write in the next chapter about everything that happened inside the ghetto walls: about the changing hierarchy of values and social structure, about the need to retain normality, about space, time hunger, illness and death. I would like here only to draw attention to what is apparently a minor difference between the area of the ghetto and the rest of Warsaw: in the ghetto there were no trees, grass or greenery. All the parks and open spaces were outside its walls. You could view them from the bridge over Chłodna Street or from the upper storeys of houses standing beside the ghetto walls. The poet had reason to write:

> I have a window on that side
> an impudent Jewish window
> onto lovely Krasiński park
> with autumn leaves in the rain ...
> In the evening, the dark violet
> branches make a bow,
> the Aryan trees look straight into
> that Jewish window of mine ...[29]

But let us return to the main story, and yet more differences between the war-time experiences of Poles and Jews. For those who left the ghetto, there was a further shock when they returned to 'the Aryan side'.

On 'the Aryan side'

> I was wearing three sets of underwear, a summer costume (a very old one), a 'good' tailored suit and on top of it all a jacket. In my shopping bag, I had some spare shoes (pumps). And a few mementos, pictures and knick-knacks, photographs. A lot of photographs, a few mementos from home – which I was finally to lose in the Warsaw Uprising. My last and only property, the only property that I regret. So I went past the guard, I don't think I was checked, in the crowd, and as soon as I was through, I pulled off my armband. I heard the greasy-palmers 'mewing': that was the way they pointed out potential victims to each other. But I looked them straight in the eye so confidently that no one said anything to me.
>
> Adina Blady-Szwajger, *A Doctor's Memoirs*

A second model experience of the occupation for Jews was being on 'the Aryan side'. Organizing an exit from the ghetto was in itself a difficult and complicated undertaking. It required money (to bribe the Germans) and friends on the other side of the wall who wanted to risk their lives. For as early as October 1941 the death sentence could be imposed for leaving for the ghetto and for extending help to Jewish escapees.[30]

Because they often had to leave their families and friends there, the decision to leave the ghetto was for many of the people I interviewed one of the most difficult decisions they had had to make in their lives. When they had finally made the decision, they again crossed a frontier between two worlds – this time in the opposite direction.

> It was as if I'd entered another world. From that monstrous place where people thought only about death, starvation, and about the whole situation … (Stefan, Interview 29).

> I went along the streets and it was all normal. That was my first impression: normality. A dazed bewilderment. I thought I was a free person. When I looked out of the window in the ghetto at the people on the 'Aryan' side, it seemed to me that they were probably happy. The experience of prisoners … After all, I very well knew what a tragedy was being enacted in Warsaw, throughout occupied Poland. But I carried with me the shadow of the ghetto – starvation, typhus; the shadow of inescapable annihilation. I quickly came to my senses. It proved that when we came out of the ghetto, to pretend that we had the right to live and die on the same basis as any other Polish citizen – then we were not spared new dangers. And they were waiting for me, too: as a Pole, and a person imitating a non-Jew. Behind the ghetto wall, I didn't suffer from the effects of Polish antisemitism, but because of the racial hatred of the Nazis. I became acquainted with antisemitism on the 'Aryan' side: in the street, on trams, in shops. And most of all, I was shocked by the amazing indifference, callousness. It was as though these people lacked some gland or other, depriving them of compassion and imagination. (Helena, Interview 30)

> I went out with a work-gang, that is, with Poles who worked in the ghetto. An obliging friend of mine had sewn a torn cat-skin collar onto my coat, so that my collarless winter overcoat would not catch people's eye. (Alina, Interview 33)[31]

Stefan Ernest wrote in his diary about the dilemma of whether to seek salvation on 'the Aryan side' or to stay and build bunkers in the ghetto:

> There is a dilemma: here or there? Should we build shelters here, hiding-places with supplies to last for weeks, or should we go over the wall? It is an insoluble problem. There, on the other side of the wall, you need money – either money or friends. On that side, one false step, one piece of blackmail, can overturn all the careful planning for hiding for weeks or months. Not to mention more dramatic circumstances. And to leave aside a whole mass of unbelievable difficulties connected with 'getting settled'.[32]

It is banal to say that the position of Jews on the other side of the wall was very difficult during the occupation – much more difficult than that of the Poles. Poles had the support of their friends and neighbours, of 'every stone' in their native towns – while for Jews everything represented a threat. Those who left the ghetto had – after two years of isolation – to get to know their native town afresh.

> I didn't know where I was. I knew Warsaw well, but because of the wall, everything was different, you see. (Anna, Interview 27)

One had to show no surprise at anything, and to keep in line with the wartime Warsaw style. One had to keep clear of pre-war acquaintances, and make sure one's coat had a fur collar. Above all, however, one had to know the whole catalogue of dangers and to have mastered the verification repertoire in force on 'the Aryan side': that is, the repertoire of possible situations one might encounter, and the way to behave in them. Let us spend a moment on this.

In one of the best books that I know about the ghetto, Krystyna Żywulska's *Empty Water*, there is a scene where the heroine after leaving the ghetto gets instructions from the Pole who is helping her:

- If, let's say, a man in civilian clothes and high boots comes up to you in the street and says, 'I believe I've met you before', what do you say?
- I don't remember you at all. And I don't pick people up in the street.
- O.K. But if he follows you?
- Please go away immediately, or I'll call a policeman.
- And if a German in uniform comes up and says, '*Kommen Sie mit*', or '*Sie sind Jüdin*'. What then?
- '*Sind Sie verrückt?*' Are you mad?
- And then what?
- Then ... I laugh as though it was a wonderful joke.
- Good. But the laugh has to be natural. ... Ah – do you know how to say the rosary?
- Stop all this foolery, please. You think that every dangerous situation can be foreseen. But I bet you won't be able to guess the one in which I'll really find myself.
- Say the rosary quickly. (Żywulska 1963, p. 95)

Documents constituted the basic element in the verification repertoire – 'good' false papers, to obtain which you needed a whole chain of well-disposed people. The photograph had to be real, and to that was added an 'Aryan'-sounding name, and a place of birth which the Germans could not check – for example, the Eastern regions of the prewar Republic of Poland, in the period when they were in the hands of the Soviets. Later, this ceased to be safe, since far-off places of birth began to arouse German suspicions. The safest thing was an authentic birth certificate or baptism certificate belonging to someone who had died. This required the co-operation of Poles, and the removal of entries on death from the appropriate registers.

> I went to the parish in Podgórze, to the parish priest, Józef Niemczyński. He'd known me since I was little. I hung about the presbytery, waited till the sexton's back was turned, and then stole several blank birth certificate forms, stamping them with the parish priest's facsimile signature. And I was able to help people who had to hide. Another priest, Stanisław Mazak, wrote out the certificates in Latin. (Józef, Interview 36)

Alongside the documents, it was absolutely essential to be familiar with your new curriculum vitae. The names of parents, brothers and sisters – a whole fictional biography had to be well-learned by heart, so that you did not arouse suspicion in any situation – for example when recalling your mother's maiden name or your own place of birth.

> Then I got papers as I.T. and learnt my new life story. ... (Irena, Interview 28)

Another element of the verification repertoire was verification through Catholicism. This could be carried out by Poles, as well as in direct contacts with the 'blue' police or the Germans. Keeping up the outward appearances of being a Catholic was particularly important for people pretending to be 'Aryans' and living with Poles who knew nothing about their real origins (for example, women working as domestic servants in Polish families). It was obvious that in order not to arouse suspicion in situations like this, they had to know the prayers, the order of the mass, Polish traditions at religious festivals, etc.

I ended up in the Montelupich prison for helping Jews. They had their suspicions that I was a Jew myself as well. They ordered me to say the Rosary and the Ten Commandments. I knew it all.

[How?]

In primary school, when it was cold or rainy, the priest who was taking the catechism didn't send us out of the class, he let us stay. We did our homework, but we heard everything and I had remembered. (Józef, Interview 36)

The problem of checking up on origins via religious faith was obviously linked with the danger which affected all men – the question of circumcision. This was incontrovertible evidence of origins, and it was generally held during the war that it was more difficult to save men on 'the Aryan side' (the first thing that the 'greasy-palmers' usually said to male Jews was 'Drop your trousers!'), that men constituted a greater danger to those who were sheltering them and also for other people who might be hiding.

Attempts were made to remove the visible effects of circumcision by operations, and other explanations were also found:

I said the rosary to confirm that I was a Catholic. But they were clearly suspicious, they called a doctor, who stated that I was circumcised. I began to explain that I had had an operation as a child – what was termed phimosis. It sometimes happens that baby boys are born with a grown-over foreskin which makes it impossible for them to urinate, and in that case the doctor has to carry out a phimosis immediately after birth. The doctor confirmed that this was possible, and I was then put back in the 'Aryan' cell. (Józef, Interview 36)[33]

The third item on the check-list was verification by behaviour. Or, in fact, through a whole series of behaviour patterns in the areas of inter-personal relations, language, ways of expressing oneself, culinary traditions, etc.

It was worth being able to swear idiomatically in Polish, and to sigh, 'Mother of God!' or 'Jesus, Mary!' In general it was necessary to be able to speak Polish well and without an accent, to avoid certain phrases, idioms, or colloquialisms that might be considered typically Jewish.

This danger applied particularly to non-assimilated Jews who up to the war had lived in isolation within their own community, had spoken only Yiddish, had not had any contact with Poles and knew practically no Polish.

> I think a lot of Jews might have been saved if they had spoken Polish better: They could have got out, but that broken Polish that they spoke. ... If they had spoken Polish well, they could have tried. Their poor Polish gave them away. ... I ate *treifes* [non-kosher food] for the first time in my life then when I got out with Kasia on 'Aryan' papers and was to be with a schoolmistress. And she said to me, 'Go and buy a bit of streaky bacon'. I didn't know what streaky bacon was. I knew that it was something you got at a Christian butcher's, but up till then I couldn't even sniff it, we weren't used to it, it had a completely different smell, pork. ... And I ate a piece of bacon for the first time in my life – and I didn't like it, I really didn't. Not until a few days later – because I had to eat it. (Interview with Ms W.)[34]

Control of one's own emotions in situations where betraying them might give rise to suspicions about Jewish origins was also part of the repertoire of behaviour. I will write about this later when I describe the reaction of 'the Aryan side' to the ghetto uprising – but for the moment, a short quotation:

> I rented a room with Mrs R. She had absolutely no idea about my origins. One day she knocked on my door – 'My dear, a terrible thing!' 'What's happened', I asked. 'We've only just got rid of those Jews, and they're already bringing more of them in from Holland'. And I said calmly, 'Don't worry. They're going to Treblinka, to the gas chambers'. (Helena, Interview 30)

Undoubtedly, one of the most important elements of behaviour, which in fact was decisive in being able to survive on 'the Aryan side', was the question of a good appearance. The colour of one's hair, the shape of one's face, and especially the nose, became immeasurably important. Characteristics of one's outward appearance over which one had no influence could now be life and death issues. Everyone who has had anything – even superficially – to do with the problems of the ghetto will immediately understand the key significance of the words, 'to have a good appearance'. The model of survival, that is the form of existence on 'the Aryan side', depended to the highest degree on whether a person 'looked like one' or did not. There were three possible forms of existence on 'the Aryan side':

- a closed hiding place, that is living in a very restricted space (for example, in one room, and in times of danger in a hiding place, a cupboard) without leaving it, without going near the windows, and often even without moving; you were not allowed to walk about, so that the downstairs neighbours would not hear footsteps in an apparently empty house;
- solitary confinement, which meant that you were able to move about relatively freely, but in a restricted space: within one room or flat;
- open functioning, or in other words, normal life, within the restrictions imposed by the verification repertoire, but going about the town, often in order to help other people who were in hiding, as a contact with the outside world for people with a 'poor' appearance.

An underground activist explained:

> We made false documents, we found flats for people with a 'good appearance' who spoke Polish, and also hiding places for people whose speech and appearance were compromising. We paid everyone a monthly allowance of 500 zł. It was a difficult job, and fairly dangerous. (Helena, Interview 30)

All three elements of the verification repertoire (documents, Catholicism and behaviour) were enormously influenced by the psychological attitude of the person in hiding. The tremendous importance of self-confidence, or cheek, can be seen clearly in the passage quoted from Krystyna Żywulska's book. Even with the very best and most authentic documents, you could give yourself away by behaving nervously or uncertainly, or exhibiting a fear that was out of keeping with the situation. And the opposite was also true: even if you did not have the very best possible appearance, you did not arouse suspicion if you behaved quietly and confidently.

> I thought that I looked Jewish, but I was not all that afraid. People sensed Jews because they had fear written all over their faces. I lived for a bit with a woman who sold sausages. And because she didn't want to get up at half past four in the morning, she sent me out with the sausages. Meanwhile, since she was very religious, she prostrated herself and prayed that nothing would happen to me. (Anna, Interview 27)

The verification procedures outlined above could be carried out by other Jews, as well as by Poles and Germans. The danger from the Germans was a danger of the second degree, since they were able to check Jews only indirectly, actually only when they were already in a police station, or in the hands of the Gestapo.[35]

As we know from the literature, and as was confirmed by many of the people I interviewed, the Germans were 'not physiognomists'; unlike the Poles, they could not pick out Jews on the street, they could not tell them from Poles. It was only when someone denounced a Jew and handed him over to the Germans that the Germans could check him out. And so it was those who checked Jews directly that represented a danger of the first degree. Potentially, all prewar acquaintances represented a danger of this kind, if one did not know whether they had resisted the depraving and demoralizing mechanisms of the war.

> I went out in the morning with the gang, that is, to do various jobs on 'the Aryan side' – to be more precise, to a farm where we plucked geese 'for the requirements of the German army'. The farm was run by a German – who I suppose wanted to avoid being called up to the Eastern Front – with the help of a Pole, a *Volksdeutsch* and a Jew. I spent the night there, and the next day, I escaped. I was lucky, because I got a lift from one of my father's patients. Generally, after you'd got past the guards, new problems turned up. Jews were afraid not only of greasy-palmers and people who denounced them for ideological reasons, but also that they would be recognized by acquaintances and that the consequences might be ominous. (Jerzy, Interview 35)

However, undoubtedly the most dangerous of all were those who picked you out in the street, followed you, came to your flat, blackmailed you, robbed you and threatened you: the greasy-palmers. Almost all of the people I interviewed had at least once, and some of them several times, been bothered by these people.

> The German had been bribed. I left normally. Of course, my mistake was the same one that everybody made. It was dark, and I was wearing an awful lot of clothes, which made me terribly noticeable. Well, they caught me at once. They took everything that there was to take and then they let me go. It's one of the greatest humiliations. They didn't have time, but if they had had, then I would have been through something worse. That is, they simply took me into a gateway and undressed me. One of them was clearly going to try to rape me,

but the other one said that there wasn't time. After all, it was very close to the sentries. It was just outside the wall.

Altogether, it happened to me three times. They were Poles, young people. Greasy-palmers. ... Why be surprised – robbing Jews was such an easy way to make a living. There is scum in every nation. After all, there were also Jews who were greasy-palmers; they pointed people out. ... (Irena, Interview 28)

Once in Bielany I met on the tram someone who was in my class at school before the war. He caught my arm and called out, 'I know this Jew'. I hit him on the arm, so that he automatically let go, and I got off. It's a very difficult business. Because during the occupation I didn't personally meet with any ill-treatment from the Germans. Of course, I knew what dangers lay in wait for me. But all the same, when I was walking along the street, I was more afraid that I would meet a Polish greasy-palmer than a German. The great majority of Germans were not what you might call physiognomists. The Germans couldn't tell. As far as the Germans were concerned, I was not afraid – not afraid that they would come up to me and say, *'Jude'*, or something like that. (Tomasz, Interview 31)

Which social groups were the greasy-palmers, and also people who simply denounced Jews, recruited from? What motivated people to take part in these shameful procedures? It would seem that there were six main groups:

1. There were people from socially disadvantaged or semi-criminal groups for whom this was an opportunity to earn some easy money.
2. 'Opportunity makes a thief', or, in other words the above social groups were expanded during the war to include weaker or degenerate people who in peacetime were restrained from crime rather by fear of the consequences than moral considerations. In a situation where for bringing about the death of a fellow human being you could expect a reward (at least in the form of taking from your victim something of material value) rather than punishment, these weak degenerates could form quite a large group.
3. There were people who became greasy-palmers for ideological reasons, people who believed in the racist ideology, identified with the Nazis and had similar motives for wanting to destroy the Jews.

4. People who succumbed to totalitarianism; they did not betray Jews for ideological reasons, or because they believed that the Nazis were behaving correctly, but simply because they were afraid. Like the loyal citizens of any state, they obeyed the laws in force and feared the punishment for breaking them. And since the penalty for helping Jews was death. ...

5. People who were being blackmailed by some third party also betrayed Jews from fear. Sometimes, the Germans promised their Jewish agents that their lives would be spared if they would hand over other Jews who were in hiding.

6. Handing over Jews was also an element in squabbles among Poles. If someone wanted, for example, to get rid of a detested neighbour, or annoy him or take over his property – then the simplest way of attaining his goal was writing a denunciation that the neighbour in question was harbouring Jews (which could be the truth, but did not necessarily have to be).

> There were masses of denunciations. We had contacts in the Post Office, we knew the truth from the people who worked there.[36] They did it because of stupidity, envy that their neighbours were making money – after all, it was not just about Jews – straightforward paying off old scores among Poles. (Helena, Interview 30)

Irrespective of the motives of the greasy-palmer, the effect was unfortunately the same in all cases. It was all the same to the Jews who brought about their death and for what reasons. During the war, the motivations were not so important as the resultant behaviour.

Each of the people I interviewed told me about a range of situations in which chance or misfortune dictated that evil or stupid people brought about someone's death. Equally frequently, however, things were the other way round: good people, chance or a lucky coincidence saved their lives. Greasy-palming was after all only one side of the coin. The other was the help – whether disinterested or not – which was extended by many Poles: by friends, acquaintances and also complete strangers.

And once again, we might consider the reasons why they helped. There were probably four main reason for helping Jews:

1. Disinterested help was extended to people with whom there was some kind of link, for example, prewar acquaintances, friends, neighbours or fellow members of a political party.

2. Disinterested help was also extended to anonymous Jews for reasons of conscience or patriotism. This was treated as a kind of struggle against the Germans – not only opposition to abstract evil on grounds of moral principle, but also the opportunity to oppose concrete decrees of the occupying powers.
3. Interested help was extended as a way of bolstering up a modest wartime budget – and people like this were on the whole loyal to their tenants (often, indeed, the motivation was linked with one of the first two categories).
4. Interested help was extended as a means of making money, of getting rich quickly. Here we come back again to the question of greasy-palmers, since it happened that someone would rent a room to a Jew, demand a higher rent from him in each successive month, and when the tenant had exhausted all his resources, he could be thrown out of the house, or – worse – handed over to the Germans. Then the room would be let to the next one. ...

However, unlike the question of the motivations of the greasy-palmers, to the Jews it was not all the same who helped them and from what motives and in what way. Good is not the obverse of evil: there is no symmetry between the two. One remembers it differently, one speaks about it differently in recalling. We need to remember that in order to save one Jew the co-operation and effort of many people were needed – while to betray him one person was enough.

The subject of the help that Poles gave during the war to Jews has a much larger bibliography than any other theme that I have raised in this study. For this reason, I am not going to devote to it as much space as it certainly deserves. I will limit myself to one or two quotations:

> Not only my friends helped me, but strangers as well. One has to remember that you risked the death penalty for hiding a person of Jewish origin, and despite that 25 or 30 people risked their lives so that I could survive. They included a handful of my friends, but there were also complete strangers, who not only took me in but also fed me. (Władysław, Interview 25)

> I didn't know where to go. I didn't even have an address in my head. Some lad in the forest had given me an address and said, 'You can

definitely go there'. They gave me a packet of lard, so that I could pretend to be a smuggler. I looked absolutely terrible, wearing men's boots, bedraggled and unwashed after three months in the forest. I got onto the train, and some man just stood in front of me and hid me from the view of other people; he asked me whether I needed anything, he gave me some money (I gave him the lard), and afterwards he put me on a tram, standing close beside me all the time and got me to that address. I don't know anything about him. You have to tell people about this kind of thing as well. (Irena, Interview 28)

Apart from these two extremes of 'the Aryan side' – greasy-palming and help – probably the most general everyday experience was the indifference of the Poles to the fate of the Jews. What were the reasons? They can, for example, be interpreted in the categories that I have proposed for experiencing of the occupation: a dyad for the Poles, a triad for the Jews.

Probably the difference between the fate of the Poles and Jews during the occupation, the separate nature of these fates arranged by the Germans, favoured the intensification of indifference. I would however distinguish between exhibited and experienced indifference.

Exhibited indifference was probably above all the product of inability to act, lack of possibility of extending assistance, helplessness, absorbing personal unhappiness. It was a kind of lack of emotion that was also demonstrated by Jews in the ghetto as they passed by the corpses lying in the street.

I heard comments like, 'It's a good thing they're burning them', 'Hitler did the right thing', etc. I met perhaps not with indifference, but with something like – let's cut ourselves off from this, it's too terrible. Do you understand? Perhaps it wasn't indifference, but rather a defence. For after all, what could the man in the street do? (Anna, Interview 27)

Indifference of the kind that Poles exhibited towards the fate of the Jews might also have resulted from their concentration on their own wrongs, from anxiety about the dangers, from lack of imagination. But there was also another kind of indifference – tinged with contempt, a feeling of superiority – which the 'Aryan' sector of Warsaw showed towards the Jews during the ghetto uprising. The Jews on 'the Aryan side', in line with the verification repertoire, not only hid their origins but also their emotions, their pain at the drama of the uprising, in order not to arouse suspicions. They felt that they were linked indissolubly with their dying brethren, while the experienced indifference of 'the Aryan side' deepened their alienation and loneliness. It was one of the most dramatic of their experiences at that time.

It was for me the most painful experience on 'the Aryan side'. It was quite simply a cataclysm. It was the time of the Easter holiday. There were crowds in the streets going on foot to pay visits to their family or friends. I was also going to friends, in Żoliborz.[37] I heard passers-by say, 'The Yids are frying, they're spoiling our holiday, it's because of them that we have to walk'. I felt as though I was walking to Golgotha. People were dying in the flames, and someone could say that they were spoiling the holiday. ... If only even one person had said that it was terrible. I walked and wept. I suddenly realized that I might give myself away. I got a grip on myself. (Helena, Interview 30)

It was one of the most terrible experiences. You had to hide your feelings from your neighbours. In the house at Boernerowa where I was living at that time, the lady of the house had two daughters whose husbands were officers in PoW camps. *Frau Kapitän* and *Frau Major*: they ran the 'Question Mark Bar' in 6 Sierpnia (6 August) Street that was favoured by the Gestapo. These ladies were terribly pleased by what was happening in the ghetto. And when the uprising was crushed, they were among the first to run there to find some loot – vases or God knows what. People said that it was ex-Jewish, or in other words it was going begging. And they went there, for them it was very exciting, you could always find something. (Irena, Interview 28)

I was still in Saska Kępa[38] at that time. My brother-in-law and I were invited out to Easter breakfast. We sat at the table, we shared eggs and from the windows you could see the smoke. Someone said, 'It's the ghetto burning'. At that, the sister of our hostess, who knew who we were, said, 'What a good thing that those Jewish bed-bugs are burning'. I was a bit surprised that she said it in front of us. (Alina, Interview 33)

The one period when the differences between Poles and Jews disappeared was during the Warsaw Uprising. Their fates then ceased to be separate; sometimes, Poles and Jews fought side by side. The Jews came out of hiding, they experienced the same things as all other citizens of Warsaw: they either took an active part in the uprising, or hid themselves in the cellars together with the civilian population.

When the Uprising started, everything changed completely. Because I went out into the courtyard, I went out into the street, and I was just the same as everybody else.

[Did you experience some kind of freedom?]

Yes, yes, of course. Everything changed immediately. (Stefan, Interview 29)

I was living in Koło[39] when the Uprising broke out. My husband was in the Old Town, and so on the morning of 2 August I went there. In the Old Town Square, there were red and white flags; it was an indescribable feeling, a feeling of freedom. I met up with my husband there, we were together and we fought together. He was killed in the Old Town, and I got out - wounded in the leg and head - through the sewers. I was already pregnant. (Anna, Interview 27)

We went on sitting in our flat, right up to 6 August, when our house began to burn. Stasiek ran up onto the roof to put out the fire, which caused an understandable sensation among the neighbours. Later we decided that we had to move out, and we moved to an enormous camp in the region of Ceglana, Prosta and Waliców streets, where there was a camp for several thousand people in the ruins of the old Merchant Company School. There were wells there, and not far away the Haberbusch and Schiele brewery, the Makowski wine business and the Ulrich seed warehouses provided a source of supplies.

['Didn't you think of taking part in the Uprising?']

Look, at that time the goal of our lives was survival, if one of us had taken that decision, he would have risked not just his own life but those of the whole group. If, for example, Stasiek, with his appearance, had volunteered for the Uprising, I doubt whether they would have taken him. We weren't heroes who could do any fighting, but deeply frightened people who were trying to survive. (Alina, Interview 33)

But there were exceptions to this short-lived (barely 63-day) experience of a common lot. Some Jews even then were afraid to come out of hiding, and others were not allowed to fight alongside the Poles.

I couldn't come out, the Uprising caught me on the front line.

[At Aleje Niepodległości 223]

Yes. The Germans burnt that house on 13 August. After a moment I noticed a glow from all sides, down below there were SS-men everywhere. I didn't want to be burnt alive, I swallowed 30 sleeping tablets but they didn't work, they must have been old. ... Well, how could I go out? I was pale as death, I didn't have any documents, only a forged *Kennkarte*.[40] I had a beard, I was dressed in rags, I was unwashed. They would have locked me up at once. (Władysław, Interview 25)

You see, there are some things. ... How beautiful all legends look. We were in Miodowa Street [in the hospital], they came to us from Leszno Street – that is, Marek Edelman, Antek[41], all the staff of the ŻOB (Jewish Combat Organization). They came to us, and they weren't accepted.

[Why?]

Because they didn't want Jews. ... And they went to the A.L. (People's Army[42]). They were in the A.L. It was terrible when they went and we stayed there. It seemed that we'd been through it all together, and that we would never see one another again. (Adina, Interview 13)

The Uprising failed. The Jews, yet once more in the course of this war, were faced with a dilemma: together or separately? To stay together with the Poles, exposing themselves to the danger of being recognized and handed over to the Germans; or – once again alone – to hide in the ruins of Warsaw.

When we realized that the Uprising was going to fail, we had to take a decision about what we would do next. We could either leave with everybody else, or create conditions under which we could stay behind. We were afraid of the Germans, we were afraid that someone would betray us, and so we decided to go on hiding. We prepared a shelter beneath the cellars of the school and we went in there when everyone left Warsaw. What was the shelter like? A normal little room, with a few straw mattresses, a store of food and water. (Alina, Interview 33)

I didn't leave after the Uprising. I stayed in Warsaw. My parents were old, they were Jews, and so it was dangerous; they were old people, and there was no danger of their being taken off as labour, but I was a young man and capable of working, and I was afraid that I would be found out, and then as a Jew I would be executed. And so I stayed in Warsaw from cowardice. I hid in the cellars at 131, 133 and 127 Marszałkowska Street. (Stefan, Interview 29)

*

The fates of Poles and Jews during the Second World War were entirely different. Although both nations were persecuted by the Germans, subjected to daily terror and persecution, nonetheless, from the beginning of the war, there could be no doubt that the Germans were going to treat the Jews differently from the Poles. The objective differences were obvious and are well known; the subjective differences were influenced by many factors that I have tried to describe above. This analysis was confirmed by the third model of wartime experience: the experience of the concentration camps.

In the concentration camp

> I saw chaps who stole a bit of black bread from a fellow-inmate. When a chance of survival depends on a thin slice of black bread like that, when the life of a man hangs on the blackish hair of gluey bread, and to steal that bit of black bread means that you are pushing your fellow-inmate towards death. Stealing that bit of black bread means that you are choosing the death of someone else in order to save your own life, or at least in order to increase the probability of survival. … In a camp a man becomes an animal who is capable of stealing a piece of bread from someone else, thereby pushing him towards death. But in the camp man also becomes an unconquered being who is capable of sharing his last fag-end, his last piece of bread, his last breath in order to bolster up his fellow-beings. That is, it is not in the camp that man becomes this unconquered being. He is already that before. It was a possibility that always existed in his social nature. But camps create extreme situations, in which the division into the human and non-human is carried out more brutally than elsewhere. To tell the truth, we didn't need the camps to tell us that man is a being capable of the best and the worst.
>
> Jorge Semprun, *The Great Journey*

The third model of wartime experience that I have distinguished is that of the concentration camp. Even though this theme is probably the best-known and interpreted exemplum of totalitarianism, it remains one of the greatest intellectual challenges of our century. It will suffice to recall here authors like Tadeusz Borowski or Primo Levi.[43] This approach to the interpretation of Auschwitz involves understanding it as a human existential experience. It is an anti-heroic and antimartyrological approach. It locates evil in the nature of man, rather than outside him: in the Germans or in supernatural forces. It sees the prisoner's experiences as an initiation into evil; the victim and his persecutor are on different rungs of the same ladder which leads towards evil. According to these authors, the concentration camps did not represent an anomaly, a marginal feature in the history of mankind, an evil stemming from outside, but were a consequence and at the same time a product of the disintegration of European culture. Both Borowski and Levi set the seal on this pessimistic view of human nature – the uselessness of Auschwitz, in the sense that it changed nothing – by their own suicide, Borowski in 1951, Levi in 1987. Before his death, and forty years after the war, Levi wrote *The Drowned and the Saved* (1989), summing up his camp experiences; there he confirmed his pessimistic view of human nature and the fact that the world did not react to the experience of the concentration camps. Since, however, a description of the models of wartime experiences would be incomplete without the concentration camps, I will deal with three selected problems linked with this experience.

Reasons for being in a camp

This discussion must begin by recalling the well-known fact that there were two kinds of camp: *Konzentrationslager*, or in other words labour camps (mainly for 'Aryans') and *Vernichtungslager*, or death camps (almost exclusively for Jews). Some camps combined the two functions. Poles who were sent to a camp as a punishment for some form of opposition to the occupation forces, or picked up in street round-ups, were sent to concentration camps. Jews, generally speaking, went to death camps. These camps were the third and final stage of the solution of the 'Jewish question', following the processes of identification and isolation: this was the stage of extermination. It was a logical consequence of isolating the Jews from the rest of society and shutting them up in the ghetto. The differences between a labour camp and an extermination camp, between Auschwitz and Birkenau, were clear to the prisoners there. Tadeusz Borowski wrote:

> They call us 'our colleagues from Birkenau', partly out of sympathy that our fate is so awful, and partly out of shame that theirs is so good. The view from the window is innocent, you can't see the kremos. People are in love with Auschwitz, they say with pride, 'In our place, in Auschwitz ...', and they greatly despise and pity us, people from Birkenau, where there are only wooden stable barracks, no pavements, and instead of bathrooms with hot water – four crematoria.[44]

Auschwitz was designed for labour, Birkenau for extermination. This explains the different living conditions in these camps, even though in both there was the same danger of death, and it was easy to cross the frontier between the two.[45] Nonetheless, the concentration camps offered a better chance of survival than the death camps.

For this reason, for Jews to find themselves in Auschwitz rather than Birkenau was a stroke of luck, like winning the lottery. Many who decided on some form of resistance to the Germans, on conspiratorial activity, knew that their only chance of survival if they were caught was not to reveal their origins. One of the people I interviewed, who was arrested as a Pole, for helping Jews, said:

> What a lot of luck I had in the camp, and in prison, and with other people as a whole. After all, one of my mates might have whispered to someone that I was a Jew, and they could have finished me off. Inside the camp, a Jew had the right to live for only 24 hours. Due to good luck, my fate was that of a normal 'Aryan' prisoner. (Józef, Interview 36)

In the same way, Krystyna Żywulska, whom I have already quoted, was arrested by the Gestapo for acting as an intermediary in procuring forged documents for Jews; at the Gestapo headquarters in Aleje Szucha, she made a great effort to ensure that she was considered to be a Pole, and not a Jew. In her story, *Also From the Theatre*, she described her interrogation:

- – 'What's your name?'
- – 'Żywulska, Krystyna'.
- – 'Place of birth'.
- – 'Łódź', I said, after a moment's indiscernible hesitation. Instinct warned me not to give a place that they couldn't reach during the war. If they can't check your birth records, it always arouses suspicion that the person interrogated is a Jew. In the territory of

the Reich a copy of entries in a parish register could be obtained in a few hours. When I announced Łódź, I wanted to eliminate the possibility of the worst crime of all - origins. Why should they check something that is so easy to establish? Maybe they wouldn't ask for the documents to be sent at all. (Żywulska 1963, p. 151)

In my view, the reasons why people found themselves in concentration camps must be seen as one of the most important differences between Jews and non-Jews. That is, the 'Aryans' (apart from hostages, people from round-ups, etc.) were sent to the camps as punishment, for some more or less abstract crime, mainly for active or passive resistance against the occupying authorities. When they decided on war against the Germans, they had to take into account the consequences of their choice; they had to take into account the possibility of being arrested and sent to a concentration camp. Thus for the majority of non-Jews, as Jorge Semprun maintains,[46] being in a concentration camp was a manifestation of free will, a conscious choice.

The essence of the common history of all of us who have been arrested now in '43, is freedom. ... It was exactly to the degree that we participated in this freedom that we ran the risk of arrest. It is therefore our freedom that we should consider here, and not our state of being deprived of freedom, not the fact that we are prisoners. I am, of course, ignoring the smugglers and underground profiteers. For them, the common essence is money, not freedom.

I am not of course saying that we all share to the same extent in this common freedom. Some - indeed, there are probably a lot like this - share in the common freedom by accident. Maybe they chose voluntarily to join the partisans or the resistance movement, but from that point on, events took over and they lived involuntarily with this act of free will. ... When a German soldier at Auxerre asked, '*Warum sind Sie verhaftet?*' [Why were you imprisoned?] there was only one answer. I am in prison because I am a free man, because it is imperative for me to realise this freedom and because I have accepted the inevitability. (Semprun 1964, p. 47)

One of the reasons for finding oneself in a German concentration camp during the Second World War was therefore that you had manifested free will. The second reason was bad luck, or accident. The third was destiny. For the Jews, unlike the 'Aryans', had no possibility of choice. They were sent to the camps on the basis of a fate decided from above, and not because of the consequences of their own decision. It seems to me that this difference in the reasons why prisoners found themselves there influenced their psychological functioning, their endurance in the camps and their survival strategies. This is confirmed by the American Holocaust researchers George Kren and Leon Rappaport, who found that a factor they called *the illusion of innocence* could, in the case of Jews, have bearing on the passivity of prisoners (1980, p. 74). In line with this theory, the complete innocence of Jews could work against them. In seeking some kind of rational reason for their position, they arrived at illusory conclusions: they decided that their situation was the result of a temporary misunderstanding, which would soon be cleared up. A belief in their own innocence meant that they stood the camp conditions worse than others (than those who were in the camps 'for something'), that they felt sorry for themselves, and so wasted the energy that they needed to survive.

Anna Pawełczyńska, in her exhaustive sociological analysis of the experience of the concentration camp, also mentions understanding the causes of one's own imprisonment as one of the elements influencing possibilities of adaptation, and consequently, survival. She also draws attention to the problem of freedom of choice and its consequences for prisoners.

> Possibilities of adaptation were also influenced by the division of prisoners into those who had found themselves in Auschwitz for fighting against the occupying forces, and those who had found themselves there 'by accident' (e.g. round-ups, hostages, etc.). The first group reacted differently to the camp, being aware of the fact that they were taking the consequences of conscious action. It was, however, more difficult for those who were in Auschwitz by chance to accept their fate – most of them were psychologically unprepared for the terror of the camp. (1973, p. 73)

Strategies for survival

Six of the people I interviewed had been in concentration camps. None of them said that they owed their survival to themselves alone. On the contrary – they all stressed the significance of the help of others. When they considered the reasons why they had survived the camps, they revealed their survival strategies. Basically, they all believed that they had survived thanks to help from others and chance. On the basis of their accounts, it is possible to distinguish two models of camp existence: passive and active.

The passive model consisted in not opposing the camp terror, submission and even inner resignation. Prisoners of this type, like one of my interviewees, M.S., did not try to get extra rations, or help from other prisoners. If someone helped them, it was rather by chance or on the basis of prewar acquaintanceship.

> You were completely passive, you had no influence on what happened and as a result the one way out was somehow to exist with it all. I experienced it fairly passively. I was a prisoner: they transported me here and there, it was a question of living through it. … I tried always to be somewhere in the middle. I remember how they took us in to Majdanek. There were SS-men on both sides of the column who pushed the prisoners on the edges about. I understood then that it was safest in the middle. Later on, whenever possible, I tried to be somewhere in the middle.
>
> Some people somehow looked after me a bit. I remember a doctor who knew my father; he worked in the camp hospital and he looked after me for a few days. Some people went out with the gangs to work outside the camp, and they brought various things back in with them. I worked within the camp, sometimes I helped to hide something, or pass something on, and for that I got something to eat. Apart from that, some people [but not Jews] got parcels from home. I remember that I made friends with a Yugoslav, a very ordinary and good man, who helped me several times, and perhaps even saved my life. … I did nothing myself to save it, I survived by accident. One transport went to the gas ovens, and the other to Majdanek. There was a selection procedure: it was often an accident whether you went to one place or the other. I can't find any reasons why it should have been me that survived, and someone else who died. I can't explain it any other way, there were no rational reasons. I treated it as a cataclysm, a scourge of God, a final annihilation. I simply gave in to what happened to me. (Marek, Interview 37)

The other strategy for survival was an active attitude. Some prisoners, like Ewa or Barbara, believed – often on the basis of earlier experiences in the ghetto – that it was not possible to survive alone. They therefore tried to organize some prisoners' self-help activity, some group or other, which would provide mutual psychological support and whose members would help one another.

> In August 1944, as a result of the final liquidation of the Łódź ghetto, I was transported to Auschwitz. Both in the ghetto and in the camps, I was saved by a lot of people, thanks to the fact that self-help groups formed to support one another, and think out some common tactics for behaviour towards the camp authorities. Straight away, during my first days in Auschwitz, we formed a close-knit, self-help group. At the beginning, there were several of us: children aged 15 to 17, and two older women – I was 38, Sara was 30. I am convinced that the existence of this group saved our lives. In that situation, a lone individual, even if he was not murdered, would not have had a chance of survival. He would have died of hunger, cold, dirt and terror. … In Magdeburg, a few of the children from our group worked in the kitchens. That saved us. They were dressed in working overalls, not rags, and they stuffed their pockets with spare bread and brought it to the block. The children from the other groups did the same – and like ours, they shared the bread with those who didn't work in the kitchens. There can be no doubt that the manager of the kitchens, a German woman, knew well enough what was going on, but she pretended that she didn't notice. (Barbara, Interview 9)

These two strategies for survival, the passive and active strategies, were models of behaviour transferred from a completely different world. They represented rational behaviour, which was often inadequate in the irrational world of the 'concentrationary universe'. In the most general terms, these same strategies for survival could be seen in the ghetto.

The death camps: the final supplement to the Jewish fate

In writing about the camps, it is worth recalling the ways in which the experience differed from that of the ghetto. In a certain sense, the experiences were complementary, because the ghetto was the gateway to the camps. Without the ghettos, and their proven modes of operation, the extermination camps could not in my opinion have functioned so effectively. And if, furthermore, the isolation of the Jews in the ghettos had not been so successful, if this 'test' had not been applied, perhaps the mass extermination would not have taken place, and the camps of the Second World War would have remained simply labour camps.[47]

The extermination camps were a final supplement to the Jewish fate during the Second World War, and were an alternative to existence on 'the Aryan side'. If someone was not able to, or did not want to, or could not manage to organize an escape from the ghetto for himself, he was condemned to transportation to an extermination camp. If he was not designated immediately 'for gassing', but held to be capable of labour before he died, he was directed from the ramp 'to the camp'. In the camp at least four varieties of degradation and reification awaited him:

1. Separation from his family. After leaving the waggon on the camp ramp, the prisoner was separated from his family, and was left alone to face the Nazi machine of terror, with uncertainty about the future, or even the present; his fear and dread were magnified by worry about the fate of his dear ones. This, from the first moments of his existence in the camp, weakened his will to live, and made him defenceless towards the camp. Separating families threw into question the sense of the sacrifices made in the ghetto, the sense of that most basic human community, where love reigns. The most important inter-personal links, which had survived the degrading circumstances of the ghetto, were wiped out.

2. Initiation and reification. A person was deprived of individual characteristics - mementos, hair, his own clothes - and became, in line with the German idea, only a number. Shaved, in striped uniform, all the prisoners looked alike, dehumanized, reified. They found themselves in the sphere of influence of a new hierarchy of values: only things - like, for example, 'old' or 'new' numbers, which indicated the degree of adaptation to the camp and the likelihood of survival - began to count.

3. The anonymity of the camp had one 'advantage' over the functioning of the Jews on 'the Aryan side': here, prewar friendships were no threat - quite the contrary, they represented a chance of survival. Among people deprived of their own families, all elements of even superficial ties

took on a special significance. These elements might consist in coming from the same country or town, or even casual acquaintance from before the war. These things became a pretext for some kind of community, ersatz links, which nullified the anonymity and sense of loneliness.

4. A degradation of inter-personal communication also took place in the camp. Words changed their sense and meaning. The camp language, 'camp esperanto', became a caricature of normal language, a conglomeration of words from different languages, just as the prisoners were of different nationalities. The matter of language was very important, although apparently not fully appreciated by the Poles. As Primo Levi, for example, pointed out, you needed to know German (at least enough to understand the German orders) and Polish (in order to be able to communicate with the predominant group of prisoners)[48] to survive the camp at all. One of the people that I interviewed noted the same thing:

In 1944, they started to bring in transports of Jews from Hungary, 700,000 people. They could have used them for labour. But they murdered them all. And they did it so quickly: in July, August and September, they murdered all those 700,000 people. At that time, when they brought in these Hungarian Jews, plus a few Greek and Dutch Jews, the gas chambers and crematoria were not able to cope with the burning, the destruction, the murder. There was such an enormous quantity of corpses. It was worst for the Hungarians, because they didn't know German, they didn't understand what the Germans were saying to them. They just kept saying, '*Nem tudam Deutsch, nem tudam Deutsch*'. They murdered them like cockroaches, like bedbugs, like locusts. (Józef, Interview 36)[49]

Not only communication, but in general inter-personal relations in the camp were degraded, reified, personal relations were replaced by relationships based on the exchange of goods. All links which did not fit into this scheme of things helped people to survive, provided some hope. All prisoners who were not reduced to a purely biological form of existence, who did not become things in the hands of the Nazis, helped others to retain their faith in the dignity of man.

To end this chapter, I would like to return to more general questions connected with the differences between the wartime experiences of Poles and Jews, and to raise, very briefly, three further problems: differences in experiencing time; life that was not pretence; and different deaths.

Differences in experiencing time

As I wrote at the beginning of this chapter, for the Poles the war was a sacred, heroic, lofty time. For Jews it was a cursed, shaming time. It was not a curse symbolically offering the possibility of penance and purification; it was a final curse of degradation, which offered no possibility of defence or escape. The sign of this curse was 'racial' origins – something very difficult to pin down, which could not be measured in any objective, scientific or physical way.

Both as sacred time and as cursed time, the period of the war in general is marked by irregularity, a change in the rhythm of life and temporal horizons.

The irregularity of time[50] is reflected in the fact that it is not continuous, it is measured by events, and not by weeks or months, which are the calendar of peacetime. The rhythm of life is changed. For example, a new breakdown of time in the day is enforced – if only by the imposition of a curfew. The temporal horizon, which usually comprises some vision of the past, the present, and a prospect of the future, is limited to one single dimension: to the present. The temporal horizon in the future is delineated by the end of the war. The majority of past experiences prove useless and unnecessary, and for Jews in hiding are downright dangerous.

The present of Poles was more capacious than the present of Jews, which was nearer to the limits of the finality of time. The number of threats, dangers and hopeless situations – which I have attempted to describe in this chapter – was greater for the Jews than for the Poles. For example, every encounter with a greasy-palmer could end tragically; revealing one's origins if arrested by the Gestapo could lead to immediate execution or transport to an extermination camp. A Pole arrested by the Gestapo, on the other hand, could count on his family's making attempts to buy him out, or that he might be sprung by his Organization, that he might escape from the transport to the camp, or in the final resort, survive the camp.

Cursed time lies nearer to the very limits of time than sacred time. Cursed time is *saturated with finality*, it is ontological and final – with a specific point of reference. For Jews, this could only be death: their own, that of their family, their community or their nation. Poles had before them – in spite of everything – prospects of life, some kind of 'tomorrow', the time that would come after the war.

It is also worth drawing attention to differences in experience of time in the Uprising of the Poles and the Uprising of the Jews. The Warsaw [Polish] Uprising fitted into a certain cyclicity of the social time of Poles; it is, as Kazimierz Wyka wrote, 'a common historical term in Poland' (Wyka 1984, p. 29). Uprisings represent a model of collective behaviour which is popular in Poland; their time, like the times of struggles and war, is also a model of 'sacred time', which embraces all the positive aspects. Even the traditional endings of uprisings – military defeat – is reinterpreted by both the participants and later generations as moral victory. The Warsaw Uprising, although it was started with major prospects of military success, ended like the rest – in defeat, which was transformed into a victory of ethics over politics.

Uprisings as a noble model of behaviour are also part of the tradition of the Jews. Admittedly, for various obvious reasons, they have had them less frequently than the Poles, but they remember them equally well. The Ghetto Uprising was in a certain sense the quintessence of the idea of an uprising condemned from the outset to failure, the aim of which from the very beginning was exclusively moral, and not military, victory. It was – in line with the interpretation of the wartime experience of the Jews as a triad – collective behaviour that demanded a reaction not only on the part of the Germans, but also of the Poles. It was addressed to the Germans as an expression of courage, aggression and revolt, and to the Poles as a cry for help. But the Poles, in line with their dyadic interpretation of their wartime experiences, did not pay sufficient attention to it. Their own uprising wiped out of their collective memory recollections of the uprising which had been the first to take place in wartime Warsaw. Although in fact, from the point of view of Polish stereotypes, the ghetto uprising was an ideal, indeed model, example of the uprising *à la polonaise*.

Life that was not pretence

The experience of total war was a total experience at the social level, too. People were forced – thanks to a handful of absurd regulations and decrees – to organize their lives around the problem of how to manage, beginning with the problem of acquiring foodstuffs, through a variety of ways of getting round the regulations (fortunately, the Germans were not above taking bribes) – all of this formed a whole which Kazimierz Wyka termed 'life by pretence'. This is how he described a life of this kind:

> A foreign occupation, which receives no ideological or political approval from the human community to which it is applied, becomes a completely curious psycho-social and constitutional fact. Man, as a social being in all his functions, is placed in a peculiar situation. The state organism falls apart. ... Contrasting orders of reality intermingle and up to a point co-exist. The average man has to live, earn his living, fall ill, and procreate in the imposed conditions – while at the same time denying that these conditions have any ideological sense or permanency. ... An occupation is like a bill of exchange which both sides treat as negotiable after a more or less defined period. ... People divide their existence into the apparent and real. They fulfil the basic obligations of their profession, working within the framework of an officially existing society – they make a pretence of living. When they shut themselves up with those closest to them, they really live. For at that time, they are living in the sphere of experiences to which they have expressed their agreement, now and in the future. (Wyka 1984, pp. 8-9)

Social and economic life during the occupation was a fiction in which the Germans also participated. This fiction of course came to an end at the point where real terror began, where people were killed.

The Jews did not take part in this game of living by pretence. They had their own lives, which were not pretence – lives in which everything was real. There was very real hunger and death by starvation, and there really was no way of buying extra food, and no means with which to buy it. And the Germans really without cause shot people in the streets of the ghetto, and the wall was really there. Real death was a lot closer for the Jews than for the Poles. The frontier of finality was so near that it made it impossible to keep up any fiction for long. A make-believe life was possible in sacred time. In cursed time, everything – including life and death – was irreversible and absolutely real.

Different deaths

> Your death and our death
> are two different deaths.
> Your death – is a powerful death
> pulling you to pieces.
> Yours is amidst grey fields
> fertile with blood and sweat.
> Your death – is a death from bullets
> for a cause – for the Motherland.
> Our death is a stupid death,
> in the attic or in the cellar,
> our death creeps out from around the
> corner of the street.
> … Your death – is an ordinary death,
> human and not difficult,
> our death – is a rubbishy death,
> Jewish and nasty.
>
> Władysław Szlengel *Dwie śmierci* (*Two Deaths*)

Comparing the Polish and Jewish experience of the occupation, it is impossible to ignore the differences in the experience of dying. For not only was the life of Jews during the war worse than the life of 'Aryans', but also their death was worse. The Polish death was a martyr's death, heroic; the Jewish death was felt to be shameful and humiliating. One of the people I interviewed put it as follows:

> For a certain time, I was very religious, I prayed that if I had to die, I would die like a Pole, if possible in the Grey Ranks, or something of the kind (after all, I was brought up on the Lwów Eaglets).[51] I felt that I was linked to the Polish side. The Polish side was getting ready to fight, wanted to fight. The Jews just died, they were killed, and I didn't want to be killed.

> [Were you afraid?]

> Very much. Of death and humiliation. Jews died in a way that was humiliating for me; they were killed. I didn't want to be killed. I didn't want to die in that way. It was important to me that if I had to die, it should be like a Pole. Not that I thought that Poles were anything

better than Jews, but ... a Polish death was better than a Jewish death. (Tomasz, Interview 31)

Jorge Semprun wrote about a friend of his, a German Jew who was in the French Resistance:

> Hans said to him: 'I don't want to die a Jew's death, that is, I don't want to die just because I am a Jew'; he couldn't accept that his fate should be written in his body. (Semprun 1964, p. 188)

The problem of a better or worse death is linked with the problem of rivalry in martyrology between the victims. This is a social phenomenon that we can observe post facto, although I do not know whether it was evident during the war. It seems, however, that both Poles and Jews want to have certain exclusive rights over suffering during the Second World War. Both nations count their own sacrifices and announce that they are in the lead, before all other nations. Rivalry in martyrology is linked with the indifference to the sufferings of others that I have already described. Perhaps suffering cannot be ranked and graded, or – as Kazimierz Wyka writes – 'the ability to participate in the suffering of others has certain limits'.[52]

Victor Frankl believed that 'human suffering is similar to the behaviour of gas. When we pump a certain amount of gas into an empty space, the gas fills it completely and evenly, irrespective of the size of the space. In the same way, suffering fills the soul of man and his consciousness, irrespective of whether there is a little of it or a lot of it' (Frankl 1962, p. 50).

Every individual, concentrating on his own suffering, completely filled with it, had no spare place (in his head or heart) to think of the suffering of others. One of the women I interviewed also spoke of this:

> You have to remember one thing.... There is a wise saying – everyone has his own lowest point. The lowest point, as it were, for the 'Aryans' (– I'm using that term deliberately, rather than 'Poles', because we were all Poles – let's say, people who were not afraid because of their origins) – their lowest point was a little higher up. They were afraid of round-ups, bombs – the same fear of bombs, air raids, Germans, the Gestapo, round-ups [as the Jews had]. Here [in the ghetto] the lowest point was even a little further down the scale. But everyone thinks that he reached his lowest point. Everyone thinks that what they went through was the worst of all. (Adina, Interview 13)

Perhaps rivalry in martyrology is a consequence and heritage of totalitarianism. One of the people I interviewed drew attention to this:

> There are things I can't bring myself to say about the Holocaust – [for example] that it cannot be measured against or compared with anything else; because if you are fanatical about that, then you cannot understand smaller misfortunes. A Pole will say, 'You put yourselves forward as the [only] victims, but after all we suffered too, and we would have been next'. But a Jew will say, 'You [dare to] compare yourselves with us! To compare what happened to you with our torment and extermination?' When discussions of this kind get the upper hand, it means that we have forgotten that during the Holocaust one of the most terrible things was competition between victims, just as now you can see rivalry developing between the heirs of those sacrifices. And this is an ominous trap. In 'the time of humiliation', and 'the epoch of the ovens', and in history in general, it led to fighting with each other rather than with the enemy or adversary. Individual people and whole persecuted groups or nations fall into this trap, as though the truth about the mechanisms set in motion by Nazism and other forms of totalitarianism, chauvinism or doctrinal utopianism could not get through to them. (Jerzy, Interview 35)

During the war, as I have tried to show in this chapter, there was no community of fate between Poles and Jews. Perhaps it was exactly this absence of a feeling of community which was one of the causes of a postwar competitiveness about levels of sacrifice. Another interviewee gave a dramatic example of this absence of community:

> Can you talk about a community of fate with the Poles? I'll tell you about something that happened: we were on our way out of the ghetto one time to work. We were walking along in the road, for as you know, Jews weren't allowed to walk on the pavements. I was sixteen years old then. And, lad that I was, I wanted to show off, so I walked along the curb. Suddenly a gendarme seemed to appear from out of the ground in front of me. He took me to the police station and there they gave me a beating with a bull-whip with lead balls at the end. I don't know how many strokes, because I passed out at the ninth. I couldn't walk for two months. And now I'm asking the question: how could I have any experience in common with the people who walked on the pavements? They treated me like a beast because of my origins, not him. (Edward, Interview 26)

Could things have been different? Was any kind of different relations between Jews and Poles during the war possible? Is it not a necessary precondition for an effective totalitarian regime that it should divide society as much as possible? Under the pressure of totalitarianism, highly varied and hitherto very strong links between people were broken. There is therefore perhaps nothing surprising in the fact that links which for a long time had been very clearly strained also broke.

Notes

1. In 1939, one US dollar was worth 2.6 Polish złotys.
2. *Nowy Kurjer Warszawski*, 30.10.1939, quoted in Matywiecki (1994).
3. The history of the curfew in occupied Warsaw strikes me as very interesting. Between September 1939 and July 1944, it was changed 19 times. For Jews, the period under curfew was at first an hour longer, and later, as much as four hours longer.
4. *Próby świadectwa VIII* (*Attempts at witnessing VIII*), in Strzelecki (1989).
5. Commander of the Bundist forces in the Warsaw Ghetto Uprising. Edelman remained in Poland after the war, became a renowned cardiologist, and was a prominent activist in the Solidarity movement in 1981-2. He is the last surviving commander of the Warsaw Ghetto Uprising, and currently lives in Łódź.
6. (Editor's note) The disjunction of which Dr Engelking speaks is characteristic of the German occupation, but not of the September Campaign against Germany, when Jews took a most active part in the defence of their country. Nor is it true of the interlude of the Warsaw Uprising of 1944, when Jews served in Polish units as well as a separate Jewish unit. Throughout the war, also, Jews were to be found fighting in Polish forces abroad.
7. R. Hilberg, the American historian of the Holocaust and author of the classic study, *The Destruction of the European Jews*, distinguishes five stages in the Nazi plans for the extermination of the Jews: identification, expropriation, concentration, deportation, killing.
8. (Editor's note) Occupied Poland was divided into a zone that was incorporated into the Reich (the 'Incorporated Territories') and the 'General Government', ruled from Cracow by the German Governor General, Hans Frank. In the General Government, Jews were required to wear white armbands with a blue Star of David. In the Incorporated Territories, Poles had to wear a rectangular patch with the violet letter 'P' sewn onto their outer clothing and Jews a yellow Star of David bearing the word *Jude*.
9. (Editor's note) Jews were, on the other hand, seized for forced labour in work camps in Poland, where conditions were a good deal worse than those encountered by Poles working in Germany. The conditions in the

Jewish labour camps in no way differed from those in the concentration camps, and the death rate was appallingly high. For an eyewitness account of such a camp, see Huberband (1987).

10. (Editor's note) This description is puzzling. During the Great Deportation in the Summer of 1942, which reduced the official population of the ghetto from 350,000 to 35,000 (with perhaps another 25,000 'illegal' or 'wild' Jews), the Warsaw ghetto was converted into a series of labour camps or 'shops' (the English word was used) and passed from civilian to SS jurisdiction. At this point, the authority that controlled all official economic transactions between the ghetto and the outside world, called the *Transferstelle*, ceased to exist, and the Jewish Council, which had distributed food imported through the *Transferstelle* according to a system of ration cards, lost most of its authority. Food importation and distribution were henceforth the responsibility of the owners of the various 'shops' and of the *Werterfassung*, an SS agency that employed Jewish labourers. The rationing system became superfluous at this point, and no new ration cards were issued. Contemporary sources do record hunger during this period; for example, Abraham Lewin (1990) wrote in his diary on 27 November 1943:

> The issue of survival, that is, the question of bread, is a very pressing one in the ghetto. Those who work in the factories or for the Germans ... receive a quarter or half a kilo of bread and one or two portions of soup six times a week. No working person can live on this. ...

Lewin (1990, p. 217) added that the 'illegal' Jews, if they were unable to live by smuggling and selling goods on the black market, 'simply do not have a crust to bite on'.

The witness was perhaps associated with the small circle around the Jewish Council, which had its own food supplies.

11. This hypothesis is supported by Szarota (1978, p. 5). Discussing various categories of occupation legislation, Szarota writes: 'Repressive, segregational, expropriational, practical and economic legislation was harsher in relation to Jews than to Poles; regulations governing public and cultural life were probably a little more liberal.'

12. (Editor's note) Poles of German descent who, by signing the *Volksliste*, declared themselves to be Germans. *Volksdeutsche* were entitled to higher rations and wages than Poles, though lower than those allocated to German citizens (*Reichsdeutsche*), and enjoyed a range of privileges. They were regarded by the Polish population as collaborators.

13. Kaplan (1963), cited from Matywiecki (1994, p. 265).

14. (Editor's note) Ludwik Landau, a converted Jew, was the chief statistician in the Demographic Statistics Division of the Economics Ministry in the pre-war Polish government. During the war, Landau kept a chronicle with the official blessing of the Polish civil underground. Although Jewish under the Nuremberg laws, and so required to enter the ghetto, Landau remained on the 'Aryan side' so that he could continue his work. He disappeared on 29 February 1944 and is presumed to have been arrested and murdered by

the German police. His chronicle is one of the fundamental sources for the history of Warsaw during the occupation.

15. (Editor's note) The popular name of the authoritarian government party, followers of Józef Piłsudski, which ruled Poland from 1926 to 1939, and which claimed to stand for the 'moral sanitization of public life'. More formally, it was called BBWR (*Bezpartyjny Blok Współpracy z Rządem* – Non-Party Bloc for Co-operation with the Government) under Piłsudski and OZN (*Obóz Zjednoczenia Narodowego* – National Unity Camp) under his successors. BBWR was ideologically amorphous and centred on the personality of Piłsudski himself, who had formerly been a leader for the Polish Socialist Party (PPS) and was generally regarded as progressive. Under Piłsudski, the party opposed antisemitism and was regarded with favour by the Jewish community. After Piłsudski's death in 1935, however, it took a sharp turn to the right and dabbled in fascist ideas. OZN introduced a number of anti-Semitic measures, and on the eve of war, was apparently about to deprive Jews of their citizenship.

In writing that 'Anti-Semitism today is not a natural development', Landau was doubtless placing wartime developments in the context of the Polish-Jewish reconciliation that took place in the first months of the war, when the quite rabid popular antisemitism of the years 1936–39 'vanished as if touched by a magic wand', according to Ringelblum (1998b, pp. 38–39).

16. 'Z pamiętnika Stanisława Sznapmana' (From Stanisław Sznapman's diary), in Grynberg (1988, p. 23).

17. Entry for 12.02.1940, cited in Matywiecki (1994).

18. 'Z pamiętnika Marka Stoka' (From Marek Stok's diary), in Grynberg (1988, p. 27).

19. (Editor's note) Łódź, the 'Manchester of Poland', was the second largest city and the most important textile centre in prewar Poland. It had a Jewish community numbering some 200,000, one-third of the population, and a substantial German minority. After the conquest of Poland, the western and northern portions of the country were incorporated into the *Reich*, either as the new *Reichsgaue* of Danzig-West Prussia and the Wartheland (the so-called 'New Reich'), or were added to the existing *Reichsgaue* of Upper Silesia and East Prussia, becoming part of the 'Old Reich'. Łódź, renamed Litzmannstadt, was the main city of the Wartheland.

20. The currency of the Łódź ghetto from June 1940. They were 'Mark-Quittungen' issued to replace the German mark, and were popularly known as *rumki* after the Chairman of the Jewish Council, Mordechai Chaim Rumkowski (1877–1944), at whose initiative they were introduced. Rumkowski, derisively called 'King Chaim' by his 'subjects', also had internal postage stamps issued and appointed a poet laureate and official artist. Despite his megalomaniacal tendencies, however, which still give rise to controversy today, there can be no doubt that it was thanks to Rumkowski's actions that the ghetto lasted to 1944, and his internal organization was exceptionally effective.

21. A merchant from Bremen, nominated head of the Getto-Verwaltung, the

German organization which administered the ghetto. Biebow, who himself carried out many murders in the ghetto, was condemned to death by the Łódź district court in 1947.

22. (Editor's note) This was called the 'Goebbels calendar'. In Warsaw, the first German action that Jews attributed to this calendar was the bombing of Warsaw in September 1939. The Jewish High Holidays occurred soon after the German invasion of Poland, and it was thought that the bombardment was especially heavily concentrated on the Jewish district on Rosh Hashanah (the Jewish New Year) and Yom Kippur (the Day of Atonement).

23. Cited after Gutman (1993, p. 87). Cf. Kaplan (1999, pp. 207–8).

24. Colonel Roman Umiastowski, head of propaganda on the staff of the Commander-in-Chief 'on the seventh day of the war, in a voice shaking with emotion, announced (over the radio): The enemy is at the gates of the city, everyone to the building of barricades, men capable of carrying arms and young people should leave the city'. Cited after Gutman (1993, p. 16).

25. (Editor's note) Polish and Russian historians are presently arguing over the numbers of people deported from these regions in 1940–41: the Russians, relying on KGB records, put the total number at 300,000, while the Poles, who prefer to trust the intelligence reports of the Polish underground, hold out for 1 million. Both groups agree that 21 per cent of those deported were Jews, the rest Poles. The numbers deported therefore did not exceed 210,000 Jews and 790,000 Poles, out of a population of 1.4 million and 5.3 million, respectively. The Jewish deportees were drawn mainly from the 300,000 who had fled from the German to the Soviet occupation zone in 1939.

26. (Editor's note) The Polish First Army, led by General Zygmunt Berling, fought on the Eastern Front under Soviet leadership. The Second Army, under the command of General Władysław Anders, made its way through the Middle East and around the Cape of Good Hope to Britain. It fought on the Western Front, particularly distinguishing itself at the battles of Tobruk and Monte Cassino.

Numerous controversies surround both armies: the Berling Army is accused of being instrumental in establishing Communist rule in Poland; the Anders army, limited in numbers at Stalin's insistence, restricted enlistment of members of non-Polish minorities to 10 per cent of the total. Jews in the Anders army encountered rank-and-file antisemitism; on the other hand, during the army's sojourn in Palestine, some Jewish soldiers, including Menachem Begin, left to join Haganah or Irgun. Most Jews remained with the Polish army, however, and Begin, at least, acted with official permission. This was nevertheless the basis of the popular belief that Jews had deserted *en masse*, a belief that helped stimulate antisemitism both within the army and in Poland.

27. *Centrala Opieki nad Sierotami* (Central Orphans' Welfare Agency); a charitable arm of the Jewish Council.

28. (Editor's note) This description pertains to the assimilated, Polish-speaking middle class, who comprised a distinct minority of the Polish Jews but the

great majority of the survivors who remained in Poland – and hence of the witnesses interviewed here. In Warsaw, where assimilationism was the strongest, perhaps 10 per cent of Jews met both criteria of assimilation, as it was understood in Poland: Polish was their native language, and they regarded themselves as Poles rather than Jews by nationality. Jews were traditionally isolated from Polish society; only a minority had become integrated before the war. In Warsaw and Łódź the ghettos were set up in the prewar Jewish districts, but in most smaller centres the Jews did have to move to new areas.

29. W. Szlengel, 'Okno na tamtą stronę' ('A Window on that Side'), in Szlengel (1979).

30. The basic German decree in this matter was issued on 15 October 1941 by Governor General Frank: 'Jews who without authorization leave the district designated for them are subject to the death penalty. People who knowingly offer hiding to Jews of this kind are also subject to the same penalty.' This was reinforced on 10 November by a still more draconian proclamation from Ludwig Fischer, Governor of the Warsaw District:

> Recently, Jews who have left the housing districts designated for them have in many cases been responsible for spreading typhus. In order to avoid the consequent danger to the population, the Governor General has decreed that a Jew who without authorization leaves the designated housing district will be punished by death.

> The same punishment is decreed for those who knowingly harbour such Jews or help them in any other way (for example by providing them with lodging, means of support, giving them lifts in vehicles of any kind, etc.). Cases will be heard before the Special Court in Warsaw.

> I draw the attention of the whole population of the Warsaw Region to these new regulations, because they will from now on be applied with merciless severity.

31. All furs belonging to Jews had been confiscated at Christmas time, 1941; they were to be used by the Wehrmacht on the Eastern front. Consequently a winter coat from which the fur collar was conspicuously missing served to mark the wearer as a Jew. (Editor's note: This was generally believed at the time by Poles and Jews alike, but may have been more a matter of subjective perception than reality. Many Jews supported themselves by selling second-hand clothing ('*tsukhes*') to Poles illegally, so that a good many furless Jewish coats must have been in circulation 'on the Aryan side'.)

32. Z pamiętnika Stefana Ernesta /From the diary of Stefan Ernest in Grynberg (1988, p. 95).

33. (Editor's note) Strictly, phimosis is the condition described ('contraction of the orifice of the prepuce, so that it cannot be retracted' – OED), rather than the operation, which is called surgical circumcision.

34. As I have said before when writing about the survivors that I interviewed, they form a specific group. They are not representative of the whole population of Jews who lived through the war. Unassimilated, Orthodox

Jews for the most part left Poland after the war, and I have not interviewed people in this group. However, in order to present a fuller account of the problem that I am discussing, I have not limited myself to quoting from the people I interviewed personally. I have also made use of other publications and of interviews quoted elsewhere. This quotation comes from an interview conducted by Lena Inowlocki in 1989 in Germany, which was presented at a seminar on the biographical method held at Kassel in September 1990.

35. (Editor's note) The Germans could and did ferret Jews out on their own initiative. This was accomplished in three main ways. First, traps were set, of which the most notorious was the Hotel Polski affair. Second, house searches were carried out. The largest such operation, which took place on Good Friday in 1944, involved surrounding the larger part of the district of Żoliborz, about 10,000 households, and searching every house from attic to cellar. This search yielded 100 persons, including Jews in hiding and members of the Polish underground. Searches on a smaller scale were a daily occurrence. Third, use was made of agents and informers, either members of the criminal underworld who worked for money, or persons – including Jews – who had been 'turned' by threats against themselves or their families.

    Official German estimates seriously underestimated the number of Jews in hiding: one estimate, cited by Hilberg (1985, p. 514), puts the number in Warsaw at 6,000. Since some 4,000 were caught at the Hotel Polski, the Germans must have thought there were very few left, too few to warrant a serious hunt.

36. (Editor's note) The Post Office was infiltrated by members of the Polish underground, who routinely intercepted letters addressed to the Gestapo. Ringelblum writes of the 'blessed arm of the Polish underground' which 'twice reached out and saved me from denunciation' in this manner. (Ringelblum 1988a, p. 27).

37. A northern suburb of Warsaw.

38. 'Saxon Wood'; an eastern suburb of Warsaw, on the right bank of the Vistula.

39. A north-western district of Warsaw.

40. Identity card, issued by the German authorities in 1941 and compulsory from mid-1942.

41. Itzhak Zuckerman.

42. Pro-Soviet Communist underground fighting organization set up in January 1944.

43. P. Levi (1919–87). An Italian Jew, arrested while serving with the partisans and sent to Auschwitz in February 1944. In 1958, he published *Is This a Man?* (Polish edition, 1978), in the Introduction to which he wrote:

    The history of the death camps should be an evil omen for everyone. ... The need to tell 'others' about it, making 'others' into fellow-participants, became in us, before liberation and afterwards, an impulse as direct and violent as other basic needs. This book was written to pacify that need; above all, then, for inner liberation.

In his view of the camp experience – without pathos or self-pity – Levi is very similar to Tadeusz Borowski. A shame, therefore, that only this book and one book of selected stories have been translated into Polish. Levi wrote four books about his camp experiences and four volumes of short stories. (Editor's note: Tadeusz Borowski (1922–51), like Levi, was a prisoner at Auschwitz, a brilliant and sensitive writer, and ended his own life. He is best known for his collection of short stories about the camp, *This Way to the Gas, Ladies and Gentlemen.*)

44. T. Borowski, 'U nas w Auschwitz' ('In our place, in Auschwitz') in Borowski (1979). (Editor's note) Auschwitz (strictly, Auschwitz I) and Birkenau (Auschwitz II) were the two largest of the 39 camps that made up the Auschwitz complex. Most of the other camps (collectively called Auschwitz III) were labour camps, connected with specific factories which they supplied with slave-labour; the largest was at Monowitz (Monowice), associated with the 'Buna' (synthetic rubber) plant belonging to I.G. Farben Gesellschaft. A substantial industrial complex also grew up in the territory separating Auschwitz I and Birkenau. Even the labour camps in the Auschwitz complex also served as punishment camps, at which much of the work was pointless and intended only to break the prisoners' spirit. Auschwitz I (the *Stammlager* or base camp) was a former Austrian cavalry barracks, with well-constructed two-storey brick housing blocks and paved streets, while conditions at Birkenau were much worse (as the previous citation points out). The mass extermination facilities were at Birkenau, but Birkenau also housed the Gypsy 'family camp', the womens' camp, and a substantial number of men's barracks as well. It was about five times the size of Auschwitz I.

45. (Editor's note) The 'frontier' of which Dr Engelking speaks was an administrative boundary; physically, the two camps were about two miles apart. Prisoners were frequently transferred from one camp to the other, however, and labour-gangs (*Aussenkommandos*) from both camps worked in the territory between them.

46. Jorge Semprun was born in Madrid in 1923; he left Spain in 1936 for political reasons and from 1939 settled in France. He studied philosophy at the Sorbonne and took part in the resistance movement. In 1943, he was arrested and sent to Buchenwald. Sixteen years later, he described the journey to the concentration camp, which lasted four days and five nights in a sealed railway waggon, together with 119 other prisoners, in *The Great Journey* (Polish edition, 1964).

47. (Editor's note) In a purely historical sense, the death camps were not extensions of the labour-camp system but purpose-built installations, and their organizational antecedents were not the ghettos but the so-called 'Euthanasia' programme – in which thousands of physically and mentally infirm individuals were murdered in gas chambers – and the special police units (*Einsatzgruppen*) which carried out massacres of Jews behind the Eastern front. The death camps were devised as a more efficient alternative to the *Einsatzgruppen*, designed and staffed by personnel drawn from the 'Euthanasia' programme. Ghettos were also not an inevitable part of the

killing process: they were established only in German-occupied parts of Eastern Europe, whereas in Western Europe it was not ghettos that served as the 'gateway' to the death camps, but holding camps such as Westerbork in the Netherlands or Drancy in France.

Dr Engelking, however, is writing about the Jews of Poland, and primarily about their states of mind. In this respect she is undoubtedly right that the ghettos were a necessary preliminary to the 'Final Solution'. The ghettos represented the Nazis' first attempt at dealing with the large, compact communities of Jews in Eastern Europe, and the success of this experiment (or, conversely, the too-slow rate of extermination through hunger and disease) may have emboldened them to take more radical steps. More pertinent to the present purpose is that the Polish Jews, starved and demoralized after having been isolated in ghettos for more than a year, were certainly more malleable than they would otherwise have been. For example, Emmanuel Ringelblum wrote that in Warsaw 'thousands' of Jews had submitted to 'deportation' (to the death camps) voluntarily, seduced by the offer of three loaves of free bread each. (Ringelblum 1988a, p. 419)

48. (Editor's note) About 400,000 registered prisoners passed through the Auschwitz complex, of whom 205,000 (51 per cent) were Jews and 140,000 (35 per cent) were Poles (Piper, 1992). Many of the Jews were from Poland, however, so that Polish was understood by the majority of prisoners. Auschwitz I was originally built in the Spring of 1940 as a concentration camp for Poles, and its predominantly Polish character was well established by the time the first Jewish transports began arriving (from Slovakia) in the spring of 1942.

49. (Editor's note) The transportation of Hungarian Jews to Auschwitz began in May 1944 and ended in July. In the course of this action, some 400,000 Jews (not 700,000) were killed.

50. G. Gurvitch, in differentiating eight kinds of social time, defines irregular time as follow: 'It is changeable, incidental time with an irregular rhythm. Domination of the present over other areas of time, the time of social roles, collective attitudes, non-structuralized groups, social classes in the process of formation, global societies in periods of transition'. Quoted after Tarkowska (1987, p. 106).

51. The Grey Ranks (*Szare Szeregi*) were the underground organization of the Polish scouting movement. The Lwów Eaglets (Orlęta Lwowskie) were the scouts of prewar Lvov.

52. K. Wyka, 'Dwie jesienie' ('Two Autumns') in K. Wyka (1984, p. 119).

2
Daily Life in the Ghetto

Vivere non est necesse. Life is not in itself anything so very important, and passing into a non-organic material state is not something so very important. Life is important as an opportunity to experience and to do things for which it is worth living.

Stanisław Ossowski, *Z nastrojów manichejskich*
(*In a Manichean Mood*)

I stopped by a bed where a child was lying. I thought that it was sick and they'd forgotten about it. I bent over and saw that the child was dead.
And at that very moment in came a little toddler and put a slice of bread and jam on the dead child's pillow.
'What are you giving him that for?'
'Because it's his share.'
'But he's already dead.'
'I know that he's dead …'
'So why have you given him the bread?'
'Because it's his share', said the little boy, impatient that I was asking needless questions, and that I, a big doctor, didn't understand such simple things.

Janusz Korczak, *Uczciwość, która nie rozumuje*
(*Honesty, Which Does Not Reason*)

Hannah Arendt (1989b, p. 332) wrote that the basic assumption of totalitarianism was that everything is possible. The reality of the ghetto, if we take it to be a kind of consummate totalitarian utopia, seems to confirm this analysis. For the ghetto proved that it was possible to construct a society in which the previously accepted social, cultural and moral norms were suspended. It became possible for people to die in their thousands in the streets and for others, still living, to dream of a quiet death. It was possible to create situations in which you had to choose whether your mother or your father should die, whether you or your children should die. This was all possible – as long, naturally, as certain pre-conditions were met.

Why were the Jews not sent straight away to concentration camps, which were an accepted and tested mode of operation for totalitarian regimes? After all, theoretically, it would have been possible to build a gigantic concentration camp,[1] where all the Jews could be placed, just as various 'enemies of the Reich' had been incarcerated earlier. What was the purpose of organizing ghettos, when it would have been possible to apply the tried and tested system of camp terror? The basic reasons cannot have been of a practical nature, since the future prisoners themselves could have built a sufficiently large camp, and it was anyway already necessary to transport Jews in trains and concentrate them in larger groups. Perhaps it was thought that the building of a gigantic camp, and the transport to it of millions of people could not be kept secret – something that the Germans at first wanted, not knowing how the world would react to their plans for 'a final solution of the Jewish question'.

The ghetto would therefore also to some extent provide a camouflage, both for the world, and for the Poles and for the Jews themselves – a camouflage which made it possible to get the future victims ready, to soften them up psychologically. The creation of ghettos did not – at least ostensibly – in itself constitute a threat. After all, ghettos for Jews had existed in Europe before: they were nothing new in history.

However, I do not think that the traditional existence of ghettos in European culture was the basic reason why they were set up. In re-creating ghettos in the twentieth century, the Germans in a sense inverted current trends in the development of European Jewry – which were assimilationist and emancipationist. A return was made to a system of marking, stigmatization and isolation. It would seem that when they shut up the Jews in ghettos, the Nazis had another aim as well – obviously apart from total annihilation.

The ghetto was much less isolated from the rest of society than concentration camps: it functioned behind a 'half-drawn curtain'. Perhaps the experience of the ghetto is difficult to understand precisely because it was not a concentration camp. Camps were after all one of the logical consequences of the totalitarian system, one of the basic institutions in the organization of totalitarian power (Arendt 1989b, p. 333). The ghetto was in a sense half-way between the normal – which was not so far off as the camps – and the camps themselves. The ghetto was not, in line with the Germans' plans, a completely isolated district; it had all kinds of links with the normal (naturally, 'normal' in terms of the occupation) world, both through personal contacts and economic exchange.[2] The existence of the ghetto seemed in a certain sense illogical; it is not unequivocally 'black', but is a kind of 'grey' experience that is difficult to decode.

The contrast between the ghetto and the 'Aryan side' served – for example – to frighten the Poles, although this was not its sole purpose. The ghetto was intended to confirm that guiding principle of totalitarian propaganda which Arendt called the principle of the infallible prophecy.[3] The Nazis formulated their threats in the form of prophecies which came true when they put their plans into action, and then their prophecies became a 'retrospective alibi'. In order to prove that the Poles were a nation of idiots, they murdered the Polish intelligentsia; in order to prove to the whole world that Jews were sub-human, they shut them up in ghettos in which sub-human conditions were created. Later, in order to demonstrate that they were insects, they killed them with insecticide gas.

The Jews could not be in 'normal' concentration camps for the additional reason that they were more important to the Germans than 'normal' citizens. The concentration camp was too trivial, too simple a method, of 'solving the Jewish question'. After all the Nazis constructed their own identity and that of their movement in opposition to the Jews, they made antisemitism a principle that served the purpose of self-identification (Arendt 1989b, p. 281), and they therefore could not treat the Jews like other people, because if they did they would lose their point of reference. They had to employ some 'special treatment' in their case, they had to show them as sub-human, thereby justifying their own position and identity as – in contrast with the Jews – super-human.

As we know, at the beginning the Nazis did not have – apart from a general desire to destroy world Jewry – a precise picture of the 'final solution'. There was a great deal of improvisation in what they did, a great deal of trial and error. I think that their own success and the ease with which they ruled the conquered society encouraged them to take further measures. How was it that they managed to achieve that initial success? Arendt (1989b, p. 332) wrote that total rule, attempting to organize the infinite variety and diversity of human beings so that they simply become one person, is possible only on condition that everyone can be reduced to constant, repeatable reactions, when each set of reactions can be changed to another one at will.

The effectiveness of totalitarianism lay in changing individuals into interchangeable objects, deprived not only of rights and free will, but even of personality. This kind of reification was, as Arendt writes, achieved gradually, in three stages, destroying their future victims' legal identity, moral identity, and person-ality, or individuality.

Arendt described these Nazi activities in the context of concentration camp prisoners, but I think that these categories can also be used to interpret the experiences of the ghetto. I have written in the previous chapter about stripping Jews of their legal identity; from the beginning of the occupation, many decrees were issued depriving Jews of all kinds of rights: from the right to buy philatelic special issues, to a ban on travelling, to a ban on leaving their designated dwelling area. The destruction of moral identity and individuality in the ghetto was, I believe, less effective than in the concentration camps, which is one of the things that I wish to discuss in the present chapter.

This chapter will deal with everyday life in the ghetto in the categories that I have proposed. I will also refer to the categories proposed by Hannah Arendt, and will try to demonstrate how the Nazis' activities worked to destroy the moral identity and individuality of their victims. I will try to present a picture of the everyday life of the ghetto in the form of a psycho-social map which illustrates various elements: both material living conditions and the psychological and spiritual conditions. These two categories are not strictly separated, but rather inter-related: living conditions have a strong effect on people's psychological functioning, and the ghetto provided a cruel illustration of this. Nonetheless, in trying to systematize the experience, one has to make use of some criteria, while remaining aware that they are far from ideal. In trying to understand the inner life of the ghetto, one has to make use not only of historical knowledge or eyewitness accounts, but also one's own imagination and intuition.

I will describe in turn particular categories of everyday life in the ghetto, on the basis of historical information and what the people I interviewed told me, also providing my own interpretation. When I distinguish and describe various elements of the everyday life of the ghetto, I am aware that only when we take them all into account, as well as the relationship between them, can we imagine the situation in the ghetto. I am going to present the situation in the ghetto in the form of a map – because when we read a geographical map we also have to supplement our knowledge of topography with imagination in order to be able to see rivers, mountains, and the whole landscape on the map as well as colours and lines.

It is obviously impossible to divide the categories that I propose rigorously from one another, and therefore categories from the 'material' sphere will be intertwined with those from the 'spiritual' sphere, in order to offer a more adequate picture of the conditions and atmosphere of life in the ghetto.

*

It is also possible to see the ghetto as a place where totalitarian oppression was reflected in cultural oppression, and in particular in the oppression of three dimensions of culture: time, the Other, and *'eligere'*. I will write about time and the Other when I analyse the dimensions of everyday life in the ghetto. *Homo eligens,* or in other words a man who makes choices, is in my view one of the more important criteria, which penetrates all the dimensions of ghetto life. A man who cannot make any choices and who at the same time is compelled to make them – this dichotomy defines the status of the inhabitant of the ghetto.

Contemporary researchers into everyday life tell us that lifestyle is a manifestation of the principle of choice in models of everyday behaviour from among the repertoire of those possible in a given culture (Siciński 1988, p. 56). If we try to apply this definition to the ghetto, where the possibility of choice was small, we have to conclude that cultural oppression was reflected in the lifestyle of *'homo non eligens'* – the impossibility of making choices. It will probably be more fitting in the context of the ghetto to use the terminology that Primo Levi applied in relation to the concentration camp – that it was the land of *impotentia optandi*. It is precisely this *impotentia optandi* which is in my view the fundamental characteristic of everyday life in the ghetto, the property of that reality, without which it is impossible to describe or understand it.

*

Everyday life in the ghetto had its own dynamics, was constantly being transformed. Newly established patterns of behaviour and ways of orientation were instantly changed because of new German decrees or a changing external situation. A shaky stability was constantly being disrupted.

Because the majority of the people I interviewed had been in the Warsaw ghetto, this has become the model for my discussion. At least four basic phases of its history can be distinguished:

- from the closing off of the ghetto on 15 November 1940 to 22 July 1942;
- the first deportation action (22 July to 12 September 1942);
- the residual ghetto – to the outbreak of the Uprising (September 1942 to 19 April 1943);
- the period of the Ghetto Uprising and its final closure.

In describing various aspects of everyday life in the ghetto, I shall also try to show the dynamics, the way that things changed in various periods of the ghetto's existence. Where necessary, I will comment on problems connected with ghettos other than that in Warsaw. Remembering that various elements of ghetto life were inter-related, that they were impermanent and constantly subject to change, and following the cognitive directives of the 'enlightened citizen', let us try to describe everyday life in the ghetto, and to read its psycho-social map.

The place

And one day, in full view of people on both sides, bricklayers began to build a wall along Żelazna and Sienna streets, along

Wielka and across Bagno, Próżna and Plac Grzybowski and Iron
Gate Square as far as the market hall, closing off the southern
district. That was the Little Ghetto. And then the wall went on
along Chłodna to Ptasia, Przechodnia to Długa, Mylna to
Przejazd, Świętojerska to Ciasna, Koźla to Przebieg via Pokorna,
Stawki, Dzika and Okopowa, closing off the northern district.
That was the Big Ghetto. And across Chłodna, near St. Charles'
church, there was a wooden bridge to join the two districts that
were divided by a tram line.

> Bogdan Wojdowski, *Chleb rzucony umarłym*
> (*Bread Thrown to the Dead*)

The first essential element of this map is a description of the
place where the events took place, in other words of 'the Jewish
residential district'. On Yom Kippur, Saturday 12 October 1940,
it was announced that by Thursday 31 October in that same year
(later this deadline was extended to 15 November) all Jews had
to move to the area of the ghetto that was being set up. This
decision introduced one of the many lines of division within the
Jewish community. A division was introduced between those
who lived in the area where the ghetto was being set up, and
those who lived elsewhere and had to move in to that area.

The latter group had four weeks to find a flat in the
designated area, agree the terms of a possible exchange of
accommodation (Poles who lived in the area of the ghetto had
to move out), decide what things to take with them, and sell the
rest or find people who would agree to store them.

> My parents lived in my brother's flat at 5 Zielna Street, and I moved in
> there too, and we lived there until they set up the ghetto. Zielna wasn't
> included in the ghetto, and so we moved from there to 2 Wielka
> Street. We exchanged my brother's flat for the tiny flat in Wielka with
> no financial compensation. (Stefan, Interview 29)

It was necessary to decide what would be essential in the new
place of residence. Winter things, or summer clothes, too? Would
the war last through to next year, and would summer clothes be
needed? Or would you be able to go home in the spring? What
part of all your previous life would be truly necessary in the new
place? Bed linen, a few pots and pans, books? How many books
could you take with you? Children's toys, photographs, memen-
toes, old letters, photograph albums …?

It is difficult to organize life in a new place in four weeks. Exchanging flats was in itself an enormous problem. On 16 October 1940, Ludwik Landau noted in his *Chronicle:*

> Everything is still caught up in the question of the move. Carts with people's things are on the move again. ... In every office the only thing that people are doing is looking for flats, if not for themselves then for someone close. In the doorways of houses there are cards describing flats 'for exchange', and at some points 'on the frontier of the two worlds', for example on Wielka by the corner of Chmielna, there are whole walls covered with these little cards offering flats for exchange or looking for them. But the transactions don't go very smoothly. It's not easy for people to find themselves a flat in these conditions. (Landau 1962, vol. I, p. 743)

Many people were not just moving within one city, but moved to Warsaw from other towns – for example, many people came to the Warsaw ghetto from Łódź. It was believed at the time that it would be easier to survive in Warsaw, or people fled from impending persecution elsewhere.

> On 18 December I went to Warsaw with my mother and grandmother. It was terribly cold, we got a lift in a lorry. ... Łódź was in the Reich; they'd introduced yellow patches. ... People were convinced that things would be worst there, and so they moved to the *General Gouvernement*. (Ryszard, Interview 34)

> My father, who was a well-known public figure, was in danger of arrest in Łódź. And so he and my mother decided to escape to Warsaw. On 11 November, they shot most of the council of the Jewish community. That made up my father's mind: he had a lot of friends in Warsaw from his younger days. My mother went with him, of course. (Arnold, Interview 9)

Transporting Jews (who from 26 January 1940 had been forbidden to travel by rail) from one town to another became of course a source of income for those who had means of transport at their disposal. According to Tomasz Szarota, in the spring of 1942, 'for transporting a three-person family from the Łódź ghetto to the Warsaw ghetto, they charged 15,000 złotys' (Szarota 1978, p. 70). And under the date 17 May 1942, Mary Berg noted in her *Diary*, 'A few days ago, a handful of people from the Łódź ghetto got through to Warsaw with the help of Kohn-Heller.[4] They had to pay 20,000 złotys per head.' (Berg 1983, p. 162)

However, the majority of migrants to Warsaw or other large ghettos did not go voluntarily, but under constraint. The Germans, who planned to concentrate the Jews in larger groupings, compulsorily transported them from from small towns to larger ones, where they set up a collective ghetto for the whole region. A lot of Jews from nearby towns were transported to the Warsaw ghetto. Not all of those who came had family or friends in Warsaw who could take them in. These people found themselves in the worst situation: they were quartered in deportees' centres which - because of terrible sanitary conditions and accommodation - became rife with disease and poverty.

> We got to the centre. The thick, almost palpable smell of human secretions, rotten left-overs and sulphur from a recent fumigation was stunning. You had to pick your way carefully up the staircase because there were streams of excrement coming down all the way across. ... And I was immediately dreadfully cold.[5]

Initially, those who did not have to move house were in a better position - those who had the 'good luck' to live in the area of the future ghetto. They did not have to pack all their earlier life into suitcases. On the other hand, large numbers of close or distant relatives and friends moved in with most, if not all, of them.

The 'privilege' of staying in your own home in the territory of the ghetto proved short-lived, since the boundaries of the ghettos were frequently changed - the Germans annexed or excluded particular streets, parts of streets, or even individual houses. The boundaries of the ghetto became a bargaining counter even before the ghetto was set up. As Chaim Kaplan noted in his diary:

> When it came time to carry out the ghetto order, everything became chaotic. The Polish side began to haggle - in this district they have a church; another is inhabited mainly by Aryans; here is a beautiful school building; there is a factory employing thousands of Aryan workers. How can the rightful owners be driven from all these places? Thus they excised piece after piece, street after street, of the Jewish area, and the boundaries of the ghetto grew more and more constricted. (Kaplan 1999, p. 211; entry for 22 October 1940)

And Ringelblum, writing about the establishment of the boundaries of the ghetto, noted:

> The priests are collecting signatures from [the inhabitants of] all the streets, asking that mixed streets should be left outside the ghetto. They're demanding that even Nowolipki, an exclusively Jewish street, should be outside the ghetto, because of the church there. (1988a, p. 179)

And so those who had at first been in a better position could suddenly find that they had to move, and now without the opportunity to exchange flats, since nobody was moving out of the ghetto, there were no empty flats, and you had to find some corner in an area that was already exceptionally overcrowded.

> At first we still lived at 24 Senatorska Street. My father went on in practice, seeing patients. Then we began gradually to sell things; or we left them with people to keep for us, or simply gave them away. We had to move to the ghetto, to a smaller flat that belonged to my uncle on the corner of Leszno and Przejazd streets. And then everyone kept moving house all the time, those Jewish chattels on the move everywhere. You became convinced that they were not just leaving their owners, but that they were going to outlive them. (Jerzy, Interview 35)

The opening of the 'Jewish residential district' took place efficiently and without complications. This was confirmed in a report dated 20 January 1941 by Waldemar Schön, the head of the Deportation Section in the Office of the Governor of the Warsaw District:

> In all, we succeeded in moving 113,000 Poles and 138,000 Jews. ... It is astonishing that a deportation action involving c. 250,000 people was carried out in a relatively short space of time (6 weeks), without bloodshed, and only in the last phase with the use of police pressure. This was to the credit on the one hand of the Polish mayor, and on the other of the Jewish Council.

> On 16 November 1940 a major police action was begun ... during which all areas of the city apart from the Jewish district were searched again; 11,130 Jews were caught and forced to move to the Jewish residential district.[6]

The exchange or loss of their former home was the first of many 'losses' which Jews were to experience during this war. It meant – not only in the symbolic sense – the loss of home, of a feeling of security, roots, awareness of belonging, being 'in one's place', and of the resultant sense of one's own worth and dignity. This loss of 'home', the experience of being uprooted, was a common experience for individuals and societies during the Second World War.

Up to July 1942, despite the death of tens of thousands of people from hunger, disease and the many deportations, the number of inhabitants of the ghetto did not fall. According to pre-war estimates by the City Administration, there were 380,000 Jews living in Warsaw on 1 September 1939. In January 1941, there were 410,000 Jews living in the ghetto, and in March 1941, 460,000. In July 1942, before the final action, there were 380,000, and in October 1942, 60,000 (Berenstein and Rutkowski 1958). And so in the period from November 1940 to July 1942, more than 400,000 people were living in an area of 170 hectares (c. 420 acres). 'Inside the walls there was an extensive cemetery, a sports ground and 73 of the 1,800 Warsaw streets. The whole of this area was surrounded by a wall three metres high topped with barbed wire, 18 kilometres in total length' (Gutman 1993, p. 96).

On average in the ghetto, there were 15.1 persons per flat, and 6 to 7 persons per room.[7]

Overcrowding

> They were still living people, if you could call them that. Besides their skin, eyes and voices, nothing human remained in these shattered figures. Everywhere there was hunger, misery, the life-sapping smell of decaying flesh, the piteous whimpering of dying children, the despairing cries and breathing of people struggling for life in the face of the hardest circumstances. ... The whole population of the ghetto seemed to be on the street. There was hardly an inch of open space. When we picked out a path through the mud and rubble, a pair of shadows stole past us which had once been a woman and a man, chasing after something and with eyes flaming with some insane hunger or craving.
>
> Jan Karski, *Story of a Secret State*

The space in which he finds himself is one of the things that has a major influence on a person's behaviour and the way that he feels. This sounds rather banal, but nonetheless, the behaviour of an individual in the space around him has long been the subject of academic research. Proximics, the study of human spatial behaviour, claims that each of us has, apart from the boundaries of our own body, boundaries of our own territory, a certain external space that surrounds us, and which is 'an extension of the human personality', an extension of the 'I'. The most external of these spaces is, as Edward Hall (1976, p. 152) calls it, 'a permanent space', in which is found the interior of home, the layout of streets in our district etc. Nearer to us is the 'semi-permanent' space which is variable, and nearest of all, the boundaries of our own organism, 'informal space'. Hall describes the arrangement of these spaces around an individual as a series of contracting and expanding fields which supply him with varied information (1976, p. 167). These spaces denote the distances that regulate social behaviour and symbolize the nature of ties with other people: the closer the tie, the smaller the distance in contacts with the person involved. Edward Hall distinguishes four distances: intimate, individual, social and public. These demarcate the behaviour of an individual in space.

What happens when these patterns of behaviour are disrupted by the impossibility of keeping distance from other people because of overcrowding? Hall calls situations like this a behavioural swamp and describes them as a state in which people can be inhibited by the space in which they have to live and work. They feel that they are being forced into behaviour, ties and emotional reactions which prove exceedingly stressful for them. ... As the levels of stress rise, their sensitivity to the overcrowding also increases – people become tenser – and they need ever more space just when they are getting ever less of it (1976, p. 186).

Among other things, the ghetto was a behavioural swamp of this kind. One of the many stresses it imposed was undoubtedly the constant overcrowding. This element of living conditions, the crowding and noise that the people I interviewed stressed, was exceptionally tiring and annoying, and was an additional factor reducing the psychological resistance of the people shut up in the ghetto. Ringelblum often made the same comments in his *Chronicle*:

> There is a terrible crowd in the Jewish streets. There are people all over the roads as well as the pavements. It's very difficult to move along.[8]

The crush in Karmelicka Street is indescribable. There's a dense wave of people on the pavements and on the roadway as well; it's unbelievably difficult to drive along there and it takes ages.[9]

It was completely dark in the streets at night, both because of the blackout that was in force and also because 'the electricity rarely worked, ... it was always pitch dark in the streets.... People milled about the streets and bumped into each other in the dark. Even phosphorescent brooches pinned onto your coat didn't help'.[10]

The constant presence of other people minimized if it did not entirely remove the sphere of privacy. The life of the individual in the ghetto was subordinated to the life of the collective. In normal conditions, interference with the sphere of privacy arouses aggression towards the intruder, and when this is impossible (for example in a lift or tram), it gives rise to attempts to avoid contact (if only eye contact). What happens when a situation of this kind lasts months or years? There is no point in aggression, it is impossible to withdraw, and so stress and depression grow.

Living in cramped conditions, living in a crowd, is something terrible. For years and years, I didn't want to live in the town, in the town centre, because I couldn't stand being locked up behind that wall, I had to have something green in front of me. Because, you know, it was like this: it was impossible to go for a walk, because you were always in a crowd, in a crowd in the street, in a crowd at home, it was all horribly overcrowded. (Irka, Interview 20)

You were never really alone. I mean, you couldn't just sit down and read a book; because first of all there was the family, and then people dropped in on one another all the time – this bit of news, or that bit of news. (Stefan, Interview 29)

Victor Frankl wrote of the longing for solitude which concentration camp prisoners also experienced:

Constantly being with the whole crowd of one's companions in misery, living with them all the time even when you were carrying out the most banal of all everyday activities, gives rise to an irresistible urge to get away even for a moment from that constant, compulsory community. You are overcome by a terrible longing to be just by yourself and with your own thoughts, by a longing for solitude. (1962, p. 57)

In a crowd like this, the human distances of privacy were infringed. The Other constantly intruded into the individual's psychological space, reinforcing the totalitarian oppression of the ghetto. The impossibility of getting away from the Other – in both the physical and psychological dimension – could lead to a disturbance of one's own identity – of an identity understood as the separateness of oneself from other people. The intimate and individual distances – so important for the defence of one's own identity – were drastically curtailed, were almost impossible to maintain. Oppression by the Other was complete.

> Your nerves were on edge, they cried out at every touch. Everything led to constant quarrels among the women crowded around the kitchen stove. Every pot was quarrelled over, every spoon gave rise to anger, every child's shout brought a reaction from the mother. The ghetto lived in a constant yell of uncontrolled nerves. ... Even the nights, which on the surface were quiet, only represented a smothering of the ceaseless loud howling.[11]

The social and public distances became confused. The whole spatial social structure was destroyed in the ghetto, was chaotically and swiftly changed.

In the ghetto the urban spatial structure was also changed. The earlier fixed spaces – courtyards, streets, squares – had new functions imposed upon them. After the curfew, courtyards became places where a lively social life took place, where information was exchanged: they became an active additional social space.[12] Streets, because of the overcrowding, became places where, instead of social or public distance, individual or even intimate distance was predominant. Human death and dying – in European culture rather intimate matters – suddenly began to happen in social space, and lost their individual, private dimension. During the first deportation action, squares – which in urban culture had hitherto been places for religious ceremonies, entertainments or executions – became the central sites of fear, the beating heart of ghetto-space, and acquired a primary cultural meaning. In the Umschlagplatz, later to become a symbol of the twentieth century, there had not been earlier a synagogue or a theatre or a gallows. There were only railway lines – the symbol of a journey into the unknown.

Over almost two years when the ghetto existed, its inhabitants got used to the crowded spaces and the behavioural swamp. While people still retained their individual identity they placed its stamp on every scrap of space, however small, that they managed to arrange for their needs. Certain rules governing distances in the world of the ghetto necessarily became established - not on a permanent basis dictated by the rationalist tradition, but by creating new principles of urban topography ad hoc. Everyone tried to to get used to the dimensions of the space - both the restricted fragment of private space and the compulsory, imposed social space.

Who ruled over the distances and social space in the ghetto? Naturally, the Germans. It seems obvious that the distance from them was, in Hall's categories, the greatest, the public distance. What happened when Germans appeared in a street in the ghetto? Because of the overcrowding the public distance could not be maintained: closeness and sometimes physical contact was impossible to avoid. The Germans did not like this either. Trying to maintain their own prestige - which was easiest to keep up at the public distance - they ordered the Jews to get off the pavements into the roads, so that they would not be 'polluted' by the unavoidable touch of an *'Untermensch'*.

The very presence of Germans brought chaos into the intuitive rules that regulated social distances in the ghetto. When the news spread that they were approaching (they usually moved in groups, and almost never walked singly), the streets emptied. The Germans also proved to have little resistance to the disruption of these distances. I think that they were helped in maintaining a subjective public distance - in addition to the ban on walking on the pavements - by lack of eye contact with Jews. Even in a chaos of social distances such as the ghetto represented, the final breaking of what remained of the rules dividing the public distance from the intimate - like looking people in the eye from an enforced proximity - had to catch the Germans, too, off balance, undermine the role they were playing.

> One night I went to a girlfriend's place in Ogrodowa street, to see whether she was still alive. In the gateway, I bumped into a young German. He must have been my age, he had an intelligent face. An old man with a white beard had come into the gateway along with me. The German took out a pistol - I was still there - and killed the old man.

[Why not you?]

> Exactly. Why? He even looked at me [in other words, he changed the rules on maintaining distance between Germans and Jews – B.E.], but he put the pistol away. Why not me? (Anna, Interview 27)

If the distance dividing Germans and Jews in the ghetto was a distance that was – for those days – public, how could the distance between the ghetto and the world on the other side of the wall be described? It was a distance not only in space, but also in consciousness, destiny, time.

I would like to raise one more problem connected with the chaos in the social space of the ghetto. That is, in this confusion of all distances, people were subjected to close physical contact with strangers. If we remember how primitive hygienic conditions were in the ghetto, then we must add another element to the experience of the behavioural swamp: the experience of smell. It is not difficult to imagine how unpleasant enforced contact with the unwashed bodies of strangers can be. His attitude to hygiene was, I think, one of the measures of how far a man still was from a state of complete indifference and submission to death.[13] Could people dying of starvation still think about washing themselves? Caring for personal hygiene is probably one of the culturally enforced habits that disappears most quickly in conditions like this.

The impossibility of maintaining basic hygiene certainly increased the stress which resulted from the constant infringement of the boundaries of safe distance from others. The smell of the ghetto was not just the smell of fear, of dirt, unwashed bodies, unwashed clothes; it was also the sweetish stink of corpses and the characteristic smell of diseases like typhus, tuberculosis, wounds that would not heal, ulcers.

There was also the smell of the streets: in the summer dust, bricks; in winter, mud, rain, frozen earth and frozen people. And spring? Was that first whiff of spring – so exciting in normal circumstances – equally pleasant in the ghetto? Or did it rather, by reinforcing the sense of one's own slavery, deepen depression?

Mary Berg wrote in her *Diary*:

> On the other side of the barbed wire it is full spring From my window I see young girls with bunches of violets walking along the 'Aryan' side of the street. I can even smell the sweet scent of the buds opening

on the trees. But in the ghetto, there is no trace of spring. Here, the rays of sunshine are absorbed by the heavy, grey paving stones. ... What has happened to my wonderful spring days of earlier years, happy walks in the park, and the narcissus, lilac and magnolia that filled my room? Today we don't have any flowers, or any greenery at all. (Berg 1945, p. 64)

And Abraham Lewin noted on 18 May 1942:

I can remember a spring day, also 18 May, several years before the war, which has become engraved in my memory. ... I was enthralled by the sea of green, the splendour of the tree-lined avenues and the wonderful radiance of the light, the tranquillity. This is why that morning is so deeply etched on my memory. Where can we find today a patch of green, a tree, a field and the chance to walk without terror over God's earth. (Lewin 1989, p. 77)

And snow? In the ghetto, there was no white, fluffy, calming snow. If snow fell, it changed into mud and water, reminding the inhabitants of the ghetto that they had no fuel, that they were cold and hungry.

There is still a terrible frost and it's getting worse, against all the norms, it's gone on for several weeks. And this is happening when coal costs a king's ransom. ... At the same time as our bodies are constricted by cold, our flats are also shrinking. The lives of whole families, both small and large, take place in one room, which is inadequately heated but where it is a little warmer because more people are breathing in it.[14]

In January 1942, Ringelblum (1988a, p. 354) wrote of the many deaths from cold:

The number of those frozen to death is rising daily, it is simply a commonplace.

In the ghetto, even the weather was against the Jews: spring brought dangerous memories, summer wore them out with its unbearable heat, autumn encouraged diseases and winter brought death by freezing.

Time

Time – and time. Sometimes it stretches like rubber, and at other moments it is different, like a dream, like smoke. Now it

stretches out terribly, without end, so that it's killing. The war
has been going on for nearly two years.

Lejb Goldin, *Kronika jednej doby*
(*The Chronicle of One Day*)

The ghetto was an island in time, governed by its own laws. There
was no past there, or at any rate it was better to forget about it.
There was only the tormenting, all-embracing, disturbing and
uncertain present. I think that we could speak of the oppression of
the present, of momentariness, in the ghetto. Time was in fact one
of the forms of totalitarian oppression expressed through cultural
oppression. Stanisław Ossowski wrote in 1943:

> Time has been unleashed. Since that September, months and years
> have passed which are not included in the current of our private
> time. Time is passing by without us – in Europe, in Asia, in America –
> marking its passing with the chronology of historical events. But the
> time which is sometimes our personal life, has lost its dimensions, its
> directionality. We do not plan weeks, months and years. ... We do
> not look look back with regret over the hour, the day, the month
> which is disappearing into the past. We wait for the moment that will
> come we know not when. We survive. We survive outside time, even
> though so much is happening in time. ... The inhabitant of present-
> day Warsaw is waiting with no date in view. Or, rather, he sets
> himself dates: he waits until the next spring, and then to the next
> autumn, but they are dates which do not turn into reality, dates
> which pass one after the other without moving time on. (Ossowski
> 1967, vol. III, p. 190)

I think that the experience that Ossowski wrote about – 'life in
the margins of time, in that margin which is dimensionless, in a
way like a temporary eternity' (p. 191) – was most distinct in the
ghetto. In the previous chapter I have already mentioned the
differences in the time of war for Poles and Jews. Let us now try
to interpret more accurately the type and quality of time that
existed in the ghetto.[15]

The basic characteristic seems to be a deformation of the
temporal perspective in all its dimensions. The horizon of time,
which in peace divided time into past, present and future, was
suspended in the ghetto. The first type of deformation was a
stretching out of the present. The war had suspended the future,
it was taking place in the present, and everyday life became an
'endless surviving', as Ossowski termed it. The horizon of time

became dominated by the present, which was all-embracing and dictated behaviour, thinking and ways of action. A condensed, thick present was the standard in the ghetto. In view of the complete unpredictability and uncertainty of tomorrow, in the ghetto you lived for today, with its dangers and hopes. There was a disproportionately large amount of the present in the ghetto, it was 'over-represented' in relation to other elements of the horizon of time. This deformation of the time perspective was noticed by those who were locked up in the ghetto. Chaim Kaplan noted in his diary:

> One of the greatest curses described in Deuteronomy has come upon us: 'And on the morrow you will say, let it be dusk' (28:67). Years pass with the speed of lightning, and moments drag out terribly. It is only now that we have learned the bitter taste of winter. And therefore we constantly long for tomorrow.

A second kind of deformation of time was the exclusion of the future, which in the ghetto turned into eternity. Eternity replaced the future: in the last analysis it was a lot closer, a lot more certain and palpable than the uncertain tomorrow. Eternity was clearer than the future, not only because of the indefinite surviving, but also because:

> Eternity was coming closer to us for yet another reason. It was brought closer by the fact that every day we came up against the categories of existence and non-existence. The end of life ceased to be some kind of distant event, about which you knew that it had to happen, but about which you knew only theoretically, almost in a way not particularly believing in it. (Ossowski 1967, p. 191)

Daily encounters with death, so omnipresent in the ghetto, brought its inhabitants closer to the eternal boundary of time. Were they aware of the special quality of time existing in the ghetto – a *two-dimensional time*, made up in overwhelming proportions of the present and eternity? It would seem that some were. One of the people I interviewed said:

> To tell the truth, it seemed to take place in two different times. One was everyday time, today's time, in which you lived and in which you behaved as you were supposed to behave. The other time came up unobserved: it was a great, absolute time, which had little in common with the first.

> You'd like to understand how these two times were related? It seems
> to me that the everyday – fear for your own life, worrying about your
> own skin, completely wiped out the other time. (Ryszard, Interview
> 34)

The two-dimensional quality of time in the ghetto, the mixing up
of the present and eternity, life 'on the margins of time',
disrupted the sense of continuity of one's own life. Many of the
people I talked to felt that from the perspective of the present,
life in the ghetto seemed unreal; they see it as some kind of a
break in the history of their lives, some kind of interruption of
the chronology and continuity of the course of their lives:

> I, who lived through it, no longer believe in it all, I don't believe
> that's what happened, even though I saw it all myself. (Władysław,
> Interview 25)

The third kind of deformation of time in the ghetto was a
foreshortening of the past. In the world of the ghetto, 'the past'
always meant 'yesterday'. A yesterday that you survived was a
success. Everything that happened yesterday was already
known, you'd got used to it, it had become an element of the
structure of the predictability of the future; everything that had
already happened might be repeated in the future. This created
the characteristic feature of time: repeatability. It seemed that
every situation which had happened once in the ghetto could be
repeated again, becoming an element of a reality that you were
used to and leading to the development of a false feeling of
security among the inhabitants of the ghetto, making it more
difficult for them to believe in what was unimaginable. Naturally,
the repeatability of time in the ghetto was illusory: the
inventiveness of the Germans in thinking up ever new torments
and an escalation of the terror was so great that 'yesterday' was
only ever repeated to a minimal extent; and 'tomorrow' was
entirely unforeseeable. Some of the people I interviewed had a
very strong sense of the momentariness and transitoriness of the
passage of time:

> When something is going on, you can't divide it up into stages, you're
> the same person all the time, and you go about in the middle of it all as
> though you were in a fog, and all the time you seem to remember
> what happened yesterday, you adapt to the fact that today things are
> completely different. (Adina, Interview 13)

The deformation of the horizon of time – past, present and future – influenced later possibilities of understanding and interpreting the experiences of the ghetto by those who participated in the events. The reference point for understanding events – for classifying them as normal, typical, explicable – is the past, our own knowledge and that of earlier generations which is passed on to us in the form of experience. This knowledge – in the form of 'stores of handy knowledge' (Schütz 1984, p. 142) – plays the role of a system of reference. In the world of the ghetto the only point of reference available was the experience of Jewish ghettos in the middle ages. This comparison did not evoke any particular concern in the Jewish community; on the basis of the experience of earlier generations, the Jews had no reason for thinking that this time they were destined for a completely different fate.

*

In the previous chapter, I wrote about a different, qualitative categorization of time, and its division into ordinary time and sacred time. Mircea Eliade writes that these two kinds of time differ primarily in that sacred time is essentially reversible (Eliade 1974, p. 86). The author is thinking here of the cyclical nature and mutability of ordinary time and festive time. Ghetto time was however certainly not reversible time. This was one of the reasons why the experience was so extraordinary: that in the ghetto, time was irreversible. And so while it would be possible to say that in a qualitative sense, ghetto time was, in contrast to everyday time, sacred time – yet because of its irreversibility, we must again call it 'cursed time'.

This specific time undoubtedly exerted an influence on destroying individuality and personality in the ghetto. Cursed time wiped away the differences between people, depriving them all equally of the past, condemning them to the present and confronting them daily with eternity.

Hunger

Why do people not commit suicide today? The torments of starvation are after all more terrible, more murderous and suffocating than any illness. Because, you see, all other illnesses are human, some of them even humanize the patient, ennoble him. But hunger is something animal, wild, primitive – yes, it's really an animal thing. If you're starving, you cease to be human, you become an animal. And animals don't know what suicide means.

Lejb Goldin, *The Chronicle of One Day*

In the Warsaw ghetto from November 1940 to July 1942, eighty thousand people died of starvation (Gutman 1993, p. 8).

*

During the occupation foodstuffs were rationed. The food rations, both for the Polish and for the Jewish population were always insufficient and changed in various years of the war. But on the whole, Jews received smaller rations than the Poles. For example, in 1941 the average caloric value of rations for Poles was 669 calories daily, and for Jews 253 calories (Szarota 1978, p. 240).

What lies behind this enigmatic calculation of the calorie ration per head? As Israel Gutman says, 'the energy value of the allotted products constituted barely 15 per cent of the biological minimum' (Gutman 1993, p. 106). In 1941, the population of the ghetto received monthly ration allowances of 2.5 kilograms of bread (from November 2 kg) and 180–200 grams of sugar per head. Other articles – for example, potatoes or jam – were allocated sporadically, in minute quantities. Rationed foodstuffs could be bought at 'fixed' prices, much lower than the black market prices. The price of bread was 30 groszy per kilogram in the shops and 8.5 złotys on the black market in the ghetto.

Relative prices become easier to understand if we look at the figures on income and expenditure of the population worked out by the Statistical Office of the *Judenrat*. Its authors point out that

The average earnings of manual workers in the ghetto were 6.4 złotys daily, and thus 160 złotys for a 25 day month. After paying the rent (35 złotys), light and gas (15 złotys) and other expenses (clothes, shoes, repairs, doctor etc. – 50 złotys) 60 złotys remained to feed a four-person family. The daily cost of food for one person was in April 1941 5.33 złotys, or in other words, for four people, 639 złotys per month. Even if the daily food for a four-person family was only one loaf of bread (purchased at free market prices), then expenditure on food would be 255 złotys. (Gutman 1993, p. 241)

Stanisław Różycki in a diary written in the ghetto, noted in November 1941,

Let us take for example the budget of a four-person family living in one room. The father of the family works, let us say, in the council office and gets a few allocations and extras and earns a salary of 235 złotys. His little son works as a messenger boy in the office and gets as much as 120 złotys. In addition, the father has a regular allowance because of his pre-war employment of 45 złotys per month, and apart from that earns a bit 'on the side' in various ways, always bringing in at least 200 złotys. His monthly budget amounts to 600 złotys. It would seem that he could get by on that. But four people. His wife, whose health is not good, works in the house from morning to night; his 10-year-old daughter is growing up beautifully, but has the appetite of a lion, and is hungry all day. A kilogram loaf of bread, the cheapest black bread, costs at least 7 złotys, and every day they eat at least 1.5 kilograms of it, even while trying to economize, which means 10 to 11 złotys daily. Let us calculate, optimistically, 300 złotys a month for this, since there is a bit of ration-card bread to make it up. They get a bit of sugar, jam and honey on ration cards as well. He gets more or less the same products as an allocation from the office, and so together with expenditure for saccharine and coffee, this comes to only 45 złotys per month.

And so breakfast and supper have somehow been patched together. But there is still dinner. Let us assume that the family gets four portions of free soup from a charitable organization, and that they have to add to that 1 kg of potatoes daily, this comes to 105 złotys per month.

They can't buy meat or butter because they can't afford it, and so they buy 1 kg of bacon fat per month at 54 złotys, or in other words 250 grams per month per person, and so not even 10 grams of fat per person per day! After breakfast, the family waits impatiently for dinner, after dinner for supper – but at least they are not starving. The rent is only 70 złotys, other charges are 6 złotys for lighting and 20 złotys for candles, making altogether 600 złotys. There is no room here for the unplanned expenditure which is bound to come up in any month; there is no room for fuel, soap, laundry, illness, the cobbler, cigarettes, sweets – but it is difficult to find any extra – even 10 złotys – in a budget of 150 złotys per person, particularly when exactly 50 per cent goes on bread alone. ... I don't know what budgets that are not based on a steady income look like. I suppose that they don't look like anything at all. You sell something, and you buy bread and potatoes, you pay the rent-collector. Your money runs out – and you pull out whatever you have left to sell. But matters look worse when there's nothing left to sell. That's the end. And that is the fate that's waiting for the majority, because in the end all reserves run out. It is only a question of time and providence. But there is only one final way out, and when it happens is just a matter of when your turn comes. Each of us is in the queue. (Różycki 1967)

The price of food on the free market changed, in response not to supply but to demand. One of the people I interviewed spoke about this:

Food prices [on the black market] were not so much dependent on supply as on demand. They rose very greatly for example at the moment when the German Jews, who still had some reserves of cash, came into the ghetto. The price of a loaf of bread jumped then from 60 pfennigs to 100 Marks. (Arnold, Interview 9)[16]

The demand for foodstuffs brought permanent inflation, food prices constantly rose. On 9 May 1940, Chaim Kaplan wrote in his diary:

The situation in the market for foodstuffs has got worse. Prices have jumped by three times again. There are some things that you can't get at any price. With the coming of spring, formal starvation began.[17]

The problem of food – or, rather, lack of food – is linked with another question which I shall discuss later: that of the gradation and stratification of society in the ghetto. Over the two years of the ghetto's existence, as the general pauperization progressed, successive social groups were pushed onto the brink of starvation. Financial reserves were exhausted, caring for the welfare of the weakest – deportees, the sick, children, the old – became ever more difficult. Stefan Ernest calculated the proportions of people in the ghetto who were starving and who had enough to eat as follows:

There are twenty thousand, perhaps thirty thousand, people who really have enough to eat; these are the social elite. They contrast with the quarter-of-a-million-strong mass of beggars and paupers who are only struggling to postpone death by starvation. ... And in between these two is a group of about two hundred thousand 'ordinary people' who more or less manage, and retain some sort of human face. They are still clean, dressed, their stomachs are not swollen from starvation.[18]

The opportunity to acquire extra food was on the one hand a prerequisite for survival, and on the other hand the fundamental element in all privileges, and a source of bribery and blackmail. For example, the police in the ghetto received higher rations, according to 'Aryan' norms.[19] Other groups of the population were also – on grounds that were not entirely clear – privileged by the Germans. For example, doctors in the hospitals got allocations of pure spirit:

> For example, we got ridiculous rations in that hospital, we got 100 grams of bread with some fat or beet jam and we got some sort of bowl of soup – it was really boiled rye, you know, mouldy rye flour and water, they made a base of that and boiled it up in salty water. And then that glass of raw spirit. It was very little. Probably, each of us had something else to eat at home, and we didn't get to that brink of starvation that others had reached, especially the deportees, above all those people who'd been driven out of all those villages, little towns, who didn't have anybody, didn't have anywhere they could go, didn't have anything to sell.
>
> The doctors and nurses on both sides of the wall got that pure spirit, it was the spirit that saved us. There was some purpose in it, to give as much alcohol as possible to the Poles, a certain amount went for their own consumption – but we sold the alcohol and thanks to that we survived. (Adina, Interview 13)

The intended policy of the occupying forces was to divide and fragment the occupied society as much as possible. They made use of the natural divisions of the society and they created new ones. Mary Berg wrote in her *Diary of the Warsaw Ghetto*:

> The Christians have their own soup kitchens; the biggest of them is next to the demolished church near the Iron Gate [Żelazna Brama]. It looks as though they are favoured by the Nazis, for the meals there are better and cheaper than those in other kitchens in the ghetto. This is supposed to be bait in the missionary work carried out by the neophytes. (1945, p. 130)

The gradation of hunger on the one hand, and the distribution of privileges on the other, was an important element in German policy towards the civilian population in the occupied countries. Deprivation of food – one of the aspects of the ghetto world which led to restriction of possibilities of choice, including moral choices – was an instrument through which the Nazis exercised power, including power over people's behaviour, and this was a power which was essential for them in view of the aim that they had in mind. It is most dramatically discernible in the ghettos and concentration camps. Hunger is an important signpost on our psycho-social map of the ghetto.

Bread was the basic foodstuff during the war. Bread in itself has many symbolic cultural connotations. Bread is a guarantee of the right ordering of the world, it is an archetype of food and peace. In the ghetto, the symbolic became literal.

Bread ceased to be a cultural totem. It became the most real symbol of food, a synonym for food in general, a hope of survival. It became a dream which for many was unattainable – even though it was within arm's reach. Its price was the price of human life. You could buy it in the streets of the ghetto, it provoked you with its smell and tempted the hungry to steal.

> Bread, bread, bread. Fine rye, fine white, fine light, fine dark, baguettes, luxury loaves, square loaves. A blinding prodigality. ... At every step, bread, bread, bread. I'm tempted to go up to the stall and touch it, squeeze the fresh rye loaves, satisfy the tips of my fingers with the soft, brown-baked dough. No, better not. It only sharpens the appetite and nothing more.[20]

In wartime, when the norms of peacetime are suspended and society is governed by other rules, all goods which are rationed or difficult to acquire become a source of speculation and a source of income. This was true also of bread. The quality of the flour left much to be desired but in addition a great variety of all kinds of substances were added to the bread to increase its weight. Its quality, and consequently its food value, was very low.

> This bread was distinguished by an ever worse quality of flour, an ever greater quantity of added ingredients, and ever worse baking. The flour that was allocated to the bakers in the last months contained barely 50 per cent rye flour of the worst grade; the rest was made up of oats, millet, barley, potato, sweet corn, mixed wheat and rye flour, and other mysterious additives. ... German wartime norms allowed bread to be sprinkled with sawdust. (Szarota 1978, p. 327)

The problem of the quality of the bread was also raised by the people I interviewed. I will cite part of a conversation with one of them, someone who worked in the *Judenrat*, who came into direct contact with the problems of bread quality and provisioning in the ghetto:

> The matter of the quality of the bread. ... We had a committee, to check whether – because you know, it was about the quality – there hadn't been theft of the flour. And so there was a committee made up of several people, and we did everything we could, only we didn't try the bread. That is, we only touched it to see whether it was well-baked, that it wasn't too doughy, but as to eating it – well, we didn't eat it, just in case. (Stefan, Interview 29)

Ration cards that were left over when someone died were a valuable commodity in the ghetto. The dead person's family tried to keep them; the *Judenrat* was obliged to take them back:

> There were situations when there were more coupons than people, you had to manipulate the allocations. I worked on checking the ration cards. There were more than 100,000 or 150,000 illegal ration cards. People died, people left the ghetto – but the cards were still there. Well, you know, there were infringements of the regulations. It was very unpleasant work for me, because I went to see the worst poverty that you could ever find – I had never seen things like that in my life before and I don't think I ever will again. (Stefan, Interview 29)

In his *Chronicle*, Ringelblum confirms that ration cards were bought and sold and that the dead were hidden in order to keep their cards:

> Trading in ration cards is one of the saddest phenomena in the ghetto. The administrators and shopkeepers, like leeches, take advantage of the situation of the poor, who have no money to buy bread, and buy up from them some of their bread coupons and all of their sugar coupons.[21]

> At 7 Wołyńska street a mother hid her dead child for a week in order to make use of the dead child's ration cards for that period.[22]

The ration allowance per head in the ghetto amounted to 253 calories per day; in order to survive you had to get hold of extra food. According to a survey on food consumption conducted in December 1941 by the Statistical Department of the Provisioning Section of the *Judenrat*, the number of calories consumed was very different for different groups of the population. The clerks of the *Judenrat*, for example, consumed on average 1,665 calories per day; the unemployed intelligentsia, 1,395 calories;

manual workers in the 'shops',[23] 1,229 calories; and beggars, 785 calories (Sakowska 1993, pp. 114–15). It is clear that the gap between the ration allowance of calories and the consumed level was made up by the black market. The smuggling which supplied that market became one of the new professions that developed in the ghetto. There was 'minor smuggling', mainly on an individual basis, in which the children of the ghetto showed an extraordinary courage and determination, often becoming the chief suppliers of their starving families. There was also 'major smuggling', carried out on a large scale, and a source of wealth for some Jews, Germans and Poles. Smuggling is an integral part of the picture of the ghetto; it is described in all the accounts and memoirs. Without it, the ghetto would simply not have been able to exist. The Germans – proponents of institutionalization and organization – combated minor, individual, 'non-licensed' smuggling. However, they were themselves fairly susceptible to bribery, and thanks to this, organized smugling existed which could get anything at all over or under the ghetto walls: food and people in one direction and valuables and furniture in the other. In many memoirs and accounts of the ghetto, it is mentioned that you could buy anything there:

> We were not doing too badly, which only meant that we had something to eat and something to sell. My father still had occasional patients, and my mother kept a kosher kitchen [you could get meat from a kosher butcher's in the ghetto – B.E.] and made sure that if someone came round they would not go away hungry. Should I pretend today to be ashamed that I still had something to eat? But it's true that when you're hungry none of the other shortages and deficits count. (Jerzy, Interview 35)

Accounts like the one above were however rare. Hunger was the general experience in the ghetto. It was felt, to a differing degree, by all the ghetto-dwellers.

> All the children, unless they came from very rich families, experienced hunger. I remember how my nephew played, 'Table, lay yourself'. He told himself a fairy story and thought up some wonderful dishes which would appear in a moment. There were a great many of them. I asked him whether he would invite me to join him at the table. He replied, 'Miracles don't happen to old ladies'. (Helena, Interview 30)

We naturally do not know about the worst experience of

hunger, leading to death, from first-hand accounts, but others described what they witnessed:

> I was never swollen from hunger, I put it down to the alcohol, a little drop of alcohol, we weren't hungry – I remember that people used to say, 'Oh God, I'd like a bit of white bread with butter and jam', but that wasn't *that* kind of hunger. From what I've seen, I think that hunger is the most terrible thing. That real hunger, the hunger of the camps, the hunger of the ghetto, the hunger that kills. It is a feeling that can make a man lose all his human qualities. That's why I don't think that I was right at the bottom. (Adina, Interview 13)

The majority of the people I interviewed were, as they themselves emphasized, somewhere in the middle – they were hungry but not starving.

> I was in the middle group, where there was no wealth and no besetting hunger. It was dirty, dark, we had lice, there was nowhere to wash, but we had something to eat; things were very bad, but we were living. ... We owned only more or less what we had on our backs. Someone we knew had a warehouse and from time to time we got from him half a bucket of rotten potatoes, sometimes I brought something. For a real holiday we bought two litres of horse blood and made something to eat with it. (Ryszard, Interview 34)

One of the most shocking descriptions of hunger was given by the Jewish writer Lejb Goldin in the essay that he wrote in the ghetto, *The Chronicle of One Day*:

> The last soup was yesterday at twenty to one. The next one will be today at the same time. So much time has already passed. How much is left? Eight hours. Even though really you might as well not count the last hour, the one after twelve o'clock. Then you are already in the canteen, surrounded by the smells from the boiler, you're already getting ready. You can already see the soup. And so there are really only seven hours left. Only seven hours. It's ridiculous! Seven hours – you say, you idiot, that 'only' seven. Well, how is it possible to get through those seven hours, or even the next two hours ... Eat, eat ... Now it's coming not from the stomach but from the palate, from the temples. If there were only just half a slice of bread, just a piece of crust, even burned, blackened, charred. I drag myself out of bed, a sip of water brings some relief, quells the hunger for a moment. You get back into bed and collapse, your legs won't do what you tell them, they're swollen. They hurt. But you don't groan. How many months is it since you learned not to groan even when it hurts. From the

beginning of the war, when you lay awake at night on your bed and thought about the situation, or in the morning when you had to get up and a sigh often escaped from you. There's an end to that now. Everything now is happening as though you were an automaton. Or perhaps – an animal again? It's not impossible.[24]

One aspect of hunger is discovering how greatly psychic functioning is dependent on bodily well-being. Someone who is starving can think of nothing apart from food. It is the true experience of being 'deprived of dignity and freedom'. Even the strongest will-power can do nothing here, when someone is reduced to mere instincts – in fact to one instinct, that for survival. It is the only desire: to eat; it governs the whole hierarchy of needs and values of the person who is hungry. Starvation is an illness. Hungry people, even when they are very hungry, do not think of themselves alone, but for example also about feeding their children. But gradually, as the illness of starvation grows worse, a typical state of indifference to everything but food develops. All the thoughts and activities of the starving man are concentrated on food. This is the state of the 'muslims' – about whom we know from the literature – in the concentration camps. And the starving inhabitants of the ghetto were similarly indifferent to their surroundings. Dr Julian Fliederbaum, one of the doctors who conducted research into hunger in the ghetto, described starvation sickness as follows:

The psychological condition of the people that we have examined is marked primarily by a change in disposition. Young people, who earlier were cheerful, are now miserable, they are in a state of depression. The sphere of interests of the person concerned is very limited. The psychological condition is marked by paucity of thought. The ability to make connections slows down – you could call it 'bradythrenia'. ... Long-term starvation leads to gradual loss of body weight, which can proceed to a very marked degree. ... Active, energetic and enterprising persons change into apathetic people without initiative, who are lethargic and sluggish. They lie in bed all the time. They are almost always sleepy. They wake up only to eat their meagre meals or to answer physiological needs. The passing from life to death takes places slowly, is sometimes almost indiscernible. ... The pulse and breathing rate slow down gradually, and it is increasingly difficult to make psychological contact with the patient, until finally he dies. Some fall asleep at night in bed or in the street, and in the morning they are found dead; others die with a crust of bread in their mouths while they attempt to make some physical effort, for example when running to get hold of some bread. (Apfelbaum and Fliederbaum 1946, p. 111)

Hunger deprives human beings of one of the important attributes of humanity: it deprives them of dignity. It is also a threat to the dignity of those people who are witnesses to starvation. Helplessness in the face of someone else's hunger, the experience of being unable to do anything about death by starvation, strikes at one's sense of one's own value and – even years later – leaves a bitter after-taste of guilt.

In considering the dramatic power of hunger in the ghetto, one has to raise the question of cases of cannibalism. We know that this occurred in concentration camps, and probably there were also cases in the ghetto. Czerniaków wrote in his *Diary* about one case:

Just now (11.33 a.m.) Colonel Szeryński, the head of the Security forces, has reported to me a case of cannibalism in the Jewish quarter. A mother and child. Here is the report:

'D. Szwizgold, group 1845. This report concerns a case of cannibalism. I report that at the request of the local constable of the IVth district of the Jewish Volunteer Forces, Nirenberg, I went to 18 Krochmalna Street, flat 20, where I found Rywka Urman, aged 30, lying in rags, who testified before witnesses (Mr [sic] Niuta Zajdman, the secretary of the House Committee, and Mr Jankel Murawa, aged 30, chairman of the House Committee) that she had committed an act of cannibalism on her own 12-year-old son, Berek Urman, deceased on the previous day, by cutting off a piece of his buttock.

'Signed D. Szwizgold group 1845
taken down by M. Grossman 393, J. Murawa, president. 19.II.42.'
(Czerniaków 1983, p. 255)

Hunger was an ally of the Germans in their attempts to deprive the Jews of moral existence and identity. The behaviour of a starving man is governed by instinct, and not the norms of co-existence in society; a starving man is deprived of the possibility of passing moral judgement on his own actions. Hunger is often interpreted as an experience which bestializes man, stripping away layers of culture that now prove to be superficial.

> When a man is so hungry that he cannot think of anything else, so thirsty that he can only think of a glass of water, then he becomes a savage. You could see that in the faces. To this very moment, I remember those faces with the eyes starting out – people who could think only about food. They had become animals. (Ryszard, Interview 34)

For some it it incomprehensible that people who were suffering so greatly from hunger did not commit suicide. Primo Levi (in the context of the concentration camp, but it applies equally well to the ghetto) writes that when you exist at the level of instincts, thinking, judgement and choice become impossible (1989, p. 155). Suicide is something human and not animal – it needs ability to judge and to employ moral categories. It is for this reason that suicides were more common after liberation from the camps – when the prisoners regained their ability to judge and employ moral categories – than in the camps themselves. It seems that the specific nature of time was also of some significance: the density of the time of every day, the necessity of getting hold of food, running around arranging everyday affairs, and also the omnipresence of death, meant that there was actually no time to think about death.

> A child swollen with hunger and moreover unconscious – how can you talk here about dignity, or about the dignity of a child who grabs a posy of flowers and eats it. How can you talk about dignity – how can you talk about the dignity of a man who is lying in the street and dying of hunger. ... It is the absolute bottom of the barrel, if you can still think about dignity. It seems to me that this is the most terrible thing, hunger, which at a certain point completely debases a human being, he is prepared to do absolutely anything, almost anything – after all, not everyone stooped to cannibalism; not everyone, they really didn't, there were only sporadic incidents during the war. I didn't hear about it in the ghetto ...

> To retain your humanity, that's just a bit higher up the scale, it's a condition when someone is exceedingly hungry but is still conscious, and then later there's a point when nothing any longer ... (Adina, Interview 13)

The experience of such intense deprivation as the hunger in the ghetto changes a man's perceptions and also changes his sense of time. The cursed time experienced in the ghetto reinforces the dimension of discontinuity on the one hand, and on the other of density. Biology becomes the clock, time is measured in meals and the intervals between them, which are filled with thoughts of food.

> You've only been living on soup alone for something like four months. And yet those few months drag out thousands of times longer than the preceding twenty months, or than your whole life to date. A whole eternity divides yesterday's soup from today's, and I can't imagine that I could manage to hold out through yet another period of nearly 24 hours like it, with hunger like that holding me by the throat. Despite all this, the last four months also seem just one dark and terrible band of nightmare. All attempts to dredge something up out of the period separately, to remember some detail worth noticing, fail. It is one black, impenetrable mass. (Goldin, in Sakowska 1986)

The picture of hunger and death by starvation is probably the most widespread surviving image of the ghetto. It was one of the most important determinants of everyday life in the ghetto, and for this reason has come up, and will continue to come up, in this chapter when various other aspects of ghetto life are discussed.

What I have written above about food supply is based mainly on the Warsaw ghetto. But the situation was similar in other ghettos. The person I interviewed who survived the Łódź ghetto, talked about the hunger that reigned there and ways that people coped with it:

> The daily ration was about 1300–1600 calories. But that fact does not tell you about the true state of affairs. Because the foodstuffs supplied to the ghetto were always of the worst quality - rancid margarine, mouldy flour, rotten vegetables. And apart from that, a lot of food got stolen on the way to the kitchens. However, the most killing thing was not so much the shortfall in calories as the shortfall in protein and fats and the lack of vitamins. We saw in the ghetto the least known forms of vitamin deficiency, up to and including fatal dysentery.

> Human initiative in the field of cheating hunger is boundless. Various kinds of ersatz made a great career in the ghetto - for example, potato peel. It was greatly in demand, people actually fought over it. The Jewish authorities therefore issued a decree that you could only get potato peel on a medical prescription! Potato peel as medicine! It was also cooked in all kinds of different ways. Usually it was added to soup, or served as potato cakes fried in stinking rapeseed oil (which

was supplied to the ghetto in minimal quantities). It was also fried in oil obtained from lubricating oil. Pigweed, beet leaves and above all grounds from corn coffee all made a similar career for themselves in the ghetto. (Arnold, Interview 9)

Perhaps the situation was a little better in other, smaller ghettos which were in rural regions or were less well isolated from the 'Aryan side'. For example in the Białystok ghetto, as another person I interviewed told me, there was no drastic hunger:

There wasn't any special hunger in the Białystok ghetto. I had all kinds of friends and acquaintances from before the war. Anyone who hadn't had any contact with Poles before the war was in a worse situation now. Some people wouldn't of course admit now that they'd known you before the war. But I knew one really good man who was our contact point. Other people just traded normally. Well, of course, they took advantage of the situation, they charged a bit more. But well, good lord, business is business; they had to take account of the risk. It was easiest to trade with Polish workers who, like the Jews, were sent by the Germans to forced labour.

Look at me, do I look like the kind of person who would allow himself to be starved? There were a few militant lads. We knew our town well. It was no problem for us get out of the ghetto at night, go a long way, to the other end of the town, wrench the padlock off some hutch and take a rabbit or a chicken. We wouldn't have died of hunger. We bought cows (it wasn't difficult, there was plenty of farming country round Białystok) and brought them into the ghetto at night. We sold them on in the ghetto for big sums. The money went for the organization, to buy arms. (Edward, Interview 26)

Living conditions in the ghetto changed in various periods; they had a dynamics of their own. Many of the people I interviewed indicated that hunger in the ghetto in fact really ended after the first deportations when 300,000 of the inhabitants were taken to Treblinka. In the previous chapter I quoted from one of the interviews: 'Officially, the Warsaw authorities did not know that the population of the ghetto had fallen from four hundred thousand to forty thousand. ... And they went on giving out ration cards, maybe not four hundred thousand, but perhaps three hundred thousand.' Daily life in the ghetto moved then in accordance with a different rhythm. Living conditions also changed (there were plenty of empty flats, there was no more overcrowding, everyone was forced to work in the 'shops', they were supplied there with food, ration cards were plentifully available), as did psychological conditions (both uncertainty and hope came to an end: everything had become clear). One woman I interviewed told me:

> After that first action, there were ten or eleven of us in that three-roomed flat in Gęsia Street. And we could afford to buy a loaf of bread, a half-kilo baker's loaf, from the smugglers. I learned to cut it: look, I've still got the callous to the present day. I learned to cut it so that there were perfectly even portions. First of all, you cut it all round, taking off the crust, pieces like the crust, leaving what you might call a more or less square piece, and then you cut that into as many pieces as there were people, and then afterwards you cut up all the crust pieces nicely. ... I got very good at it and so I did it. It's unbelievable, can you imagine that you might cut bread in a way that made sure that none of your children got even a quarter of a centimetre more than another ... (Adina, Interview 13)

Hunger and starvation are almost a synonym for the ghetto. But there were also other illnesses.

Sickness and death

> Oh, those coupons, I won't give up my coupons,
> 'Cause Pinkert* is on call
> That bastard takes them all,
> Oh, those ration coupons.
>
> > Popular ghetto song

In the ghetto, the most widespread disease – apart from starvation sickness – was typhus. In fact this in the end was used as the pretext for closing down the ghetto. The Jews – as potential carriers of typhus germs – had to be, for the good of the remainder of humanity, isolated in the ghetto. Warsaw was covered at that time with posters proclaiming: 'Jews – lice – typhus'.

Typhus is a communicable disease carried by parasites, usually lice. Nine to fourteen days after infection, a high fever develops, accompanied by headaches, depression and great

---

* Motl Pinkert was the undertaker in the Warsaw ghetto (see p. 120 below – Ed.)

physical weakness. Three days later, the characteristic rash appears. The patient is somnolent and in the worst cases unconscious. If there are no antibiotics, the majority of typhus patients die. Stefan Ernest wrote in his memoir about the outbreak of typhus in the ghetto:

> In the summer of 1941, an epidemic of typhus broke out in full fury, after a period when there had been plenty of cases, but still only sporadic ones; the epidemic was to last unchecked for almost a year, to the spring of 1942. At the beginning there were several dozen deaths daily, and in the months when it was at its worst, in October, November, December, January, it yielded 200 corpses daily. Death statistics give 6,000 registered deaths in each of these months. And nobody knows how many additional nameless knights of absolute poverty – who died in the street from hunger and cold and were buried in common, unmarked graves in the Jewish cemetery – went unrecorded.

> Poverty, hunger and the camps happen to the least well-off and the weakest. But typhus is more democratic. It carries off victims from all social classes, spheres and professions. And by a strange stroke of luck, the poorest are more resistant to the disease than those who are well-off.[25]

There were various epidemics in the ghetto: dysentery, typhus and typhoid fever. There were many cases of tuberculosis, which was often a side-effect of starvation. In the terrible sanitary conditions of the ghetto, making hygiene impossible, and with the dreadful overcrowding, it was not difficult to get infected. But the symbol of disease in the ghetto, perhaps thanks to German propaganda, was always typhus. One of the women I interviewed had caught it:

> I was seriously ill. In the afternoons, when my temperature rose, I was overcome by depression and wept. I was haunted by hallucinations. I saw the whole galaxy of Polish kings, I counted them off in succession to my brothers and sisters. Another day I heard Beethoven symphonies. When I got to the Eroica, the funeral march, I cried bitterly. When I finally got out of bed, I was so weak that my brothers and sisters had to teach me to walk all over again. I got to know that ghetto disease very well; I visited and bade farewell to many who were dying of typhus. (Helena, Interview 30)

The people of the ghetto were afraid of disease and epidemics. Every new threat or affliction was a grave blow, which increased the already enormous burden of stress. Illnesses made unforeseen additional expenditure necessary.

Despite the punitive regulations issued by the occupying authorities, cases of typhus were often not reported because this entailed compulsory quarantine, and the fumigation of the whole apartment house during which the steam would destroy the poor remnants of the ghetto inhabitants' property. People tried to avoid contact with the sick and places where you could become infected.

> Altogether you walked about in the ghetto as little as possible. You only went out when you had to arrange something. We were frightened to walk about, because after all there were [Nazi] fanatics who shot blind, some trouble or other was always flaring up. And apart from that, people were terribly afraid that they might catch typhus somewhere. (Irena, Interview 28)

Typhus inoculations, usually smuggled in from Russia, were extremely expensive.

> Lately typhus serum has been imported from Lvov, which has fallen into German hands. The Soviets, when they evacuated Lvov, left behind a great store of typhus vaccine in phials. Now this valuable medicine is being smuggled into Warsaw. But only the rich can afford it – the price is as much as several thousand złotys for a phial. (Berg 1945, p. 91)

One of the women I interviewed, who came to the Warsaw ghetto from Lvov, brought this kind of vaccine with her, the sale of which was an important source of income for her family.

> My parents were happy that I had arrived, but were very embarrassed. They wanted to give me something to eat, and they didn't have any scrap of bread, any drop of soup in the house: nothing. Luckily I had with me a bit of money and two Weigel injections. These were typhus injections that were greatly prized in the ghetto. You could sell them for a high price. My middle brother, who lived with my parents, ran out straight away to the shop, bought something to eat, mother made some soup, and only then did we start talking. (Anna, Interview 27)

Supplies of medicines in the ghetto were, like all other supplies, inadequate. There were pharmacies and wholesale pharmacists in the ghetto who sold medicines from their pre-war stocks, or goods that were smuggled – which greatly increased their price.

There were official allocations of certain medicines and the Germans made it possible to purchase them. There were not many of them, and so the distribution was through medical prescriptions, with only a few - like the popular 'Cockerel powder' - being generally available.

It would seem that pharmacies did well in the ghetto, and their owners were in the highest income group. Mary Berg noted:

> The best business in the ghetto is being done by doctors and pharmacists. The doctors work in the hospitals and have big private practices, but they are helpless when it comes to writing out prescriptions. They know that even the most essential medicines cannot be obtained in the chemists' shops in the ghetto because the Nazis allow only minimal quantities to be delivered here. The pharmacies are controlled by the Jewish Council, and the pharmacists employed in them are public employees. (Berg 1945, p. 142)

There is a further interesting question - which today is difficult to answer unequivocally - connected with the problem of medical supplies. What kind of access was there to products necessary for feminine hygiene? It is difficult today to say. One of the women I interviewed, when I asked about 'women's problems', claimed that in the ghetto women often (as was the case in the concentration camps) ceased to menstruate. This was probably a reaction to stress, and a side-product of hunger or other illnesses; it is not today possible to decide clearly about this, or to deal with the question in statistical terms.

I would like to deal with one more problem in the area of medical treatment. Is it not surprising that in these conditions, amidst poverty and hunger, with corpses lying in the streets, and against the background of a tremendous sense of danger and uncertainty, hospitals continued to function at all? Major and minor surgery was carried out there, of the kind that was normal in peace-time. Doctors devotedly saved the lives of people who shortly after they left hospital were to die of hunger or from German bullets.

> During the first winter of the war, there were many serious cases of frostbite, but still then and later the operations most commonly performed were in the field of internal surgery; there were quite a few broken limbs in older people. Then bullet wounds appeared on the

scene, mainly men, more rarely women and quite often child smugglers. Later on, I worked on the typhus ward, where we had to have two patients to a bed during the epidemic. I wrote a sketch - I was writing satire then - claiming that this was a medical break-through because when there was a pair [in Polish, *para*] of patients in a bed, typhoid automatically became paratyphoid, which wasn't so dangerous. I think there was a need for black humour like that. (Jerzy, Interview 35)

We are dealing here with the question of defence of human dignity, a free axiological choice exercised by doctors in the ghetto. Treating patients who were condemned to death anyway was a part of fighting against the Germans. Every victim who was saved from death even for a short time - a week, a month, perhaps a year - was a success in this unequal battle. Perhaps during the extra time that was given to him, someone would fall in love, experience wonderful friendship or read a fascinating book ... .

As in Warsaw, so in Łódź the ghetto had its public health service to take care of the inhabitants. One of the people I interviewed worked there as an emergency service doctor. He described the illnesses typical of the Łódź ghetto as follows:

Apart from starvation sickness there was also another illness that came from inadequate nutrition: tuberculosis. On the other hand, the enforced diet meant that there were relatively few illnesses connected with digestive problems. There were not many cases of diabetes or of kidney stones. Housing and sanitary conditions meant that dangerous epidemics were constantly breaking out in the ghetto. Tuberculosis and typhus were really endemic; in 1941 there was a great epidemic of dysentery, and in 1942 of typhus. All of the epidemics were brought under control by the health services of the ghetto, which were excellently organized. Obviously, there was a shortage of even the most basic medicines. Some of them were produced in the ghetto by cottage industry. But often we used what is called today a placebo - distilled water or soda water. (Arnold, Interview 9)

Most illnesses in the ghetto ended in death. Death was one of the most generally familiar elements of everyday life in the ghetto, a significant point on its psycho-social map. The language of the ghetto absorbed death in its typical way. People did not say 'to die' but 'to hand in your ration card'. This euphemism summarized and emphasized the meaning of bread and ration cards – the most valuable things in the ghetto. Krystyna Żywulska wrote: 'A ration coupon is the equivalent of 300 calories daily, and has long been worth more than a human life' (1963, p. 14).

Death was the norm, and dying was a style of ghetto life. A style of life understood literally, as a manifestation of the principle of choice of models of everyday behaviour from among the repertoire of possible behaviours in a given culture. In the totalitarian cultural oppression of the ghetto, choice of a lifestyle was nothing more than choice of a way of dying. The best-known example of choice in this area was the ghetto uprising, of which Marek Edelman said exactly this: that it constituted a choice of a way of dying (Krall 1977, 1986). The inhabitants of the ghetto were at various stages of dying, and the stage was determined by various factors which are being described in this chapter. In the world of *impotentia optandi*, in the ghetto, the style of dying was one of the few choices available.

The death of some made possible a prosperous life for others. Many new undertakers opened in the ghetto. Henryk Bryskier noted in his memoirs, which he wrote while he was in hiding on 'the Aryan side':

> Before the war, the opening of a rival undertaker's business, beside the only one then in existence, caused a great fuss. Now it is a sign of the times that undertakers are springing up like mushrooms after rain, and black caps with white piping have provided a temporary refuge from the snatchers of the living for snatchers of dead bodies. (Bryskier 1968)

The best-known undertaker in the ghetto was Motl Pinkert, whom Ringelblum dubbed 'the king of corpses'. He was the owner of a well-established firm called *The Last Rites*, and was – as we would say today – an enterprising and energetic businessman. Ringelblum wrote that 'Pinkert is continually opening new branches. He's just opened one in Smocza Street, where he offers a "luxury" funeral, i.e. with bearers in special uniforms, for 12 złotys' (1988a, p. 245). Apart from funerals of this kind, and 'normal' funerals, *The Last Rites* also dealt in collecting corpses from the streets of the ghetto and burying them in common, anonymous graves in the Jewish cemetery. People died in the ghetto streets – from hunger, illness and cold.

In addition, many families who did not want to give up the ration coupons of the deceased, or who had no money to pay for a funeral, carried their dead at night out of their homes into the street, where they were picked up next day by Pinkert's carts. In an entry in his *Chronicle* dated 26 August 1941, Ringelblum wrote about this as follows:

> The problem of corpses in poor homes is very pressing. If they don't have money to bury their dead, they often throw them into the street. In some tenements, they close the gate and will not let the tenants out until they give money for a funeral. The district policemen meanwhile, wishing to avoid the bother of formalities connected with the matter of corpses, carry the bodies from one pavement to another. At the cemetery, they are buried in common graves. At the very front of the cemetery, and therefore in the oldest part, there are high mounds of sand which have been formed in this way.
>
> On hot days such a strong odour wafts from these mass graves that you cannot walk past them without holding your nose. The mass graves are – evidently – dug too shallow, which is why there is the smell. Undertakers, especially the Pinkert brothers, are doing excellent business. Some undertakers have special carts for particular tenements which supply them with 'the goods' every day.
> (Ringelblum, 1988a, p. 309)

We should add that one of the main smuggling routes from 'the Aryan side' to the ghetto ran through the cemetery. Forbidden goods were often carried in coffins along with the corpse.

> A friend died and we had to go in a lorry from the Czyste hospital, which was then outside the ghetto, to the Jewish cemetery. There were a few other things in it apart from the coffin, but only the coffin was 'legal'. I had to stand up and report to the guardpost, show the pass. The pass stated that the corpse had died of typhus, and so the German let us through without searching the lorry, because the Germans were terribly afraid of *Fleckfieber*. Relief.
> (Jerzy, Interview 35)

In the ghetto, death was generally anonymous. Corpses lying in the streets were stripped not only of clothing, which might still be of use to others, but also of surnames and first names, of their identity. Buried in mass graves in the Jewish cemetery, they were to remain anonymous for ever. Ringelblum noted in his *Chronicle*:

> There is no way of establishing the identity of the majority of corpses, especially those from the streets found with no documents. It's only rarely that anyone from the family turns up, and then it's only to claim the dead man's shirt. (Ringelblum, 1988a, p. 245)

There was co-operation between life and death in the ghetto. It was not the utilitarian attitude to corpses which the Germans demonstrated when they turned them into soap – but rather a certain kind of bond between the living and the dead. The beggar friends of those who died in the street took off their clothes and boots. A sheet of gutter newspaper was substituted for the traditional Jewish shroud. Leaving the dead alone and even disowning them violated certain cultural norms. In cursed time, death lost its exceptional, sacred character, the barrier of intimacy was broken. In the ghetto, the living took advantage of the dead. For some they were a source of income, prosperity and even wealth; for others they simply made it possible to survive longer. The ration cards that they left behind, and their property which could be sold, gave the families of the dead the hope of assuaging their hunger. A coffin with a corpse was a chance of carrying a man out of the ghetto and of bringing food or documents into the ghetto: corpses offered a chance of salvation.

Switched-off morality

> Today I saw Janusz Korczak[26]
> As he walked with the children in the last procession
> And the children were in clean clothes
> As though it was a Sunday walk in the park.
>
> Władysław Szlengel, *Karta z dziennika akcji*
> (*A Page from a Diary of the Action*)

People were not visibly moved that it was Korczak walking along, there were no salutations (as some claim), there was certainly no intervention on the part of emissaries of the *Judenrat* – no one approached Korczak. There were no gestures, there was no song, there were no proudly raised heads, I don't remember whether anyone was carrying the banner of the Orphanage, they say that they were. There was a terribly tired silence. Korczak dragged one leg after the other, he was somehow bent, he was muttering something to himself from time to time ... I thought he muttered the word 'why'. These were not moments of philosophical reflection, these were moments of dull and silent, boundless grief, where no one asked questions to which there are no answers.

Marek Rudnicki, eyewitness to the events

Maria Ossowska (1966, p. 48) differentiates between moral philosophy and ethics on the basis that moral philosophy is constructed from descriptive statements, while ethics is constructed from evaluations and norms. Moral philosophy would therefore not in any circumstances make judgements, but would be exclusively a description of certain human patterns of behaviour and opinions. I think that only this kind of descriptive, non-evaluative approach is possible when presenting questions of morality in the ghetto. The morality of wartime, of an exceptional time, had its own norms and rules of behaviour, which were different from those typical of peace time. Because of their different and exceptional nature, I suggest that we call the morality of the world of the ghetto – paraphrasing Kazimerz Wyka's term – 'switched off morality'.

Are we anyway today – well-fed and peaceful – entitled to dare to describe morality in the ghetto, and by so doing designate spheres of 'immoral' behaviour? Since I have many reservations on this point, I will impose two limitations on what I say. Firstly, I will only write as much about morality in the ghetto as I heard from the people I interviewed. Secondly, in the words of Maria Ossowska (1966, p. 215), I will assume that 'a person can be subjected to moral judgement only when acting consciously'. This excludes from descriptions of moral behaviour people who were forced into 'immoral' actions by hunger or mortal fear.

In the opinion of the people I interviewed it was fear which made them aware of the fragility and relativity of the norms and rules of behaviour which had hitherto been accepted, and also the sense of evaluating the behaviour of other people according to these norms.

> It is difficult to imagine what people are capable of when they are in extreme situations. It's difficult for me even to speak about it. ... I saw mothers abandoning their children. ... Terrible things. ... The fact that I saw what people are capable of when they are in the grips of fear of that kind influenced my attitude to people later. (Irena, Interview 28)

Fear is the feeling which annuls all normative rules of behaviour. Fear of death, of pain, of starvation. People acting on the impulse of fear do not act consciously, they do not have the ability to to understand the consequences of their own actions, they do not have free will – and therefore they cannot be judged from the standpoint of peace-time ethics.

> You know, when such a terrible time comes for people, it reveals some kind of other human nature. I myself saw mothers who took food away from their children. … You can reduce a human being to that state. (Anna, Interview 27)

In view of this, what criteria can we accept to describe switched off morality? What, according to the inhabitants of the ghetto, was moral and what was not? Moreover, moral choices in the ghetto were not 'moral' in the sense that they did not fulfil the Kantian condition of freedom to undertake them. Kant claims that freedom relates to internal circumstances. That is, in a moral act, there is no discord between the motives and the aiming of the act at a defined goal. In this way, to act as 'a free man' means something very similar to 'willingly'. A moral act is a free act if, when we take a particular course of action, we wish to achieve the goal towards which the action is aimed. The primary characteristic of moral choice is that it is a sovereign act of the subject (Czerwiński 1988, p. 174).

People who were hungry, sick, frightened or dying could not perform Kantian moral acts, because their free will and their possibility of taking decisions were limited. We therefore have to look for indirect indicators of 'moral' behaviour . One of these could be attitudes to the community of which everyone had been forced to become a part. I will write more about this when I describe social gradations within the ghetto. For the moment I would like to draw attention to a certain specific attitude to the community which was linked with questions of morality – attitudes to the police and to the *Judenrat.*

> My dear, when someone's fighting for his life, he does it to the point of complete debasement or to the point of heroism. Living in the ghetto was a ceaseless struggle for survival. Some people betrayed others in order to save their own lives, others gave up their own lives in order to save someone else. It was attitudes like this that produced moral criteria. We despised the police, we felt bitter about people

whose egoism was stronger than a feeling of solidarity with the whole community. In a controversial situation like that, you lose your objectivity in judging what is going on around you. ... The will to live is clearly stronger than morality. A man is suddenly stripped bare. It is strange how easily you give in to evil and identify with it. After all, those people who became butchers and hangmen would, if they had lived in normal circumstances, have been ordinary average men. But they took money in return for promises of rescuing people and then committed crimes. To be fair, one has to say that there were some among them who tossed aside their police caps and went to their deaths along with their nearest and dearest. But there were too few of them. (Helena, Interview 30)

Attitudes to the police in the ghetto were unambiguously negative, all the more so because the part they played in the great deportation action from the ghetto to Treblinka influences contemporary judgements. The Germans announced that if policemen wanted to avoid being deported themselves and protect the members of their immediate families, they each had personally to deliver five Jews daily to the Umschlagplatz. The carrying out by the police of this decree was a clear example of excluding themselves from the community – from a community which had been condemned to death.

Fighting for your own life obviously had a place in the criteria of switched off morality, but it was understood rather as avoiding death, and not surviving at the expense of others. This norm was anonymous, indirect, because in a certain sense – in the face of the absurd randomness of death – every life that was saved was saved at the expense of someone else's death. The Germans laid down daily quotas for deportation, that is, a specified number of people had to be deported: five thousand, then ten thousand. If therefore someone succeeded in hiding and so survived, someone else, who for example hid himself less effectively, was deported 'instead'. In the place of an anonymous inhabitant of a house which on a given day was to be cleared, his anonymous neighbour was deported, who would perhaps not have been sought for (and found) if the Germans had met their quota earlier. The norm of indirectess, of the anonymous interchangeability of the victims, was permissible from the point of view of switched off morality. From the point of view of the Germans this was of no significance, since in any case sooner or later all Jews were to go to Treblinka. However, the norm of saving your own life at the direct expense of other people, as was the case with the behaviour of the Jewish police, was unacceptable, or at least years later was judged negatively.

Attitudes to the *Judenrat* were somewhat more complex than those to the police, as can be seen from what was said by people I interviewed:

> Attitudes to it were decidedly negative. ... Some thought that the *Judenrat* was doing what it was forced to do, and that maybe other people would be worse. But after all, they did terrible things. (Irena, Interview 28)

> I'm not going to find a common denominator between the *Judenrat* and the police. Its members included both worthless individuals and people of calibre, who were aware of the enormous responsibility that they had, and of the impossibility of coping with it. Engineer Adam Czerniaków was a great man. (Helena, Interview 30)

The problems of 'switched off morality' became even more dramatic and complex in the period of the mass deportations from the ghetto to Treblinka – that is, in the period of greatest terror and mortal fear on a mass scale. Many of the norms of peacetime which it had been possible to keep more or less in place up to July 1942 were now totally abandoned. One of these was the norm of fidelity and mourning for the dead.

> A lot of those who overnight lost their nearest and dearest, their family, were understandably in a state of shock, many became extremely apathetic. But they had to think about the fact that they needed to eat, work somewhere, earn something, look after anyone close who was left, hide somewhere, look for a chance on 'the Aryan side'; the thought of fighting was still only in its infancy, although you could see some livening up of the political groupings. Others formed new relationships, and not only those who had been single before, but for example – today they took his wife away, tomorrow he's already with another woman. It was not necessarily promiscuity, just that people wanted to be together, to live. You couldn't be alone any more, you had to snuggle up to some kind of warmth to find the strength to survive, a way out to some sort of hope. There was an atmosphere a bit like Beaumarchais: let's lap life up, maybe the world will last for another three weeks. Sometimes those three weeks shrank to one day. (Jerzy, Interview 35)

People lived together – when they'd taken away his wife, when they'd taken away her husband – they went to bed together. It was normal. I know one man who had worked before with Korczak; they took his wife, you'd think that it was the worst thing that could happen to anyone. But he somehow survived it and quite quickly found consolation. It didn't seem shocking in those conditions; people said – well, tough luck, today they're dead, tomorrow it will be me. (Ryszard, Interview 34)

Marek Edelman spoke in his conversation with Hanna Krall of the need felt in the period of the mass deportations to be together, to be close to another human being.

To be with someone was the only possible way to live in the ghetto. You would shut yourself up with another human being – in bed, in the cellar, anywhere – and then until the next round-up you were not alone. ... People at that time wanted to form relationships more than ever before, more than ever in normal life. During the last deportations they ran to the *Judenrat*, looking for a rabbi, or anyone who would marry them, and they went to the Umschlagplatz as man and wife. (Krall 1977, 1986, pp. 48–9)

Another norm that proved impossible to observe during the period of the deportations was the duty to take care of children and take responsibility for them.

I don't know myself why mothers threw their babies out of the trains, I've never been able to provide myself with an answer to that question. Either they thought that they could somehow save them, or it was the opposite – it was known that women with babies usually went straight to the gas chambers in the selection procedure. Children had to be hidden all the time, and the fact that mothers threw their babies out ... In the face of fear, all norms disappeared, in the face of such terminal danger. (Adina, Interview 13)

Are there any prior indications of how someone will be behave in a situation where all the moral intuitions of peacetime prove totally useless? Is there any kind of guarantee against behaving independently of all the norms of morality? I think not. We today cannot in the least say how we would have behaved in the world of the ghetto.

The philosophy of war consists in the fact that everything that you knew about a man before turns out to be worthless. You could never know how someone would behave. People that I'd regarded as absolutely despicable behaved heroically, and people that I'd thought were my best friends hid bread from me. You didn't know yourself how you you would behave. … I was afraid of myself, terribly afraid, all through the war I carried cyanide with me, because I really didn't know how I was going to behave. (Irena, Interview 28)

The people I interviewed were from a specific group of those who, as they said themselves, kept up a 'middling' standard of living in the ghetto that protected them from starvation sickness, and – through a variety of plans or opportunities to get out of the ghetto – offered them a minimal feeling of security. The fact that they themselves did not depart from certain norms confirms in a way the fact that they were in a privileged situation. The norm of switched off morality became for many to act in accordance with their instincts: hunger and fear. It was hunger and fear that determined rules for behaviour, at first for those who were hungriest, and at the time of the deportations – for everyone. Morality was a privilege in the ghetto; like all goods in limited supply, it was not available to everyone.

Krystyna Żywulska was an exception among the people I interviewed in that she experienced almost the depths of poverty and hunger. My interview with her, which was made after I had finished collecting the rest of the material, was in many respects an exceptional conversation, different from those that had gone before. Krystyna Żywulska, who for many weeks was swollen with hunger, had the following to say about morality in the ghetto.

[What moral judgements were passed in the ghetto?]

None. This is how things are, you've got to hold on, there's no escape, what can you do … it was miles away from what we were interested in, we didn't talk about it at all.

[What did you talk about? What were you interested in?]

There was a lot of silence; where to find something to eat, where else you could go. … There was a kind of total apathy. … I can't give an opinion about it, you can't sum it up in any categories. … It's something completely different, if you live in a relatively free space, various things are happening round about, you are listening to news, and then time – of course, it is somehow comparable – at the moment, I'm here, then here – I go away, I come back. And in the ghetto – it was just to survive to the end of the day. That was all, the whole point.

[And what was the situation with prostitution in the ghetto?]

You know, the prostitution ... if they could earn themselves a bit of bread ... it was understandable ... they were not condemned or anything. That kind of discussion had no meaning.

[And the police?]

The policemen ... they were people who hoped to survive at the expense of others. No one dared judge anyone else, you know.

[And collaboration with the Germans?]

There were people, Gancwajch and others, who had their Gestapo, apparently they handed over a lot of people, there was an action. ... But you can't apply any normal criteria to the ghetto. I didn't wonder about what was moral and what was immoral. What we were concerned with was what to do to get hold of something to eat – we didn't bother our heads ...

The destruction of solidarity between people which was carried out through stratification and the construction of a maximally complicated system of social gradation in the ghetto was one of the stages in depriving its inhabitants of a moral identity. It was, as Hannah Arendt wrote (1989b, p. 342), the decisive step in the preparation of living corpses. It would seem that the reduction of living beings to a point when they were governed exclusively by their instincts was the Germans' greatest success in preparing the 'living corpses'. During the mass deportations, the next stage in the totalization of human beings was also partly successful: depriving them of individuality and personality. People were anonymous, interchangeable victims; one could be exchanged for another, both at work in the 'shops' and on the train to Treblinka. What could protect the inhabitants of the ghetto from being turned into passive participants in the totalitarian world? Hannah Arendt has written that human conscience could still stand up to the attack on the moral entity, saying that it was better to die as a victim than live as a bureaucratic murderer. Totalitarian terror achieved its most awful triumph when it managed to cut off the moral being from the idea of individual escape and made decisions of the conscience absolutely unquestioned and ambiguous. What decision is a man to make when he is faced with the choice between betraying and thereby murdering friends, and sending his wife and children, for whom he is in every way responsible, to their deaths, and when even his suicide would mean the immediate deaths of his own family? The choice is not between good and evil, but between murder and murder (Arendt 1989b, p. 343).

One of the men I interviewed talked about the dramatic necessity of making inhuman choices, of the impossibility of doing good and of the selection made among themselves by the victims:

> I was back working at that time in the hospital at 1 Leszno Street. I remember a scene when a young doctor, Jurek Bzura, came into the hospital and showed us what was known as a *Lebenschein* – a permit for living. He had only one. 'Well, gentlemen: my mother or my wife?', he asked. How can you make a choice when you can only save one person and by so doing you have to condemn the other to death? Situations like that, that kind of inhuman choice, were a matter of course in the ghetto. Some people didn't want, or couldn't manage, to make choices like that. Instead of saving themselves and either their mother or their wife – they went along with them both to the railway waggons.

> These are choices that you shouldn't have to make in life. As Jerzy Szaniawski showed in 'Two Theatres'*, people are sometimes faced with this kind of decision not because of the orders of executioners, but for example when there are natural disasters. And what do you do then? Avoid making a decision? But if there is a choice like that to be made, you can't avoid it. Do you accept the deaths of three people if two of them could have been saved? There were situations like that, and people who were not at all contemptible chose in inhuman situations a way out that in the light of normal moral codes would be wicked, some would say contemptible. There are people who see everything separately and view this kind of behaviour completely detached from its inhuman context; they mercilessly censure the unfortunates condemned to make choices like that. They think they're superior, they consider themselves irreproach-able, while the fact is that they weren't there and life didn't force them to make that kind of choice. They lack imagination and humility. (Jerzy, Interview 35)

---

* Jerzy Szaniawski's three-act comedy *Dwa teatry* was first performed in 1946. Based on the author's wartime experiences, it had an enormous influence on the style of postwar Polish theatre – Ed.

Those who were able in the midst of the greatest terror and the greatest fear to stand up to their own instincts, who took responsibility for making choices, who obeyed the dictates of their own consciences and thereby prevented their own moral existence from being destroyed and totalitarianism from enjoying victory, were heroic. Heroism, however, cannot be the norm of morality or the standard for behaviour: it is always a free choice and not a moral constraint.

What did heroism in the ghetto consist in? Let the people who were there say:

> During the first action, Icchak Malme killed two Germans. They in return immediately dragged a hundred people out of their houses and shot them. They announced that if he did not give himself up, they would shoot another thousand. Did he have any kind of choice? He gave himself up. Where they hanged him is now Malme Street. Was he a hero? He couldn't take the death of a thousand people on his conscience. And so he went voluntarily to his death. It's difficult to judge, especially today with hindsight. I don't think anyone living has the right to judge those who died, if they haven't been through what they went through. (Edward, Interview 26)

> You could call it heroism that mothers handed over their food to their children, that parents went to the Umschlag in the place of their children – I saw a lot of things like that. But heroism is usually connected with some kind of conscious action, and was all that conscious? I don't know. Maybe it was a reflex action. I'm afraid to talk about heroism, because I wouldn't like to detract from anyone if he's considered a hero, or to add anything to anyone. If someone is dead you can't take anything away from him, because he's already got nothing. All my objections stem from the fact that whatever we say which is derogatory about those times, the people can't defend themselves. You know, I'm not terribly concerned about the truth. I'd rather not tell the truth if it was going to harm anyone. And on the other hand, I can't say that all those who died were heroes. Heroes and despicable people died. I don't want to set myself up as a judge and that's one reason why I don't want to say anything. The brave people, and those who were a bit less brave, all of them, deserve a kind thought.

> I think that perhaps heroism comes out when you are serving some kind of cause, some kind of idea – good or not, true or false – but then you act against your own interests and against your own fear. (Ryszard, Interview 34)

Heroism was a way of not giving in to totalitarianism. It was one of the choices available within the framework of the ghetto lifestyle. Often heroism was in fact a demonstration of choice of a way of dying. But also, frequently, it was heroism at that time to act in ways which would in other circumstances be seen as entirely ordinary.

Adaptation

> In the winter of 1942 you saw people barefoot in the ghetto streets. It didn't even make much impression by then. People had become impervious even to the sight of children who were still alive, but couldn't walk any more, with dry, wrinkled faces and dull eyes. No words came out of their mouths any more, but some awful gabble, you couldn't see fear in their eyes any more, or hunger, but just death. And you already walked calmly past these children, who were usually sitting by the court building, next to corpses and human scarecrows.
>
> From a memoir by an unknown author

Were things in the ghetto 'normal', could you treat the ghetto world as 'normal'? Yes, in fact it would seem that there were two kinds of normality there. The first was what we might call 'prewar' normality, for which the point of reference was the prewar world. Awareness of that world, memories of those times, made it possible – by contrast – to define wartime as abnormal and exceptional time. Situations which developed in the ghetto which were familiar from prewar times were considered to be elements of normality. That previous life was a point of reference, a certain standard for normality, for the usual and normal course of life. The prewar period seemed usually unreal and far away, the distortion of the temporal horizon meant that in the ghetto, the past was only 'yesterday', which was quickly forgotten because of the dreadful 'today', which was in turn under threat from the uncertain 'tomorrow'.

In this short and uncertain space of time, every succeeding day in the ghetto constructed its own normality, and the inhabitants adapted to it. It was a temporary and illusory normality, a normality that was mutable and endangered, but the human need for a feeling of security meant that even the world of the ghetto was absorbed. Everyday life did not lose its importance and sense, but went along according to its own rhythm because 'the world of the everyday is a universe which has meaning for us. It is a structure of sense which we must interpret in order to find our place in it and get to know it' (Schütz 1984, p. 16). One of the women I interviewed described as follows elements of prewar normality that existed in the ghetto:

> While you were still alive, it only needed one normal day, one day without illness, death, deportations – for everything to go on as it used to go on normally. You went to do the shopping, you ate dinner, someone dropped in for tea made from potato peel. ... It's difficult to imagine how strong is a human being's will to live and how strong is his ability to organize a normal life for himself. It only needed one half-normal day for everything to be as it ought to be, and for conversation to centre on how I'd got hold of some tomatoes and there would be tomato soup. ... And it was like that right through the occupation. We lived relatively normally, we ate, we slept, we made love, we were unfaithful to one another, we experienced completely civilian tragedies. ... It's deep down in human beings, it wasn't really conscious, it's a defence mechanism. In the end, we're living normally now although we know that we'll die in the end. It's the same in wartime. The fact that death is nearer and may be violent isn't particularly important. Otherwise we would all have gone mad, and as it was we came out of it relatively normal. (Irena, Interview 28)

In the abnormal world of the ghetto, every 'normal' moment, 'normal' behaviour took on great significance, was of exceptional importance as a contrast with the abnormal world of everyday. How difficult it was in the world of the ghetto to behave 'normally' in the sense of the standards set by prewar life. Behaving according to those standards was a defence of freedom, refusal to accept life on the terms imposed by the occupying forces, a demonstration of one's own personality. When physical resistance to the Germans was impossible, psychological resistance was a method of struggle against them.

> We tried to live normally. Normally, you understand, given the conditions. I used to tell my fellow-students that we ought to shave, and have clean shoes, smile at the patients, because it was all good for the patients – and anyway, we had to keep up appearances, just to stand up to what they wanted to do to us. We debated heatedly how you could feel even a little free, but it was accepted that our work was

something that protected us not only physically but also psychologically. (Jerzy, Interview 35)

This normality constructed in accordance with prewar standards as a contrast with the everyday life of the ghetto could be called external normality. Its opposite or complement is the other kind of normality – the internal normality of the ghetto which might be better termed adaptation.

In order to survive, you had to adapt to the conditions obtaining in the ghetto. Anna Pawełczyńska (1973, pp. 166 and 152) has written about the defensive adaptation of prisoners in concentration camps. Her ideas can also be applied to the situation in the ghetto:

> A necessary pre-condition for adaptation to conditions obtaining in the camps was to reduce your needs. People who had hitherto been convinced that everything that contemporary civilization offered them was essential for living – managed to adapt to the condition of primitive man, deprived of all equipment and objects to protect him, weak and defenceless against his environment. ... One can speak of complete defensive adaptation when the prisoner begins to exhibit the ability to experience the camp as everyday life, in which (even if in fundamentally different proportions) alongside defeats and causes of despair there are also moments of major and minor joy, a feeling of closeness to other people, things that are funny, to which you can react with humour, when interests and the need to act appear – both connected with the system of your present life, but which also constitute a continuation of your former biography.

There is something fascinating in the fact that people could manage to adapt to the realities of the ghetto, that they could absorb them and that they became 'normal'. But it had to happen: after all, you cannot live simultaneously in two worlds, calling the first – in the past – 'normal' and denying the second – in the present. This would lead inexorably to schizophrenia.

People always consider the everyday world that surrounds them 'normal' in the sense of the given reality. You have to get to know it and try somehow to interpret it, in order to act in it and behave rationally. Alfred Schütz (1984, pp. 167-8) gives the following definition of 'rationality' in everyday experience: 'We can say that a man is acting rationally when for us, his partners or observers, the motive and course of his action is understandable. And this is so when the behaviour is in accordance with a socially approved collection of regulations, prescriptions for dealing with typical problems by applying typical means to achieve typical goals.'

What, in the terms of this definition, would constitute 'rational behaviour' in the ghetto? Survival, living through it, has to be accepted as a typical goal for inhabitants of the ghetto; hunger, danger and death were the typical problems; and adaptation to the conditions of the ghetto, by which I mean a specific 'rationality of the ghetto', was a typical means of attaining the goal. One of the women I interviewed offered a picture of this kind of rational adaptation to life in the ghetto:

> Yes, you saw corpses covered with newspaper lying in the street, even in the centre of the town. I didn't venture into the poorest, most Jewish streets … I remember how my sister's mother-in-law came home one day from town very upset, because some little street urchin had snatched a packet of butter from her hand and eaten it. Those street urchins snatched anything, you know, it was absolutely wild. Because the majority of deaths from starvation were very quiet, people simply faded out, they died and that was the end of it. It was terrible, but you know it would have been difficult to weep over every corpse of that kind. On the other hand, if someone you knew died, or a neighbour, if it wasn't one of those anonymous deaths, then you were very upset. (Alina, Interview 33)

The essence of the rationale of adaptation to ghetto conditions was clearly summed up by another person I interviewed:

> I saw people being hanged in the ghetto. Three Jews who worked in the oil plant were hanged because they had stolen a few sunflower seeds. I was at the hanging. Everyone was seized by fear. In fact there was constant fear, terror, but after things like that life went back to normal. People had to live. Not everyone was going to lie down in the street. (Edward, Interview 26)

Janina Bauman (1982, p. 69) called this rational adaptation to conditions of life in the ghetto 'unhealthy stabilisation':

> I remember that second winter in the ghetto as a time of unhealthy stabilisation. I learned to live in a sea of suffering, which came right up to the threshold of my home. The evil that was growing all around me and engulfing ever new sacrifices became as obvious to me as heat in summer and frost in winter.

From today's perspective, what seems most surprising and disturbing is that one can get accustomed to the omnipresence of death. We feel disturbed by the fact that dying can constitute a style of life. Death in the ghetto, anonymous death from starvation, the death of unknown people, became after a time the norm, it became an element in what was real and obvious. It became an objective fact, to which rationality enjoined you to adapt.

> How could you rebel against it when it was the norm? You saw so many people dying that it became the norm. I remember that during one of the deportation actions, there was a decaying corpse outside the room where I spent the night. You stepped over the corpse and went on. There was nothing to be done. (Ryszard, Interview 34)

The process of adaptation, getting used to the conditions of the ghetto, occurred gradually. The world of the ghetto became daily for its inhabitants ever more the 'norm', the only experience of reality currently available to them, in which every day that they lived through became a point of reference for approximating to the future. Although the fact that the Germans often changed the 'rules of the game', and new regulations and the difficulties of everyday life hampered their orientation in this world, their ability to foresee the future or evaluate their own chance of survival, nonetheless, the desire to survive enforced the rationality of adaptation.

> People gradually became indifferent to suffering. At the beginning, you know, when you saw a dead man, a corpse in the street, or a man dying of starvation in the street, you couldn't walk calmly by. But when it went on for months, when you'd seen numberless corpses like that, and you couldn't even help them, then you became indifferent, it's normal in everybody, a defence mechanism. Just the same you know, as in the Warsaw Uprising, at the beginning it was this one wounded, that one - but when you see the corpses - this one killed, that one killed - then you think of yourself. (Stefan, Interview 29)

> The first time I came across it, I stood still and I couldn't move - either forwards or backwards. But slowly I began to get used to the picture of everyday life. The street crowds walked along, shouted, lived. But whether you become indifferent, or whether you turn to stone with despair, or whether you think 'When is it my turn?'. It's some kind of atrophy of feeling. Beggars snatched everything edible from the

hands of passers-by with unbelievable dexterity and ate it with the speed of light. You're helpless in the face of what's going on. (Helena, Interview 30)

Everything that you saw in the streets: hunger, corpses, and the people who were dying but still had a spark of life. ... You soon – perhaps too soon – got used to it; otherwise it would have been more difficult to hang on to the will to live, to keep up your energy, you wouldn't have been able to do anything normally, even work. This was not callousness towards what was happening, but a callousness which grew because of the fact that you could do nothing about it, there was no effective way to help. You simply couldn't do anything – or very little – for those people. Even though a lot, really a great deal, was done, but it was a drop in the ocean compared with the needs – I'm thinking here of the people working in charity organizations, or individually, who tried to relieve the enormous want that was constantly extending the reach of hunger and poverty. But for people from outside who came into the ghetto, that was what was most striking – that people walked apparently indifferently past the dying and the corpses in the streets. But what could you do? At the very most, buy a newspaper and cover somebody's corpse with it. (Jerzy, Interview 35)

It would seem that one way of surviving the ghetto, not only in the physical but also in the psychological sense, was to adapt to its inner rationality and normality. Remembering prewar standards of normality and applying them, rather than applying the principles of rational behaviour which obtained in the ghetto, did not make survival easier, but only increased the suffering – both moral and physical – of its inhabitants. It was depriving people of moral dignity that was the second element (the first was depriving them of their legal existence) in the totalization of society, in the preparation of a society of 'living corpses', as Hannah Arendt called it. She points out (1989b, p. 342) that depriving people of their moral identity was also effected by, for the first time in history, making martyrdom impossible. By making death anonymous, Arendt says, the Germans took away its true significance as the end of a fulfilled life. In this sense, they deprived the individual of his death, proving that from then on nothing would belong to him and he would belong to nobody. His death would only finally confirm the fact that he never really existed (1989b, p. 343).

Sensitivity to the anonymity of other people's deaths observed daily in the ghetto evoked fear of anonymity in one's own death, fear of disappearing without trace, without leaving any memory of one's own existence. It would seem that a great deal of testimony from the ghetto (and the people I interviewed also talked about it) on the impossibility or difficulty of adapting to this anonymous dying shows that not everyone managed to shake off their moral identity.

> My mother ... despite an undoubtedly sensitive nature, is somehow internally coping with it better. She simply deals with it in categories of what she can do officially and privately, and not - like me - in categories of conscience. You do what you can, and if you can't do anything - well, hard luck, it's war time. I can't be like that. I expect miracles of samaritanism from people - and there are no miracles. I do things myself that are beyond my capacities, and yet it's not even a drop in the ocean, but only an atom of a drop. ... I've 'fallen asleep' in sympathy. That is the only adequate description of my state of mind. I'm only afraid that I shall burn up completely, be lost in this ocean of 'alienness' which is already a major part of me myself.

> I am more isolated than ever before, even though I'm surrounded by many people close to me. ... It's as though someone has opened a crack in the door in front of me, through which I can see some goal shining, some way, but I don't know yet how to open it wide myself, and nobody's showing any signs of throwing it open for me.[27]

Totalitarianism, with its slogan of 'everything is possible', was a contradiction of common sense. But, as Arendt writes, it was common sense that to a certain extent made its successes possible. It was common sense that made it impossible to believe in the effectiveness of totalitarianism, to believe that it would be able to carry out everything that it shamelessly and openly predicted. And later it was the common sense of ordinary people that prevented them from believing in the crimes that were being committed.

Hannah Arendt (1989b, p. 331) wrote that the normality of the normal world constituted the most effective protection against revealing the mass crimes of totalitarianism, and that the common sense reluctance to admit the existence of monstrous things constantly reinforced the totalitarian ruler himself.

An example of behaviour of this kind can, for example, be found in the language of Nazism, which in order to describe terrible things used terms from the 'normal' prewar language.

Let us, however, return to the problem of normality and adaptation in the ghetto. It has to be stated clearly that adaptation to the ghetto did not mean acceptance of the ghetto. Adaptation was a kind of mimicry, fitting in, the only rational way of behaving in view of the necessity of surviving. Awareness of the need to adapt was for many ghetto inhabitants an additional source of suffering. One of the women I interviewed put this into words:

> The most terrible thing was that you had to make some kind of shell for yourself, because otherwise you wouldn't have been able to live. It was obvious that I couldn't share my bread with everyone who needed it. I had to learn to eat without looking at the people who were dying of starvation. Because I did after all eat, things varied, but all the same we ate. (Irena, Interview 28)

Adaptation to the realities of the ghetto was revealed in patterns of behaviour which I called in the previous chapter exhibited indifference. But indifference of that kind did not exclude – according to one of the people I interviewed – sympathy and sensitivity to other people's suffering.

> [In conditions like that was there any place at all for sympathy?]
>
> Yes, there's always room for sympathy. There's always room for trying to help others. I don't think that I ever got rid of that feeling.
>
> [Where does the boundary lie between sympathy and indifference?]
>
> Indifference appears when you are absolutely finished physically. While you're not yet in a state of bestiality and are somehow managing – then there's sympathy. (Ryszard, Interview 34)

It would appear that the retention of sensitivity among the inhabitants of the ghetto is evidence on the one hand that the attempt to deprive them of moral identity and conscience was not successful; and on the other hand that retaining sensitivity was a kind of luxury in the ghetto. People who were not 'right at the bottom of the barrel' could afford it, and most of the people I interviewed were in this group.

Information

> Everyone was very careful. Before you left home you asked the question: How are things out there today? And you tried to keep a watchful eye out for danger in a crowded street. People walking along exchanged words of warning which could suddenly change the whole direction of movement in the street. One word of danger, one gesture, squeezed a crowd of several thousand people into gateways, leaving an empty street, suddenly stripped bare.
>
> From Natan Żelichower's memoirs

In the life of any society – including the society of the ghetto – the quality and circulation of information play no small role. In wartime, the role of information is probably greater than in peacetime. Information plays a significant regulatory function – it is the basic source of speculation about the future. During wartime, when the temporal horizon is restricted, the possibility of making a prognosis about the future is of particular importance.

Information in the ghetto was of three kinds: official information, unofficial information and rumours.

Official information consisted of all the German decrees and instructions published on the order of the German authorities by the *Judenrat*, and posted on the walls of the ghetto. The only official newspaper in the ghetto, the *Gazeta Żydowska* (*Jewish Gazette*), also conveyed this type of information, as did street loudspeakers. The *Gazeta Żydowska* was published in Kraków and was the German authorities' official newspaper for all the ghettos in the *Generalgouvernement*. Loudspeakers were a means of mass communication widely used during the war, also on 'the Aryan side'. They broadcast German propaganda texts and various decrees; they announced repressive measures being taken by the authorities. In the ghetto, as throughout Warsaw, the loudspeakers broadcast in Polish.

I do not know how many loudspeakers there were in the ghetto. Ringelblum (1988a, p. 385) mentions three: 'on the corner of Miła and Zamenhofa, on the corner of Gęsia and Zamenhofa, and on the corner of Nalewki and Nowolipki'. Throughout Warsaw they operated from July 1941, and, according to Tomasz Szarota, were 'usually installed in squares. Twice a day they broadcast news; they also broadcast the texts of decrees, and lists of names of those who had been shot in public executions were read out over them' (Szarota 1978, p. 348). It would seem that in certain periods the loudspeakers became a source of valuable information.

> I remember when the German-Soviet war broke out. There was one loudspeaker - not far from here, where the monument to the heroes of the ghetto now stands - that broadcast communiqués from the front. Lots of people gathered there, I went along as well. There was a belief then that maybe things would be settled on that front. (Ryszard, Interview 34)

The demand for information was so great in the ghetto that people even bought on the black market the official German papers published on 'the Aryan side' - naturally at higher prices. Ringelblum (1988a p. 281) noted on 6–11 May 1941 that:

> Newspapers are smuggled and (naturally) are more expensive. *Nowy Kurjer Warszawski* costs 35 groszy instead of 20, and the *Krakauer* [*Zeitung*] - 50 groszy.

In this situation of information deprivation, any kind of news that helped people to foresee the future was exceptionally valuable. It allowed people to have, even if only temporarily, some orientation about what was really happening in the world. In the ghetto, where all the rules for orientation familiar from an earlier life had ceased to apply, people were completely adrift. There were no signposts which permitted them to foresee what would happen in an hour's time, a week's time or next day, or which told them how to behave appropriately to the things that happened. And therefore various kinds of unofficial information were of great significance in the ghetto.

Unofficial information consisted chiefly in underground newspapers. According to Ruta Sakowska (1993, p. 244), 61 titles appeared in the underground press of the ghetto, of which 56 titles appeared fairly regularly - as weeklies, bi-weeklies and monthlies - between June 1940 and July 1942. The papers were the mouthpieces of various political parties, many of which carried on underground activity in the ghetto. The most extensive activity came from the Communists, the Bund and left-wing Zionists. Were these papers generally available, outside the circle of party members and sympathizers? It is difficult today to find out. The people I interviewed had contradictory views on this – depending, I think, on their ideological and social contacts:

> No, not underground papers, there was some sort of Jewish paper which came out, I didn't even read that, there weren't any opposition papers published in the ghetto at all, a few got in from 'the Aryan side', but a really small number, or at least I hardly saw any of them. (Stefan, Interview 29)

> From the moment when the party was formed I was very busy – there was the press, which had to be distributed, and meetings, and educational activities ...

> [Weren't you afraid to distribute the underground press?]

> You didn't need to be frightened about that at least, even my parents read the underground ghetto press. (Irena, Interview 28)

> We had underground papers all the time. I don't know where they came from. I remember that it was me that brought them home and that at first I was very afraid to do it. (Ryszard, Interview 34)

On 20 October 1939, Dr Otto, the *Reichskommissar* for Warsaw, issued a decree that all radios were to be confiscated immediately, and they were to be handed in by 5 November (Bartoszewski 1982, p. 84). As a result, the Jewish population was deprived of a major source of unofficial information long before being imprisoned in the ghetto. It is difficult to discover today whether listening to the radio illegally was as widespread in the ghetto as on 'the Aryan side'. One man I interviewed listened to the radio in the Łódź ghetto:

> I was once at a session when we listened to the radio; of course, the penalty was death. It was a detector set which picked up the news in German. It was the only big radio set in the ghetto, which in fact was later discovered and confiscated. (Arnold, Interview 9)

The most powerful source of information in the ghetto, the source with the widest circulation, was rumour. Rumour was a major element in the psycho-social map of the ghetto.

In his book on *The Psychology of Rumour*, Klaus Thiele-Dohrmann (Warsaw 1980) makes a distinction between gossip (talking over somebody who is not present) and rumour (information on general matters). He writes that rumours appear above all in periods of political and economic crisis. They were therefore bound to thrive in wartime.

> There were a lot of rumours. About major victories by the Red Army, that Hitler had died. (Ryszard, Interview 34)

> That Hitler had committed suicide, and that the English had landed outside Warsaw ... (Stefan, Interview 29)

The rumours in the ghetto were of two kinds: favourable and unfavourable for the Jews. They were almost entirely about wartime events, dealing directly with military developments or events that might have bearing on them. The purpose of rumours was to keep people's spirits up, to give them some temporary hope – and they therefore usually spoke of a coming end to the war, or about events that might speed up the end of the war.

> There was general poverty, general hunger, you thought about how to survive, that was most important. People cheered themselves up with all kinds of news, like, for example, that the war was going to end soon. And so you had to hold on, you had to survive, that was basic. (Stefan, Interview 29)

Chaim Kaplan wrote in his ghetto diary (1963, 1964, p. 364) that

> The last week has been dominated by 'cheering news'. This is usually a product of the imagination of some armchair politician who can't differentiate between reality and daydreams. There is no press, but news of this kind circulates like lightning through the whole community, which longs for good news. The miserable will even believe in the impossible: e.g., in a sudden collapse of the front. A people whose existence is based on a miracle is prepared to believe in miracles.

One of the elements of ghetto life was the informational chaos that obtained. Chaos, lack of orientation about the world, and lack of a possibility of assessing the future created an information gap which was entirely filled by rumour. The level of disorientation about the surrounding world rose in the ghetto with the passage of time. In the period of relative calm, the 'minor stabilization' to July 1942 (in the case of the Warsaw ghetto) there were certain local rules for assessing the future. In the first period of the ghetto's existence, you more or less knew what to expect, ways of getting used to the circumstances developed, some kind of modus vivendi existed. The population of the ghetto developed skills in orientation in the world that surrounded it. Smugglers knew when they could relatively safely get past the sentries, and which Nazi was bribable; and that when 'Frankenstein' was on your beat, you should stay away because he shot at anything that moved. This kind of information was – literally – essential for living.

This original orientation in the world of the ghetto proved completely out of date from the moment when the Germans started to carry out their plan for 'the final solution of the Jewish question'. At that point there was unbelievable informational chaos, and the rules that had been learned ceased to apply.

The specific character of time, where the horizon was restricted to the present, was also not without significance in determining the susceptibility of the inhabitants of the ghetto to rumour. The present seemed to drag out into all eternity. The disintegrating character of life in an unending present stems for example from the impossibility of planning your life for longer than the next moment – which evokes strong anxiety and a feeling of uncertainty. It is difficult to plan one's own behaviour when one does not know the rules according to which the world around operates. And hence a willingness to believe the strangest and least credible rumours.

Ringelblum noted carefully all kinds of rumours that circulated in the ghetto, as did Czerniaków and other chroniclers of the ghetto. It is a characteristic of rumour that you forget it very quickly – and therefore the people I interviewed could not remember them in detail fifty years later. But they remembered that there were rumours, and what they were about in general.

> When I found myself in the ghetto in Warsaw, I thought that the mood there was optimistic. They constantly thought that the war would be over soon, that everyone would survive. It's difficult to imagine the quantity of optimistic information that was in circulation in the ghetto. We were continually discovering something wonderful. … Bad news only came from the *Judenrat* – that food rations were to be reduced, that there were to be deportations. (Irena, Interview 28)

It is worth pointing out that rumour played a dual role: it was not only informational, but also emotional. Apart from the passing on of what quickly proved to be false information –

but information that satisfied the hunger for information, for news – rumour also reduced the level of fear and provided hope. Rumour was a major element in the ghetto psychosis of hope.

You could say that the ghetto constituted a rumour laboratory. This would be the opposite of the 'rumor clinics'[28] set up by the Americans during the Second World War to combat demoralizing rumours which undermined the national morale. The ghetto, on the contrary, was a laboratory, a hatchery, for rumours. In the first phase of its existence rumours that were full of hope, and favourable to the Jews, were predominant. On 18 May 1941, Ringelblum (1988a p. 286) noted that

> On 16 May the news spread like lightning that at 11.30 it had been announced on the radio that Goering had died from his wounds. Apparently half the town had heard it. But you couldn't find one person who had heard it with their own ears. ... On the basis of this, the ghetto built castles in the air: there was talk of an armistice, of peace, toasts were drunk to the occasion, and people relaxed for a moment. ... With the eye of the imagination they saw the walls pulled down.

This rumour has all the typical, definitive characteristics set out by Thiele-Dohrmann (1980, p. 165):

- it has significance and arouses interest;
- the content is ambiguous and the interpretation depends on the needs of the audience;
- the source of the information is unclear;
- the information contains 'a grain of truth'.[29]

Although they cannot refrain from listening to rumours and passing them on, people are aware of the difference between rumours and confirmed, real news. Every rumour contains, in addition to the informational content, an emotional component (referring to the content) and a probabilistic component (referring to the probability of the events which the rumour is about). I think that in the ghetto, too, people were able to estimate the probability of the truth of the rumours that were in circulation.

But it is difficult today to say with any certainty whether the inhabitants of the ghetto believed in the rumours that circulated or not. Reality very quickly verified them, and some of them proved untrue. The stock of particular rumours rose or fell in line with the probability of the events predicted in a particular rumour coming to pass. Most rumours were very quickly bankrupted, proving to be complete nonsense, or information so distorted that they completely changed the meaning of the event reported. I think that in the first period of relative stabilization in the existence of the ghetto, its inhabitants learned – and this was one of the factors in orientation to the situation in this world – not to believe rumours. And this was one of the reasons why people believed the official information about deportations to the East, and did not want to believe the rumours that the Germans were shipping them direct to the gas chambers.

Moods: between hope and fear

> Between gibberish
> and rusty spittle
> between the lichen on the wall
> and the corpse of a passer-by
> with cruel china eyes
> between stone
> and mad screaming
> stood Salcia in a red dress
> but the colours were soaked with venom
> and an apple rotted in hands
> that were pale. From the stench
> a white maggot wriggled.
> Withered apples rotten apples
> and mother was dying.
>
> Tadeusz Różewicz, *Żywi umierali*
> (*The Living Died*)

One of the typical elements of everyday life in the ghetto was the way that public life, collective life, invaded personal life. Individual life had its own rhythms, and its problems of a private nature. However, even the most intimate dimensions of everyday life were penetrated by the public dimension. The personal lives of the inhabitants of the ghetto depended on what was happening in the collective life of the ghetto and on the mood that obtained there. The dimension of personal life in the ghetto was – as was the case with the time dimension – reduced to skeletal forms, and was really only quasi-private. It was difficult to retain intimacy and privacy if only because of the over-crowding and the reduction of social distances in the ghetto. Public moods in the ghetto were influenced by both external and internal factors.

External factors meant the influence of the situation outside the ghetto: what was happening on 'the Aryan side' and generally in the war. News from the outside world, from the fronts of the war, undoubtedly influenced the mood of the ghetto (as was also the case on 'the Aryan side'). One typical example of external factors influencing mood can be found in the increase in pessimism among the Jews after the fall of Paris:

> After the fall of Paris, there was an observable collapse of optimism in the ghetto, disillusion after the shattering outcome of the German offensive. It was an especially difficult thing for me personally to take, since I was a francophile, and for someone of my age and opportunities knew quite a lot about French history and culture. For me, Paris was the centre of the world. And to give in to the Germans so easily, a lot more easily than Poland. That's what we felt then, that's how it seemed. And not too long afterwards, the loot began to appear in Warsaw restaurants: Sauterne, and I think Barsac, and then champagne and sardines. (Jerzy, Interview 35)

Stanisław Sznapman confirmed this in the diary he kept in the ghetto:

> In our terrible distress, we were full of trust, optimism and faith, that the two democratic powers, England and France, would wipe out the black phantom which was strangling the whole of Europe.

> Then came May 1940. It started. And ever more dreadful news came through. We were dumbfounded. We didn't believe it. We weren't able to understand what had happened. We fooled ourselves that the situation would change at any moment. ... But unfortunately what followed was the sad, the tragic reality. France capitulated. We were overcome at that point with boundless despair and hopeless depression. It was then that people broke down and suicides began. We trembled with fear that England would give up the struggle and begin negotiations.[30]

After the outbreak of the German-Soviet war, there was however a prevailing optimism in the ghetto:

Among the Jews there were very many people who opposed the Soviet Union, but also very many who sympathized. And the fact that from mid-1941 Russia was on the right side in this war, together with the Allies, did a lot to clear the atmosphere. Polish society had a deeply rooted conviction that there were two enemies, but a lot of Jews didn't choose to see Russia as an enemy. And that was why it was possible to feel a wave of optimism in the ghetto. People stood under the loudspeakers, listened carefully to the communiqués, and reading the underground press became more and more widespread. (Jerzy, Interview 35)

However, very soon, this optimism turned into anxiety and disillusion:

Unfortunately, this optimism changed into real despair. It turned out that Russia, our potential liberator, was falling apart. We heard every day that one division after another had capitulated to the Germans. People began to fear that they would not live to see the liberation. They had believed, they had known for sure, that whatever happened, the outcome of the war was somehow predetermined, that the Germans were bound to lose. It was only a question of time. People used to say humbly: for God's sake don't let the war last longer than the Jews can manage to hold out. (Jerzy, Interview 35)

The most important internal factors in mood in the ghetto were hope and fear. These are important categories, without a closer interpretation of which we cannot fully understand the ghetto. The opposite of hope was despair, and it was on this 'continuum of mood' that the emotions of the inhabitants of the ghetto were placed. They wavered between hope and despair, between faith and doubt, between fooling themselves and resignation. All of these feelings, irrespective of which kind, were terribly intense, because of the specifics of time in the ghetto, close to the dimension of eternity.

Tomasz Szarota writes in *Everyday Life in Occupied Warsaw* (1978, p. 505): 'You can picture the psychological space of life in the form of a surface divided into two parts – on one side is the zone of fear and terror, and on the other that of faith and hope; the relative size of the two zones would reflect the mood.'

The same point could be made about moods in the ghetto, but with one reservation: the direct threat to the lives of the inhabitants of the ghetto was incomparably greater than that to the lives of those on 'the Aryan side', and therefore the intensity of both hope and fear was stronger in the ghetto. It seems that the Germans needed the Jews to have hope, to remain to the end unaware of the fate that awaited them. It was thanks to concealing their intentions that the Nazis could be successful in carrying out 'the Final Solution of the Jewish question'. On the one hand, therefore, hope was an internal need of the Jews, and on the other it was kept up by the Germans for their own ends.

Rumours of all kinds undoubtedly helped to keep up hope (Szarota suggests that some of them were spread by the Germans themselves). Hope was also bolstered by various prophesies and predictions, which were exceptionally popular during the war. Ringelblum (1988a, pp. 219 and 313) wrote:

> I heard recently about some little boy from Pańska Street who had predicted the liberation. ... There are rumours again about the end of the war. People cite Ossowiecki, the clairvoyant, who died recently,[31] leaving us with the information that the war would end on 23 October. I heard from the clairvoyant Mme Merlińska that a revolution would shortly break out in Germany, that the Jews had hard times still to come, but that the war would end in January.

Hope in the ghetto also had an historical source. This was after all a community that for centuries had experienced various kinds of persecution. From the beginning of their history, the Jews, who were faced everywhere with dislike or hatred, had learned various responses to antisemitism.

The genocidal antisemitism of the Holocaust, however, proved the first kind of antisemitism in history to which there was no response, and on which you could not turn your back. Other forms of hatred of the Jews were not so holistic, they left some escape route, some way out to evade persecution.

Religious antisemitism could be evaded by changing your faith, by converting. Ethnic antisemitism could be evaded by assimilation, by moving from the 'alien' group and going native. Emancipation provided protection from social antisemitism. Emigration offered a possible escape from political anti-semitism: Zionism was a political response to this kind of aversion to the Jews. It was only genocidal antisemitism which put the Jews in a position where there was no way out, there was no room for any kind of apostasy.[32] The long centuries of experience proved useless. But they proved useless only after

July 1942; up to that time, the Jews – remembering the experiences of their nation, which were the only point of reference available to them – had hope.

One of the men I interviewed drew attention to the role of historical experience in maintaining hope in the ghetto:

> I think that if he [the chairman of the *Judenrat* – B.E.] had said, 'The Germans are going to murder you', what would have happened? They would have shot him, and would have put somebody else, perhaps worse, in his place ... I think that the *Judenrat* in a way represented the millenia-long history of the Jews: you have to keep quiet, maybe it will be all right, don't take any risks, don't annoy them. ... Those were the views of the Jewish diaspora. (Edward, Interview 26)

One of the ghetto diarists also wrote about the historical background of hope:

> The Jews did not believe that they were lost. At the very heart of their 'temple of meditation' was God, who had brought them through the Red Sea and who would pull down the walls of the ghetto. They responded to the executions with horror – their hearts were squeezed with unbelievable terror – but they left themselves a rational way out: you could get rid of thousands, or several thousands in that way, or even, let's say, several tens of thousands, but not the half-million strong ghetto. Not everyone will be killed – and that gave everyone a chance that he would not be among those caught. Before execution you have to arm yourself with faith, an unshaken faith in divine protection.[33]

The Germans were successful in 'the Final Solution of the Jewish question' exactly because the Holocaust was the first event of its kind in the history of the world, and people were therefore unable to foresee what was in store for them. They had hope up to the very end:

> People asked – are there still any orders from Germans coming in? Because if there were, if some murderer had ordered himself a pair of boots and they were to be ready, say, in two weeks, that meant that the ghetto would last two weeks more. And perhaps the Russians would arrive during that fortnight ...? There was hope right up to the end. (Edward, Interview 26)

The inhabitants of the ghetto did not lose hope up to the end. Even during the Uprising, when the Germans fired the neighbouring houses, Marian Berland (1992, p. 68), hiding in a bunker under the rubble next door, wrote:

Either we die here, or we have the way ahead there, opposite, via the *Umschlagplatz* to the gas chambers of Treblinka. For the time being, I'm still calm, balanced. I work, I do everything that I ought. I put out fires, I save people, I cook, I dig people out. Why this is going on, why I do it, I don't know, it's hopeless and senseless. What is the point of the riddle? Where is the strength that will help me to bear it all and fulfil it? In Samson it was in his hair, in me it lies in the fact that we're together, that I have a family. That's the only incentive for pulling through. Somewhere in the depths of my being there's still a little spark of hope which allows me to believe in a better tomorrow.

The presence of those closest to you, family ties, were often a source of strength and the will to survive. Hope was, however, often illusory and delusive. It was only loss of hope that gave a realistic chance of survival. Not the kind of loss of hope that led to passivity and death, but the kind that stirred you to action, made you aware that there was no point in counting on a miracle, but that you had to save yourself. Hope was therefore a phenomenon with ambivalent meaning: it could help or hinder, assist survival or make it more difficult. I think that for survival a certain optimal level of hope was needed, since both too little and too much could prove fatal.

*

The second factor determining mood in the ghetto was fear. Its basic, most visible characteristics were: universality, inductiveness, gradability.

The universality of fear was reflected in the fact that it transcended all divisions and differences between people, ignored the gradations of the ghetto hierarchy and social rank. None of those who lived in the ghetto was free of fear:

Remember that in spite of all the differences, people were levelled by fear. The pressure of fear and misery was enormous and increasingly paralysed thought, and consequently behaviour. (Jerzy, Interview 35)

People were afraid. I saw that people were terribly afraid, fear is a big thing. (Irka, Interview 20)

The inductiveness of fear lies in the fact that like hope it was an infectious feeling, it was passed on to others: fear is an adhesive, infectious emotion that is easily spread about.

> I went down for a moment to the shelter and I immediately escaped again. I wasn't able to bear that huddling, shrinking, and fear – oh, shooting, oh, a bomb! That kind of fear is terribly infectious. ... Everyone had his own fear and to that he added the mood of others. (Ryszard, Interview 34)

The gradability of fear has its own dynamics. In the very concept of this characteristic lies the assumption that there is a certain 'basic level' of fear. The population of the ghetto adapted to omnipresent danger, absorbed fear, which became an element of the normality that I have described earlier.

> When the smuggler got me and a few other people over the border at Zaremba Kościelna, I was afraid that I might not get home to Warsaw. I was afraid that I might not get there, that I might never see my parents again. This was reinforced in Małkinia when I saw the first German shouting 'Jude' at a friend who was walking behind me. It was a different kind of fear from the kind I'd been through a few months earlier during the bombardment of the road to Siedlce. But in both cases I felt a particular fear of an anonymous death. Later I discovered other fears, for example the fear in the ghetto, that fear before the beginning of the July–August deportation action. By then, it wasn't a sudden, sharp fear, but was somehow tamed. You didn't distinguish it any more as a feeling of fear – it was integrated, mixed with anxiety, helplessness, it had become a part of the ordinary, the routine, almost the natural life of the ghetto. (Jerzy, Interview 35)

There were, however, events in the lives of the inhabitants of the ghetto when the feeling of fear – this time stronger fear than the general level of being frightened that they had got used to – dominated all others, even hunger. This was usually at times of deportations, when the threat to life became more immediate than before. It was then that you could see how greatly fear could be gradated.

> Fear became something general. I think that there are certain limits to the level of fear that you can take. In the ghetto when you woke up and knew that you hadn't anything to eat for the whole day ahead – then hunger was stronger than fear. Hunger is gradated differently. But when you got up and knew that there was to be a deportation, then the fear was greater and stronger than the hunger. Fear kills hunger – you are in its grip. (From a conversation with Krystyna Żywulska)

Marian Berland (1992, p. 22) also writes in his memoirs about the disappearance of hunger among the Jews hiding in the bunker:

> It is already four o'clock in the afternoon. Since yesterday evening we have had nothing to eat. Nobody thinks about it, everyone is filled with his own misery.

This experience of the strongest kind of fear is often reflected – and even many years later – in the dreams of those who went through it in the ghetto. One of the men I interviewed talked about this:

> Later, there were new fears, constantly new ones. That terrible fear in the period of the action that began on 22 July 1942, even though after a few weeks I was more or less anaesthetized to it for personal reasons. And then the fear from the time in hiding, which went on for months. To the present day, I don't like to tell the story of the time I spent in hiding, especially not in the evenings. Because then I always have the dream. The same dream. I dream that I'm buried in sand up to the neck, with only my head standing out. And the Germans are coming. I don't know how the dream ends, because I wake up. And we use the word 'fear', but it's a very imprecise label, because what we're talking about is really a much more complex emotion, of which the fear is a part – sometimes a very big part, and sometimes a small part. (Jerzy, Interview 35)

In psychological categories fear can be interpreted as a type of powerful stress, or, rather, distress. Hans Selye (1977) distinguishes three stages of stress: alarm reaction, the stage of resistance, the stage of exhaustion.

The length for which each stage of stress lasts is differentiated on an individual basis and depends on the social situation in which the stress is taking effect. After a certain time, in the stage of exhaustion, indifference and adaptation to the stress – or in this case to fear – occur.

The last property of the feeling of fear to which I wish to draw attention is linked with its gradability: the relationship between fear and the instinct to preserve your life. It would seem that these two feelings are linked. The stronger the fear, the more directly life is threatened, the stronger is the instinct to save your life. This of course holds good up to a certain level of fear, which when it is reached totally disintegrates the functioning of the human organism. At that point, fear paralyses human behaviour, makes it impossible to take rational decisions, and prevents control not only over one's own thoughts and actions but even over physiological functions. This threshold of disintegration has a relative value, depending on individual psychological characteristics, and also an absolute value which depends on the social circumstances within which the individual is functioning.

One of the factors that can strengthen tolerance to fear is long-term existence in conditions of constant fear, which allows an individual – as is the case with long-term stress – to adapt to it. In this case, the frontier point of fear, which disorganizes the functioning of the organism, is postponed. In situations of extreme tension caused by long-lasting fear, people behave as they would 'normally' have behaved. Years later, they themselves find their behaviour at that time incomprehensible and often reprehensible.

> When they took my mother – that is, I came home and she wasn't there – I ran about all night, looking for some kind of help. In the morning, Dr Makower went to the Umschlag. But I didn't go with him, I stayed outside the gate. It was the instinct to stay alive, you know, I'm not sure whether I thought about it then, but to go in there? You might not come out, it was probably subconscious, but I stayed outside. I mean, he left me there, and I didn't say that I was going with him, I didn't run after him. When it's a matter of life and death, people are capable of all kinds of things. Before that, I didn't somehow imagine it. (Adina, Interview 13)

Apart from structural characteristics, fear in the ghetto had also differing contents. You could fear for yourself and your family: would they manage, would they avoid death? You could fear illness, hunger, terror, greasy-palmers, in fact all the categories of daily life in the ghetto could constitute a source of fear. People were also, obviously, afraid of the Germans. In addition to individual fear, affecting your own fate and that of those closest to you, there was also fear for the whole community and the fate of the world. Many people thought with anxiety about what might happen to the world if the Germans won the war.

In his diary written in the ghetto during the war, Stanisław Sznapman makes reference to this:

We deluded ourselves that the Germans couldn't bring it off, that the world could not sink into a deep pit, that civilization could not go back a thousand years.[34]

Fear and hope were two strong emotions which dominated and in a way 'ordered' the emotional life of the inhabitants of the ghetto. Paroxysms of fear and hope were of significance for the functioning of individuals and human groups and for the decisions that they made. Fear and hope changed the sense of the passing of time: fear dragged it out and hope shortened it.

Work

> Shaking, with my teeth chattering, I shuffle towards the gas ring. I light it. I lean my face over the steaming pan. I close my eyes. I think: I must go out and look for work ... nobody will go for me ... I can't just lie about, I've no right to lie in bed ... I must go out ... nothing will help me ... nobody will help me ... I must go out into the street ... into the frost ... and make contact with a world condemned to destruction.
>
> Krystyna Żywulska, *Pusta woda* (*Empty Water*)

The question of work was a significant part of the 'psycho-social map of the ghetto' that we are trying to recreate. For the inhabitants of the ghetto, work constituted a chance of survival. But many prewar professions lost their prestige, proving quite useless in the ghetto, while new professions appeared on the scene. In order to discuss the problem of work more clearly, I think we should divide up the inhabitants of the ghetto into:

- those who continued to practise – of course in a changed, and often distorted form – their prewar occupations;
- those who were forced by the situation to break completely with the work they had done before the war, and who often made a living from casual and accidental employment;
- those who had no work at all, and kept themselves by selling things, begging and receiving help from the *Judenrat*.

The people I interviewed stressed that those who were able in the ghetto to continue with their prewar occupations, at least in some residual form, were in a better position than the rest:

> For instance, it was very important whether you could practise your profession or go on with your education. If you could, even worse material circumstances were easier to bear. But people who, for example, like pianists and violinists, instead of appearing in concerts had to work in the 'shops', or do hard manual labour, destroying their hands which after all were the tools of their trade, felt much worse. So did engineers or barristers who did a bit of illicit cottage manufacturing or trading. They managed to save their lives, but their lives seemed terrible and senseless to them. (Jerzy, Interview 35)

Before we look at who had a chance of continuing their prewar occupations in the ghetto, we must make one further distinction concerning the typology of occupations. I propose in this chapter to use two terms: calling/service and work/occupation.

Let us begin with service. This is a specific kind of work, which stems rather from inner motivations and a particular kind of psychological need, rather than from the desire to earn money. It was often people for whom work was service who had the opportunity in the ghetto to continue with their prewar professions. This is true for example of doctors and teachers – exemplified by Janusz Korczak.

It was relatively easy for doctors and dentists to continue their work – they are needed in any situation. Within the ghetto there were several hospitals in which many of the doctors had already been employed before the war, and where others – including many famous names – found themselves forced to work during the occupation. Two of the people I interviewed, and the fathers of two more, worked in hospitals in the Warsaw ghetto; another was a doctor in the emergency service in the Łódź ghetto. H.M., who is a child psychologist by training, and who before the war worked in a child psychology advisory clinic, also continued in her calling: helping the children of the ghetto.

> From the beginning of the war, all activity connected with care of children centred on Centos[35] which had previously only cared for Jewish orphans. The *Judenrat* carried on social work, there were professional organizations, religious bodies and the Society for the Protection of Health. Initially, people's canteens were opened where children and adults could get supplementary food. Everywhere house committees were organized, which worked quite effectively. I worked in the individual social work section and helped to organize house common rooms. We set then up in every apartment house or for a

group of several houses, it depended on the number of people in care. The aim of the activity was above all to provide extra food, but we also tried to take an interest in the children's intellectual development. We got meals (the richer families helped the poor); the younger ones had a substitute for a kindergarten and the older ones had lessons. In the boarding houses, day boarding centres and day centres in the ghetto, all kinds of entertainments, concerts and performances were organized. This modest cultural activity was enormously important. The children locked up in the ghetto didn't know anything about animals and plants: they asked what cows looked like.

In the building of the Traders' Union at 16 Sienna Street, Janusz Korczak told stories. I once took my four-year old nephew to one of those evenings. I saw a large gathering of hungry children who couldn't take their eyes off the extraordinary story-teller, listening as only children can listen. He fed them with those stories. If only I could remember even one of those stories, if I'd written something down – nothing! (Helena, Interview 30)

Another of the women I interviewed, Anna, who had worked before the war with handicapped children, continued to do the same through the whole occupation. At first, after fleeing from Warsaw to the East, she worked in Lvov, and when she returned to Warsaw after the outbreak of the German-Soviet war, she worked in the ghetto in a children's home.

I worked in a children's home in the ghetto, as a teacher. It wasn't a big home, it had twenty or thirty children – it was just a big flat. I don't remember the name of the person who funded it. He rented a flat and bought all the furniture himself. After all, there were very rich people in the ghetto – he was from outside Warsaw, a banker of some kind. But the children in the home were dying chidren collected up from the streets. My God, how strongly those children wanted to live! It was the worst job I've ever had in my life.

[Could you do anything at all for them?]

I could play with them a bit. I fed them. They lay in their cots and I gave them something to eat – a very little, they couldn't be fed much. I told them that they were getting better, that they looked nice. I gave them a little bit of hope, but they usually died. It was all too late, they were already too exhausted. They knew that they had no parents any more; they asked in little piping voices, 'Will the Germans kill me?' It was terrible. There were two of us to look after all those children. I

was there day and night, I did the washing, ironing – I did everything.
(Anna, Interview 27)

Unlike service or callings, the other kind of work in the ghetto was just an occupation. Under this heading, some people continued what they had done before the war, while others sought employment in a new field.

During the war there was a complete change in the meaning of the term 'work' which had earlier been accepted in our culture. In the ghetto, the word lost its meaning because work was often not work, and pay was not pay. The money that you were given for working had no value: it was not enough to buy food and did not make possible the essential goal of existence in the ghetto – in other words, survival. Therefore parallel to the passage of time and changing conditions, and as the fact that the ghetto would be closed down became more and more evident, make-believe pay for make-believe work – the value of which was measured exclusively in terms of the chance it gave of survival – became increasingly general. The make-believe pay consisted in food, and later, the chance to enrol as a worker in a 'shop', or a *Lebensschein*, a permit to live.

Work also lost its meaning in the sense that it often ceased to be a profession, and was only an occupation offering a chance of survival, it was an activity in itself: a make-believe activity. Work did not create the normal relationship between employer and employee: it was any kind of occupation, any kind of skill, that offered a chance of survival. Most of the new jobs that grew up in the ghetto belonged to this category of random occupations: they grew up as a result of necessity and human invention – for example smuggling, or being paid to stand in for people taken to compulsory labour batallions. There were also new special branches of previously existing occupations, like for example the printing of identification armbands. There were about twenty other kinds of armband in use in the ghetto, apart from the compulsory identificatory white band with the blue star; the additional bands were worn on the right forearm for example by the Security Service (yellow with a red inscription), by the ambulance service and doctors (white with a red star), by *Judenrat* clerks and officials (dark blue), by omnibus employees (dark purple), by undertakers (black with a white border and white inscription), etc. Henryk Bryskier (1968) wrote about the armbands:

> The armbands generally got dirty very quickly, became crumpled and torn; those that had a printed inscription could not be laundered and very soon looked terrible, like rags. If it was an ordinary identification band, then you washed it, or bought a new one from the street sellers. But if it was an official band, then it was very difficult to change it, or sometimes completely impossible to get another. To avoid these problems, the owner would have his armband bound. Sometimes institutions had them bound wholesale. Cardboard was put underneath and it was backed with canvas; then the front was covered with cellophane and the whole thing fitted with a strap and clip. This guaranteed that it would last. The variety and number of the armbands created a whole new branch of the bookbinding business.

The world of the ghetto also forced into existence new occupations on 'the Aryan side' – for example, greasy-palmers and people who hid Jews.

Since the people I interviewed were all people with higher education, the majority of my comments deal with this social group. Their accounts form a very subjective and unrepresentative picture of work in the ghetto. I shall therefore use other sources in an attempt to consider other aspects of the question.

Craftsmen, like some of the intelligentsia, continued their pre-war occupations. They formed quite a large group in the ghetto. At this point it might be worth looking at the social structure of the ghetto, of which Ruta Sakowska (1993, p. 55) writes:

> In September 1941 8.4 per cent of the population of the ghetto was registered in the Arbeitsamt as professionally active (compared with 43.3 per cent in August 1939). ... The data from the Arbeitsamt do not cover people employed in the underground sector of manufacture and commerce. People engaged in smuggling, teachers in clandestine schools, street traders and the whole mass of people turning their hands to a variety of odd jobs did not figure in the statistics.

In reality the number of people who were professionally active in the ghetto must have been a great deal higher. Adam Czerniaków in his *Diary* calculated the number in April 1942 (including those in forced labour gangs) as 79,000 – or in other words, 22 per cent of the population of the ghetto at that time.[36] If we accept that Czerniaków's calculations are nearer to the truth, then all the same, one working person had to maintain and feed at least three who were not working.

I think, however, that the figure of 22 per cent does not reflect the true situation in the ghetto. It does not cover the 'grey area' of people engaged in smuggling, trade, and offering a variety of services. The crowding of the ghetto streets that was stressed by the people I interviewed suggests that the majority of its inhabitants were 'on the move', that they had some occupation, they were doing something (for example, looking for work). There was after all a black market in the ghetto and a range of associated occupations which do not figure in any statistics. In any event, the practices of everyday life in the ghetto appear to suggest that more than 22 per cent of its inhabitants were working (in the sense of being occupied).

Other estimates show that 55.2 per cent of the professionally active group were engaged in small-scale craft manufacture and industry; 24 per cent in commerce; 6.9 per cent worked in public and voluntary institutions, education, culture and the health service (other occupations: 6.9 per cent) (Sakowska 1993, p. 79). And so the members of the intelligentsia whom I interviewed were part of a fairly small minority in the ghetto. And yet it is this group which is best represented among those who survived. The answer to the question of why this was the case forms part of a different chapter, and we will return to it later. For the time being, let us go back to the problem of work in the ghetto.

> Everything was produced in the ghetto. In little rooms, in cellars. In attics. Everything that could be made, they made. (Stefan, Interview 29)

As I think is fairly generally known, the ghetto was a great factory, producing for the needs of the Germans and 'the Aryan side'. Up to a certain point it seemed that being useful to the Germans might be an effective survival strategy (Chaim Rumkowski in Łódź was almost successful in bringing this off). In other ghettos, too, it was believed that the Jews would survive by making themselves useful or necessary to the Germans. The man I interviewed who survived the Białystok ghetto said:

> The whole Białystok ghetto was turned into a gigantic labour camp. Workshops large and small, factories large and small. ... It was mainly the clothing trade. It was generally believed that people would

manage to survive thanks to that work, and that they were necessary to the Germans. (Edward, Interview 26)

Incidentally, it seems strange that the Germans, who had introduced such rigorous principles of racial segregation and deemed all contacts with Jews to be 'unclean' (sexual contacts were particularly severely punished) were not bothered by the fact that they were wearing uniforms and boots (the uniform! – the symbol of German dignity) sewn by these *Untermenschen*.

The majority of inhabitants of the ghetto had to seek work in a field other than that for which they were trained. Barristers were not needed because there were no courts, writers were not needed because no books were published, rabbis were not needed because people were not allowed to worship. A chance of a job was offered by the opening in the ghetto of new places of employment – both the 'shops' working for the Germans, and the fairly extensive ghetto administration. Israel Gutman (1993, p. 132) claims that 'the administrative apparatus of the *Judenrat* grew until it reached 6,000 employees. By comparison, the prewar Jewish community council employed about 350'. Many barristers found employment in the ghetto police force.

> There were a lot of lawyers in the police – they thought that through that work they could ensure some sort of law and order. (Alina, Interview 33)

> The lawyers only really had two choices – to join the police or to become janitors. To be a janitor was the height of luxury, you know, it was a very respected job. Dustmen also had good social standing, the ones who carted the rubbish out of the ghetto – it was a contact with 'the Aryan side', you could bring things in and take things out. (Stefan, Interview 29)

It was the intelligentsia above all who had to seek new ways of earning their living: their skills became devalued more quickly than the skills of manual workers or craftsmen. Only some of the intelligentsia managed – at least for a time – to carry on with their prewar professions.

> Yesterday's engineer was pleased to get a job as a janitor; yesterday's lawyer – as a door-to-door salesman of sweets; a merchant who was wealthy until lately – in the queue for free soup; a professor of music – a street musician; a lady barrister – the janitor in the lock-up; but the

street trader stays on in his old job. Here is the whole gallery of socially displaced persons. (Bryskier 1968)

As was the case with the Polish intelligentsia on the other side of the wall, among the Jewish intelligentsia it was common to give private tuition, especially since the schools were closed.

I worked, I gave private lessons in Polish and French. It's ridiculous, but people in the ghetto were learning French. (Irena, Interview 28)

Make-believe work did not only provide make-believe pay which offered a chance of survival. Make-believe work was a specific ghetto variety of make-believe living, analogous to that described by Kazimierz Wyka as the experience of Polish society during the occupation. Any kind of activity was of psychological significance – it constructed a structure for the days and weeks, it ordered time, it gave a sense of meaning, of being useful and necessary. One of the women I interviewed talked about this:

I tried to find something to do, and quickly, and I got private pupils through a friend's sister. First one, then some more. I had, I think, seven altogether. I taught them the whole primary school course. First I had one little girl, Haneczka, who was 11, and then her cousin who was the same age, and was also called Haneczka. They were very intelligent little girls. I went to their home every day, six days a week. I got 30 złotys a month from each pupil – that was the price of two and a half loaves of bread. Altogether I earned about 200 złotys a month. (Alina, Interview 33)

Although to work in a calling was possible for only a few, still any occupation was highly placed in the ghetto's hierarchy of values. Everyone was looking for a job that would offer a chance of survival – whether in the form of earnings, or of getting food, or – later – of a certificate of employment.

The age at which you began work fell considerably, and even teenagers had occupations.

We were living at a fairly poor level. I started to work, to get a bit of extra money. I worked for a very nice tinsmith, pan Kociński in Długa Street. He was a very interesting man. Before the first world war, he'd been all round the world with his melting pot, and had a lot of stories to tell about it. That was my first job. I worked there for a few months – I cleaned the buckets, I cleaned up, you know, what a boy does at a tinsmith's. Later on, I did odd jobs in various places, and then for a longer spell in a factory in the ghetto. I also brought in, down my trouser legs, tubers from the Jewish cemetery in Okopowa Street. At first I worked for a horrible man in the 'Metro' company, making handles for drills. Then I was taken on at the Schultz factory. (Ryszard, Interview 34)

We tried various occupations. My father tried to set up a timber yard – I used an axe, a saw, I carted the wood about. Later on, I had a rickshaw – that was the most common form of transport – and I found all sorts of jobs. (Rysiek, Interview 11)

Those who did not find work in the ghetto, or whose earnings were not enough to keep them (which was generally the case), had to sell their things. They were exchanged for food, and they were sold either in the ghetto, or – at a better price – on 'the Aryan side'. Usually friends or trusted acquaintances (often prewar servants) sold the things for them and sent the money into the ghetto. This of course applied to people who had had some resources before the war, who were relatively well-off. And as it happened it was from this group – the relatively wealthy middle class – that most of the people I interviewed came. And so I heard accounts similar to the following from most of them:

My father sold a house before the war and had some money. All our things stayed with our housekeeper, and she sold them gradually and kept us supplied. (Irena, Interview 28)

Later on, we began to sell things gradually. My father was still in contact with a few – to be more precise with two – of his former patients on 'the Aryan side'. They helped us a lot, right through to the end. Pan Stefan was later to save our lives. Pani Irena kept some of our things and helped to sell them, including valuables, to give us something to live on. My father still earned a bit, he saw patients, and either charged them or not, but that wasn't enough and so we were selling things. (Jerzy, Interview 35)

I have made two distinctions in this chapter on the question of work. The first on the basis of whether people could continue in their prewar professions, could not continue in the same profession, or could not find any employment at all. The second was on the basis of whether people worked in a service/calling, or in a job/occupation; to these should be added the category of vegetation/survival.

The people who were in the worst situation were those who had no work, no resources, and nothing to sell. They did not think of following a calling, or of an occupation, but only of survival. They were condemned to vegetation. Vegetation was a variety of dying, and was also one of the ghetto lifestyles.

Various voluntary organizations worked in the ghetto under the patronage of the *Judenrat* to deal with care of the hungry: people's canteens which offered soup free or almost free, and associations which tried to find money for example to open children's homes. This subject is currently dealt with in most studies of the ghetto, and also in many memoirs and diaries; I do not therefore intend to go into the question in detail. I shall limit myself to saying that despite the heroic efforts of many people of good will, the help that they were able to give to those in need was not enough.

The largest number of those in need were deportees from other ghettos – people who had often been forced on German orders to pack in a quarter of an hour, and had been allowed to bring only the bare necessities.

> There were Jews who had been driven out of little towns near Warsaw – they were terribly poor, they'd been driven out with what they stood up in. They arrived with absolutely nothing. And that was real poverty, it was absolute poverty, because they hadn't any hidden property, maybe sometimes they had relations, but they didn't have any things, even really rich people. (Stefan, Interview 29)

People like that obviously did not have time or opportunity somehow to place their property in safe keeping, and even if they did (they gave it to their neighbours to keep, 'to be collected after the war'), they could take with them only moveable property: money, gold, valuables, which lost their value relatively quickly in the ghetto. It was among these people with no means of livelihood that a majority of the starving were to be found, and they also constituted a majority among those prepared to undertake forced labour for the Germans.

As I noted in the previous chapter, Jews aged from 14 to 60 were compelled to work. As early as October 1939 the Germans used them as an unpaid labour force for various kinds of work like cleaning and tidying barracks, etc. Later, special 'establishments' were set up where Jews were compulsorily employed outside the territory of the ghetto. On average they employed from 1,500 (January 1940) to 10,600 (August 1941) people daily.

Unqualified workers were employed in clearing up rubble and cleaning (for example, in private German residences); the qualified worked in tailoring workshops, cobblers' workshops or various repair workshops. Work in the 'establishments' lasted for 12 hours a day, and the pay was theoretically from 3 to 8 złotys a day, depending on qualifications. I say theoretically, because the employers (state-owned and private German firms) were notoriously behind with the payments: 68 per cent of earnings were never paid at all, 20 per cent were covered by the *Judenrat*, and the German employers paid only 12 per cent (Sakowska 1993, p. 79). In practice, therefore, work in the 'establishments' was unpaid labour for the German occupying power. This was what gave rise to the need for stand-ins for forced labour – which satisfied both sides. People who were threatened with being recruited for an 'establishment', and who had some kind of occupation in the ghetto that was a source of livelihood which they did not wish to lose, hired stand-ins. They were paid some small sum, but that at least gave them a guaranteed income which was not offered by the Germans. At a later date, the 'establishments' acquired special significance. This was during the period of massive exodus to 'the Aryan side' just before, during or immediately after the action to close the ghetto. For the most usual way of getting out of the ghetto was to attach yourself (after bribing the appropriate person) to one of the groups of Jews leaving in the morning for the 'establishments'. On the other side of the wall, you took off your armband and at the right moment separated from the group.

The Germans organized all kinds of 'establishments' in Warsaw and district, and there were also special expeditions – for example at harvest time – to distant places. One of the people I interviewed took part in an expedition of this kind:

> I went once in '41 – they organized recruitment in the ghetto to work on a landed estate near Hrubieszów. And I went there for the harvest. It was the summer of '41, very hot. There on the estates of Count Potworowski, a senator, we took in the harvest – a group of boys and girls from the ghetto. We were paid peanuts. It was hard work, it was a real effort. (Rysiek, Interview 11)

Because workers in the 'establishments' received some rations of food (again we find the element of degradation of remuneration for work), there was no shortage of volunteers.

> Well, and so, you know, those people worked as well as they could. There were labour camps, like the one in Falenty. The Germans took Jews there to work. It was funny, there were street round-ups and the Germans caught Jews who still had some strength, who looked more or less fit. But the people who really tried to get in to work there could hardly stand – because whatever it was like, you could get a bit to eat. (Stefan, Interview 29)

The categories I have presented – people who carried on their old profession, people who found a new occupation, and those with no source of livelihood – were very fluid. As I wrote at the beginning of this chapter, the rate of change in conditions of existence in the ghetto was very variable. The whole population of the ghetto was very quickly pauperized (there were, of course, exceptions: the nouveaux riches, about whom I will write later), and all the distinctions in the ghetto were subject to very swift and chaotic change. Usually for the worse. That is, people who at first worked and somehow managed might at any moment find themselves among those who were barely vegetating. It all happened so fast, in such condensed time. Possibilities of finding work and financial reserves shrank, and the *Judenrat's* ability to finance charitable work was also reduced. From month to month, the number of people who were ill, starving and dying grew. There were ever more beggars, who gave the ghetto a specific appearance, smell and sound. Henryka Lazowert (1941) probably wrote about this the most expressively.

> For half an hour a swollen beggar woman has been howling outside the window (there is what is known as a 'rich house' opposite). 'Good people, five groszy, only five groszy'. A moment ago two new voices joined in for an accompaniment. I know them. It's two children. They sing a strange song. It begins, 'Four miles outside Warsaw ...', but then there's nothing about the wedding of the hoopoe and the jackdaw, only a bad father whose children propose various ways that he can commit suicide. The elder sister brings him in turn a knife, an axe, a rope. 'Hang yourself, father, Hang yourself, father ...'; 'Kill yourself, father, Kill yourself, father ...'. It sounds more than realistic. Authentic, macabre. The children singing are 10 years old. And I know already know who will 'perform' later today.

There will be the boy screeching for hours in one place, '*Ots rachmunes ...*' (Have mercy) and the girl with '*Ots mitsleich ...*' (Have pity), and something tiny, you can't tell whether it's a girl or a boy, with its '*Vorf arup a shtikele broyt*' (Throw down a bit of bread). There will be two brothers, horribly swollen, who only moan. Their legs – red blocks with big blisters as though they'd been scalded, and faces like Kalmucks: yellow globular cheeks, with the eyes simply lost in the swelling. There will be an old woman, who crawls about the roadway on her back. There will be my nice little perhaps-seven-year-old 'orator' with a big basket, who pulls along his three-year-old brother with a bandaged head. The 'oration' is always as follows: 'Respected ladies and gentlemen, dear ladies and gentlemen, have pity on these two poor little children, give a little bit of bread, give a crumb of bread, or an old crust, or one potato. And in return, you will never be hungry and will never have to beg yourselves. Respected ladies and gentlemen, give a bit of bread for these two little hungry children.' And then the twelve-year-old boy: '*Yidishe kindoch, ich beite*' (a Jewish kid, I beg you). And two skeletons – two red-haired girls with tuberculosis. And a father with two (I'm sorry, one's already died) children. And a swarthy, raven-haired mother with a beautiful, dark two-year-old. And later on, after the gate has been closed, a terrible, twisted crippled boy with long arms like an ape, and legs bare to his bottom (he only wears bathing trunks and a strip of shirt).

And then in the night and at nine o'clock in the morning, there will be 'Miss Marysia'. Miss Marysia is twenty-five years old and is said to have a matriculation certificate. She has a pleasing, pure, girlish alto voice. She has an old mother and a tiny flat somewhere near here. Apart from that she's got nothing – just swollen legs and half her wits for the last half-year. She sings, 'Where have you gone to ...', and another hit and 'Sister, give me your hand. ...' (I suspect that this is her own composition). It begins, 'Life has dealt me a shabby blow, sister, stay with me, sister, give me your hand!' Occasionally, when her wits are in a worse state, she also asks for a white collar (she's dressed very carefully) or an old jacket ('Please, sirs, men are more obliging than women ...').

*

To end this section, I would like to raise two further questions. The first is connected with the link between the meaning of work and the variable rate of change in the situation in the ghetto; the second to strikes in the ghetto. What I have had to say so far has applied basically to the the period of the ghetto's existence before the first action.

During the closure action, which lasted from 22 July to almost the end of September 1942, about 350,000 Jews were transported from the Warsaw ghetto to Treblinka. The first to die were those whose earlier existence had been in the category of vegetation/survival. Patients from the hospitals were taken, deportees from the displaced persons centres, beggars, those dying in the streets, children from children's homes. A large number of those whose work fell into the category of service/calling died with them. It was a consequence of their calling: an intellectual, social, religious or cultural testimony.

People who were employed in work/occupations, and who had developed skills in fixing matters which were invaluable in wartime, redoubled their activities and efforts. The status of work was totally deprived of meaning during the deportation action. There was no longer any talk of pay – on the contrary, people paid to be taken on to work in a 'shop'. People went along with their own tools, sewing machines or typewriters etc., to ask for work.

> My sister had her own typewriter, and so they took her on in a shop.
> (Alina, Interview 33)

In the first phases of the closure action, it was thought that a certificate to say you worked in a 'shop' would save you from transportation. And so people tried to get this at all costs. But there were no rules by which you could assess the value of particular certificates – the Germans sometimes took them into account and sometimes did not, one day they would honour a certificate from only one particular 'shop' and the next day from another. There was total chaos. Even a certificate obtained at a high price stating that your work was of essential importance for German interests gave no guarantee of safety.

> I started to work at Hoffman's (it was a factory in Smocza Street) to get some bit of paper. That bit of paper sometimes gave you protection and then the next day not. It was all completely random. There was bribery, of course, but I didn't have anything to pay bribes with. My mother also had a bit of paper that seemed to be a good chance. But it wasn't. They picked her up in Ogrodowa Street, in a courtyard, I don't even remember exactly what day it was. Some time at the beginning of the action. I went over to the other side at that point, and that was it.
> (Ryszard, Interview 34)

The guarantee of having work, even if it was not a real one, nonetheless gave a feeling of security, constituted an imagined guarantee of prestige – a stronger position for survival. The extent to which the concept of work had been degraded is shown by the fact that after the action, the workers in the ghetto 'shops' did not receive any pay at all. Ruta Sakowska (1993, p. 317) writes:

> The German management of the 'shops' drew payment for the Jewish labour force working for the SS from the workers themselves, who paid 3 złotys a day per head in tax, and 2 złotys for food.

The other problem which I wish to raise is that of strikes in the ghetto. I have tried to show above that the culturally conditioned concept of work was degraded and lost meaning, and that the relationship between employer and employee was turned upside down. But all the same, certain ideas from the past, and modes of behaviour that stemmed from them, were retained. For example, the porters in the ghetto went on strike demanding back pay that was due to them and a pay rise.

> It was very difficult to talk to the porters. They were constantly demanding pay rises, they called us rotten intellectuals, they threatened to strike. And finally they did strike. Suddenly, Korczak appeared. He'd clearly heard what they were planning and had come to see them because he was worried about deliveries of food for the Orphanage. He started to talk about his life, his work, his time in Russia. ... It was different from when he told children's stories, a different kind of fascination. We listened, and everyone forgot about the strike. (Helena, Interview 30)

Something similar happened in the Łódź ghetto. There were even trade unions there, defending the workers' interests in an organized way.

> The leadership of the Union Left[37] organized strikes in the workshops to combat poor working conditions, unaccountability of managers, and cheating in the kitchens. May Day demonstrations were also organized. These were aimed at the people running the ghetto, and above all at Rumkowski. (Arnold, Interview 9)

> There were lots of fine young people in the organization, who were also determined to make an armed stand against the Germans. But since there was no chance of this, their activity was limited to fighting

with the Jewish administration which was servile to the Germans, sabotage in work places, and more generally – to surviving with dignity, which in the conditions of the ghetto often required a heroic attitude and risking your life. (Barbara, Interview 10)

It might seem that strikes would be a totally inadequate riposte to the working conditions obtaining in the ghetto. They were a reaction that belonged to a different, prewar past. They did however have enormous psychological significance – they were a demonstration of attitudes, a struggle to defend your own dignity, rights and humanity. They were also of ideological significance, especially in the Łódź ghetto, where they were organized by the very active Communist group.

Study

My dear lady, these aren't goods, and this isn't a shop, and you're not a client, and I'm not a shopkeeper, and I'm not selling you anything, and you're not paying, because after all these bits of paper are not money. You're not losing anything, I'm not earning anything. Who's cheating whom at the moment and why bother? But you have to do something, don't you?

Janusz Korczak, *Diary*

On 4 December 1939 all Jewish schools in the *General Gouvernement* were closed down. The Warsaw *Judenrat* applied to have the schools re-opened at its own cost. In August 1940, permission was given for vocational training courses to be started (by now in the ghetto). After two years of trying, permission was granted on 5 September 1941 for primary schools to be opened in the Warsaw ghetto.

During the one school year which was officially conducted in the ghetto, 20 schools were opened – or came out into the open – there: six run by religious organizations, eight by various political organizations, five by teachers of the old state elementary schools, and one run by the Catholic association 'Caritas' for Jewish Catholic children. In all, there were 6,700 pupils in these schools (Sakowska 1993, pp. 187–93). This represented 13.4 per cent of all school-age children in the ghetto (or, according to other calculations, 6.7 per cent).[38]

It would seem that by the time the schools were opened the problem of education was not as pressing in the ghetto as it had been two years earlier. The ghetto population had become so pauperized and degraded that the problem of educating their children was no longer at the front of their minds. None of the people I interviewed went to school in the ghetto, or taught in a school there, and no one even mentioned the existence of schools (with the exception of A.M., who talked in detail about the organization of the Łódź ghetto, including the schools). There seem to be several reasons why this was the case:

- the secret teaching of children that had been carried on since the beginning of the ghetto under the guise of children's canteens was much more important;
- many of the children in the ghetto, if not a majority, were occupied in getting hold of food or money, and so had no time for learning, or their parents could not afford it;
- the children were too weak and hungry to learn anything.

To make our description of the psycho-social map of the ghetto more precise, it is worth dividing the question of education into learning, getting knowledge, teaching.

Each of these learning-related activities had a slightly different meaning and significance. They were all forms of mental or intellectual effort that were a way of fighting the Germans, forms of resistance to the occupying power. They often constituted a spontaneous reaction to being classified as a sub-human, a method of defending one's own value, dignity and self-respect. Let us look in more detail at the three categories I have proposed.

Learning can be interpreted in temporal categories as an activity directed towards the future. Learning is a certain kind of investment made in the present which will come into its own in the future. In the ghetto, where the temporal horizon was deprived of the future, learning must have had a different meaning. What would have been the sense of learning when faced with inevitable destruction? It put into practice a certain ethos of the intelligentsia which stressed the value of learning for itself. The Jews, known for a few thousand years as 'the people of the Book', had a culturally deeply rooted conviction that knowledge was very important, that it was important to have learning.

The decision about learning was not made by the children

themselves, but by their parents. In the conditions of the ghetto, this decision must have reflected an attempt to achieve a particular quality of life, or a conscious axiological choice. However, only a certain number of the better-off inhabitants of the ghetto could allow themselves the luxury of putting these values into practice. This was pointed out by the woman I interviewed who had given private lessons in the ghetto:

> Parents who had some ambitions and didn't want their children to go completely astray tried to arrange for them to have private lessons. (Alina, Interview 33)

Perhaps force of habit lay behind decisions of this kind, or a desire to organize their children's time, or a belief in salvation? Perhaps it was a desire to prepare their children for life after the war, a refusal to accept the lack of prospects for the future, the limitation of the temporal horizon? Perhaps it was an attempt to maintain normality at all costs? It was also, and perhaps primarily, a defence of one's own dignity and rights, an effort to protect moral existence and individuality, to resist degradation. The children in the ghetto understood this, because those who were able to learn did so willingly:

> My pupils were exceptionally nice and wanted to learn. They were well aware of the situation and worked very hard. Between January and May we went through the whole curriculum for the fifth class of primary school, and started on the next one. Both of them were killed. (Alina, Interview 33)

I think, however, that despite the enormous value of the cultural tradition of learning, its ranking had seriously fallen in the ghetto. In the face of the threat to life, various kinds of practical skills, which offered a chance of getting a job, earning something, survival, took on a greater pragmatic value. Vocational courses, which offered exactly these skills, were very popular in the ghetto. Young people attended them (if they could afford to, as they were all fee-paying), including two of the people I interviewed:

> I attended courses of some kind in the ghetto. There was a much-talked-about course given by Professor Centnerszwer[39] from which I was ceremoniously expelled.
>
> [Why?]

I don't remember. There was a big row and they kicked me out. Another course that I attended was run by Toporol.[40] We had theoretical classes and practical work. For the practical work I had an absolutely stinking job – I looked after the chickens in the incubators, being raised to provide food for the ghetto. One day they got chicken cholera and they all went to the devil. (Ryszard, Interview 34)

In that first period, I even attended some courses, there was a first-rate mathematician, from the university, his name was Zalzwasser – and I remember that I went to his lectures, and they made an impression on me, but that soon came to an end. Later on there were courses in physical chemistry run by Professor Centnerszwer from the University of Warsaw, and I think I attended those for about six months, and then, well, it all came to an end, things started to get worse, the end was getting nearer, people's resources were running out. ... (Rysiek, Interview 11)

Secret university-level courses were also organized in the ghetto. I would categorize this kind of intellectual activity as obtaining knowledge. The decision about this was not taken by parents but by the students themselves. One factor in the decision was the age criterion, but this was not the only one. Of course, obtaining knowledge was often linked with seeking opportunities for earning money or getting food. Nonetheless, if these were the goals, there were other ways open to attain them. And so what were the real goals of people in the ghetto when they set about obtaining knowledge? What was the sense of obtaining knowledge when faced with destruction? I think that there were two reasons.

Firstly, the need for satisfaction of an individual kind, the pleasures of cognition stemming from the mere fact of obtaining knowledge, and acquiring skills in solving problems. This need to obtain knowledge has been common to many people in many epochs, in various situations, and despite external conditions is analogous to the category of service/calling which I used when discussing work in the ghetto.

Secondly, in the social, supra-individual dimension – the need to contribute to human knowledge and experience in general. It was in this spirit that research was carried out in the ghetto into starvation sickness, published as an academic study after the war (Apfelbaum and Fliederbaum 1946). Obtaining knowledge was, like learning, a form of struggle against the

Germans, a demonstration of independence and strength of the human spirit, which – unlike the body – will not allow itself to be locked up behind walls and barbed wire. Jerzy, one of the men I interviewed, stressed exactly this aspect of obtaining knowledge: a way of putting freedom into effect. He himself took part in the underground academic courses in the Warsaw ghetto.

At the beginning of the war I was a third-year medical student. At first I worked in the hospital at Czyste and then in Leszno Street on the surgical ward. For a novice like myself, relationships on that ward were very curious, extremely hierarchical. Maybe there was a war going on, but the head surgeon was still a feudal lord and the elite surrounding him were the courtiers. But somehow it wasn't objectionable. Maybe because of the charm of the people concerned, or perhaps we young people needed something like that in those difficult days. With time, the ice broke, and some sort of local community took shape that brought people of different generations together. While I was still at Czyste, I was elected chairman of the student group. There were a few dozen of us, and nearly all of us were working without pay. Only a few were employed as medical orderlies. As the student leader I came into contact with various attitudes and matters, which were often unpleasant, but sometimes stimulating. Some students made extra money by giving injections outside the hospital, some took on the full colours of doctors and saw private patients in the town, but others were simply wonderful people. After eighteen months, I decided to move to Stawki Street where there was internal medicine and typhus wards. Students didn't much want to go there, but I explained that after the war it would count as an internship, although the point really was to persuade people to go to the fever wards where there weren't enough doctors. So as the leader of the group, I set an example, and in fact I found myself in an excellent ward, where the doctors and students were splendid.

Apart from working, I was continuing my education with the underground medical school. This was at a high standard both for the first years of the course and especially during the clinical training. But it was the art of medicine that made the biggest impression on me. I had an opportunity to come into contact with really big names from all over Poland who had ended up in the ghetto. Not many of them took part in the student lectures. But instead they taught us on an everyday basis – and how! They had found an asylum in the hospital and they valued it.

They wanted to pass on their skills and experience, and the young doctors and students lapped up the opportunity. We grew. There were academic sessions, which were a miraculous oasis for people wanting to get away from the depressing and crippling reality that was all about us. Scientific research went on. How proud we four students on Jakub Penson's ward were when in order to support one of his hypotheses we agreed to drink diluted urea. It was a tiny scrap of freedom. I'd like people to realize that in that ghetto, in that paralysing and debasing life, beautiful and proud things happened. People who had the sentence of death hanging over them, who were in what was at the time the biggest jail cell in the world, even if it wasn't quite Auschwitz, or Treblinka, and it wasn't yet the time of the closure action – how those people loved one another, worked, wrote academic studies, organized theatre performances, concerts, tried to help their family and friends, despite the fact that at the same time they were subject to the pressure of apathy, despair, helplessness, and in the end indifference. These influences with time flooded the shrinking area of hope where a human being can defend his rights to life and at the same time to humanity. (Jerzy, Interview 35)

What was the sense of teaching others in the face of annihilation? I think that there were two aspects to teaching in the ghetto. The first was part of ideological life, connected with the political and ideological education of future members or activists of the party that you belonged to. One of the women I interviewed talked about this:

As soon as the PPR[41] was formed in the ghetto in 1942, I joined it. The party immediately organized educational activity. I was in charge of a group of five young people, a 'five', that I was to educate. Not only in the Marxist-Leninist religion, but we educated those unenlightened, uneducated young people from small towns, who often could hardly speak Polish, in general. We believed then that they would all get out and join the partisans, and that we had to prepare them for life on the other side of the wall.

Fighting fives were also set up, but of course, there wasn't any military training, there wasn't anybody to instruct them. (Irena, Interview 28)

The second aspect linked with non-ideological educational activity falls within the category of service/calling. There were many eminent teachers in the ghetto, who provided evidence there of the exceptional strength of their calling. Janusz Korczak symbolizes them all. A great deal has already been written about him, but I would like to quote what one of the women I talked to said:

> The directors and teachers of other institutions met with the same fate as Korczak. They did the same – they consciously went to their deaths together with the children. You only hear about Korczak's heroism. People need symbols, stone monuments. If there hadn't been a Holocaust, those nameless substitute parents would have gone through life equally namelessly, while Korczak, as a writer and educationalist, would have been in the encyclopaedias and the histories of literature and education anyway, as a supporter of children's rights. I saw how they escorted Korczak and the children out. There was a deathly silence. Korczak, the children and Mrs Stefa Wilczyńska.[42] She is undeservedly overshadowed. Korczak was a difficult, stubborn man; she was sensible, communicative, resourceful. I remember the last time I met her at Centos, when she came as usual to arrange food supplies. She said then, 'Our children don't know what lies in store for them, and they're not going to know until the last moment. Why should they?'

> Korczak was a bit of a poet in what he did, his head was in the clouds. He created an ideology for dealing with the problems of orphans. He loved children, every child – Jewish or Polish. In the ghetto he wore a Polish army officer's coat, and he served a prison sentence for not wearing an armband. (Helena, Interview 30)

To conclude the discussion of the question of education in the ghetto, I would like to raise two interesting details connected with this phenomenon, which add to the psycho-social map. Firstly: what was the language of instruction in the ghetto? In December 1940, the Germans issued orders that Jewish children were not to be taught in German or Polish. And yet the schools, with the exception of the religious schools, used Polish as the medium of instruction (only religious education classes were conducted there, traditionally, in Hebrew).

The official language of the ghetto was Polish:

> You know, those megaphones, the loudspeakers, were only in Polish. Polish was used in the ghetto in contacts with the *Judenrat*, with the supply organizations, in the street, etc. Yiddish was not an official language. For example, I worked in the supply organization, before that I worked in Patronat, and I didn't have any difficulties because I didn't speak Yiddish, I could communicate without any problem. (Stefan, Interview 29)

Another interesting detail is connected with the Łódź ghetto. The man I interviewed who was a survivor of that ghetto told me:

> Rumkowski's administration made it possible to operate a schooling system that covered almost all the children in the ghetto. In 1940-41 all children born in 1933 or earlier were obliged to attend school. There were 45 schools in the ghetto, including special schools - for the deaf and dumb, the mentally handicapped and for young offenders. There was a music school and an industrial training school. In 1941, gymnasia and lycées were opened, which managed to get their pupils through the first stage of the matriculation.
>
> On 29th July 1942, on the basis of a German decision, all the schools were closed down; in September, all children under ten were transported. The rest had to work in the workshops. (Arnold, Interview 9)

As I have already noted in the previous chapter, the Łódź ghetto was exceptional in many respects, including, as we can see from the above account, in the matter of opportunities for education. Was this the result of Rumkowski's activities alone? Or did the fact that the Germans initially had different plans for the Łódź ghetto (it was to be a labour camp, not subject to extermination; this seems to have aided Rumkowski, who saw it as a chance for survival) play a role?

We can leave the debate about the exceptional status of the Łódź ghetto to the historians - and in fact they have been conducting it for years. I have quoted this account here in order once again to indicate the variations in German behaviour, the inexplicability and ambiguity of their conduct. Schools were opened in the Łódź ghetto at a time when in Warsaw it was barely permitted to run vocational training courses; and they were closed down when in Warsaw the extermination action was already in full swing. Why did they allow schools for handicapped and educationally sub-normal children to operate, when quite unquestionably German plans from the very beginning envisaged their 'euthanasia'? Or perhaps the Łódź ghetto had so much autonomy that the Germans, at least initially, did not interfere to the extent that they did not know of their existence? I think that other events - for example the strikes which I have mentioned that were organized in the Łódź ghetto - argue in favour of the latter interpretation.

Social and cultural life

> Hoe, saw, pliers, rake,
> Do you still remember mate?
> Apenszlak, Ordonka, PKO
> That was the life, pal, who'd say no? [...]
> Spotted trousers, pliers, rake,
> Gone for good and no mistake,
> but next year, think back and see...
> again. – 'Sztuka'. Wiera Gran ... [...]
> You got real coffee in the 'Sztuka', Anigsztajn's fine cakes and mocha,
> whores and hits and no more said,
> as long as ... the smuggling paid ...
> Hoe, saw, stick, shoe,
> gone for good or nothing's true ...
> suddenly – Alarm! the action's on ...
> everything down below – it's all OK!!
> Hoe, saw, wardrobe, chest
> Lejkin, Szmerling and Treblinka,
> rucksack – waggon – block or square
> shed, ausweiss, flask, sore head ...
> Hoe, rake, pliers, broom,
> Hop in, brothers, there's still room ...
> And tomorrow ...? don't waste time ...
> The living news bulletin's still on ...!!

Władysław Szlengel, Resume, or Krakowiak Macabre

In the ghetto, according to what I have described so far, people worked, studied, fell ill and died. People who had at least a middling standard of living, and whose spiritual and cultural needs had not been entirely stifled, had opportunities of satisfying those needs in the ghetto. Depending on living conditions and income levels, people made contact with other people, made new friends, read things, and entertained themselves in various ways. What kinds of ties were formed between people in the ghetto; how did they spend their 'free time'? Social life in the ghetto fell into three spheres: the family, neighbours and friends.

The family constituted the basic social environment of the inhabitants of the ghetto. Against a background of danger, the necessity of getting hold of food, families consolidated, and the mechanism of family egoism appeared. Families extended to take in their near and more distant relations: if people had lived outside the area designated as the ghetto, they moved in with members of their families who had flats within the area. If you had any possibility of helping others, you helped in the first instance your relations – in the broadest meaning of the term. As time passed, the families shrank again, their weakest members fell by the wayside: old people, the sick, children. Families suffered dramatic losses during the transportation action:

> Maria knocked on the door. There were some people there. A man, an old woman, a young girl and a child. A patched together family. The man had lost his wife and children. The girl was his sister. The old woman was his grandmother and the child was his nephew. (Szajn-Lewin 1989, p. 23)

Families changed their composition in the ghetto – distant relations took the place of near relations who had gone, making a reintegration and renewed consolidation of the family possible.[43] The traditional division of roles and hierarchy within the family also underwent change. The role of the head of the family altered: often the father ceased to play this role, which passed to whoever earned their living, provided food, and was not afraid to take decisions. One of the men I interviewed, who during the war was a young boy living with his mother and grandmother and earning a living for this three-person family, said:

> My mother wanted to feed me best, but I said that I was either going to eat the same things as everyone else, or not at all. One day, I saw that she was giving me more than my fair share of butter, and from then on I wouldn't touch butter at all. (Ryszard, Interview 34)

Krystyna Żywulska (1963, p. 25), who was also for a certain time the only working member of her family, wrote:

> For two weeks I received a portion of bread every evening. ... Every evening they waited for me while I was dashing along the streets tightly clutching the bread I'd earned. ... When I put the bread on the dish, father took a knife and cut it slowly into four equal parts. ... The expectant silence, the ceremony of the sharing out, being aware that I was useful – all made me dazed with happiness.

Family life in the ghetto functioned in a deformed way. Both the structure and the role of the family were different from those of peace-time. Families disintegrated; because of numerous losses in the immediate family circle, whole clans began to be linked by close family ties. The internal structure of the family was also deformed: children or young people became the breadwinners, and decision-making – which was earlier an attribute of adulthood – was no longer the exclusive province of parents. Children became independent and grew up earlier, which is in fact a characteristic of wartime in general.

Apart from family ties, ties with neighbours also developed, within the framework of one apartment house: this was aided by the activities of the House Committees, and also by the curfew.

> There was a curfew – 6 or 7 o'clock, they changed it. After the curfew, life went on within the framework of one apartment house.
>
> [What form did it take?]
>
> Well, you didn't watch television … Normal family life, meetings with neighbours, and walking backwards and forwards about the court-yard. (Stefan, Interview 29)

Friendships were intense, sometimes based on a common ideology – for example, in Communist circles, which fought the Germans by publishing underground papers and training young people. Other friendships dated from before the war – from school or work. And people also made new friends in the ghetto.

> There was no normal social life, because there was the curfew; at first there were the house common rooms, but they died a natural death. You made friends easily. Firstly – because of the curfew – in the house where you lived. These died out when you moved, but you made new ones. I had a few friends from Łódź, and a few new ones. I was closest to a boy I'd known in Łódź and who lived not far from here, on the corner of Leszno Street and Orła Street. He worked in a photo-grapher's. I sat and talked to him for hours; we had a wonderful collection of photographs of Nazis. Later on, they arrested him for taking photographs in Plac Bankowy, and he was in prison in the Pawiak. His mother destroyed the collection of photographs at that point. It was a pity they were lost. He went away later to Bochnia and died there. His name was Chaim Krupka. I remember that I was reading Bergson at that time, and we thought up together sculptures that would reflect the Bergsonian ideas. (Ryszard, Interview 34)

The Germans initially closed down all the cultural institutions in the ghetto: cinemas, theatres, libraries, bookshops, etc. However, in 1941, when there was an increased flexibility in their behaviour towards the Jews, some of these bans were lifted. The 'Eldorado' revue theatre got a concession, or in other words permission to operate legally, in December, and later four other theatres were licensed. Of these five theatres in the ghetto, three played in Yiddish and two in Polish; three were revue theatres and two offered drama. Because of the curfew, performances began at 5.30 p.m., and on Sundays and holidays there were matinées at 3 o'clock. Ruta Sakowska (1993, pp. 215–26) writes that these theatres were very popular; there were premières every month, with audiences running at 80 to 100 per cent of capacity (there were all together 3,000 seats in the five theatres, and the tickets were relatively cheap). I have however heard this information about theatre audiences contradicted. Krystyna Żywulska said in conversation with me:

> Not many people went [to the theatre] ... If there were twelve people in the audience in a theatre in the ghetto, it was a big deal. It was all naturally a parody ...

The dramatic theatres had a fairly ambitious repertoire (Jakub Goldin's *Mirla Efros*, Szalom Asz's *The God of Revenge*, Sholom Aleichem's *The Great Haul*), but in the interests of the box office they were obliged to put on lighter things too – it was what the people of the ghetto, tired by the difficulties of everyday life, wanted.

Cultural life also went on in cafés, where concerts (with outstanding musicians), recitals and other evening performances were held. Apart from the licensed professional theatres, there were numerous amateur groups who performed in canteens or rooms made available by the House Committees. They usually did all kinds of one-act plays, and also commentaries on current events which they often wrote themselves.

As well as musicians playing in cafés in the ghetto, there was also the licensed Jewish Symphony Orchestra, which did not stick to the German ban on playing 'non-Aryan music'. Janina Bauman (1982, p. 72) wrote about this:

> So many eminent musicians had been blessed with Jewish origins that a really high-quality orchestra was formed in the ghetto. The

conductor was Szymon Paulin. I didn't have a clue about classical music and I'd never been to a concert before. It was Hanka who first took me along there. ... People sat motionless in the dark hall, deeply moved. ... After that first concert, I couldn't wait for the next one, and after that I didn't miss one, until the Germans banned them. The orchestra was finally disbanded because they played German music, which was strictly banned for Jews.

People tried to offer children – apart from food, which was the main concern of their parents and guardians – at least the bare minimum for intellectual and spiritual development. It was very difficult because hungry children could only with difficulty concentrate on anything apart from food. One of the women I interviewed, who looked after children in the ghetto through Centos, had the following to say about this aspect of her work:

> We were very concerned with the children's intellectual development. In the boarding houses, day boarding centres and day centres in the ghetto, all kinds of entertainments, concerts, performances were organized. My friend Klima Fuswerk lent us puppets and other props. She went around in a circus waggon and gave performances in courtyards based on Stefan Themerson's book, 'How Mr Tom built his house'. The lead part was played by Michał Znicz, a distinguished actor from the Polish theatre. This modest cultural activity was enormously significant. The children locked up in the ghetto didn't know anything about animals or plants, they would ask you what cows looked like. (Helena, Interview 30)

As time passed, a certain unwritten code of decency took shape in the ghetto, dictating where it was socially acceptable to be seen, and where it was not. There was a certain accepted hierarchy of entertainments. I do not know whether this applied to all social circles, but certainly among the intelligentsia, where the great majority of the people I interviewed belonged, there was a strong sense of this unwritten code. One of the women I talked to said:

> I went to concerts. I even went to a cabaret twice, with a rich girl friend. But that upset me. I felt that it wasn't *appropriate to go to the 'Paradis'* (my emphasis – B.E.) at a time when everything was as it was. (Irena, Interview 28)

The parents of this rich friend had a wholesale pharmacy

business in the ghetto, and therefore were, it seems, doing very well. One of the ways that these two young girls spent their free time in the ghetto was playing 'there's no war':

> I used to go to see her and we would play 'there's no war'. ... We ate good things. We didn't drink alcohol in those days, but we talked about things that amused us, we played records, people came round, we danced. 'There's no war' ... (Irena, Interview 28)

When trying today to reconstruct the hierarchy of entertainments in the ghetto, we might say that at one end of it came the concerts and dramatic performances. These were not only the most intellectually 'elevated' entertainments, but above all they provided a livelihood for unemployed musicians and actors, who because of the 'superfluous' nature of their calling were in a very difficult material situation.

But it was not socially acceptable – which seems perfectly understandable in the situation in the ghetto – to enjoy yourself too ostentatiously. Nonetheless, in the winter of 1941, shortly after the area had been sealed off, the traditional carnival season dances took place in the ghetto:

> There was a carnival dance in the 'Melody Palace' with a competition for the best legs. The ghetto danced. (Ringelblum 1988a, p. 233)

It was undoubtedly not socially acceptable to be seen in cafés and restaurants whose owners were German collaborators, exploited the poverty of others or made fortunes from smuggling. Places like this were at the other end of the ghetto hierarchy of entertainments. In fact, we do not know a great deal about them, for there is rarely any information about them in accounts from the ghetto; nor did the people I interviewed speak about them. We only know that they existed – but not how many or where. Places like this were often connected with certain types of 'services' provided for the clients. Krystyna Żywulska (1963, pp. 23-4) worked in one of them briefly:

> You know, don't you, that a lot of smart guests come here?
>
> Yes.
>
> Yes, well, they work hard to get smart. They smuggle goods past the guards and their nerves are on edge all the time. Afterwards, they need to relax. ... If my guests want you to, you've to go with them

and do whatever they ask you to do. And not give them any trouble. They have pockets stuffed with money. If you're nice to them, they won't stint. ... There's a war on, you can't stand on ceremony. That other waitress is fifteen years old and she doesn't make a fuss about it.

How many places were there like this in the ghetto? The number probably varied. Apart from the best-known, 'good' places like the *Sztuka* ('Art') or *Nowoczesna* ('Modern') cafés, there were a number of second and third rate places. On 6 April 1941, Ringelblum (1988a, p. 260) wrote that 'There are 61 cafes, restaurants and other entertainment establishments in the Warsaw ghetto.'

Ruta Sakowska (1993, pp. 229–30) lists fifteen cafes and restaurants. However, one the of the men I interviewed said:

The number of those places of entertainment, cafés, elegant restaurants that I've heard about everywhere – it's terribly exaggerated. I know that there were two or three cafés, but they weren't big cafés, and a few tiny restaurants, where you could eat really well, but which could seat ten or twelve people. I was in a café maybe twice, maybe three times, that's all. (Stefan, Interview 29)

He does not seem to remember, or he did not know of, the existence in the ghetto of places lower on the scale of the ghetto hierarchy of entertainments. The discrepancies between the above accounts indicate how time distorts the memories of people who were participants in events. I think that Ringelblum, who noted the events in the ghetto as they happened, was probably nearest to the truth. And I suspect that years later the ghetto hierarchy of entertainments may be a filter imposed by memory.

The problem of cultural life in the ghetto is seen through a distorting filter because of the over-representation of the intelligentsia among the survivors. They survived because they had a greater adaptability and more opportunity to adapt (Sakowska 1993, pp. 229–30). I do not know of any data on the educational patterns of survivors, but one could imagine that certain social groups are only marginally represented among them. If we remember the criteria for verification that I proposed in the previous chapter, we can see that certain groups of Jews had less chance of meeting the criteria for survival on the 'Aryan side'. Their poor or non-existent command of Polish, their 'poor appearance', or inability to behave adequately to the situation, all told against them. The majority of the prewar poor, manual workers and some craftsmen were the first to topple over the edge of the chance of survival. It was they and the deportees from other towns who were the 'muslims' of the ghetto, and like the 'muslims' from the camps represent only a tiny proportion of the survivors.

*

Alongside the collective model of the reception of culture which has been described above, there was also an individual model of reception. Instead of spending your free time in company or in a café or restaurant, you could – as far as conditions permitted – occupy yourself with reading. One of the men I interviewed recalled the time he spent in the ghetto as a period of intensive reading and individual study:

> There was some sort of substitute intellectual life. When I got home from work, I used to get washed and I always read something. I remember that at the beginning of the war I bought a lot of books from a stall (there were stalls on Długa street, full of books from burned-out houses), on chemistry for example, but things like Bukharin as well. Two volumes, published just before the war. I very much wanted to study. And I studied. Maybe some of it was a bit odd – for example ancient history; in 1940 I went through the mathematics course for the polytechnic. I wasn't studying for the future, or in order to survive, but just because it gave me pleasure. (Ryszard, Interview 34)

Not everyone was, however, able to read in the living conditions imposed by the ghetto. Housing conditions, the psychological pressure caused by the overcrowding in the ghetto, hunger, illness and exhaustion, all influenced this. Living under stress, and constant oppression by the Other, made concentration impossible.

One natural human reaction in difficult situations is to relieve the tension through humour, jokes, laughter. The ghetto did not prove an exception.

> Even in the worst period of the closure action, there was a pathological sense of humour in the ghetto. I remember how during

> the action those who had survived would gather in some corner of the courtyard at night and yell with laughter. I don't know whether I ought to talk about it. ... But it was some kind of compensation, relief of tension. (Ryszard, Interview 34)

There is one further problem connected with cultural life in the ghetto. Many chroniclers note that there were a lot of people in the ghetto who wrote poetry, memoirs, who drew and painted and composed music. One trend in this creative work dealt with 'immediate' questions – that is, the current problems of the ghetto; another was 'timeless' and dealt with general problems. People wanted to record and pass on to others their own experience, they were aware that they were taking part in something unique, something uniquely terrible. They wanted to warn others, to protect humanity from a repetition of anything like it again in the future. This was the goal that inspired Emanuel Ringelblum, who with an historian's objectivity collected information on various aspects of the life of the ghetto.

The chroniclers of the Łódź ghetto also did impressive work, noting (daily) things like the weather, births and deaths, suicides, arrests, street demonstrations, rumours – and also gave a detailed account of the activities of the *Judenrat*, and of its chairman, Chaim Rumkowski.[44] Unfortunately, most of the literature, art and music produced in the ghetto perished with the ghetto's inhabitants; only a small part survived.

Creative activity in the ghetto was, like academic study or work, a form of psychological resistance to the Germans. It was a way of preserving your inner freedom, of protecting your inner self from the terrible outside world. Ideas about what you had seen and heard, and the need to pass them on to others, to bear witness, were a defence of the human dignity and individuality that the Germans were denying.

Social distinctions

> During one of the last mass executions, Tobiasz Mokotowski was being taken to his death. Constable Noj was dancing round him like a spinning top, jumping up on all sides, insisting:
> – Take off your jacket, what do you need a jacket for now? Give it me!

Mokotowski held himself erect, and walked along without saying a word. Noj danced round like a madman, pulling at his sleeve, but it did him no good. And so off went one Jew, annoyed with another Jew because the latter preferred to be buried in his jacket, rather than hand it over.

Calel Perechodnik, *Czy ja jestem mordercą?*
(*Am I a Murderer?*)

The prewar social structure was destroyed in the world of the ghetto. Wartime divisions were superimposed upon the natural stratification of Jewish society. It was in German interests to destroy social ties and atomize all groupings: making the Jewish population disoriented and uncertain would facilitate the introduction of the German extermination plans. It seems fairly obvious: the factors which stablized the prewar social structure ceased to be of significance in the ghetto. A social hierarchy took shape based on different principles from those operating in peacetime. Values like knowledge, education, honesty, or even property were no longer markers of value; what counted, apart from money, was ability to network and a certain moral flexibility (flexibility of conscience), which made it possible for some people to fight for their own survival at the expense of others.

I think that social distinctions in the ghetto had two partly overlapping dimensions: the utilitarian and the moral.

The gauge of the utilitarian dimension was the chance of survival. It was the chance of survival that was a significant, if not the most significant, measure of status in the ghetto. People who had a chance of survival were higher in the social hierarchy than those who did not have a chance of survival. The various chances of survival, often illusory, changed as the situation in the ghetto changed; but let us look at the utilitarian dimension of the social structure of the ghetto from this point of view – the point of view of the chance of survival. If we take into account the second factor which was of enormous value in the ghetto – money – we are able to distinguish two main types of chances for survival – with money and without money.

Survival dependent on money basically applied to two groups of people: those who were wealthy before the war and those who made fortunes in the ghetto. Prewar resources had to be really large to make it possible to survive in the ghetto (there had to be enough to buy food on the black market for two years), for getting out of it (bribes), and for hiding on 'the Aryan side', which as I wrote in the previous chapter often entailed major expenses.

It is difficult to calculate how much money you needed to have in order to survive the war, the more so in that the majority of payments had to be made in dollars, gold, jewellery, etc. Perhaps owning a tenement house prewar, or considerable assets located in safety, were enough to ensure survival.

Probably it was the wealthy middle class and the richer capitalists who were able to survive the war thanks to their money. But possession of wealth alone was only a necessary pre-condition, and was not in itself enough to ensure survival. It was also necessary to have access to your money (Swiss bank accounts were useless) – you needed to have trusted persons on the 'Aryan side'. It was safer not to have too many valuables with you in the ghetto; the Germans requisitioned things regularly, and took valuables from Jewish homes with impunity. When they went to the ghetto, people tried to leave some property with Polish friends or acquaintances, and with their help would then be able to make use of their property. On the other hand, the more affluent tried to help the poorer members of their close or distant families (the more affluent constituted a chance of survival for their poor relations).

> I more or less landed on my feet, because we had a bit of money hidden away, a few things hidden away – here and there. But it was all very quickly exhausted. We had quite a lot of friends and quite a large family that we had to help, and we had no income at all. I didn't really earn anything at all, and my parents didn't earn anything. The hierarchy of values? Money. (Stefan, Interview 29)

The other category of people whose chance of survival was denoted by the amount of money they had were those who made fortunes in the ghetto. Here the utilitarian criterion came into contact with the moral, which I shall write about below. At any event, while the people who lived from pre-war assets did not break away from the community, and their behaviour and social position were in some sense 'normal' – part of the prewar world, and not acquired at the expense of others – the people who got rich during the war were not respected by others, all the more so in that their fortunes were usually acquired through some kind of collaboration with the Germans.

> There were a few people who still had money, they had a bit of money – they weren't great fortunes, but if someone had some rings or something, some valuables. ... There were a few nouveaux riches, I mean people who were involved in smuggling.
>
> [There were big fortunes made in the ghetto, too.]
>
> Big fortunes! That's a big exaggeration, but, well, there were people who managed to make money in some way, schemers, who often collaborated with the Germans, they had some contacts, those were the nouveaux riches, they were seen as Croesuses. (Stefan, Interview 29)

Money, of course, did not guarantee survival: it only constituted a chance of survival; but it was, undoubtedly, one of the basic factors in determining social ranking in the ghetto. Those who did not have money, those who came totally expropriated to the ghetto from other towns, were the first to die of starvation.

The social structure in the ghetto was funnel-shaped, that is, ever wider circles became pauperized and degraded and were sucked down to the depths of poverty. Even people who before the war had been rich or relatively well-off, gradually exhausted their resources and were faced with hunger. Piotr Matywiecki, in an analysis of the memoirs written in the ghetto, said: 'The authors of the ghetto diaries observed the passing of generations of beggars within months: they came first from among the deportees, then from among the pre-war poor, and at the end from among the intelligenstsia. They died one after the other' (Matywiecki 1994, p. 285).

Chances of survival not dependent on money changed in parallel with the changing situation in the ghetto. They were linked with your own initiative or with receiving help from others. Those who had rich families, or friends who were willing and in a position to share, received help from others.

Your own initiative could be shown by organizing smuggling for your own needs, selling things, etc. Initiative could also be shown in finding appropriate work – that is, work that offered a chance of survival.

Work in the *Judenrat* was considered to be of this kind: fairly secure and reliable. It gave a source of livelihood, but was at the same time judged ambivalently: many of the inhabitants of the ghetto considered the members of the *Judenrat* to be collaborators and thieves. Undoubtedly, contact with goods that were in short supply (and in the ghetto, everything except death was 'in short supply') made many people corruptible and willing to take bribes. Ringelblum (1988a, p. 314) wrote very critically of the *Judenrat*, calling its chairman 'that duffer, Czerniaków':

> People have such a poor opinion of the *Judenrat* that they think it's capable of any dirty trick. That's the most accurate judgement of the *Judenrat*.

Israel Gutman, in his *The Jews of Warsaw, 1939–1943* (1993, p. 132), also criticized the activities of the *Judenrat*:

> The policies of the *Judenrat* led to the petrification of deep social divisions. The *Judenrat* made no attempt to take money from the rich – or at least it did not take even a tiny fraction of their wealth – to help those who were condemned to hunger and death from starvation. Of course, moves of this kind would not have changed the situation greatly, but they might have slowed down the process, and consequently have made possible a better use of the Jewish community's own potential resources.

The activities of the *Judenrat* are controversial to the present day, although I do not intend to go into this: I wish simply to note that attitudes to it were ambivalent.

Working in the *Judenrat*, or in one of the institutions that it controlled, was linked in the first place with privileges of some kind, and so there was no shortage of applicants for jobs. For example, the Jewish police force – later hated because of the part they played in the closure action, which for them was to be a guarantee of safety (which later proved illusory) – also had a higher ration allowance. On 23 June 1941, Adam Czerniaków wrote in his *Diary* (1983, p. 195): 'Aryan rations for the service, but from the general allocation'. This meant that the police got higher food rations at the expense of the ordinary people of the ghetto.

Even greater privileges stemmed from collaboration with the Germans – which was obviously to a greater or lesser extent veiled, but still evident. Two well-known collaborators from the ghetto, Kohn and Heller, who did unbelievable business with the Germans, and were the owners of the horse-drawn tram service running in the ghetto, known as the 'kohnhelerka', were even given permission not to wear armbands.[45] All privileges of this kind, even very minor ones, deepened social divisions within the ghetto, and meant that new groupings were constantly appearing there who were pursuing their own interests, which were often in conflict with the interests of the ghetto as a whole.

But were there in fact any 'interests of the ghetto as a whole', apart from survival? It was precisely this goal which caused conflicts of interests between particular groups and sub-groups. Each of them strove to retain their concessions, privileges or apparent privileges. All 'centrifugal' tendencies of this kind, which loosened the social structure from within, were in the interests of the Germans, who acted on the principle of divide and rule. Through creating various kinds of illusory privileges, and by seemingly ceding responsibility for this state of affairs to the Jews themselves, they managed to divide the community into mutually competitive groups with conflicting interests, which was later to be one of the factors making it possible to carry out the final closure action.

> The Germans managed to bring about a situation where everyone was fighting just for his life. Two and a half years were enough to destroy all bonds. (Ryszard, Interview 34)

The most typical characteristic of social ranking in the ghetto was the enormous range and the huge contrast between those dying of starvation in the streets and the rich who could afford anything. Calel Perechodnik, a Jewish policeman from the Otwock ghetto, in memoirs that he wrote while in hiding on 'the Aryan side', said (1993, p. 17):

> Life in the ghetto was rather strange, everything was available, you could get anything there if you had the money. ... The rich man lived, dressed himself, ate, and drank without fear that he would be sent to a camp; you could always buy yourself off if you had the money. Meanwhile, the poor man swelled up and died of starvation in full view. Most people accepted it.

It was these contrasts, condensed because they were concentrated in a small area, that above all attracted attention. Even if there were not so very many rich people, their existence, and also the existence of an infrastructure adjusted to their requirements – well-supplied shops, restaurants – stood out from the background poverty of the rest of the inhabitants of the ghetto, and emphasized the contrasts that existed there.

> It was horrible in the ghetto. Those Jews were an absolutely class-based society. Alongside the terrible poverty there were cafés where you could get anything. (Ryszard, Interview 34)

The majority of the people I interviewed regarded their own situation as average, although I think that they meant different things by the concept of 'average'. In the situation in the ghetto there was no objective point of reference for the term. It was subjective, but at the same time very elastic: it covered everything that came between the two contrasting ends of the ghetto spectrum. When the people I talked to described their own situation as 'average' they were using a relative measure: each of them had seen people who were in a better position than themselves; each of them had seen people whose situation was worse. And therefore they thought that both those who like R.H., quoted above, were on the verge of starvation, and those who for as long as they could maintained a kosher kitchen, and those who had a cleaner, were 'average'.

> To the present day, I don't really know what we lived on. My brother-in-law's sister had married a rich Englishman before the war; I think that maybe she had in some way provided security for her parents. They had a lot of different prewar connections, many people helped them. Thanks to that, we were not so terribly poor, just ordinarily poor. We would boil some buckwheat grits – they were brought to the boil on the stove and then wrapped for hours in a blanket, to save fuel. But every now and again, a woman came in to clean at my brother-in-law's parents, and that was a certain kind of luxury in the ghetto. (Alina, Interview 33)

It was not only Alina who was aware that her own position was privileged; many of the people I interviewed were similarly, and sometimes painfully, conscious of it.

> When things began to get steadily worse, before the final apathy and despair set in, I was helped by the absurd 'defensive' formula that even in the new, crippled scale of comparison, I was in luxury conditions. I recognized very early on the principle that was later best put by Stanisław Jerzy Lec, that is, that when you think that you're

absolutely at the bottom, you will one day hear someone knocking underneath. (Jerzy, Interview 35)

The situation where divisions and gradations in ghetto society, based on chances of survival, were made more clearly and dramatically visible was the period of the great deportations which began in the Warsaw ghetto on 22 July 1942. All social divisions were revealed at that time with exceptional intensity. Only work constituted a chance of survival, since it seemed that only those who were working in the 'shops' for German requirements would remain alive. Therefore overnight getting employed in a 'shop' became a guarantee (again, as it proved, illusory) of safety. And once again, money became significant, since it provided the possibility of getting a certificate of employment, as did family ties or friends who might be able to arrange for you work in a 'shop'.

> In July my parents and I somehow managed to wriggle out of it, and that was because I somehow managed to fix myself up in Toebbens 'shop'. They were clothing workshops, sewing uniforms for the Wehrmacht. I started to work there and my parents fixed themselves up somewhere else, taking advantage of the fact – and that was what it was all about – that one of my father's brothers-in-law had had a small boot factory before the war. And he set up a 'shop', that is, he wasn't the owner, he was in charge of a workshop at Schulz's 'shop', which was in Nowolipie Street. And they started to work there. (Rysiek, Interview 11)

> The manager of the 'shop' was our neighbour in Podwale Street and thanks to him, we got taken on there. (Irena, Interview 28)

The utilitarian dimension, measured in various survival chances, was only one of the aspects of the structure of social differentiation in the ghetto. The second was the moral aspect. The gauge of this dimension was attitudes to the community.

According to German assumptions, everyone there was equal before the fate that had been reserved for them. The highly gradated prewar Jewish society arrived in the ghetto with highly differentiated external baggage; it was only when whey were in the ghetto that they were levelled down. 'Glajch, glajch' sang mad Rubinsztajn as he ran about the ghetto.

> Sometimes I'm haunted in my sleep by nightmares about the ghetto streets. There was a madman called Rubinsztajn who ran about and

shouted 'Glajch, glajch!' – everyone's equal, everyone's the same. He was shouting what we could all hear being shouted inside our own heads. He was right, in a sense we were all equal, even if the rich were eating salmon, Swiss cheeses and ham; but they were poor just the same. They couldn't bring themselves to give up these vanities of the world, they really didn't know how to. They thought that money could buy everything, but in fact the same annihilation was hanging over them, too. (Helena, Interview 30)

Rubinsztajn was famous, and was written about by many of the diarists of the ghetto, including Samuel Puterman:

The king of the Warsaw beggars, 'Glajch, glajch', went about jolly and well-fed, he made a career for himself. He had various ideas, he knew how to dress, he was a constantly new and welcome attraction for crowds of passers by. He appeared in the streets in various costumes, and he explained why he was wearing them by jokes that were quickly on everyone's lips. He'd put on a lady's dress? Because I don't have a wife, today I'm my wife, that's a good one isn't it? He put on bathing trunks and said he was on the beach, that's a good one isn't it? For a few days he went about in a frock coat, because he was attending a meeting at the *Judenrat*, or the Supply Department, that's a good one isn't it? He was so popular that the management of the 'Melody Palace' put on a revue entitled 'Glajch, glajch'. And for the last number, the most popular madman in the ghetto appeared in his own person in a frock coat. ...[46]

The ghetto was a community of fate and of destiny. There were people there of differing social backgrounds, from very different circles and with differing senses of their own identity and national allegiance. There were people who were completely assimilated into Polish society, who spoke, thought and felt exclusively in Polish, and were often also Roman Catholics; there were people who were Zionists and spoke Hebrew by choice; and there were Orthodox Jews and Hassidim, who spoke Yiddish and often did not speak any Polish.

I remember how when I was walking on a Saturday with a girl in the ghetto, I lit a cigarette. A Hassid came up to me and slapped me on the face. I didn't hit back, he wouldn't have stood a chance. And he said, 'Has the Good Lord not punished you enough already, that you smoke cigarettes on a Saturday!' It was a different mentality. (Edward, Interview 26)

All of these social and group differences proved insignificant in the light of Nazi ideology. What became fundamental was the brand mark of origins, which many of these people felt was of no importance at all, or was secondary.

A new structure created by the conditions of war was superimposed upon the prewar social structure, and had a great deal of significance for many people. In the ghetto, it was not only prewar status and property or contacts – which might constitute a chance of survival – that were important, but also natural or cultural differences which revealed themselves in attitudes of Jews themselves to the fate prepared for them.

I think two types of differences of this kind, defining attitudes to the community, were of fundamental importance: cultural differences and religious differences.

Cultural differences were the first of the reasons leading to acceptance of the community, or rejection of it.

> In the ghetto you could sense the heritage of pre-war differences of tradition amongst various social groups. After all, a Jew from Nalewki Street and a Jew from Królewska Street were from two completely different worlds. There was more that divided them than united them. There were many people among us who felt more Polish than Jewish. They didn't turn themselves into stereotypical Jews, but only a few rejected the community. The majority found a bond with Jewishness in the ghetto because of the common destiny. That didn't lessen the feeling of Polishness, but it increased the feeling of belonging among people sharing a common fate. With time, new divisions began to take shape. Groups of people came together who in another situation would have had nothing in common; people were brought together by their professional position, a common workplace, living in one tenement house, and they were divided by physical distances, differences in the standard of living, current incidental arrangements – like pawns on a chessboard. And it was really a very complex pattern. Some people felt uncomfortable with it, you could see that they still had the feeling that they were from a different world, that they had been forced into this. Others – like myself, for example – found a place in this imposed world and felt all right there. (Jerzy, Interview 35)

> From the first moment I felt linked with that world behind the walls. I was no longer a Polish woman of Jewish origin, I was Jewish – that's how racism had categorized me, that's how I categorized myself. (Helena, Interview 30)

The cultural dimension divided Polish Jews and could constitute the marker of their attitude to the community. The same dimension, in a more drastic form, separated Jews who came into the ghetto from outside Poland from the rest of the community. As we know, many Jews from other countries were brought into the ghettos. From the beginning they formed a separate group, making the pre-existing divisions stronger. I have already referred frequently to deportees from small towns in Poland whose social status was, it would seem, the lowest in the ghetto, and who were the first to die of starvation and illnesses. Another group of deportees who stood out from the community in the ghetto were the German Jews. They were mainly assimilated into German culture, and they were German patriots – which evoked an understandable aversion to them in the territory of occupied Poland.

> A lot of Jews came into the ghettos from other ghettos that had been closed down. This didn't bring any protests. But – although this is perhaps to over-generalize – the German Jews were not at all welcome in the Warsaw ghetto, all the more so in that they made it clear that they were German patriots. They despised the Ost-Juden, or in other words all of us, and they were waiting for the Germans to win the war, because they thought that then the Nazi episode would come to an end and everything would be all right. There was something of this in it, although like all generalizations, it involves over-simplification. (Jerzy, Interview 35)

There was a similarly unwelcoming attitude to the German Jews in the Łódź ghetto:

> Very sharp conflicts broke out between the German Jews – cultured, educated, proud and usually assimilated – and the poor local population, on the one hand with the religious Jews and on the other with the left-wing ones. The Łódź Jews however had the advantage over the rich Jews from Germany – in 1941, they were a lot better adapted to life in ghetto conditions. Culture, education and social polish proved worthless there, and even at times was a hindrance, making life more difficult. Those with more cunning, the more resistant, those with contacts and friends, who understood the customs or interests of the ghetto, came out on top. (Arnold, Interview 9)

Religious differences constituted the second dimension which defined attitudes to the community. There was a group of

Catholic converts in the ghetto, which if perhaps not particularly large was fairly noticeable and stood out from the rest of the community. As I have already noted, they got permission to open a separate school, the Christian charity 'Caritas' provided them with extra food, and they had higher food rations. In September 1941, Ringelblum (1988a, pp. 317–18) wrote:

> The neophytes ... want to have their own school and they will have it, since they get everything they ask for. ... They also get more products than other people. Lately 4 or 6 kilos of sugar. In the *Judenrat* and in the police etc., they have the highest posts. They support one another.

It is true that many Catholic converts had positions in the *Judenrat*. This was probably because the Catholic converts were mainly, if not exclusively, educated people, often from the free professions, who before the war had occupied a high position not only in the Jewish, but also in the Polish, social structure. During the interwar period, it was made difficult for Jews to reach major positions in public, social or academic life. And therefore they often changed their religion (and surname) for reasons of status. The Germans, in line with their policy of introducing as many divisions and conflicts in the ghetto as possible, promoted the converts; for example, the commandant of the ghetto police, Jakub Szerzyński, was from this group.[47]

The converts formed a fairly tightly knit group in the ghetto. They mainly lived in Sienna Street, the most elegant street in the pre-war Jewish district, which Ringelblum (1988a, p. 324) somewhat maliciously called 'The Avenue of the Neophytes'. There were also three churches in the ghetto: in Plac Grzybowski, where Father Godlewski was the parish priest and was responsible for rescuing people of Jewish origin; in Leszno Street, where the priest was a well-known convert called Tadeusz Puder;[48] and a third in Nowolipki Street, which did not function as a church during the ghetto period.

Of course, in a situation where some social group is given greater privileges than another group, the number of its members rises. And there was no shortage in the ghetto, either, of people willing to change their faith. It is difficult to say today how many authentic conversions there were, and how far they resulted from a desire to belong to a privileged group.

Ringelblum at the time saw it as a 'psychopathological' development. In October 1941, he wrote (1988a, p. 327):

> Changes of faith are taking place quite frequently. On the day of Hosanna Raba,[49] more than 50 people were baptised. The reason: 'Caritas' is taking care of the neophytes. And the hope that baptised Jews will manage to get out of the ghetto.

The people I interviewed also spoke critically about the converts, as people who broke away from the community in the ghetto:

> In medical circles, and especially among students, Professor Hirszfeld was very unpopular. Obviously not because he was an assimilated Jew, who thought of himself as a Pole, because after all, there were plenty of those, and not because he was a Christian, because there were quite a few of those, too. The point was his peculiar arrogance, if only in the way he formed sentences, the demonstrative way that he stressed his difference, his superiority to the ghetto community. For him, even his laboratory in the hospital was Europe, and everything round about was the ignorant backwoods. He voiced his 'Christian ideals' in a very unpleasant way – and the term should be in inverted commas. He treated his enforced stay in the ghetto as a mission to put these ideals into practice. He boasted that he was there to free us of our belief in racism and its significance, as though we – the students – believed (in the ghetto!) that there was some truth in Hitler's ideas. He announced that he would lift this curse from us, and that he would do it during his first lecture. He didn't know that if it had not been for a request from Dr Izrael Milejkowski, the head of the Health Service at the *Judenrat*, the Warsaw students would have put a stop to that lecture. We remembered Hirszfeld's behaviour before the war, when he failed to protest against the quota system introduced for Jewish students, the approving way in which he had defended the anti-semitism of the government and society, the scorn he had shown for Jews who considered themselves Jews – without seeing it as a stigma – while at the same time being no worse Polish patriots than himself.
> (Jerzy, Interview 35)

*

Apparently what made it possible for the Germans to eradicate the ghettos efficiently was the fact that they had introduced a maximum number of divisions within the community, and a maximum number of groups with conflicting interests and goals (apart from that goal that was common to all: of survival). They strengthened through all kinds of concessions to groups who broke away from the community.

I think that in this, the Nazis made use of their own experience of seizing and retaining power. They used a similar social technology in relation to the Jewish populations of the occupied countries. A successful implementation of their aim – total extermination – required the creation of a new society in place of the established social structure in which various groups had a defined place and ways of articulating their own interests that were sanctioned by tradition – a new society that was declassed, atomized, divided into random interest groups. As Hannah Arendt writes. (1989b, pp. 247–70), totalitarian movements are possible where mass society replaces class society. It was the masses who provided support for Nazism in Germany. And they apparently applied the same tried and tested social technology in the ghettos. The Nazis worked to create there mass societies, which they understood in the way that Hannah Arendt reinterprets: the term 'masses' is applied only where we are dealing with people with whom – because of their very number, or passivity, or a combination of these two things – it is impossible to form any organization based on a community of interests, any political party, municipal authorities, professional organization or trade union (1989b, p. 250).

The final solution of the Jewish question

> As an old National Socialist, I have to say that if the Jewish tribe in Europe were to survive this war, while we are sacrificing our best blood to save Europe, then the war would be only a partial success. This is why my hope in respect of the Jews is that they will cease to exist. They have to be removed. ... But what should we do with them? Do you believe that they should be removed to territories designated for settlement in the Ostland? In Berlin they told us: why go to all that trouble, we don't have any role for them in the Ostland or in the Reichskommissariat; get rid of them yourselves.
>
> Governor Hans Frank, 16.XII.1941

To end this chapter, I would like to discuss two questions linked with the final period of the existence of the ghetto. The first is the problem of the selections carried out during the period of the deportation action; the second is the question of when the Jews came to believe that Hitler wanted to murder them all; the question of when they understood what the 'final solution of the Jewish question' involved.

Hannah Arendt wrote that after the destruction of morality in people, the one thing that still remained to prevent their being turned into living corpses was individual differences, the uniqueness of the individual identity. The destruction of individuality meant the destruction of spontaneity, of man's ability to start something new on the basis of his own resources, something which could not be explained as a reaction to the environment and events. Nothing then remained but hideous puppets with human faces, who without exception reacted in a way that could be exactly predicted even when they were going to their deaths, and whose lives were made up exclusively of reflex actions (1989b, pp. 343–5). Arendt was referring to prisoners in concentration camps, but what she had to say can also be applied to the ghetto, which was after all an experimental laboratory for totalitarianism. The reduction of human personality to reflex actions, the total interchangeability of the victims, was put into effect through the mechanism of selection.

Various kinds of selection were one of the basic elements of terror, a way of dealing with the civilian population which was applied from the beginning of the occupation to both Poles and Jews. Jews were first of all selected for all kinds of labour gangs (for example clearing rubble in Warsaw), for work camps, etc. This soon became a part of normality and everyday life in the ghetto and its inhabitants adapted (as did the 'Aryan' part of Warsaw) to various kinds of street round-ups and deportations.

Selections were from the beginning of the war one of the instruments which divided Jewish society into different interest groups: if only for example into those who were and were not able to buy themselves out of compulsory labour. The greatest strength of selection, used as a basis for the treatment of the civilian population, came with the great deportation action in the Warsaw ghetto. Before the deportations, the atmosphere in the ghetto thickened: terror was stepped up, tension grew. Lejzor Czarnobroda noted in his diary at the time:

For several days people have been muttering about the terrible sentence that the enemy has pronounced on us, and that the hour when it is to be carried out is approaching. There have been shootings for several weeks. Anxiety is rising. At night, without cause, the butchers have shot hundreds of people on the pretext of combatting smuggling, have shot them on the spot, in their homes, in the courtyard, in the street. Until recently, they still did it under cover, in the gaols, work camps, concentration camps, on gallows, in gas chambers or electric chairs, but now they're doing it shamelessly, in full public view, in order to terrorize, to break entirely and demoralize a Jewish population that is already exhausted, hungry, decimated by epidemics and death from starvation. The ghetto has been reduced in size, the number of exits to the 'other side' has been reduced, in order to squeeze us more tightly, to make all attempts at rescue, escape to 'that side', impossible.[50]

According to the German practice of linking important events with Jewish religious holidays, the deportation action began on Wednesday, the eve of the Ninth Day of the Month of Av. In Jewish tradition, this is a day of fasting and mourning, connected with the destruction of the First and Second Temples and the driving of the Jews from Spain. The action ended on the Day of Judgement, or in other words on 21 September. According to 'official German sources, during that period of 46 days, 253,471 Jews were sent to their deaths. The daily contingent varied from 13,596 people transported on 8 September to 2,196 transported on the last day of the action; on average, it was about 6,000' (Gutman 1993, p. 292).

The people I interviewed divided time into before and after the action. Some of them had already got out to 'the Aryan side' before it started, and here I will only quote those who lived through the action in the Warsaw ghetto itself. The selection here was something new in that the Germans had brought about such divisions in the Jewish community, had given rise to the existence of groups with such totally conflicting interests, that the victims made the selections among themselves.

The Germans solved the problem of the selection of victims in a macabre way. From the beginning, they divided Jewish society into those who already had a sentence passed on them and those with an indefinitely suspended sentence - it could be for days, weeks or even months. And then later they handed over the process of selection to the

Jews themselves. The victims had themselves to choose who would go first to a labour camp or to deportation, in other words to death.

> I remember how in the early stages of the July and August action, we – that is, a few hundred young doctors and medical students – were sent one day to the *Judenrat*, allegedly to replace officials there who had urgent business to conclude. There in the courtyard, surrounded by rifles and with the Jewish police standing by, we were told we had to go into the houses in Leszno Street and check the certificates of the Jews living there. Those who had no employment certificates were to be brought into the street, because they were to be deported for labour in the East. We had to supply them with so many people, and if we couldn't find them they would make the numbers up from among us. I remember the stony face of my brother, who wouldn't know how to hand anyone over, and the face of one of our colleagues, who exhibited exceptional keenness. In fact that action was successful, but only because people came down by themselves without persuasion, they only asked whether they would get the 3 kilos of bread and 1 kilo of jam offered in the announcements straight away. That day has left an awful memory, but it was still 'small beer' compared with what came later. (Jerzy, Interview 35)

What did people who took part in the selections feel like? They were situations where human behaviour – under pressure of fear, terror, and hope – was reduced to reflex actions, making rational behaviour impossible.

> People didn't talk at that time. It was as though one person was divided from another – and they were divided. For after all, they were being hunted like animals – they were being killed, in the street and not only in the gas chambers. I don't remember any conversations from that period. You didn't know then what was happening to other people. And because there were Germans everywhere, you could only talk in the night. (Anna, Interview 27)

A certificate of employment in a 'shop' protected you from deportation from the ghetto, and then later a 'permit to live', of which the Germans printed about 60,000 and ordered the Jews to divide them up among themselves. Everyone who was able, who had any kind of way of fixing it, arranged work for themselves and their families in a 'shop', or at least a certificate of employment.

> I was entered on the list of bakers, I don't remember whether there were numbered tickets, but there was a list. I could put one additional person on the list. I entered my father, and – I thought it was worth a

try - my mother as well. She didn't work in the supply depot, but was hiding with me. We all came out and there was a German there and it was: to the left, to the right - everyone had the papers, so I gave the certificate to my mother, but she didn't take it and went to the left. Yes, that's what it was like, you know. (Stefan, Interview 29)

There were also selections in the 'shops' - people who were hiding there without the appropriate papers were caught.

I survived several selections in the shop where I worked. The Germans came in unannounced with an order - all workers out into the courtyard. They formed lines - some to the right, some to the left. ... What was the point? Life or death. For the time being, the point for all of us was life, of course. Everyone was frightened, helpless. You were ashamed that you'd evaded the bad luck, and shamelessly overjoyed that you'd been saved. That was the formula for happiness. But in the depths of your soul there was a stifling bitterness. After every selection, I ran home terrified about whether I'd find my mother behind the wardrobe, whether my sister had come back from the courtyard. (Helena, Interview 30)

Another way of protecting yourself from deportation was to arrange a fictitious marriage with someone who had a certificate of employment - since the Germans had announced that these would also protect the closest members of their family.

A week after the deportation was announced, I made a fictitious marriage. On 22 July, I married Jurek, my present husband's cousin. In the ghetto he worked as a lecturer on the chemistry courses set up by Professor Centnerszwer. These were under the auspices of the *Judenrat*, and it was thought at the time that this would offer protection against deportation both for himself and his wife - in other words, me. (Alina, Interview 33)

Nonetheless, most of the inhabitants of the ghetto, who did not trust the Germans or the certificates of employment, simply hid themselves, packing themselves away into all kinds of holes and corners. These were usually collective hiding places, where people sat motionless for hours, making sure that no child cried and that no one coughed, because that could give everyone away. One of the men I interviewed however thought that hiding on your own was safer:

When we knew that there was going to be a round-up - a rumour always preceded it - I put my hands into my pockets and went into a ruined building. There were islands in the ghetto where people lived; I went outside those islands. I found myself some corner which seemed safe and waited until the action was over. There was always a problem with food. There was water, electricity, gas. I made myself something to eat on a gas stove if I found a bit of flour … (Ryszard, Interview 34)

After the mass deportations to Treblinka had ended, the Germans announced that all the remaining inhabitants of the ghetto were to report on 6 September in an area demarcated by a quadrangle of four streets: Miła, Niska, Stawki and Zamenhofa (hence the name: 'the quadrangle action'), where a great, final selection would take place. In the Ringelblum Archive, there is the following proclamation of the *Judenrat* written out very carefully by hand:

On the orders of the plenipotentiary for matters connected with the resettlement, the *Judenrat* in Warsaw announces the following:

1. By 10.00 a.m. on Sunday, 6 September 1942 all Jews without exception in the territory of the large ghetto should collect for registration in the district bounded by Smocza Street, Gęsia Street, Zamenhofa Street, Szczęśliwa Street and Parysowski Square.
2. It is also permitted for Jews to make their way there during the night of 5 to 6 September 1942.
3. Food for two days and drinking vessels should be brought.
4. Flats may not be locked.
5. Whoever fails to comply with this order and remains to 10.0 a.m. on 6.9.1942 in the ghetto (excluding the region specified above) will be shot.[51]

One of the women I interviewed described the action:

Later there was a proclamation, posted up everywhere, that all the inhabitants of the ghetto were to report on 6 September in a square between such and such streets. I think there was a separate selection in the 'shops'. But we had to report in the area of that quadrangle. The selection consisted of the crowd turning into a procession which moved along to a certain point where there were Germans. From there some people were taken away and the rest went back to the ghetto. I wasn't completely aware of the moment when the selection itself took place.

I remember how we went back in that procession. I remember that there was a man with a linen basket on his back, and that when he went past some inspection point, they took a child out of the basket. When I got back into the ghetto, I met my brother-in-law, who had come back with his disinfection column, and we waited for my sister to come back. She hadn't come back by three, but you could hear that the Germans had come back - we heard music, they were celebrating after the end of the selection. She had still not returned, and we understood that now she wouldn't return. (Alina, Interview 33)

Was it possible at that time in the ghetto to defend yourself effectively against totalitarianism? It seems that what was involved was rather instinctive behaviour, for example by people whose sense of responsibility for others was stronger than fear for their own lives. But in order to do that, to think of saving your own life and the lives of those close to you - you had to lose hope. You had to believe that deportation to the East meant death. This was one of the paradoxes of life in the ghetto - only loss of hope gave a chance of survival.

Hitler's intentions towards the Jews, although they had been announced in *Mein Kampf*, were not clear - either to the Poles or to those who were subject to the Nuremberg Laws. It was difficult to believe that you could simply murder a whole nation - just like that. There was no precedent in the history of mankind - which is why all attempts to find rational motives for German behaviour, all analogies, were suspended in a vacuum. Reason prompted you to believe that you could not totally without cause just kill people, that the world would not allow it to happen, that nobody would waste so much free labour, and finally - that you do not give people going to their deaths bread and jam. In all the interviews that I conducted there was the repeated refrain of 'People didn't want to believe it'.

Here are a few quotations representing various attitudes to the problem. Some people knew from the beginning what awaited them:

The Germans caught my brother as he was crossing the frontier and he was in prison here, in the Pawiak. ... Because he was a real textile expert, they took him to the workshops so that he could work in prison. The foreman there was a German. That German told him that he didn't for a minute believe that the Jews would survive the war. He wasn't trying to frighten him, he told him about pogroms, about what you had to do to kill Jews, to finish them off. ... When I met my brother in 1941, he was convinced that he wouldn't survive - because of that German with whom he'd had a lot of conversations. ... When you went into the ghetto and were a person who thought a bit, you could see that this was a collection of people condemned to annihilation. If you allowed people to die in their hundreds in the streets, if corpses were lying about covered in newspaper, if typhus was raging – and you didn't do anything about it; if a young German can go along the street – I saw this – and shoot older people, and just kill people, it's obvious. It's obvious that you're condemned to annihilation. (Anna, Interview 27)

I well knew that the Germans, the Nazis, held the Jews responsible for all evil. ... And I understood that really nothing could stop them doing it. What could stop them? I was completely aware ... and I was convinced that nothing would stop them from it, I knew. (Arnold, Interview 9)

Others came to believe it only after the war:

On the question of attitudes to what was happening, I wasn't aware. It was only after the war that I found out what had happened to the Jews. I remember that I first came across information about it in the ghetto. There was another schoolgirl with me in the workshop – she was 10, her name was Hanka and she came from a small town – I don't remember which one. She was in the ghetto with her mother and a baby sister; her father had stayed in a labour gang in that town. I remember a scene when she stood up and cried and said that they were supposed to be taking all the Jews away in motors and gassing them – I remember the word: 'gassing'. I told her that I thought it was completely impossible – I wasn't just trying to comfort her, I really meant it. ... I found out after the war. There was no chance to find out in Auschwitz – those who were on the side of life were on the side of life. If I had found out there, I wouldn't be telling you all this today. In Auschwitz some rumours got through to us. ... They pointed to the chimneys, they talked – but you still had to believe it. ... And after all, in Auschwitz they twice took us to the baths. (Ewa, Interview 17)

Between these two extreme attitudes – a catastrophic conviction of the inevitability of death, and rejecting the testimony of your own eyes – there were many intermediate positions. But among other things, your chance of survival depended on whether you believed in annihilation. For becoming aware that all were threatened by death mobilized many people into activity, into seeking for salvation. Perhaps many others could be pushed by the same knowledge into final despair, passivity, apathy and inability to take any decisions. The majority of these died. One of the women I interviewed said:

> It's not that a person wants to die, I didn't want to. As you can see: I'm alive. It isn't just coincidence, but my will to survive. (Anna, Interview 27)

It is not surprising that people did not want to believe in the Nazi plans for the extermination of the Jews – strong defence mechanisms always protect us from admitting the necessity of our own death. One can imagine how strong are the mechanisms protecting us from accepting consciously that our death will be so cruel, and at the same time so stupid, so completely unnecessary. Some cannot to the present day believe that it was all possible.

> No one believed it, I tell you. You couldn't believe it. I didn't believe it. I only found out when I was going out to work as an ordinary labourer, four or five weeks later – someone told me that it was to the gas. Someone pulled me out from just in front of the waggon – a policeman who knew me from the concert – and I struggled with him because I wasn't afraid of going. I only knew that I was going off to work. That's why I was keen to go – I wanted to go with them to that work. (Władysław, Interview 25)

Even if people knew, or sensed, what was waiting for them, hope made them believe to the last moment in a chance of salvation, the possibility of rescue. Lejzor Czarnobroda noted in his diary:

> The pogrom is still going on. The Inquisition is systematically working to destroy those who have managed to survive. They have squeezed us more tightly into a few workshops and factories, in order to be able to deal with us at one blow. There are some among us who believe. Who believe in a miracle. They pray for a miracle, for personal salvation.[52]

For many of the inhabitants of the ghetto, the event which warned them of Hitler's real intentions was the suicide of the president of the Warsaw *Judenrat*, Adam Czerniaków:

> Up to a certain moment nobody believed it, nobody believed that something like that could happen... but then when they announced the deportation, with the death of Czerniaków, everything became clear. (Adina, Interview 13)

Some people only came to believe when they were in Auschwitz:

> I didn't believe it. We didn't believe it till the end, even though it was so obvious, so open. ... It was in Auschwitz that I found out about it definitely. (Barbara, Interview 10)

Usually people were forced to believe in it when they came into contact with eyewitnesses of genocide:

> I remember that a boy came back from the Umschlagplatz, where he had been trying to get his parents out, without success. And he told us what the loading onto the transports looked like. I didn't have any illusions after what he told us. (Irena, Interview 28)

> It was in September in '43, I was already with the partisans and a friend of mine brought in Jew who had been hiding in the forest. He was called Ruben. ... He was the only prisoner from Treblinka that I ever saw in my life. He'd taken part in the uprising in Treblinka, in the camp. My friend had found him walking from Treblinka in the direction of his home town – maybe he was still counting on being able to hide in the Białystok ghetto? And he was the first to tell us what happened. Well, the death of one person you can understand, but that they took people ... and poisoned and burnt them all, it's, it's ... it was only what he told us, when he told us ... [that I believed it]. He told us how those corpses fell – he was in the *Sonderkommando* – in what way the corpses fell out of the gas chambers ... crammed together, some blue, some red – like young trees pressed together ... (Edward, Interview 26)

Those who already believed in what lay in wait for them wanted to warn others – those who did not believe yet – to warn them not to go voluntarily to their deaths, to try to hide or to go over to 'the Aryan side'. But those who did not want to know would not be convinced:

> People didn't believe it because it was unbelievable. They simply didn't believe it, even when the action began in the ghetto. I had a friend there to whom I went and said that it wasn't any kind of resettlement – she'd volunteered to go. I said that it was to death, that I knew for certain. And she said that it was all untrue, that people just said things like that, and she took a huge, packed rucksack and went off herself. ... In the morning I saw her from the window, down below in the courtyard. A group of people had gathered there in the courtyard, together with various kinds of bedding, with small children. Letters were being passed round allegedly sent saying that it was fine

there, that it was in the East, that they'd been given flats – that kind of thing. And I'd had a telephone call [from 'the Aryan side'] that they'd had information from Polish railway workers that the transports went to Małkinia, where the people got out and didn't go anywhere, and the empty trains went back. And so they thought that it was a concentration camp of some kind, or an extermination camp. ... I saw that group of people down below and I went down, though my brother thought that there was no point. But I went down and said that I'd had information from 'the Aryan side' that it was to death, that they shouldn't go, that they shouldn't get ready. They surrounded me, they wanted to beat me – they said that it was a German trick, that the Germans sent people like me so that they would rebel, and then the Germans would finish them off. And at that point my brother came down and somehow got me out of it. (Anna, Interview 27)

It would seem that the success of German plans for extermination can be explained by the total irrationality of the idea. If the victims themselves did not want, and could not manage, to believe in the fate that had been prepared for them, then is it surprising that the whole world did not believe it either?

Notes

1. In Western Europe, where there were fewer Jews, it did become usual for the Nazis to confine Jews in camps (such as Drancy in France and Westerbork in the Netherlands) prior to deportation to death camps. In Poland the Nazis at first considered the idea of a so-called 'reservation' for Jews in the Nisko area, near Lublin. Several thousand Jews from Austria and Czechoslovakia were transferred there. The Nazi ruler of Poland, Hans Frank, opposed the Nisko plan on the grounds that there were already too many Jews in the General Government; in addition, he did not want the SS to get an upper hand in running things in his territory. He therefore appealed direct to Hitler, and, as Israel Gutman (1993, p. 36) puts it 'in April 1940, all traces of the experiment near Nisko were liquidated'. The Nisko plan was not without further consequences, however: the Majdanek concentration camp in Lublin and a substantial number of labour camps for Jews were established in the same region. Shortly after the fall of France in June 1940, another plan was seriously considered, to establish a Jewish reservation in the French colony of Madagascar. This plan was defeated by logistical difficulties. Consideration was also given to a Jewish reservation in the Soviet Union, after the expected German victory.

2. (Editor's note) Ghettos varied in the degree of contact they had with the outside world. In smaller centres, ghettos were often 'open', that is, the Jews had to live there but were allowed to move about in the surrounding town within curfew hours. The Łódź ghetto, at the other

extreme, was hermetically sealed off from the outside world. The Warsaw ghetto was an intermediate case. It was 'closed', but located in a central district. Tram lines passed through it and 22 gates allowed people with appropriate authorization to enter and leave. Telephones and the postal service continued to function. There was also a considerable illegal trade across the ghetto wall.

3. The best-known example is Hitler's statement of 30 January 1939: 'Today I will once more be a prophet: if the international Jewish financiers ... should succeed once more in plunging the nations into a world war, then the result will be ... the annihilation of the Jewish race in Europe.' As Arendt points out, if you translate this into non-totalitarian language, it means, 'I want war and I intend to kill all the European Jews' (1989b, p. 276).

4. Moritz Kohn and Zelig Heller were involved in various mostly shady enterprises within the Warsaw ghetto. They are best known for operating the horse-drawn tram service (nicknamed *kohn-hellerka*) from May 1941.

5. Extract from a report by E. Karasiówna, assistant in the deportees' centre at Śliska Street, December 1941, *Biuletyn ŻIH* (Bulletin of the Jewish Historical Institute), 1975, no. 94.

6. Extract from a report by Waldemar Schön, the head of the Resettlement Section in the Office of the Governor of the Warsaw District, 20.1.1941, quoted in: Bartoszewski and Lewinówna (1969, pp. 890–1).

7. Schön report. (Editor's note: although these figures are widely reproduced and accepted as standard, they are actually based on a simple error: Schön relied on census data provided by the Jewish Council, but confused rooms with apartments. The correct census figures are reproduced by Berenstein and Rutkowski (1958). At the time the ghetto was closed there were 410,000 people in 139,644 rooms for an average of 2.94 persons per room, rising to 3.29 persons per room in March 1941 when the ghetto population reached its peak. There were 6 to 7 persons per apartment. By way of comparison, the population density in 'Aryan' Warsaw at that time was 1.89 persons per room. Though this represents a significant difference, the very noticeable overcrowding in the ghetto was more a result of the lack of open spaces and non-residential areas than of the shortage of rooms.)

8. Ringelblum 1988a, entry for 1.XI.1940.

9. Ringelblum 1988a, entry for 15.XI.1940.

10. Bauman (1982, p. 57). In the early days of the ghetto's existence, because of the crowding in the streets, the idea of wearing brooches that reflected light was publicized, because they were supposed to warn other pedestrians of your presence. But the idea was soon abandoned because it proved ineffective, and there were not enough of the brooches.

11. From the memoir of Natan Żelichower in Grynberg (1988, p. 44).

12. (Editor's note) Housing in Warsaw at that time typically consisted of three- to six-storey apartment buildings clustered around a central courtyard. To get to a particular dwelling, you entered the courtyard through a gateway from the street and then ascended one of numerous staircases through a door opening onto the courtyard. Because of evening curfews, the 'courtyard' and 'staircase' became fundamental social units of wartime

Warsaw, comprising not only the physical spaces themselves but all the dwellings that they connected and the people living there. The gateways also played a significant role, as the subsequent narrative will show.

13. It was the same in concentration camps: ignoring hygiene was the first step towards 'muslimization' and consequently to death.

14. Kaplan (1963, 1964), entry for 29 January 1940, cited after Matywiecki (1994, p. 306). This day's entry is missing from Kaplan (1999).

15. The experience of time described here does not necessarily apply only to the ghetto: some of its characteristics can also be applied to 'the Aryan side' and to the war in general.

16. This account comes from the Łódź ghetto, hence the reference to marks and pfennigs rather than złotys.

17. Quoted after Matywiecki (1994, p. 295). This passage is omitted in Kaplan (1999).

18. Quoted after Gutman (1993, p. 123).

19. Czerniaków, for example, writes about this (1983).

20. L. Goldin, *Kronika jednej doby* (The chronicle of one day) in Sakowska (1986). Lejb Goldin (1906–42) was a writer, an essayist, a translator of European literature into Yiddish, a member of the underground Ghetto Archive *Oneg Shabbat*, who worked with Ringelblum.

21. Ringelblum (1988a, p. 325), October 1941.

22. Ringelblum (1988a, p. 333), entry for 1–10 November 1941.

23. The 'shops' (*szopy*) were workshops (shoe-making, tailoring, etc.) in the area of the ghetto, producing goods for the Germans (the word was borrowed from English and the English spelling was often used – ed.). People deluded themselves that by working in a 'shop' they could avoid re-settlement. In the Łódź ghetto, the workshops were called *resorty*. (This word has nothing to do with the English 'resort' but literally means a state enterprise. Here 'shop' or 'workshop' is used for both – ed.)

24. Goldin, in Sakowska (1986), pp. 84–5.

25. 'Z pamiętnika Stefana Ernesta', in Grynberg (1988) p. 42.

26. (Editor's note) Dr Janusz Korczak (Henryk Goldszmit), 1878–1942, was a world-famous educator and child psychologist who directed an orphanage in the Warsaw ghetto. After turning down a chance to escape from the ghetto, Korczak accompanied his children to the gas chambers on 6 August 1942, in the scene described here.

27. Lazowert (1941). Henryka Lazowert was a poet, born 19 June 1910 in Warsaw, the author of a volume of poetry entitled *Zamknięty pokój* (The closed room, 1930) and *Imiona świata* (The names of the world, 1934); she held a scholarship from the Polish Academy of Literature. In the ghetto she worked with the Jewish Community Self-Help and the ghetto archive, Oneg Shabat. For a monographic study of what happened to the people living in the refugee centres she received one of the first prizes awarded in a competition by Oneg Shabbat. She wrote poetry and short stories; part of this material is in the Ringelblum Archive. Henryka Lazowert refused to go over to 'the Aryan side', not wanting to part from her mother. They both died in Treblinka in the deportation action in 1942. (Editor's note: Lazowert

is best known for her poem 'The Little Smuggler', which honoured the child-smugglers of the Warsaw ghetto.)

28. Thiele-Dohrmann (1980, p. 76) writes about this: between March 1942 and December 1943 the Boston newspaper *Herald Traveler* published weekly a series of articles in which psychologists explained current rumours.

29. In the case of this particular rumour, the 'grain of truth' was the news of the flight of Rudolf Hess to England, which took place on 10 May 1941.

30. 'Z pamiętnika Stanisława Sznapmana' (From the diary of Stanisław Sznapman) in Grynberg (1988, p. 24).

31. This information is incorrect. Stefan Ossowiecki was born in 1877 in Moscow. He studied in the 3rd military cadet corps and at the Technical Institute in Petersburg, and later worked as an industrial chemist. In 1917 he was imprisoned by the Bolsheviks, was set free a few months later, and lived in Warsaw from 1918. Before the Second World War he was a famous clairvoyant; he found missing persons and items, etc. He was shot by the Germans in August 1944 at the very beginning of the Warsaw Uprising.

32. I wrote in detail about various forms of antisemitism in my M.A. thesis (Engelking 1988).

33. 'Z pamiętnika Natana Żelichowera' ('Memoirs of Natan Żelichower'), in Grynberg (1988, p. 45).

34. 'Z pamiętnika Stanisława Sznapmana', in Grynberg (1988, p. 24).

35. Centos (*Centrala Towarzystw Opieki nad Sierotami i Dziećmi Opuszczo-nymi w Rzeczypospolitej Polskiej* – the Central [Organization] of Societies for the Care of Orphans and Abandoned Children in the Polish Republic) was founded in 1919. From the outbreak of war, the scope of activities of this society extended to cover complete care of the child community in the ghetto: in boarding houses, day boarding centres, day centres and people's canteens, and also the street children. Centos also worked together with the House Committees.

36. E. Ringelblum calculated that the inhabitants of the ghetto in July 1942 numbered 355,514. Quoted following Sakowska (1993, p. 52).

37. *Organizacja Antyfaszystowska – Lewica Związkowa* (Anti-fascist Organization – [Trade] Union Left) was led by members of the Polish Communist Party (KPP), which had been dissolved in 1938 by the Comintern as Trotskyist. It was a trade union which was very active in the ghetto, both in the area of protecting the workers against complete tyranny by the management in the 'resorts', and also organizing various kinds of resistance to the Germans. The most active young people in the ghetto belonged to the Union Left.

38. According to Sakowska (1993, p. 193), there were c.50,000 children in the ghetto. But according to estimates made by Adolf Berman (Sakowska 1993, p. 172), there were about 100,000 children under fourteen in the Warsaw ghetto in January 1942. If this figure is accepted as more probable, then it would be the case that only 6.7 per cent of the children in the ghetto received some official schooling. Sakowska (1993, pp. 187–214) describes in detail the official and underground schooling in the ghetto, the care of children, supplementing their food, and the House Common Rooms, etc.

39. M. Centnerszwer (1874–1944) – an eminent physicist and chemist, a professor of the University of Warsaw, who organized chemistry courses in the ghetto (in an underground polytechnical institute) which lasted until July 1942.

40. 'Toporol'(*Towarzystwo Popierania Rolnictwa* – the Society for the Support of Agriculture) had already existed in the inter-war period. In the ghetto, it renewed its activities from 1 December 1940. It had a small number of pieces of land under cultivation – mainly courtyards cleared of rubble – and organized farming courses, etc.

41. *Polska Partia Robotnicza*, Polish Workers' Party, successor to the disbanded pre-war Polish Communist Party, formed on 5 January 1942.

42. S. Wilczyńska, born in 1885 in Warsaw. In 1906–08 she studied biological science and medicine at the University of Liège in Belgium. In 1909 she began voluntary educational work in Warsaw which she continued for the rest of her life. From 1912 – until their extermination together – she was the closest associate of Dr Janusz Korczak in his activities in the Orphans' Home organized by the 'Help the Orphans' Society. She creatively implemented the educational systems and concepts of the eminent educationist, doctor and writer. She devoted herself with great passion to combatting the miseries of orphaned children of all ages. During the occupation, she shared the difficulties, troubles, poverty and dangers of being in the ghetto with Korczak and the two hundred children in their care – aware of the enormous responsibility she shared for the life of their charges. She died in Treblinka on 6 August 1942, together with all the inhabitants of the Orphans' Home.

43. This phenomenon became even more evident after the war, when the nearest relations of people who were often the only survivors of large families proved to be very distant relations by marriage that they had not known before – who had left Poland before the war, and now became the closest family members and support for the survivors, often inviting them to join them and helping them start a new life.

44. The Chronicle of the Łódź Ghetto was compiled by the Department of the Archives of the Jewish council in Łódź over a period of almost four years. There were ten to fifteen people working on the archive; they were all educated people, but none was an historian. From 12 January 1941 to 1 September 1942 it was written in Polish, and thereafter, to 30 July 1944, in German. It was almost entirely preserved (5 per cent gaps). After the war, the Chronicle of the Łódź Ghetto was published by the *Wydawnictwo Łódzkie*, edited by Danuta Dąbrowska and Lucjan Dobroszycki: volume 1 in 1965, volume 2 in 1966. Volume 3 which was ready for publication, was pulped in 1968; volume 4 was never published. A one-volume abbreviated version of the entire chronicle has been published in the USA, and the entire Chronicle, in Hebrew, in Israel.

45. E. Ringelblum wrote, 'Heller and Kohn have been excused from wearing armbands. Three people in the Jewish district have this privilege' (1988a, p. 292).

46. 'Z pamiętnika Samuela Putermana' (From a memoir by Samuel Puterman) in Grynberg (1988, p. 33).

47. His original name was Szenkman. Before the war he had been a state police commissioner, and worked in the High Command of the Polish Police. The ŻOB (Jewish Fighting Organization) sentenced him to death, a sentence that was to be carried out by Izrael Kanał on 20 August 1942. The attempt was unsuccessful: Szerzyński was only wounded. He committed suicide in January 1943.

48. Father Puder was known before the war because of an attack on him by the right-wing ONR. In 1938 he was struck in the face in St John's church by Rafał Michalski.

49. The seventh day of the Feast of the Tabernacles.

50. *Dziennik Lejzora Czarnobrody* (The diary of Lejzor Czarnobroda) in the Ringelblum Archive, Ring II, no. 205, quoted after Sakowska (1980, pp. 115–16).

51. Cited after R. Sakowska (1980, p. 57).

52. *Dziennik Lejzora Czarnobrody*, cited after Sakowska (1980, p. 113).

3

Why Did It Happen?

I could never complain that I was bored at Auschwitz. ... From the moment that the mass extermination action began I never felt happy in Auschwitz. I was dissatisfied with myself.

SS-*Obersturmbannführer* Rudolf Höss,
Camp Commandant at Auschwitz

People have been trying for fifty years to understand why the Holocaust took place. Sociologists, psychologists, political scientists, historians and theologians have attempted to interpret its causes, seeing them, and explaining the whole phenomenon, from the point of view of their own discipline. The main questions covered in this chapter fall under four headings:

1. What are the causes of Nazism?
2. Why were the Jews chosen as the victims?
3. Why was the Holocaust possible?
4. Why were the victims passive?

The causes of Nazism

'A sub-human' is biologically similar to a man – a creation of nature, with hands, feet, a certain type of brain, eyes and ears. However, it is a terrible creature, with only the features of its face resembling a human being, but in spiritual terms lower than any beast. An awful chaos reigns in the soul of this creature ..., an instinctive desire to destroy, primitive desire, an undisguised meanness. A sub-human – and nothing else!

Der Untermensch, Berlin 1942, leaflet published by
the Central Office of the SS, Ministry for Foreign Affairs
and Ministry of Information and Propaganda

The people that I interviewed are also looking for answers to these questions. Some of them think that the sources of the Holocaust lie in irrational factors, that Nazism, and more generally Fascism, was a European sickness. They consider it an aberration, a disruption of the normal, regular development of the world.

> It's amazing that in the heart of Europe – a nation that everyone respected, which gave the world its greatest musicians, a marvellous literature, philosophy. ... They were clean, well-kept people, they were often intelligent, they spoke foreign languages, they loved music, they sang in church choirs ... (Ryszard, Interview 34)

> I believe that the greatest possible bestialization of man took place – in cultured, civilized Europe ... (Edward, Interview 26)

This kind of explanation – Fascism as a moral sickness of Europe – was historically the first interpretation offered. In line with this interpretation, Fascism is something unusual, a disruption of the normal development of Europe; it was something sudden, unforeseeable, and at the same time 'curable': Fascism would come to an end and Europe would go back to her normal, healthy paths of development. Benedetto Croce offered the following explanation in November 1943: Fascism was not thought up by any social class, no social class wanted it or supported it, but it was a straying of consciousness, a social depression, a flush of victory caused by the war.[1] Golo Mann also considered fascism in general, and National Socialism in particular, to be a sudden outburst of irrational and demonic forces which were produced by complex factors stemming from the profound economic crisis (De Felice 1976, p. 42).

Some of the people I talked to saw the source of the Holocaust not so much in a sickness of Europe as in certain events in German history.

> Why in Germany? It was connected with the humiliation of the Treaty of Versailles. The Germans already had all that in their history – that sense of nationhood, a sense of individual dignity, a sense of cultural and economic expansion. It was that leadership, Hitler had that charisma, he knew how to take the whole nation with him, he had that ruthlessness. (Stefan, Interview 29)

Racism and intolerance run right through the history of Germany. It happens only very rarely that a child from a good home goes astray. It can happen, but as a rule, a good home brings up a good child. It's the same with nations. I'm terrified of the idea of a united Germany – a power like that! I don't believe that they've been cured and morally born again. (Barbara, Interview 10)

Historians have passed similar judgements on fascism. One of the classic historical interpretations is that fascism was a logical and inevitable consequence of the historical development of certain countries, above all Germany and Italy, linked primarily with under-development, lack of stabilization and conflicts in the economic growth patterns, the process of unification and establishing independence (De Felice 1976, p. 49).

One of the men I interviewed presented a different interpretation of fascism:

Very many factors contributed to it, and not the least was the economic situation of Germany after the first war. The active left played an enormous role in Germany, working secretly in the Communist party. That aroused strong feelings of dislike. It was easy to stir up very unfavourable attitudes to them. (Andrzej, Interview 22)

This way of viewing the causes of fascism is in line with the third classic historical interpretation, which sees fascism as a product of capitalist society and as a reactionary anti-proletarian movement. It is understood as a form of struggle against the revolutionary labour movement – against Communism and Bolshevism, particularly in Russia. This way of explaining Fascism assumes that it should be analysed in the context of the social and political structure of contemporary capitalist society, with its inner contradictions (De Felice 1976, p. 56).

One of the men I interviewed had a very interesting historical interpretation of his own of the Holocaust, containing all the 'classic' themes, but with a slight difference. He considers the capacity for genocide to be a natural attribute of the human race, and the Holocaust to be one of the manifestations of this attribute:

The Holocaust is an attribute of the human race, from the beginning of its existence. The murder of all the South American Indians was also a Holocaust, wasn't it? The murder of all the inhabitants of Australia or Tasmania was a Holocaust as well. Like the murder of the Armenians by the Turks …

[But the justification was different]

The Nazi justification was the justification of the white man whose views of the world took shape in the period of colonialism, imperialism. Christian ideology – which from time immemorial had blamed the Jews for the murder of Christ – also played no small part in the justification. ... German antisemitism became a major part of the Nazi ideology. The nation was shown the reason for all its defeats and misfortunes: the Jews. Fighting them was very simple. In my view that ideology grew out of colonialism and Christianity. You can't even see Christian ethics as constituting a brake on genocide. After all, in some sense, Nazism grew out of that ethic. It was that which justified the murder of tens, of hundreds of thousands of Amerindians, Blacks. ... Wonderful cultures were destroyed, all those people were killed. ... And so why should the same ethic not be used to justify the extermination of the Jews? Only because they were white as well? No. The best evidence comes from the fact that during the Crusades hundreds of thousands of Jews were murdered in the name of the Cross.

[Was Nazism inevitable?]

I think that things didn't necessarily have to be like that at all. But Hitler hit on the needs of his epoch. He hit on the needs of the Germans and the ideas of contemporary Europe. (Arnold, Interview 9)

Some of the people I interviewed were inclined to interpret the Holocaust from a sociological, rather than historical, viewpoint. One of the most common elements of this is to see fascism as a form of totalitarianism. They often referred to the view of totalitarianism proposed by Hannah Arendt.

I can understand why Hitler chose that path; you had to find something to integrate those people. I've read a lot on the subject and I understand that it's easy to programme something like that. I'm convinced by what Hannah Arendt writes about it. (Irena, Interview 28)

According to Hannah Arendt, totalitarianism was the new phenomenon in European culture which made it possible to solve the fabricated and inflated 'Jewish problem'. She claims that totalitarianism was a complete contradiction of the whole European tradition, which from the time of Plato had linked action with thought; it was a breakaway from continuity and from the canon of moral concepts and values which had hitherto been connected with Europe.

Totalitarianism breaks with tradition, contradicts the continuity of history, is entirely concentrated on attaining a distant, utopian goal. Life under totalitarianism takes place in the dimension of the temporary: the past, the present and the future are rejected. Everything – including the existence of individuals – is subordinated to the effort to attain the Goal. It justifies all means, often using terror and violence. Arendt says that life under totalitarianism is without the certainty of life 'en route'; that at any moment everything can change. Tradition no longer provides a signpost to the way ahead, and without tradition – which selects and defines, which passes on and conserves, which shows where the treasures are and why they are of value – there seems to be no conscious continuity in time, and therefore no past or future, but only eternal change and the biological life cycle.[2]

A totalitarianism which takes its mission to reorganize the world seriously has to effect a symbolic break with the cultural status quo and perform a symbolic act of founding the new order. The new world and the new man were to rise like a phoenix from the ashes of the old world. Arendt claims that it was precisely the annihilation of the Jews that was to constitute the symbolic breaking with the former religious and cultural canon, which was to bring about a break from God through denying the fundamental principle of religion: love of one's neighbour.

The Holocaust was interpreted by some of the people I interviewed as an effect of the actions of a totalitarian state:

> Why did it happen? How can you reply to a question like that? Why did it happen. ... These are the moral consequences of a totalitarian state, that you can bring people up like that. That you can in the end do goodness knows what with the culture of a nation like the Germans. You can order them to believe that they're doing it so as to achieve something, some higher aims. ... In a totalitarian upbringing, all moral norms are abandoned. It's a moral bestializing of an entire nation. I'd like to believe, to see somewhere, whether any of them really believed in any of it. ... Apart from that, Germans believe in orders; it's a nation that believes in orders. A nation that believes soldiers don't have to think. (Adina, Interview 13)

In this statement, one might note that one of the elements in the explanation echoes T.W. Adorno's idea of the authoritarian personality. However, the most popular of the psychological interpretations of fascism was that Hitler was mentally ill, a lunatic.

> I thought that Hitler was abnormal, that the whole of that society was in the grip of an abnormal man or beast. You would survive if you didn't fall into the jaws of that terrible monster. (Iza, Interview 32)

> I don't understand it. I've never philosophized about it much. Simply: Hitler turned up, a madman, and thought up the theory that the Jews were responsible for everything. ... He was crazy, a madman, a murderer! It's difficult for me, an ordinary person, to judge the activities of someone who was completely abnormal. In my view, all his behaviour shows that he was mad. (Władysław, Interview 25)

There are also many theological interpretations of fascism in general and the Holocaust in particular. The people I interviewed, the great majority of whom were not religious, did not cite explanations of this kind. One of the women I talked to said, when she was dicussing the passivity of people going to their deaths:

> It was a completely passive death; they couldn't defend themselves, they went quietly. It was something that they call kiddush hashem, death in the name of God. Devout Jews were prepared to make the sacrifice, to die, because they believed that God required it of them. (Adina, Interview 13)

A man that I interviewed, a religious Jew, asked himself the dramatic question of whether God was present or not present during the time of the Holocaust:

> I'm not a theologian, I haven't wondered whether it made any sense. During one of my stays in Treblinka I thought that after all, I'd been taught the Old Testament. And when I read the Old Testament, I read the history of Abraham and Isaac, and that Abraham bound Isaac and wanted to sacrifice him to God, and God defended Isaac. I believe, I am deeply convinced, that this is what happened: since God acted then to defend one person, one child, how could it be that he did not act to defend a million and a half children? (Edward, Interview 26)

The people I interviewed do not know the answer to the question of what caused the Holocaust. They ask questions, but they know that all rational and logical answers are inadequate.

The choice of the victims

> Tell me, mummy dear, what does the word 'Jew' mean?
> Is it some stigma, some kind of shame? ...
> A Jew, my dear, is suffering,
> A Jew, my dear, is a bad fate,
> A Jew, my dear, is worries,
> A Jew must withstand all blows.
> A Jew, my dear, is comfort,
> A Jew is faith in the future, better times,
> A Jew never in his life loses heart,
> He laughs though his heart sometimes trembles. ...
> A Jew - wait, I know what to tell you,
> A Jew is a big word, believe me,
> A Jew is I think the only person,
> Who knows truly bitter tears.
>
> Ghetto song

The second part of the question 'Why did it happen?' is the question of why the Jews were chosen by fascism as its victims.

'There are also not many obvious causal connections between antisemitism and the Holocaust. ... The Holocaust was the most spectacular culminating point of the centuries-long history of religious, economic, cultural and national persecution' (Bauman, 1992, p. 59). However, the 'normal', traditional antisemitism, which made use of persecution, discrimination and pogroms, could not have led to genocide. Certain special conditions and a certain coincidence were needed: historical, economic and political, social and cultural conditions, which when they came together at a particular moment in time, gave rise to the Holocaust.

One of the fundamental elements in the specific nature of the Jewish minority in Europe seems to be that all other ethnic groups (apart from the Gypsies) living outside their mother country differed from the Jews in that they came from some-where, had their own country, to which they could - at least theoretically - return. I think that the awareness of having a native country, a place on the earth to which one belonged, gave a feeling of having roots, gave security, prevented complexes. The Jews had nowhere to go back to; they were 'at home' everywhere and nowhere; their mother country existed only in the sphere of the spiritual, in religion, in books, in tradition.

Their feeling of national identity was indissolubly linked with religion, with the status of the chosen people, with the tradition of the Covenant concluded with God. In order to survive in the midst of separate, alien communities, they had to make themselves necessary to them. And they could make themselves necessary by their knowledge and/or money.

Hannah Arendt (1989b, p. 10) wrote that antisemitism reached a climax when the Jews lost their public positions and influence, and were left only with wealth, in line with de Toqueville's principle that wealth without power produced the impression that they were dispensable, parasites, and therefore that the situation was unacceptable.

Hannah Arendt has written in *The Origins of Totalitarianism* about the specific role of the Jews in Europe, about their fall and 'dispensability', and about assimilation, which other nations found menacing because it wiped out differences. She thinks that the choice of the Jews as the victims of genocide was not accidental. It followed from the age-old Jewish–Christian conflicts in Europe and from the specific position of the Jews in society. In order to understand why no other ethnic group fell victim to extermination, it is necessary to go back into the past and analyse the exceptional position of the Jews in Western Europe in the nineteenth century, when modern, political antisemitism was born.

According to Arendt, the nineteenth-century Jews, who financed various state undertakings, had considerable political power of which they were unaware. As the only important group with supra-national status, they performed yet another function, apart from the economic. In a situation of international conflicts or wars, since they did not take sides, and were not directly involved in the conflicts, they were indispensable as military suppliers, financial advisers, and negotiators for peace treaties. This role came to an end when the parties ceased to try to make peace, and wars became life and death struggles intended to destroy the enemy completely.

Arendt goes on to argue that the Jews, who because of the specific nature of their own history had no political tradition or experience, were unaware of their potential strength, and were also unaware of the growing tension between the state and society. They were loyal to governments, to those in authority as such, maintaining an often unwarranted conviction that the governments were well-disposed towards them while they remained useful. At the same time, in the era of class societies, they did not belong to any class, but because of the specific role that they played, they were the only group which could be identified with authority by society in general. And so various classes which were losing their position and coming into conflict with the state turned against those who in a way represented that state – and became antisemitic. Arendt repeatedly emphasizes that dislike of Jews grew when they had lost their importance and had ceased to play a role which had significance for the state.[3]

The Jews, who were deprived of their own place in the world and wanted to preserve their own national identity through complete separation from Christians, were a group which was ideally suited for attack in a situation of conflict. They placed too much trust in the state, which in giving them privileges made emancipation possible – but they forgot that this was a reward for their valuable services. When the model of the multi-national state was exhausted, the Jews became simply dispensable.

Internal social crises which were the result of political change, the collapse of nation states, the birth of imperialism and mass societies led, in Arendt's view, to the collapse of the position the Jews had hitherto occupied. There was no longer any place for them in the social hierarchy. They had to seek for a new position at the price of losing their religious and national identity, and it then proved that there was no escape from 'being a Jew' – Judaism became an undefined but inborn psychological characteristic.

The new situation of both the societies of Western Europe and of the Jews became the basis for an unprecedented, organized, formalized and ideological political antisemitism. It was a new form of the disike of Jews that was already well known in Europe. This dislike, which had existed in the sphere of European culture for at least two thousand years, was known earlier in other forms. In my view, four kinds of antisemitism can be distinguished:

1. Religious antisemitism, which was based on religious intolerance linked with the Christian injunction of mission and attempts to convert the heathen. Intolerance towards Judaism

was stronger than that expressed towards other religions – probably because these two religions had common roots, worshipped the same God and were based on the common source of the Old Testament. In the Church there was the conviction that by killing Christ the Jews had automatically become the enemies of Christianity. This kind of antisemitism was practically unknown before the Crusades, when the Church militant needed a clear enemy with whom it could fight in order to maintain internal cohesion, unity and strength. In 1146 (the second Crusade), Abbot Peter of Cluny wrote: 'Why set off for the ends of the earth ... to fight the Saracens, when we leave among us other infidels who bear a thousand times more guilt toward Christ than the Mohammedans' (from Delumeau 1986, p. 261). This religious antisemitism propagated by the Church led to the consolidation of dislike of Jews in the centuries that followed. Theological language spread hatred of the Jews (p. 264).

2. Ethnic antisemitism, based on the human tendency to see the world as divided into 'them' and 'us'. The source of this was the ethnic separateness of the Jews: in their language, customs and culture. This separateness was clearly to be seen and easily noticed, emphasized by dress, culinary traditions, religious customs and rituals. Ethnic differences are a source of ambivalent (for they are not exclusively negative) emotions between any two 'alien' groups: in differing from others, we find ourselves and constitute our own identity. This is the least specific kind of antisemitism, and was already known in Ancient Egypt, but is apparently currently most widespread in its 'folk' form. We should also remember that, for example, their different dress, essential for easy identification of Jews, had been imposed upon them during the period of the Crusades. Delumeau points out that the Israelites up to that time had been protected by charters, and were free people speaking the same language as the local population, wearing the same clothes, authorized to ride on horseback and carry arms, and to take oaths in court. They were thus practically part of the surrounding society. It was only an edict of the Fourth Lateran Council in 1215 that ordered the Jews to dress differently. The strength of the contemporary need to differentiate them from the rest of society and the importance of the problem for the church and

state hierarchy of the times is attested, according to Delumeau, by the fact that between 1215 and 1370, 12 synods and 10 royal ordinances ordered Israelites to wear a yellow band with a star (p. 259).

3. Social antisemitism, which was based on difference in the social status of individuals and differences between groups. The Jews (partly because of religious and ethnic antisemitism) formed a fairly closed, coherent, obvious group, which occupied a specific position in society. By tradition and law they were not allowed to practise certain professions, and were therefore predestined to practise others, which led to strong rivalry and dislike on economic grounds between themselves and the local population. We should remember that among the Jews for religious reasons every boy at the age of five began compulsory instruction in reading and writing – they were therefore in the nature of things better educated than the average members of other social groups.

The growth of social antisemitism in the nineteenth century was not unconnected with the parallel development of the natural sciences. The biological theories of race that were developed at that time popularized the idea of the superiority of some nations and the inferiority of others. This was later to provide the 'scientific' basis for racism.

4. In the nineteenth century, these three types of antisemitism came together to provide the basis for a new form: political antisemitism. It appeared together with the development of modern states, a new concept of the nation[4] and the spreading of nationalist sentiments. It was then for the first time that antisemitism was drawn into an institutionalized framework: in 1870, Wilhelm Marr formed the Antisemitic League in Germany. Institutionalization made it possible to use antisemitism in political struggles, which constituted something importantly new in the sphere of dislike of Jews. It was at that time that theories of a world-wide conspiracy began to appear, and antisemitic leaflets were published (for example, the *Protocols of the Elders of Zion*, apparently prepared by the Tsarist Ochrana). Belief in conspiracies of this kind grew in periods of political crisis, for example in France at the time of the Dreyfus affair. Barbara Tuchman (1987, pp. 237–8) wrote of this that the 'Syndicate', which was a creation of the antisemitic press, was in

the eyes of the right wing a synonym for evil. It was held to be an underground fraternity of Jews, a wicked and miserable conspiracy which was mobilizing all forces to overturn the sentence passed on Dreyfus, and to put some Christian as a traitor in his place. Everyone who spoke out for a review of the sentence, however eminent or respected, was in the pay of the 'Syndicate'. The 'Syndicate' was everywhere; it became the embodiment of the hatred and fears of the right wing. The 'Syndicate' was the enemy.

All the above-mentioned forms of antisemitism appeared contemporaneously in history, were often intertwined and mutually complementary, and it is not always possible to observe them in a 'pure' form. Each of them had its own specific shape and rate of development, but – in my view – none of them is enough to explain the Holocaust. We have to recognize that a new form of antisemitism grew up in the twentieth century: genocidal antisemitism, which was a drama-tically logical consequence of all the earlier forms. It brought together experience of earlier forms of antisemitism and took them to an apogee in the Holocaust. The categories of positivist academic disciplines, or of statistically verifiable truth, are not sufficient to explain it. Explanations are sought in historio-sophical and cultural concepts, in the social subconscious, in cultural crisis, in an assassination attempt on God. Those who have created theories of this kind basically agree that the murder of the Jews was only a means to an end, a means for achieving great things. The Jews were therefore the accidental victims of the Holocaust inasmuch as their destruction was not an end in itself; for the point was – according to the ideology of totalitarianism – to destroy the old order of culture and society. And they were non-accidental victims inasmuch as they were the only group which could become a symbolic scapegoat. They were an ideal object of persecution: they were alien, had been piled high with guilt, and they were no longer needed in Europe. According to Hannah Arendt (1987, p. 346), only the choice of the victims, and not the nature of the crime, can be traced from the long history of hatred of Jews and antisemitism.

There is no one unified interpretation of the Holocaust. Basically, there are two distinct standpoints taken by those who write about it. Some see the Holocaust simply as a bigger and better-executed pogrom against the Jews; other see it as qualitatively new.

The people I interviewed also represent these two stand-points. Some see the Holocaust as the consequence of age-long antisemitism and racial hatred, brought to life by fascism. They attribute the Holocaust to characteristics of mankind, seeing it as the result of prejudice, stereotyping, and hatred among nations.

> [Do you think that there is only a quantitative difference between pogroms and the gas chambers, and not a qualitative difference?]
>
> Quantitative. ... The number of Jews had grown so greatly that they had to find new means. ... And so primitive technology gave way to industrial techology. (Arnold, Interview 9)

> There have been things like that through the whole history of the existence of man on earth. From the beginning of the past, from classical times, and I should think that it will go on. [The Holocaust] was a pogrom in greater style than the ones that preceded it. I think that if they'd known in the middle ages or in the classical period about the organization of work and the methods of killing that the Germans knew about, they would have used them then. Hatred of people who are alien exists all over the world and in everybody, even in the most civilized countries. That otherness, whether it's in appearance, or dress, or religion, or culture, or language – it's a way of working off an inferiority complex, or a superiority complex, at any rate, it's what leads to a feeling of hatred. A feeling of hatred is necessary for everyone, because it underlines his own personality, his sense of his own nation, his sense of nationalism etc. (Stefan, Interview 29)

A second group of the people I interviewed emphasized the exceptional nature of the Holocaust, and the impossibility of comparing it with other forms of antisemitism. They see it as something new in the history of the world, something which had not previously existed, which had no precedent.

> For me it's important that it provides a terrible testimonial for mankind in general. Mankind has given itself the worst of all possible testimonials. And in that way, if I can say so, I identify with the people who carried it out, in the sense that they betrayed mankind. The point here is not individual responsibility. Something exceptional took place. I see the exceptional nature of it in the fact that no culture, no old culture – which should have opposed it – managed to stop what was happening. That means that everyone – all of us, you and me – are

at a stage where culture is only an outer skin which it is very easy to scrape off – and then only beasts will remain of any of us. (Ryszard, Interview 34)

In his book *Modernity and Holocaust*, Zygmunt Bauman considers, like Hannah Arendt, the reasons why the Jews were chosen as the victims of the Holocaust. He sees the phenomenon as an expression of fear, even a phobia about modernism, and changes which were inevitably coming. The emancipation and assimilation of the Jews were a reflection of the breaking down of the old order of the world, in which everyone had his established place. The breakdown of that old order, the uprooting, disinheriting and removing from a secure – because familiar – social position was bound to meet with resistance from all social circles which felt afraid of a change in the rules, and of chaos. He says that the defeat of the conservative rebels, and the clear triumph of modernity, led to a shift of the conflict into highly secret regions. In this new situation, resistance made its presence felt through emptiness, an unfulfilled longing for certainty, a paranoid mythology of conspiracy and a mad search for indefinable identities. The Jews became a palpable embodiment of inner demons (1992, p. 77). They were a goal for the opponents of modernity, associated with everything that they did not like in it: with capitalism, with money, with technology and with the industrial system.

The Jews were a blot on modern civilization. Bauman suggests that the Nazis wanted to fulfil the dreams of the Enlightenment philosophers, and to create a world that was beautiful and ordered as a garden. The classicist belief in the identity of good, truth and beauty, somehow twisted in a distorting mirror, took on the shape of the Nazi vision of a world without weeds. The Germans wanted, in Bauman's view, to create a world that was beautiful, ordered, planned and aesthetic. In it, the plants were to be blonde, tall, straight and strong, while all the dark, sick and twisted weeds were to be pulled up by the roots. In line with the ideals of scientism, the Nazis wanted to create a world free of deviation by the use of social engineering; they wanted to bring order by eliminating 'asocial' and socially undesirable types. This was a difficult, labour-intensive and responsible task: the mission of the gardener. First it was necessary carefully to identify the weeds, work out the way in which they could be effectively eliminated, and then carefully weed the garden. In this new and splendid world, everything was to be good, beautiful and true. The real victory of Reason was to be brought about.

The perpetrators

> I was terrified when I thought of the shootings, of the mass executions of women and children. I had had enough of executions of hostages and group shootings. Now [after successful experiments with the use of gas] I was sure that we would all be spared those blood baths, that the victims would be spared suffering right up to the last moment. That was what I was most concerned about.
>
> Rudolf Höss, *Autobiography*

The third element of the question 'Why did it happen?' concerns how it was possible to carry out the Nazi plans for genocide. It would seem that it was above all in the way in which it was carried out that the Holocaust differed from all other, earlier forms of antisemitism, and this means that it is impossible to compare it with any other manifestation of hatred for the Jews. It is impossible, at least in my view, to reduce extermination – planned and carried out with perfect precision, using all available scientific knowledge, including the fields of psychology and sociology, and modern technology – to the level of the pogrom, carried out by an excited mob, looking for an outlet for explosive aggression. You cannot compare the clerk, who during working hours as part of his duties co-ordinates the timetables of the trains running to the extermination camps, with the member of a mob which under the influence of sudden, powerful emotion, carried out a pogrom. As Umberto Eco says in *The Name of the Rose* (1994), a massacre carried out by a crowd, swept away by almost ecstatic excitement, and mistaking the diabolic laws for the divine, is a different thing from individual crimes carried out in cold blood, quietly and cunningly.

The question of why the Holocaust could be carried out has two aspects: firstly, how was it possible that some people were capable of murdering others in cold blood; and secondly, how was it possible that those others were so passive? Let us first pay a little attention to the people who carried out the Holocaust.

It would be easiest to say that the perpetrators of the Holocaust were depraved criminals, monsters, not the same kind of people that we are. But memoirs from the camps and eyewitness accounts confirm that there were not many degenerates or sadists among the Nazis. Most of them were ordinary people. Raul Hilberg (1961, p. 53) wrote that in order fully to understand the significance of what these people did we had to accept that we were not dealing with individuals who had their own, separate moral code. The civil servants who were drawn into the process of extermination did not differ in their moral principles from the rest of society.

Those who carried out the Holocaust were 'desatanized'. *Obersturmbannführer* Adolf Eichmann, the head of section IVB4 in the Reich Security Ministry (RSHA), became the symbol of a new kind of criminal: the murderer-bureaucrat. He was one of those who carried out and co-ordinated the *Endlösung* action – the Final Solution of the Jewish question. He obediently carried out the orders of his superiors, and as he said himself, would not have hesitated to send his own father to the gas chambers if he had been ordered to do so (Wiesenthal 1971, p. 13). During his trial in Jerusalem, after each of the fifteen charges had been read out and he was asked whether he pleaded guilty or not guilty, Eichmann replied, 'Not guilty'. He did not feel personally responsible for the deaths of six million Jews – he only carried out his duties: he supervised the synchronization of the routes and times of departure of the trains taking their loads to their destiny. He took care that the trains arrived punctually, without unnecessary delays en route, and that – in the name of efficiency – they had as few 'empty' runs as possible. Hannah Arendt talks about the banality of evil. She strips the evil that occurred of its mystique, incomprehensibility and secrets. She shows what unthinking obedience can lead to.

Eichmann treated the problem of transporting the Jews unemotionally – he was not an antisemite, but a good civil servant, trying to carry out as efficiently as possible the tasks entrusted to him. Hannah Arendt believes that Eichmann was not a demonic criminal, nor the embodiment of evil, nor a fanatic, nor a born murderer – he was simply and tritely unthinking. He did not think, even though you did not need to be exceptionally intelligent or particularly well versed in moral problems to do so; all you needed was to have the habit of living openly with yourself, that is, the habit of carrying on with yourself that silent dialogue which from the time of Socrates and Plato has been called thinking (quoted in Król 1987).

At the same time, Arendt points out, Eichmann was not a fool. It was simple lack of thought – which in no way can be identified with stupidity – that predisposed him to play the role of one of the greatest criminals of his day. But even if it is banal, or simply ridiculous, even if with all the will in the world you cannot find in Eichmann any devilish or demonic profundity – this is still a long way from calling what he did ordinary (Arendt 1966, p. 371).

Eichmann was a product of mass society; he was, according to Arendt (1985, p. 39), a bourgeois, with all the outer hallmarks of decency, all the habits of a good father of a family, who was not unfaithful to his wife, and honestly tried to ensure a safe future for his children. In response to the economic chaos of our times, he turned into an unwitting trouble-maker who despite his hard work and efforts was not able to predict what tomorrow would bring. In order to secure his pension, his insurance policy, to ensure the security of his wife and children, a man like this was prepared to sacrifice his convictions, his honour and his human dignity. The only condition that he made was that he should be relieved of all responsibility for his actions.

Other Nazis talked in interviews with Gitta Sereny about the ordinary, human motives that led them to working on the euthanasia programme, and later in Treblinka. Franz Stangl, later commandant of the extermination camps in Sobibór and Treblinka, spoke as follows about why he decided to resign from his job in the police force in Linz and transfer to work on the euthanasia programme in Hartheim:

> I wasn't happy in Linz. I was at odds with my boss, who had begun disciplinary proceedings against me. If I hadn't accepted the transfer that I was offered to Hartheim, my boss would have found some other way of getting rid of me anyway (Sereny 1974, p. 52).

Albert Hartl, who worked with Stangl, replied to the question of why he agreed to work on the euthanasia programme as follows:

> You want to know what were the general motives of the people who decided to work in T4 – not in the administration, but those who

worked in the Institute. Well, I always thought that the majority got their jobs through personal contacts. It was said that the work was connected with the Führer's chancellery, and that sounded good. The pay was good, and there was no threat of being sent to the front. (Sereny 1974, p. 80)

These replies confirm the thesis that evil was banal and ordinary. A well-paid job, conflict with the boss, fear of being sent to the front – these were the ordinary human motives that persuaded Germans to take up employment with the euthanasia programme or in the concentration camps. The Canadian historian Michael Marrus also writes about this kind of motivation in his book *The Holocaust in History* (1989, p. 70):

The Abteilung Deutschland, which occupied itself with Jewish questions [in the German Foreign Office], was not inspired by antisemitic fanaticism, but rather by concerns for professional competence. Its officials conscientiously applied themselves to their tasks, instinctively sensing the change in Nazi policy during the Barbarossa campaign. Careerism drove officials forward. Eager to demonstrate his indispensability, the head of the Jewish desk took initiatives to help speed the Jews on their way.

It is precisely because evil proved to be banal, boring and without any element of supernatural power that the experience of the Holocaust constitutes an exceptionally dangerous precedent in the history of mankind. For now, in particular circumstances, any other nation might prove 'dispensable' and become the victim of genocide. Contemporary history provides us with sad evidence that these fears are not misplaced. We need only to remember the drama of the Kurds murdered by the Iraqis, or the civil war in the former Yugoslavia.

At the end of *Eichmann in Jerusalem*, Hannah Arendt (1966, p. 273) writes of the

rather uncomfortable but hardly deniable possibility that similar crimes may be committed in the future. The reasons for this sinister potentiality are general as well as particular. It is in the very nature of things human that every act that has once made its appearance and has been recorded in the history of mankind stays with mankind as a potentiality long after its actuality has become a thing of the past. No punishment has ever possessed enough power of deterrence to prevent the commission of crimes. On the contrary, whatever the punishment, once a specific crime has appeared for the first time, its reappearance is more likely than the initial emergence could ever have been. The particular reasons that speak for the possibility of a repetition of the crimes committed by the Nazis are even more plausible. The frightening coincidence of the modern population explosion with the discovery of technical devices that, through automation, will make large sections of the population 'superfluous' even in terms of labor, and that, through nuclear energy, make it possible to deal with this twofold threat by the use of instruments beside which Hitler's gassing installations look like an evil child's fumbling toys, should be enough to make us tremble.

The people I interviewed noted this aspect of the question about the causes of the Holocaust – the actions of the people who carried it out – and asked themselves about the reasons for their activities:

> How did they manage it? How did they manage to brutalize such a great majority of such a cultured nation? I don't know. It isn't a question to which I would ever dare to provide an answer. If you can philosophize a bit about life – then it is made up of enormous mysteries; we permanently have problems to solve. And we're constantly faced with the same problems. (Ryszard, Interview 34)

Zygmunt Bauman offers an attempt at an answer to this question, emphasizing the role of the bureaucracy and the official hierarchy in carrying out the Holocaust. He goes further than Hannah Arendt in claiming that evil is not only banal, but also rational. In his view, the Holocaust proved that rationality – the banner of contemporary civilization – is a double-edged sword. It was rationality that led to a split between ethics and practical action, and to the division of labour, which Bauman sees as the key factors making the carrying out of the Holocaust possible.

He draws attention to the fact that in the process of the division of labour, especially in administrative work, individual people carry out each particular step without having an overview of the whole. They do not take responsibility for the final stage of the activities, but only for the stage of the work which falls to them. This division of tasks creates both a practical and a psychological distance between those who carried out successive steps of the activity and its final effect. People at the lower levels of the administrative hierarchy do not have to understand the sense or the goal of official instructions; they only have to carry them out to the best of their abilities. The division of tasks is a functional division: the task itself has no particular evaluating mark; it is only when it comes together with a series of other tasks that it proves to be serving a good or evil cause. Workers who were trying to carry out their duties effectively were freed from responsibility for the end effect of the actions in which they were participating. The particular activities for which they were personally responsible were morally neutral. A worker was only an interchangeable performer of a role, and not someone obeying a moral code in his activities. The specific official language was also not without significance here. This, according to Hannah Arendt, brings with it a dehumanization of the objects of administrative activity, that is, it offers the possibility of defining these objects by the use of purely technical concepts which are ethically neutral (Arendt 1987a, p. 149).

Bauman (1992, p. 144) claims that the effect of the administrative division of labour is the replacement of moral responsibility by executive responsibility. This was undoubtedly facilitated by the growing role and institutionalization of the state in the twentieth century. Its ever stronger, ever better organized structures made the citizen dependent on it to an unprecedented extent.

And so bureaucracy and administration had an influence on the possibility of carrying out the Holocaust. It was carried out by an unthinking product of mass society, who was additionally freed from moral responsibility for his actions, since he was barely a minor cog in the wheel of the great state machine. Moral judgement on his activities was completely separated from the activities themselves and the motivations for them. Ethics was separated from practice, something which Bauman (1993) calls a social invention and an extraordinary achievement of our civilization.

Marek Czyżewski and Alicja Rokuszewska-Pawełek draw attention to another aspect of the functioning of 'murderers behind desks' in *Analiza autobiografii Rudolfa Hössa* ('Analysis of the autobiogaphy of Rudolph Höss', 1989). They point to Höss's inability to put himself in the place of the other person, calling this shortcoming, 'a rejection of inter-subjectivity'. This kind of crossing beyond one's own point of view is made possible because 'we are able to assume that if we found ourselves in the place of the other person, we would be able to accept his point of view; and also thanks to the fact that we are able to assume that if another person were in our place, they would be able to accept our point of view.' Höss was not able to put himself in the other person's place – he was not able to look at the world around him from any viewpoint but his own. At the same time, he required that others should be able to understand his situation: 'When he talks about his enthusiasm and commitment in organizing the camp at Auschwitz, he sincerely regrets that the camp prisoners – from whom he required unstinting work like his own – did not understand his efforts and ambitions'. Perhaps this intellectual characteristic, this inability to change one's point of view, was characteristic also of others responsible for carrying out the Holocaust – was a part of the Nazi mentality.

Czyżewski and Rokuszewska-Pawełek analyse the typical kind of justification for one's own behaviour that is used by Höss. He uses the excuse of the need for absolute obedience to orders, throwing responsibility onto others (for example, onto prisoner-chargehands for the cruelty in the camp), claiming that he had no influence on anything, and so on. The authors come to conclusions that accord with what Arendt and Bauman have written about those who carried out the Holocaust. They believe that the 'technique of neutralizing the crime' which is typical of the Nazi mentality, and which is to be seen in both Höss's autobiography and in the autobiographical accounts by Eichmann and Stroop, constituted a consistent elimination of the dimension of moral responsibility.

The ideology of obedience was the philosophy of Nazi actions. In his autobiography Rudolf Höss repeatedly justifies his actions by pointing to orders from superiors: 'I didn't think about it. I had received orders and I had to carry them out' (Höss 1989, p. 142). This kind of obedience, where not only will but also judgement is handed over to your superiors, was called 'corpse-like obedience' by St Ignatius Loyola, and was recommended by him to the members of his order.

The passivity of the victims

> The wind through the window moves
> the arm of a cold shirt,
> the quilt lies crumpled,
> as though someone had snuggled up in it,
> ownerless things lie about,
> a dead home stands there,
> until the rooms are filled
> by other people: Aryans.
>
> Władysław Szlengel, *Rzeczy* (*Things*)

The final aspect of the question of 'why it happened' is the problem of the passivity of the victims.

I think that in some sense the earlier chapters of this book have provided an answer to the question. The isolating of the Jews, their gradual exclusion from the community, making both the Jews themselves and the witnesses familiar with the idea that what was happening was normal and justified – all this was an important aspect of the success of Hitler's plans for genocide. Legal discrimination against the Jews – depriving them of civil rights, placing them in a situation of social inequality, excluding them from the community by administrative methods – all this on the one hand made use of the sub-stratum of antisemitism, but on the other made possible the next stages in the isolation of the Jews. The second stage was physical isolation: deportation and locking them up in ghettos; the third stage was extermination. Everyday life in the ghetto, in restricted space and time, with all the problems, and the necessity of taking daily risks and making daily difficult decisions, absorbed all the energy of its inhabitants. Their capacity for being active was exhausted in solving ongoing problems.

The Jews were exhausted. They were worn out by their time in the ghetto, tired of looking for rescue, ways of escape, of hiding. Calel Perechodnik (1993, p. 89) describes the following event:

> An episode which is deeply etched on my memory was the execution of a group of eighteen Jews of both sexes who had escaped from the ghetto, and having nowhere to go sat in a field not far from Karczew. Among them was old Jankiel Braff, together with his daughter who was in the last month of pregnancy. Miss Braff, probably affected by

the high level of excitement, began to give birth. Her old father delivered the baby and laid it down on the grass.

A few hours later a gendarme walked through the field, saw the group of Jews, and ordered them to lie down on the ground. There was one shot, a second, a third - and then the rifle suddenly stopped working. It turned out that the German had no more bullets in his magazine. And so he sent a Polish boy to the police station in Karczew to ask that they send him ammunition. He himself sat down and waited, completely unarmed - for, as I have said, he had no more bullets with him.

What did the Jews do then? Did they throw themselves on him to avenge the death of their families? Or did they perhaps run away? ... They went on lying, with their faces to the ground and waited, waited more than half an hour for the bullets to be brought - clearly they were bullets of deliverance. Finally a Polish policeman turned up with the ammunition and the gendarme shot the rest of the Jews.

You could say that German 'public relations' (although the term was not yet used) was a masterpiece of its kind. The gradual desensitizing of both the direct and indirect witnesses of the Holocaust was a necessary precondition for carrying out the whole action. Another important mechanism in German behaviour was that of selection. Selecting representatives of some group as scapegoats meant that the remaining members of that group had a sense (often a guilty or even humiliating sense) of security, or at any rate a sense of relief. This mechanism - most widely used later in the concentration camps - was however already used earlier. From the beginning of their period in power, the Nazis had made selections within society, dividing off various groups according to their peculiar criteria. The same mechanism proved effective during the occupation in Poland: the Jews were separated off, designated as victims, thus giving the rest of society a feeling of relief that it was not they who were subject to such misfortune. It is also worth remembering that the war, with all the dramas and misfortunes that it brought for the Poles, constituted a splendid alibi for thinking only about yourself. Being unfortunate yourself is always a justification for not caring about other people's misfortunes. In a situation of selection and terror, it was not only the Jews who behaved passively; one of the women I interviewed drew attention to this:

> People speak slightingly of those who were part of the deportation actions – they went like sheep, frightened, passive. When during the Warsaw Uprising, on 13 August 1944, we came out of Zofia Dębicka's flat (she was Stefania Sempołowska's niece) and were driven with a numberless throng to Zieleniak, I said to Zosia, 'Remember, you kept on saying that the Jews in the ghetto went passively to the slaughter. And how are we going now? How is this crowd before us and behind us going?' She understood what I meant. The only truth is what you have been through yourself. (Helena, Interview 30)

I do not think it is important to decide here whether the Germans applied all the socio-technical elements on the basis of sound academic knowledge of psychology and sociology, or whether they operated on the basis of brilliant intuition. Both of these factors, supplemented by the techniques of public relations, were complementary. It would seem that there was a bit of both in German behaviour, but that to the greatest extent they operated on the basis of trial and error (for example, the unsuccessful experiment with the *Einsatzgruppen*).[5]

But to return to the problem of the passivity of the victims. It is often said that 'they went like sheep to the slaughter'. Some of the people I interviewed shared that view:

> We knew exactly how those transports ended, it was no secret. It seemed strange to me that people knew about it and yet went to the slaughter.
>
> [Maybe they had some kind of hope.]
>
> No, I don't think they had hope, but they were not brought up in the spirit of trying things, of fighting for anything. And, well, after the hunger, after the long ghetto, they had no psychological strength. I feel disgusted when I see that famous photograph with one gendarme escorting a crowd along Smocza Street. I can't understand why they didn't scatter and run away. One could have run up and killed the German, that wasn't a big deal – with that great crowd. ... Of course, they were very tired, they were people who were worn out. But in spite of that, I can't understand, I can't bear that photograph. (Ryszard, Interview 34)
>
> Jews in Israel, especially young Jews, ask as well how it was possible. For them the point is not that the Xs murdered the Ys, but why the Ys let themselves be murdered.
>
> [After all, there were gradations in dying – there were always some who were in a worse position. Well, and there was hope.]

Of course, there was always hope. There wasn't a moment when you didn't have hope, probably even when you were going to the gas chambers. Apart from that – and this is very important – a man who knows that he's going to die wonders how he's going to die. Everyone prefers to die painlessly, for example in his sleep. But the Germans had perfected the art of dying painfully. People were very afraid of that. (Arnold, Interview 9)

Zygmunt Bauman draws attention to a very important aspect of the passivity of the victims, or, rather, to their co-operation with the murderers: that the Jews, by making rational choices, brought about their own annihilation. He wrote:

> The Jews were able to make their persecutors' task easier, were able to help, to bring nearer their own downfall – all the time following in their behaviour the dictates of a rationally justified attempt to save themselves. (1992, p. 184)[6]

> The game in which the Jews were forced by the Nazis to participate was one of death and survival, and thus rational action in their case could be only aimed at, and measured by, the increase of the chances of escaping destruction, or of limiting the scale of destruction. The world of values was reduced to one – remaining alive. ... At all stages of the Holocaust, therefore, the victims were *confronted by a choice* (at least subjectively – even when objectively the choice did not exist any more ...). They could not choose between good and bad situations, but they could at least choose between greater and lesser evil. (1991, pp. 129–30)

A situation like this constituted a break with yet one more canon of European culture: the identification of the rational order with the moral order. In the choices which the inhabitants of the ghetto were frequently forced to make, the rational order was often the amoral order. Up to this date, the argument in the European tradition had only been about whether the moral order was not in conflict with the natural order; the moral order, on the other hand, had always been rooted in rationality, and had not been contradictory to it. To date, good had stemmed from Reason. The Nazis not only distorted the classicist concept of the identity of beauty, good and truth: they also distorted the concept of the rational justification of moral behaviour that was so deeply rooted in the European philosophical tradition.

The Jews in the ghettos (and to a lesser extent the prisoners in concentration camps) had the possibility of making choices in the situations in which they found themselves. They could make choices at various levels: from behaviour in the sphere of private life, to fundamental choice in the life of the community – a choice between resistance to the Germans and passivity or passive obedience. When people make decisions, they try to take into account rational factors, but in this case, lack of resistance, or even collaboration with the Germans, was the rational course. They believed, as did for example Rumkowski in Łódź, that 'being useful to the Germans' would save them. They hoped that the Nazis would not so willingly give up a free labour force. It seemed that though perhaps the weakest – the old and the sick – would die, the majority would survive. The Judenrats were basically prepared to sacrifice some in order to save the rest. The Jews' thousand-year-long tradition and ages-old experience of survival in alien or enemy societies played some role here. One of the men I interviewed spoke about this:

> I'm convinced that religion allowed the Jews to retain their identity through many centuries. But on the other hand it was religion that influenced the fact that many Jews gave up during the occupation. That they believed more in studying Holy Writ than in taking up arms. I think what I'm saying could be summed up as: you should believe in God, but you have to help Him. There's no other way. Because if you only rely on God's decisions, then I don't know whether God wanted them to go willingly to their deaths or whether he would have preferred them to defend themselves. (Edward, Interview 26)

Michael Marrus cites Raul Hilberg on the role of tradition in the passive behaviour of the Jews:

> 'The Jews attempted to tame the Germans as one would attempt to tame a wild beast. They avoided "provocations" and complied instantly with decrees and orders. They hoped, somehow, that the German drive would spend itself. They obeyed their decrees and orders immediately. They had some sort of hope that the Germans' determination would fade.'

Marrus adds:

> At times, in efforts to curry favour with the oppressor or simply to prevent unnecessary suffering, Jews even moved ahead of the Germans, in what the author calls 'anticipatory compliance'. Hilberg assumes that this response was peculiarly Jewish and can be traced to

'a 2,000-year old experience'. Throughout their long period of exile, 'the Jews had always been a minority, always in danger, but had learned that they could avert or survive destruction by appeasing their enemies'. Having responded in this manner for so many centuries, the Jews could not act otherwise when confronted by Nazism. 'A 2,000-year old lesson could not be unlearned; the Jews could not make the switch. They were helpless.'[7]

Philip Friedman voices a similar opinion:

Jewish traditions differed from the traditions of other nations and had a clearly specific nature of their own. At the same time, because of a high degree of differentiation – both cultural and social – within Jewish society, there was no unity. The intelligentsia, the educated part of the middle classes and the working classes had absorbed the traditions and values of the nations amidst whom they lived. The mass of Orthodox Jewry, especially in eastern and South Eastern Europe, approached these problems differently. Other nations developed traditions of heroism, in the sense of physical strength and military courage, while in the traditions of Orthodox Jewry the concept of heroism was linked with spiritual courage, with sacrifice in the name of faith. And that was the only way of resistance recognised by Orthodox Jewry: resistance stemming from religious dictates, resistance based on deep-rooted traditions, expressed in the statement: 'not by force of arms, not by violence, but by the spirit'. At the basis of this attitude – which had been characteristic of the Jews for generations, and which had grown up in the context of ages-long religious persecution – lay the idea that one should not combat evil in this world, or attack evil with physical force, because the battle between good and evil is decided by the will of God.[8]

Some people, even those deported to Treblinka, believed that they were going to work, because after all the Germans had given them bread and jam. The Jewish policemen at the time of the closure action in the Warsaw ghetto were faced with a choice: should they save themselves and their families (and thus behave rationally) or die together with everyone else? Rationality was limited at that stage to saving one's own life. It seemed that if you sacrificed your mother, or wife, or children, then you yourself might have a better chance of survival. The order of rationality of choice was in conflict with the moral order. But the rationality of the behaviour of the victims served the Nazis' ends and made it possible for them to effect their goals.

Notes

1. Following De Felice (1976, p. 37).
2. H. Arendt, *Between Past and Future Time*, quoted in Król (1987).
3. Zygmunt Bauman defines this specific position of Jews in society as 'lying across the barricades'.
4. One of the Polish ideologists of the national state and of antisemitism, Wojciech Wasiutyński, wrote: 'The nation is a spiritual community, of common faith, ancestors and language. A national state serves one tribe, and imposes its language and customs. ... A man can only be free amidst his own nation – in order to be a human being, you have first to be a Pole. ... There is no free nation where cultural and economic life are governed by aliens' (*Prosto z Mostu* – 'Straight from the Shoulder', 1935, nos 9 and 11).
5. The *Einsatzgruppen* were special units of the SS who accompanied the army and dealt with the elimination of individuals and groups capable of organizing anti-German resistance. In the territory of the Soviet Union, the *Einsatzgruppen* were used mainly to shoot Jews. This proved to be an ineffective method for 'the solution of the Jewish question' because of the slowness of the operation (up to 10,000 people a day) and the psychological costs, since there were cases of madness among the members of the *Einsatzgruppen*.
6. (Editor's note) This sentence, omitted from the English edition (1991), in the Polish edition (1992) immediately precedes the text that follows here.
7. Marrus (1993, p. 109), citing Hilberg (1985) pp. 1030-1, 1038-9. (Note, however, that Marrus is here summarizing Hilberg's argument, not agreeing with it. Marrus himself takes the view that historical explanations should not rely on the 'blunt weapon of long-term causality' – ed.)
8. Friedman, P. 'Hitnagdut Yehudit le-Nazism – Hebetim ve-Zurot' (Jewish Resistance to Nazism – facets and forms), in Israel Gutman and Livia Rothkirchen, eds., *Sho'at Yehudei Europa* (*The Catastrophe of European Jewry*) (Jerusalem 1973), p. 365; cited in Gutman (1989, p. 225), here after the Polish edition (1993, p. 312). (Note that after citing Friedman, Gutman immediately qualifies these remarks by noting that 'the Orthodox sector of Warsaw's Jewish population comprised only a part of the larger Jewish community, which likewise embraced a substantial population of ideologically committed people devoted to a Jewish and human tradition laden with examples of rebellion despite overwhelming odds, the obligation to defend oneself, and revolt against an oppressive power' – ed.)

4

The Psychological Consequences of Holocaust Experiences

Why is my pain perpetual, and my wound incurable, which refuseth to be healed?

Jeremiah 15:18

A review of psychological research on Holocaust survivors

International research

For every camp survivor there comes a moment when he looks at himself and simply cannot believe that he could have stood it all. Just as when the day of liberation arrived in his life everything seemed like a wonderful dream, so a day will come when everything that he went through in the camp will seem like a bad dream. But the crowning experience for all those who returned home is the splendid feeling that after everything they suffered they have nothing in the world left to be afraid of – apart from their God.

Victor Frankl, *Psychologist in a Concentration Camp*

Survivors are marked for life by their wartime experiences.

The first studies of the consequences of concentration-camp experiences were published in Scandinavia. In 1952 a report on the physical and mental health of former concentration-camp prisoners found that three-quarters of those examined displayed symptoms of neurotic or neurasthenic disorders. In 1954, on the basis of detailed research carried out in 1947, the Danish psychiatrists Herman and Thygesen described the concentration camp syndrome (*Konzentration-lagersyndrom*). This was interpreted as a wide spectrum of somatic and psychic disorders which originated in concentration camp experiences. It was demonstrated that traumatic wartime experiences had consequences lasting many years, and also affected victims' children born after the war. It was this last group – 'the second Holocaust generation' – who began to seek therapy in the early 1960s. Psychologists, psychoanalysts and psychiatrists began to analyse their problems, and those of their parents, with increasing care and depth. At first, investigation was limited to those who had sought therapy, while later attempts were made to find a broader representative sample of survivors; finally, by the 1980s, they and many other traumatized groups were subjected to systematic psychological testing to sound out various theories.

However, before the problems of Holocaust survivors had become an everyday matter, trivialized by the quantitative methods of the social sciences, a great deal of information had been gathered about them.[1] In 1968, W. G. Niederland proposed a 'survivor syndrome', consisting of persistent and numerous symptoms like chronic depression and reactive fear, sleeplessness and nightmares, personality changes and advanced psychosomatic illnesses. On the other hand Bruno Bettelheim (1990, p. 42), himself a former concentration camp prisoner, speaks of 'extreme situations'. An extreme situation, a situation 'at the limits', exerts in his view a shattering influence on the individual, who was totally unprepared for it. The victim cannot free himself from the situation, to him it seems that it will never end, but will continue to the end of his life; life itself seems constantly under threat; and the victim feels totally defenceless.

What really was the essence of the postwar sufferings of those who survived the Holocaust? Contemporary psychiatry places Holocaust survivors among those who have lived through situations of extreme shock, for example survivors of Hiroshima, floods or other disasters. The American Psychiatric Association defines situations of this kind as entailing:

1. serious threat to human life;
2. serious threat to physical integrity;
3. serious threat to the life of, or injury to, close relatives or friends;
4. sudden destruction of one's home or community;
5. witnessing the recent injury or killing of another person;
6. physical violence;
7. information about a serious threat to, or injury to, a close relative. (per Lis-Turlejska 1992)

In 1980, the American Psychiatric Association recognized 'post-traumatic stress disorder' as a separate illness and entered it in the US classification of psychological disorders. Robert Lifton (1980), who has carried out comparative studies of Holocaust survivors, Vietnam veterans, and survivors of the floods at Buffalo Creek, presents the following model of the experiences and behaviour comprising post-traumatic stress disorder.

The first element is *the imprinting of death, and fear of death*. The first kind of experience is 'major psychic shock' which imprints death and fear of death.

In this experience, it is the omnipresence of death that exercises a dominant influence on the psyche of the individual. This becomes the theme of reminiscences, dreams, nightmares and images which come to mind in the daytime. In long stretches of tortured sleeplessness, the figures of the dead pass before the eyes of the survivors; terrible scenes from the past cause a constant sense of indefinable anxiety. They feel that they have survived 'the end of the world' or 'the end of time': the destruction of everything. They are in a way immersed in images of death, which may cause a feeling of being outside time, and an inability to take any initiative in life – which from a 'mortal' perspective of this kind seems entirely pointless.

The experience of dying and mass destruction still lives on, even many months or years after the catastrophe. What before the Holocaust – in the old world – would have seemed impossible, seems now, after it has been lived through, something natural, possible, and subconsciously anticipated with exceptionally powerful fear.

My research confirms that the element of fear of death is present in the later life of survivors. This is reflected mainly in dreams:

> I dreamt that I was still in Auschwitz, that they were taking Helena to the gas chamber. I screamed at the top of my voice, woke up and jumped out of bed. Subconsciously I must have been going to help her. ... (Barbara, Interview 10)

> I often dream about the war. While I'm dreaming, I want to remember everything to write it down when I wake up. And when I really wake up, I don't know what I have been dreaming about. ... (Edward, Interview 26)

It would seem that the omnipresence of death from the period of the extreme situation leaves permanent traces. Fear of death is mobilized in moments of anxiety or danger, which for the survivors are obviously associated with the earlier situations.

The second element of post-traumatic stress that Lifton distinguishes is a *sense of guilt* (the guilt of survivors).

'Why am I alive when so many others died?', the survivors ask; they have an irrational feeling that they ought to have done something to save others. It is unbearable for them to recall their own powerlessness and helplessness during the war. Painful memories of inability to act are linked with a feeling of indebtedness towards the dead. Their own life was bought at the price of the death of others, and since it was largely accident which decided who should survive, then if they had died, others would have lived – perhaps people who were better than they were, who would have made better use of their postwar, 'spared' life. And in my research, too, feelings of guilt made their appearance:

> I have a kind of feeling that the ones who wanted to live life to the full were the ones that died. Fate treated them unfairly. ... It's not a feeling of guilt, but a feeling that maybe somebody else would have been able to get more out of life than I have managed to do. (Ewa, Interview 17)

Lifton writes of the necessity of distinguishing between psychological guilt, which is a feeling of self-condemnation, a sense of inferiority because of what one has done, or, rather, what one has not done, and moral or legal guilt, which stems from ethical or social judgements on what constitutes evil. The survivors, of course, experience psychological guilt. Most of them suffer because of something that they did not do, because of some sin of omission. My investigation confirms the presence of psychological guilt in survivors:

My younger brother asked me to fix it for him to get out. I said goodbye to them and left when I got that letter. And for two weeks I couldn't fix anything, and then I just found out that they'd taken those people from the brush factory, both my brothers. ... (Anna, Interview 27)

I took my mother out of the ghetto ... I was supposed to come back again for my brother, but I didn't go back. ... For many years I had periods of searching my conscience about it, and I still get them today. (Edward, Interview 26)

I hold it against myself that in that time of weakness, when I was ill, I didn't stand up to my father when he was going back from Białystok to the *Generalgouvernement*. I think that if I'd dug my heels in, I could have made my father get my mother out, we might have ended up in the Soviet camps, but we would have been bound to survive. ... (Rysiek, Interview 11)

I also found that the sense of guilt emerged in the form of a feeling of indebtedness, of obligation to the dead. The point here does not lie in a failure to perform some concrete action, but in symbolic escape from the common fate prescribed for all Jews. Indebtedness towards the dead takes on the form of obligations in life after the war:

I have a very strong, built-in sense of owing something. To the people who saved me, to those who helped – and by no means only to those who helped me. Of owing something to those who were orphaned and to those who died. After all, you could say that just as 'somebody has to stay awake so that others can sleep', somebody had to die so that I could live. And finally, I feel that I owe something to the whole experience of the 'era of the gas chambers', which can't be allowed to go to waste – and for the individual I think that means some private undertaking not to live just any old way. A sense of debt also involves wanting to meet new challenges, not to let people down, not to become indifferent, not to stick to the role of a museum piece rescued from death – but rather to fight to make it a worthwhile life. But all the same the sense of indebtedness can't be allowed to overshadow everything, to extinguish the desire to live life, with all its intellectual, aesthetic and hedonistic sides, to the full. (Jerzy, Interview 35)

Let us return to the question of the sense of guilt. It seems of interest that comparative studies of Holocaust survivors and survivors of natural disasters or catastrophes show that only the former suffer from a sense of guilt towards the dead. This element of experience of a mass psychological trauma is specific to the experience of the Final Solution, and distinguishes it from other experiences of a similar type. I agree with Lifton that this is so because in the case of natural disasters, and even in the case of Hiroshima, death was anonymous, impersonal, dealt at a distance. It would also seem that the length of time the trauma lasted was of some significance.

The opportunities for 'doing something' to save one's nearest and dearest are much fewer in the case of a victim of a natural disaster than in the case of someone who spent two years in a ghetto, and then two more in a concentration camp. It is therefore clearly easier to come to terms and not blame oneself in the case of sudden death, caused by abstract Nature (natural disasters) than when one has taken part in mass dying, observing death stripped down to its essential elements and inflicted by people seemingly just the same as oneself.

Perhaps also the element of the banality of evil, which I discussed in the previous chapter, is significant here. The fact that the evil of the Holocaust was entirely redundant and banal probably has certain consequences. I think that it is more difficult to accept that human beings inflicted so much suffering on other human beings than to accept suffering caused by Nature, which has not been entirely understood and tamed by human beings. Unnecessary death or useless suffering inflicted by other people was bound to give rise to questions about whether the victims and their torturers could possibly belong to the same human community.

The sense of guilt which stemmed from the experiences of the Holocaust has moreover a cultural aspect which Bruno Bettelheim (1979) has called the experience of inconsolable mourning. He stresses that cultural patterns like the funeral, the manner, time and place of carrying out mourning, created a special ritual of saying farewell to the dead. The time of visiting graves, the time of recollecting, helps us to come to terms with the death of those close to us. It is however difficult to come to terms with death when we cannot experience mourning fully because it has no beginning and no end – when the date of death is unknown, when there is no grave, when there is no community of people who also knew and loved those dear to us, and with whom we would be able to recollect them. It is impossible to part with the dead who have not been mourned.

Two of the women that I talked to spoke of 'inconsolable mourning':

> I feel it all the time about my dead – that I did not say enough, explain enough, do enough. ... (Barbara, Interview 10)

> I don't go to the cemetery, after the war I haven't been to any camps, I avoid the subject as far as I possibly can. I don't have anyone in the cemetery. ... My generation, when they come over here, they don't visit the camps. Only the graves of their relatives and friends, if they have real ones and not symbolic ones. I don't have real graves. (Ewa, Interview 17)

Yael Danieli, an American psychoanalyst who deals with the problems of survivors and their families, suggests that the sense of guilt may also play other specific roles. He believes that guilt may be a kind of defence against experiencing a feeling of total hopelessness, and that it is a line which links the Holocaust generation (1989, p. 21). This may be connected, in Danieli's view, with their fear that 'completed mourning' would mean forgetting the dead, and that forgetting the dead would mean a posthumous victory for Hitler.

> I think that life is really a parade of generations, a relay of generations. After all, when we talk about our mother country, we are thinking among other things of graves. The remains of our ancestors are in this earth. A person has to remember those who've passed on. Everyone will come to a moment when he'd like to postpone his end. ... Everyone wants to prolong his existence – and that's why he has to think about those who've gone. If someone agrees to forget, he becomes an accomplice of Hitler's. (Edward, Interview 26)

A sense of guilt can also therefore be a kind of loyalty to the dead. This is precisely what Elie Wiesel was thinking of when he wrote (1979) that those dead have no cemeteries, and that we are their cemeteries.

The third element of post-traumatic stress is, according to Lifton, *mental stupefaction*.

The symptoms of apathy, self-absorption, depression and reduced activity that are found among survivors are an extension of the state of shock induced by the catastrophe – a defence mechanism of the organism in reaction to the shock caused by omnipresent death. This is something like 'mental paralysis': the disparity between perceptions and the emotional response to what is seen. In extreme situations it is impossible to preserve a 'normal' emotional sensitivity; in order to survive one has to blunt emotional response and experience. Stupefaction that lasts after the end of the stress leads to regression, depression, despair and apathy. A life of this kind, with suppressed emotions, in a way a 'partial' life, is on the one hand a method of defence against strong fear and a sense of guilt and on the other hand, is an expression of identification with death. Mental stupefaction also occurred among those that I interviewed:

> I gave in to it. I told myself that apparently this was how things had to be. Later on, I adopted that attitude a lot. I simply adapted to the situation; in the camps, I did the same. I locked myself up in myself when I was persecuted or beaten. I treated it as a cataclysm, God's judgment, some kind of final annihilation. I just gave in to what happened to me. I was a prisoner: they transported us here and transported us there, it was a surviving phase. (Marek, Interview 37)

It would seem that a reaction of this kind is at the same time a form of natural adaptation and a way of coping with stress. Nonetheless, as Lifton has pointed out, a complete elimination of response and feeling was dangerous, since in the camps it led to the 'muslim' stage, which usually ended in death.

The fourth element that Lifton identifies in 'major psychic trauma' is suspicion of false comfort.

Survivors have a tendency to withdraw from human contacts, suspecting other people of lack of understanding and false pity. And yet in fact they greatly need these contacts. They need friendship, love and support, understanding, acceptance and strong family ties. Often they deny, or do not know how to demonstrate, their emotional needs for fear that they will be considered symptoms of weakness. They are also afraid of pity, knowing that it is difficult for those who have not lived through the same thing to understand their experiences and emotions.

This is why they often enter into relationships with people who have had similar experiences – they do not have to explain to them why they are so sad. At the same time, they are often quick to take offence, anxious, aggressive – which is a front for regret and a sense of irretrievable loss. In my research I found confirmation of fears of this kind among survivors, including the dread that others would not understand their experiences.

I have no-one to talk to about it. ...

[What about Marek [Edelman]?]

We talk about it only very rarely. What would be the point? Everything is clear to us both. (Adina, Interview 13)

You have no common language with someone who didn't live through it. How could you talk about it? Someone living in normal conditions isn't capable of grasping it. Even I can't talk about it now that forty years have passed. It was another world, different categories. I didn't [talk] about it much [with my wife]. She knew what I'd been through, and what's more she was able to understand it. We didn't talk about details: I didn't see the need and nor did she. In the end, it's not important whether something or other took place in one camp or another. The point was to understand it in broader outline, not detailed accounts. The most important thing was to feel what it was really all about. (Marek, Interview 37)

The element of fear that wartime experiences would not be understood was in a certain sense confirmed in the world's reaction to those experiences – a reaction which Yael Danieli (1989, p. 9) has called 'a conspiracy of silence'. He writes that after the liberation, as had been the case during the war, the survivors were the victims of a general reaction on the part of society of stupidity, indifference, avoidance, repudiation and denial of their experiences. For many people, the survivors' experiences were too dreadful to hear and to believe. Danieli called this 'bystander guilt'. Inability to understand their experiences entailed an element of suspicion that the survivors must have themselves done something wrong if they had managed to live through it. Making light of the profundity of their experience, and superficial comfort, led in turn to the survivors' silence.

Lifton calls the last element in experiencing an 'extreme situation' the need to understand, a need to make sense of it.

The Holocaust was 'a disaster of total loss' – loss of life, property, a social structure that had centuries of tradition, and also of a symbolic world with points of reference which stood outside time and the individual, and with a vision of a goal and the meaning of existence. The stable existence of the community, from which one could draw support, a sense of security, self-confidence – a community which provided answers to questions about ways to live one's life, suggested patterns of behaviour and rules for action – was destroyed.

The Holocaust was an uprooting revolution and brought about the destruction of time: the breaking of links between the past, the present and the future. In the face of the world after the catastrophe in which they had to live, the survivors are looking for answers to question about the sense of the Holocaust, are looking for new rules of behaviour which would allow them to integrate those experiences into the history of their lives. They are looking for ways to rebuild a universal morality which has fallen apart. It is this, in Lifton's view, which explains their frequent impulse to stand up and bear witness against Nazism.

And yet again, this element appeared in my own research:

> I gave evidence at the trials against the camp guards. In 1964, there was the first case at Frankfurt am Main; *Unterscharführer* Breitwieser was on trial, and I was able to say positive things about him. The court took that into consideration. I gave evidence in Poland, at the Central Commission for Investigation of Nazi Crimes, against Bernard Bonitz, whom I recognized in 1966 in Berlin in a group of about a thousand people. (Józef, Interview 36)

And just as frequently as they want to testify against Nazism, the survivors want to work for the cause of peace and democracy, to build a world without racial prejudice and hatred. For many, the creation of the state of Israel constituted this kind of 'survivors' mission', while for others it was the construction of a successful political system in which all men would be equal. This need was expressed by some of the people I interviewed in a desire to build in postwar Poland a new and – as they then believed – just social system. One of the people I talked to said:

> For a short time I had the illusion that everyone was going to be equal, that all men would be brothers. But I was soon cured of that. I let myself be taken in. But well, since such a lot of eminent people allowed themselves to be fooled, what's surprising if a Jewish boy from Białystok let himself be fooled too? (Edward, Interview 26)

I will discuss reasons for staying in Poland after the war, including ideological reasons, later. I would like now to present briefly Polish research on concentration camp prisoners.

Polish research

> We knew what brotherhood was. Brotherhood means identifying oneself with someone else, not separating his fate from your own; it means even more – seeing his danger more clearly than your own, the conviction that his death would be more difficult to live through than one's own.
>
> Jan Strzelecki, *Próby świadectwa*
> (*Attempts at Witness*)

At one time a great many articles appeared in the Polish specialist press[2] and in the daily press.[3] on the question of experiences in concentration camps and their later consequences. From the early 1960s serious academic research and studies of these problems have been published annually in the January number, known as the 'Auschwitz issue', of *Przegląd Lekarski*, the official publication of the Kraków Medical Association.

Most research on the former prisoners of Nazi concentration camps has been carried out up to the present date by the Kraków Psychiatric Clinic.

In 1970 Professor Antoni Kępiński (1992a, pp. 79-81) wrote that

> About 15 years ago, Dr Stanisław Kłodziński, who had formerly been a long-term prisoner in Auschwitz, approached several colleagues from the Psychiatric Clinic of the Medical Academy in Kraków and asked whether they would be interested in working on the problems of concentration camps. ... Thanks to help from the Kraków Club of former Auschwitz inmates they managed to contact former prisoners, and it was probably they who provided the strongest impetus for undertaking research into this exceptionally difficult problem. ... Further research and contacts generally confirmed the results that had been arrived at during analysis of the lives of the first hundred ex-prisoners investigated.

Kępiński (1992a, p. 81) describes varied patterns of illness among the former prisoners:

> In one of the former inmates, premature arterial sclerosis may have been a consequence of the camp; in another, general sclerosis; in another, pulmonary tuberculosis; chronic disease of the digestive tract, of the hip joint, premature involution, persistent neurasthenic symptoms, panic attacks and depressive syndromes, alcoholism, epilepsy etc. may all have been the results of the camp.

The author believed that in some former prisoners, the symptoms of disease occurred only many years after the war, while in others there were no symptoms at all. He considered this very varied picture of the symptoms of KZ-syndrome, and sought a common etiology in the specifics of camp experiences.

Kępiński drew attention to the fact that being in a concentration camp entailed the necessity of mobilizing the organism long-term, and enduring lasting psychological tension and stress. He thought that three aspects of internment in a camp played a major role in the later life of the inmates:

- the incongruity of their experiences (the hell of the camp, but also the presence of people who by their conduct restored faith in humanity and gave hope to others);
- undermining of the psycho-physical integrity of the individual (prisoners who gave up the struggle for survival, who lost hope and the will to live, very quickly became 'muslims' and died); and
- camp autism 'which consisted in discovering something to rely on within oneself that made it possible to survive the camp' (Kępiński 1992a, 90).

The research carried out by others working together with Professor Kępiński (including M. Orwid, M. Dominik, R. Leśniak, A. Szymusik, Z. Ryn and C. Kempisty – the latter carrying out periodic examinations of ex-prisoners and their children in Wrocław) showed that former prisoners suffer from what was termed the post-camp debility syndrome (another name for KZ-syndrome): nervous depressive illness, sexual disorders, premature ageing. Personality disorders were found among the prisoners (excessive sensitivity, difficulty in making contact with their environment, suspicion, fear, apathy, a sense of the futility of life, indifference to the suffering of others, thoughts of suicide, pessimism, a low estimate of their own worth, a declared absence of fear of death linked with exaggerated concern about their own health) as well as changes in their philosophy of life, which could be observed in three areas: in their relations with other people, in their philosophical and religious views, and in permanent changes in their character.

Polish research was conducted mainly through surveys: former prisoners received questionnaires with questions about their state of mind, their health etc., and then the data which were returned were analysed in detail.

While recognizing the enormous contribution made by the Kraków researchers into this problem, it has to be said that the Polish research – indeed, like Western research – concentrated mainly on the pathology of camp experiences, on their negative, dysfunctional effects. By drawing attention mainly to non-adaptational models of behaviour and difficulties of functioning in the post-trauma world, a picture was constructed of the survivor as a victim, a person who was in some sense sub-standard, ill, in fact handicapped by the experiences of the past.

This kind of picture of survivors is unrepresentative and unfair. It is bound to give rise to numerous objections.

Criticism levelled at the unrepresentative nature of the sample

> Many knew little and few knew everything.
> Primo Levi, *The Drowned and the Saved*

The first reservation stems from the selection of the sample for research. It has to be stated that this was totally unrepresentative. Above all, it was mainly 'volunteers' who were surveyed, together with those who because of their problems turned to professionals for help. Those who did not wish to talk about their experiences, or who did not complain about anything, entirely escaped the attention of the researchers. Did they experience something different, something more profound and dramatic, did they suffer more? Or had they, on the contrary, cut themselves off completely from their past, and did not want to talk about it because it no longer had any meaning for them? Attention was drawn to this, for example, by Norman Solkoff (1981), who criticized the research on survivors and their children on the grounds of the methodology employed. He claimed that the theoretical conclusions reached were based on incorrectly amassed data. His doubts stemmed from the unrepresentative nature of the sample and – in many cases – the absence of control groups.

What kind of picture of the survivor would have been formed if it had been drawn up on the basis of a differently selected sample? If people who required no help had been interviewed? If it had been possible to talk to those who had not returned the questionnaires, or who had determinedly refused to talk at all about the question, even to their closest friends and family? Would we not then have found out something more: might our picture of survivors not have been diametrically opposite to the one that dominates the literature? I am convinced that this would be the case.

It was precisely this specific choice of sample which distorted our understanding of the consequences of wartime experiences. More recently, attention has finally begun to be drawn to other than negative effects of wartime experience. David Jaffe (1985) has claimed on the basis of biographical data and his own clinical observations that in particular cases, self-renewal, or a creative restructuring of the personality, may occur after extreme stress.

Other researchers have claimed that we could obtain a fuller picture of survivors, one which does not concentrate on psychopathology, by making use of the methodology of the social sciences in research, rather than the methods employed in psychiatry (Kahana *et al.* 1988). They have proposed indicators of well-being in Holocaust survivors. Surveys (using question-naires) carried out on a large sample showed that physical health, a high standard of living, social status and speaking about their own experiences were all important in producing a feeling of well-being among survivors.

Barbara Schwartz Lee, a psychoanalyst and herself one of the survivors, has protested (1988) against seeing them as sub-standard, crippled human beings. She has pointed out that among the survivors there were many who during the war demonstrated an exceptionally powerful sense of their own identity, an imposing strength of ego, and who after the war led and continue to lead happy and successful lives which bring them satisfaction. Schwartz Lee claims that it was positive emotional relationships with their parents in their early childhood which protected these individuals from the destructive influence of their traumatic experiences in their later life. Krystyna Żywulska agreed with her, and in conversation with me said the following:

> I often wondered what gave me the strength, who gave me the strength, to survive everything that happened. I came to the conclusion that it was my childhood. I remember that I was surrounded by exceptional love, that I felt that I was loved. And that was at the bottom of everything. If I had had to go through everything that I went through without those reserves of love inside myself ...

When I was analysing the attitudes of the people I interviewed, I found myself in a situation in which my theoretical knowledge was contradicted by what actually happened. I never thought of them as 'victims'. I saw their suffering, I understood it, I sympathized with them, but I cannot say that they were people who were functioning pathologically. Some of them in fact stated categorically that they did not feel themselves to be victims, and that – paradoxically – their wartime experiences, although purchased at a great price, in some way had enriched them.

> My long life fell into a strange mosaic; every now and again I passed through various ordeals of fire in finding my own place in the world. And it was precisely the period of the occupation, in the ghetto and on 'the Aryan side', which helped me most in this: I became more profoundly acquainted with evil, but light came through to me as well – I met exceptional people, different from the boring average. They really knew how to fight, and to give everything of themselves that was worthwhile. I felt then that I was being lifted up by something other than the real, something unreal. That by the side of people like this I could manage to achieve something. Everything dangerous and hopeless that I survived thanks to people that I met on my way immunised me against the evil that surrounded me, hardened me and didn't let me give up. In spite of times of enforced inactivity, *I felt that I was alive* (my italics – B.E.). I was saved by optimism, faith in the people who passed through my life. All this made it possible for me to dream of survival, to see a vision of the future. And what about after the war? It happened sometimes that I got up in the morning and thought: what am I going to do today? It's so boring in People's Poland. ... (Helena, Interview 30)

> For me the war was the experience of gaining faith in my own
> abilities. In some sense, I was undoubtedly born again during the war.
> If I had to put a date on it, it would be the date when I got out of the
> ghetto. I see it as an experience that built me up, that gave me faith in
> my own abilities. I am a kind of self-made man. (Ryszard, Interview
> 34)

On the basis of my research, I would give an affirmative answer
to the question of whether it is in any way possible to be happy
after the experience of the Holocaust. The majority of the
people I interviewed are leading lives that satisfy them, they do
not wallow in memories of the past and the losses they suffered,
they do not expect fate or other people to compensate them for
their sufferings. One of the people I interviewed said

> I'm married for the second time (my first wife died), I have two
> children. After everything that I went through I can only thank God
> that I'm alive. I am 73. I can't complain, I mustn't say that I could want
> anything else. What I got from life and from God is just right. That's
> how it ought to be. (Józef, Interview 36)

It would seem that researchers into the problems of Holocaust
survivors, or of former concentration camp prisoners, make the
mistake of psychologism. They see an individual as a bi-partite
psychosomatic organism, an organism which can only be ill;
they do not give enough weight to the role of the traumatic
experiences which the individual confronts in the spiritual
dimension of his existence. Psychiatrists and psychotherapists
can treat a sick body or sick psyche, but they are helpless when
confronted with sickness of the soul. They leave that human
dimension to the theologians and philosophers, and by so doing
make it more difficult to comprehend the full complexity of
wartime experiences. Max Scheler has called this manner of
proceeding – ignoring man's spirituality – 'metaphysical
ignorance'.[4] In fact, I believe that the experience of major
psychological traumas has further consequences for the
spiritual life of those who have been through them.

Probably not all survivors feel that their experiences
constituted spiritual – as well as psychosomatic – suffering.
Nonetheless, one cannot ignore the experience of those
(perhaps few in number) who do feel this way: that their
experiences were also, or perhaps primarily spiritual.

I think that to a large extent the war formed me, influenced my attitudes to my surroundings. I don't even know whether this helped me in my work, in my profession. I keep things in perspective, I have a certain sense of relativity. A lot of people get upset about the major or minor trifles that make up everyday life. I often pass over trifles of that kind. It's easier for me to understand people, I can manage to talk to them. I try to accept their faults.

I know that I am a victim of the war, but I don't feel like a victim, because I believe that it was the war that enriched me. Even if it was at a terrible price, it definitely gave me something. Even though I lost my whole family, I lived through a nightmare, I lost several of the most important years of my life. ... But I don't see myself in categories involving being a victim, although I know that, objectively, that's what I am. (Marek, Interview 37)

One of the people I interviewed spoke of his Holocaust experience as of an enriching of his spiritual life, which – despite the terrible price paid – made him a better doctor.

It happened. I was here at that time, and not somewhere else, and I don't feel that because of my experiences I'm handicapped in comparison with other people; nor do I want to feel superior to those who haven't been through it. I had to put up with a lot, I lost a lot and I won something. Maybe it made me a more sensitive person, and it certainly made me a better doctor. You could say that in some way my life was enriched – although I hope nobody will ever again have to be enriched by experiences like that. The whole set of experiences linked with the awfulness of the ghetto and – although this is an entirely different dimension – the profound and painful intensity of months in hiding has obviously affected my later life. It has forced me to evaluate things differently. But to tell the truth it's neither a gramophone record which always plays the same tune, nor a cassette tape where you can wipe everything out and record another composition. The tune from those days will not vanish, but a lot more new ones have been played. You have to live up to the echoes of the past, while at the same time meeting the challenges of the present. (Jerzy, Interview 35)

One of the dimensions of spiritual suffering is, in my view, the loneliness of the survivors, and I would like now to spend a little time on this question.

A feeling of loneliness is a subjective consequence of the experience of the Holocaust, one of the consequences of which the people I interviewed spoke. It is a feeling that goes with the experience of exceptional suffering which is so difficult to convey to other people. Every human being, every one of us, knows the feeling of loneliness or the sense of being isolated. When we go through periods of depression, breakdown, or difficulty in taking some important decision, we feel that nobody understands us, that nobody can advise us – that we are obliged to fall back on our own resources. I would call this kind of loneliness situational loneliness. Holocaust survivors experience not only loneliness of this kind, but also, and above all, existential loneliness, which takes three forms.

The first is physical loneliness: the absence of childhood companions, people with whom they can recall happy times from their youth; the absence of all those people who create together our own private kingdom – neighbours, acquaintances, and also streets, and the houses along them, in which life happened. Those who survived have nobody who can say to them, 'My word, you've grown', or, 'As you get older you get more and more like your mother', or, 'Your father always complained about pains in his left knee, too'. One of the people I interviewed said,

> Very often, more and more often [I feel lonely]. Even though I have people close to me, at the same time I don't have, I have no one from my family. From my family, you know, I mean relations, and that's something different, but I have no relations in Poland. And apart from that, you feel lonely because of all these constant funerals. Of the people that I knew when I was young, more and more are passing away. (Stefan, Interview 29)

The problem of loss of 'the kingdom of childhood' appeared exceptionally dramatically in conversation with Edward:

> This is how it goes with that one stone [at Treblinka]: that's my school, those are my teachers, those are my parents, that's my family, my cousins, everyone, everyone. That's the library, that's the cinema, that's the club, that's, I know, the ones I played ping-pong with, those are the ones I quarrelled with. Maybe the girl that I kissed, or who kissed me, is there – after all, that's life! In Białystok there was Minas ha Tsedek – where's the monument to that? There was Minas Cholim – the society to care for the sick – where is it? There was the Jewish hospital – where are those doctors? There were grammar schools, general secondary schools, primary schools, all kinds of schools – it was a living world! (Edward, Interview 26)

The second form of existential loneliness is psychological loneliness: an absence of those who shared the tragedy, of those who alone understood the experiences of the war. The majority of survivors believe that,

> anyone who didn't live through it can't altogether understand it. (Barbara, Interview 10)

And so there is nobody to talk to about it, you can't tell anybody about it, it is impossible to share the experience with anyone and therefore possibly receive comfort. The element of psychological loneliness is present in the category of extreme psychic trauma that Lifton describes and which I have discussed above; Lifton calls it 'suspicion of false comfort'. One of the women I talked to expressed the essence of psychological loneliness when she said:

> How can you tell anyone what hunger is? ... You can't tell anyone what pain is, or hunger, or fear. ... I can't even convey what it means to want a cigarette as much as I wanted one during the Uprising. (Adina, Interview 13)

The third form of existential loneliness is spiritual loneliness: loneliness in the face of God, in the face of the meaning of the Holocaust, inability to answer the question, 'Why did things happen like this?' I wrote in the previous chapter about hopeless quests to discover meaning in the experience. In categories of the life of the individual, this brings spiritual loneliness as well as metaphysical suffering. This may be expressed in a painful feeling of the accidentality of existence, the senselessness of human existence.

> Sense? Was there any sense in the annihilation of the Jews? What kind of sense could there be in that? The fact that I'm alive is an accident – not an isolated one, but a string of coincidences ... I don't know whether they were lucky or unlucky coincidences, because I don't know whether it wouldn't have been better to die, I'm not all that sure. ... (Anna, Interview 27)

Existential loneliness in the three dimensions described here is one of the forms of spiritual suffering experienced by survivors. Spiritual suffering also means a sense of a wasted life, even though one survived. One of the men I talked to described this in a fascinating way:

I feel as though I had lost out on life, even though I survived. I didn't want to reject my father and mother, but I was always judged for my family background. I feel useless, unnecessary, like an intruder in my own country. And after all, a man must have a country of his own, without a mother country he's worth nothing. A mother country is not such a complicated thing: it's the earth where my roots have been put down, where I was born and where my grave – where someone might light a candle – will be. (Edward, Interview 26)

For most of the people I interviewed, their sufferings had not led to what would have been entirely understandable railings at fate:

[What has stayed with you most from the ghetto, from that experience?]

In general, from everything?

[Yes. What has stayed with you?]

Some kind of pain, some kind of general feeling of pain, that I had to go through it, that so much was lost.

[Do you feel bitter?]

No. It was the fate of a lot of people. Perhaps I had a more dramatic time, there was war – I was in a camp. … There was terrible suffering. Stefa, for example – they took her from a wedding, she cried all the time in the cell for the child that she'd left behind all by itself. And so I thought – I haven't got a child, I'm better off. Someone else nearby was always worse off than yourself, always … (Conversation with Krystyna Żywulska)

No, things like that never occur to me. How can you feel bitter at your fate …? I don't pity myself, and so I don't rail at what is called fate, I don't even know what it is. I would prefer not to have had experiences like that. I feel weighed down by it all; it's better not to have been through something like that – it's not for human beings. It isn't human. Thinking about it weighs down a human being to the end of his days. (Anna, Interview 27)

The people I interviewed do not feel bitter and unjustly treated by fate – although if they did it would be entirely understandable. I think that it would be equally understandable if they expected that after what they had been through life owed them something. This 'something' could be very individual; the point is a subjective awareness of compensation for the pain, humiliation, loss of family and friends, for the wasted years of their youth and time lost. The majority of the people I talked to claimed, however, that they did not feel like this.

> I would think that I had wasted my life if I did not have a child, or work where I could prove myself. Luckily, I have had both. I never compared other people's dramas with my own experiences. Their problems or dramas didn't seem small or insignificant to me just because I'd been through something worse. I don't measure things according to that scale. I don't believe that I'm owed anything more. I understand that things are hard for everybody. Those are the times we live in. ... I'm only afraid that the times that are coming will be worse. (Anna, Interview 27)

> [Didn't you think that after the war life owed you something?]

> My dear, I simply didn't have any time for philosophical questions of that kind. In the mornings I was a student, I went to lectures; in the afternoons I did political work; in the evenings I learnt Russian. (Ryszard, Interview 34)

Other people I interviewed expected 'everything': a happy life and compensation for the suffering they had been through.

> [Did you expect something from life after the war?]

> Everything. I had won the war! I'd survived, I was still young, I had my whole life in front of me. My generation had won. That's what we'd been through the war for, now finally to live. Life owed us everything then. (Irena, Interview 28)

> I believed that after what I'd suffered, life owed me everything. I believed that I had to get my own back. I didn't take enough interest in the children, who after all had done nothing to deserve that kind of treatment. I believed that I had a nice flat, and although other people didn't have anywhere to live at all – that was all right, why shouldn't I have a nice flat – had I spent too short a time in a camp barracks? (Conversation with Krystyna Żywulska)

What, however, the Holocaust survivors primarily expected was understanding of the suffering they had been through and respect for the dead. They expected that after the war there would be no more antisemitism. They believed that by virtue of their suffering and torment Poland would become at last a true and loving mother land for them.

Did I expect anything after the liberation on 11 September 1944 [the date when Soviet troops captured right-bank Warsaw], and in general after the war? Well, after all, emerging from long months in a mental and physical hidey hole is bound to be difficult. But what I wanted was to put aside those obvious, tangible difficulties – and in my case they were made worse by a serious worsening of my tuberculosis and the prospect of chronic and incurable intestinal illness. What I want to say is that I expected a more friendly attitude on the part of the surrounding world. I expected that when people saw someone who had survived the nightmare of the occupation – and Holocaust survivors represented a terrifyingly small percentage of the Jewish population in Poland – they would be pleased to see me. It's true that some people's reactions were exemplary. But in the main, attitudes and behaviour were very frustrating. And not only from the man in the street, where it was no rarity to hear 'We'll build a monument yet to Hitler for what he did to the Jews', and things like that, as well as the less shocking, 'The Jews will get their own back now. They'll take everything we've got' (for, after all, a lot of people had acquired Jewish property). But among people in my own social circle, educated people in the district where I lived and at the university showed quite clearly by their behaviour that antisemitism had come through the war in good shape. When I met one of the other students, who'd been in the same year as me before the war, at Boremlowo where the Faculty of Medicine was re-opening, he didn't ask me how I'd managed to stand it all, he didn't give any sign in word or action that he was pleased to see me alive. He asked me only one thing, in a sharp and inquisitorial tone, namely why I was attending a more advanced course than my pre-war record would have entitled me to. What on earth could I say? Just that since he'd been in favour before the war of the 'lecture hall ghetto' he'd now have to accept the fact that in yet another ghetto I'd taken courses that were recognized by the underground authorities. I'd longed so desperately to be dug out of my hiding place – and what I found was a sense of alienation and prejudice, and I more or less had to apologise for surviving. (Jerzy, Interview 35)

Let us return to the theme of the spiritual dimension of ghetto and camp experiences. Victor Frankl, who was himself a concentration camp prisoner, has written a great deal about the spiritual dimension of the suffering associated with these experiences in his book, *Psycholog w obozie koncentracyjnym* (*A Psychologist in a Concentration Camp*, 1962). It seems to me that his thoughts and attitude in the camp were the same as those of many people, perhaps particularly those whom Kępiński (1992a, pp. 87-8) describes as 'restoring faith in human nature, giving hope to others':

> If fate imposes suffering on a human being, he has to accept it as his task in life, his only task. He has to manage to become aware that he, together with his suffering, is something unique in the whole universe. No one can take away his suffering and no one can suffer for him. But what he achieves in life will depend on how someone who faces this fate takes advantage of his opportunity and how he bears the burden of his suffering. For those of us in a concentration camp, this was not some kind of unreal, theoretical calculation. Only thoughts of this kind could help us. For they did not allow us to fall into despair even when it appeared that we had no further chance of saving our lives. We had already long before come to terms with the problem of the meaning of life, with that naively posed problem which understands life simply as the putting into effect of a goal through some creative achievement. The point for us was the meaning of life as a whole, including death, the point was the meaning of suffering and dying. We fought for this meaning! ... For us, suffering became a task to be carried out, the meaning of which we did not wish to lose sight of. Suffering revealed to us the possibility of real achievements, the possibility that Rilke wrote of: 'how much there is to suffer!'

One must of course conjecture that this way of enduring the suffering of wartime experiences was available only to the few. And we have absolutely no right to judge or evaluate either those who did, or those who did not, manage to bear suffering in this way. We have to remember that physical experience – hunger, thirst, fear, cold, sickness – generally extinguished thought, the 'higher' levels of functioning. None of us knows how long our own spirit would manage to resist and fight in conditions like these. Even in the normal world, not everyone remembers about his spiritual life on an everyday basis. Not everyone takes care of his spiritual, as well as psycho-physical, development and health.

Why is this standpoint absent from the academic description of 'Holocaust survivors'? Perhaps it was precisely this group who understood their experience in this way, who did not complain and therefore did not become objects of research? Perhaps for them the spiritual dimension of their wartime experiences is too intimate and they do not want to talk about it? Or perhaps the 'best', the most sensitive, those who most readily helped others, were exactly those who died?

Many authors believe this. Frankl (1984, p. 9) wrote:

> Of the prisoners who were in the camps for years, were transferred from camp to camp, and finally in insignificant numbers emerged from the camps, on the whole only those who fought for life with total ruthlessness could remain alive. All of us who emerged with our lives thanks to dozens of happy coincidences or miracles – depending on what you want to call it – are profoundly convinced, and can calmly state, that the majority of the best did not return.

Primo Levi (1988, pp. 82–3) saw it much more starkly, claiming that the 'survivors' were not the best people, who were predestined to do good, or carry out a mission, and that what he had seen and been through proved something quite the contrary: that it was the worst who survived – the selfish, the violent, the insensitive, the collaborators from the 'grey zone', and the spies. This was not exclusively the case (there were no rules there, just as there are no real rules governing human matters), but nonetheless it was the case.

The objection that a non-representative sample has been used can also, of course, be levelled against my own research. I interviewed only a small group of those who define themselves as Jews and who wanted to speak about their wartime experiences. Those who perhaps 'hid' themselves better after the war, who wiped out the tracks from their past and managed not to go back to them, remained inaccessible to me. Similarly, the experiences of those who refused to talk to me remained inaccessible. For this reason, the questions and reservations raised in this sub-chapter are my own questions and reservations, and I have no answer to them.

The objection that cultural and linguistic differences have been ignored

> You don't know Yiddish
> You don't know what it means
> When someone rails in Yiddish
> You still keep asking why,
> How am I to explain,

Either you understand me, or you don't
Can I put my heart into your body?

Song from the ghetto

My second reservation results from another aspect of the selection of the sample, on the basis of which knowledge about traumatic experiences and their consequences has been more generally applied to the whole category of 'survivors'. Knowledge on the subject, which was built up mainly on the basis of American research, took insufficient notice of cultural differences between pre- and postwar communities of survivors, and the influence of these differences on their psychological well-being. Looking at the research from the viewpoint of ethno-methodology, we might consider what these particular conclusions and ways of seeing the problem tell us about the researchers themselves, and more broadly - about the society from which they come.

It would seem that the researchers take a position similar to that of wartime witnesses to the Holocaust: in discerning only the medical, pathological consequences of these experiences, they place the experiences themselves beyond the bounds of the understandable, interpretable world. They close them up in a great cupboard with a notice reading 'Dysfunction' or 'Psychopathology', which provides an alibi for not taking part in other people's suffering. For the experience of the Holocaust - the essence of suffering: physical, moral and spiritual - goes fundamentally beyond human possibilities of sharing in the sufferings of others. Researchers into wartime experiences therefore join, willy nilly, the 'conspiracy of silence' which Yael Danieli wrote about. In fact it really began with absence of reaction on the part of the world to the Holocaust during the war, and it goes on until today. Today it does not apply to the necessity of reaction to the mere fact of genocide, but the necessity of reaction to the consequences of that fact - the necessity of facing up to one's own helplessness in respect of the sufferings of others.

One other aspect - this historical - is important in the context of seeing survivors as victims. These were, after all, people who found themselves after the war with all their baggage of experience and suffering in a country (I am thinking of the

United States) whose society knew nothing of the realities of war. They knew about all its cruelty, the terror of occupation, the nightmare of the ghettos and camps only from newspapers, from second-hand sources. This must have made the behaviour and problems of people from Europe all the more incomprehensible and sick to them. The new arrival from Europe did not 'fit in to' the scale of values of American society, where satisfaction with life is ranked highly, along with not complaining and not revealing (except to an analyst) psychological or spiritual suffering. The survivors' problems could not be understood by a society that had not to the least degree shared their wartime experiences. And apart from wartime experiences, their baggage contained value systems shaped in the prewar world. This could mean that the survivors themselves had difficulty in adapting to the new universal cultural and moral values that were so different from the ones they had lost. From this point of view, some of their problems could be seen as a research artefact which resulted to a great extent not from the very essence of the experience of war, but from a confrontation between these experiences and the postwar world which did not understand them and was not understood by them, and had a different civilizational and cultural existence.

There is another side to the same question: in Poland, where everyone suffered during the war, and almost everyone lost somebody, everyone had lived through the Gehenna of war and occupation – there was probably an absence of understanding for the differentiation and gradation of wartime nightmares. The camps seemed to be the apogee of cruelty; the ghettos were not considered. They remained an exclusively Jewish problem: let the Jews worry about it. The desire to break with the past, the necessity of rebuilding the country and changing the political system – which for some was yet another defeat, and for others victory and hope – also played a significant part here.

It was probably similar in Israel: there the necessity of fighting for a new motherland stimulated people to think about the future and not the past. Moreover, it was regarded as shameful there that the European Jews had 'allowed themselves to be slaughtered', and all the greater attempts were made to show the world that Israelis could manage to fight and defend their country.

I also regard the problem of the language of communication as exceptionally important. In what language should war experiences be told? The literature on the subject was written on the basis of information in various languages. The survivors often had to tell about their experiences in languages which they had learnt only after the war (for example, English). Could they find in these languages words which reflected the realities that they thought about in other languages? Were they capable of rendering semantic nuances and emotions, as well as elements of wartime reality, in languages where no precise terms for these things existed?[5] Every language determines the areas of meanings and emotions proper to itself; it defines the way of naming and experiencing the world. It is worth noting that in most camp and war memoirs German terms and proper names are retained.

When he analysed the problem of communication in concentration camps, Primo Levi wrote that understanding German orders and familiarity with camp jargon was one of the fundamentally necessary preconditions for survival. In second place, knowledge of Polish was essential, since the Poles were the dominant group among the prisoners. Exchange of information, often warnings of dangers, the possibility of maintaining contact with other prisoners was necessary in order to stay alive. Levi writes that prisoners remembered words in foreign languages that were used in the camp, the meaning of which they did not know then and often still did not know to the present day. However, when they recalled their camp experiences, they also remembered words describing the realities of those times, if only the omnipresent Polish swearwords like 'cholera' ('blast!') and 'psiakrew' ('damn!'), etc. In the poem of the same title that opens Levi's *Awakening* (1966) and which describes a camp morning, every verse ends with the Polish word *wstawać* (get up!).

I am convinced that it is easier to talk about camp experiences in the language which one was using at the time and which had names for the things of that world. For this reason, I believe that accounts by Polish survivors in Polish are more reliable, closer to the inner truth, than accounts given in other languages.

This is linked with a problem that I raised in the Introduction. That is, my belief that one should speak of the world of the ghetto in the language proper to that world. Martin Walser has drawn attention to the problem of understanding those realities in terms of the categories that they themselves created in an essay entitled, *Nasz Oświęcim* (Our Auschwitz). He thinks that the difficulty of communicating the realities of camp life lies in the fact that the stories are told either by victims or their persecutors.

According to Walser (1981, pp. 288-9), the experience of these two groups was completely different, and a different Auschwitz grew up in their memories.

> Auschwitz is something real only for the 'prisoners' who survived. SS-men describe their activities there in the way that defensive tactics require, … they stick to their army slang. And there isn't even any certainty as to whether they're only using slang because it can be an excellent cover for individual responsibility, or whether in fact they have no language for their memories of Auschwitz. … And therefore one should not be too surprised that the accused often smile, or give answers that sound almost ironical. It is not cynicism. Even today they are unable to understand the realities of the 'prisoners' Auschwitz, because in their memories an entirely different Auschwitz was preserved, that is, their Auschwitz, the Auschwitz of the SS-men.

The problem of the language in which wartime experiences were communicated came up in one of my interviews, with someone whose first language was Yiddish. This was the language of his childhood, his memories, and for this reason writing the story of his own life is very difficult for him:

> Once or twice I've started to write memoirs but I don't know what language I ought to write them in. In Yiddish, I can no longer find the words, and in Polish, it seems to me that I'm making mistakes all the time. (Edward, Interview 26)

The fact that knowledge about the Holocaust survivors was built up on the basis of imprecise accounts is perhaps one more aspect of the artifactuality of that knowledge. The data which the researchers rely on must in the nature of things have been distorted by the necessity of using a foreign language – neither that which was the native language of the survivors nor that within the framework of which they survived the war.

And now let us pay a little attention to problems specific to the situation of survivors in Poland, which do not appear in the international literature. I would like to deal with three questions: the reasons for remaining in Poland after the war, the problem of changing one's surname, and experience of antisemitism after 1968.

The reasons why they stayed

> My sentimental country town
> Dearest town of youthful trembling
> I'll come back to Theatre Square
> On the first free sunny day.
>
> Song from the ghetto

The very way of posing the question of why some survivors remained in Poland after the war needs to be held up to inspection. When it is put in this way in the international literature, it contains the hidden hypothesis that the natural and correct behaviour was to leave Poland, and therefore staying behind needs some special explanation. I do not want a question posed in this way to predetermine a conclusion that there were key differences between survivors from Poland and those from other countries in the world. I understand the reaction of emigration: the desire to flee from the site of the annihilation, the impossibility of living any longer in the place where the death of family, friends and one's own nation took place. Some people found relatives of some kind overseas – someone who had emigrated before the war. For others – and it is difficult to be surprised by this – Poland had become one great cemetery of the Jewish nation. They wanted to leave this cemetery behind as quickly as possible, to begin their lives 'afresh' in a new place, to break away from the traumatic experiences of war. But there were also people who stayed behind in Poland exactly because it was the cemetery of the Jewish race. Perhaps this resulted from their sense of guilt towards the dead, a feeling of responsibility towards them:

> I never doubted that there was no [other] place on earth that I would want to be. But there's something more. Some people thought that you couldn't live in a cemetery, but it seemed to me that someone had to look after that cemetery. (Adina, Interview 13)

I believed that there was some sort of obligation. I believe that every one of us has some kind of duty to the dead. After all, you can't forget about it. … In the ghetto, the feeling of sharing a common fate was very strong. … If I feel guilty, it's for another reason. After the war, one ought to have dedicated one's whole life to enforcing respect for the memory of the dead. Even though I'm alive, I'm still one of them – whether I like it or not. I would like to have a place where I could light a candle for my dead and pray. I don't have any such place, and for that reason I feel completely uprooted. But maybe it's partly my own fault that there are no places of that sort, that there are no memorials, that everything is constantly misrepresented. (Edward, Interview 26)

I believe that immediately after the war for many survivors remaining in Poland, the desire to rebuild their own lives and the life of the country was something entirely natural and understandable. I think that this was the view of many people at the time. They wanted to go on living in their native land. Involvement in reconstruction, and in building a new life, was not necessarily political or ideological in character. They were simply happy to have recovered their freedom, they wanted to study, work and rebuild the country.

I wanted to start studying immediately. I met one of my teachers from before the war, and told him that I needed my school-leaving certificate. And he wrote it out for me straight away. After that, I was one of the people who organized the University. I can't remember now how I had come by a horse and cart – but I collected books for the library. I studied Mathematics and Physics, and I went to some lectures on Philosophy and Sociology. (Ryszard, Interview 34)

To explain his decision to return to Poland with his wife from Switzerland in 1919 or 1920, Ludwik Hirszfeld wrote, 'If we had stayed in Switzerland, our life would no doubt have been a bed of roses, it would have been a quiet life, filled with academic successes. But in coming back to Poland, we found ourselves in some way at the very heart of major events. Our life here was more interesting, and we never regretted coming home'. Basically, I could say the same thing about myself. In July 1939, I needn't have returned from France to Poland. After the war, I could have left without any difficulty, without worrying that I wouldn't find work and would be penniless. … Everywhere there I would have found myself in the lap of luxury. But here, in Poland, I was 'at the heart of things'. And after all, I was in my native land – something that you need for your well-being. (Arnold, Interview 9)

272

Another of the people that I talked to expressed most fully the desire to take part in the life that was being resurrected after the war. When I asked whether he had not thought after the war about leaving Poland, he said:

> No, I didn't think about it. I was in a mood at that time which you couldn't call euphoria – but it was a surprise that I was alive at all. It was something extraordinary for me. I lived for the very fact that I was alive. Some aunt of mine found me. I didn't remember her, I didn't even know that she existed, for she'd emigrated to the States in the 1920s. She found me, through the Red Cross, I think. She wanted me to go to her, she sent me the documents. I even got as far as getting emigration papers. But at a certain stage, I gave up the idea, I threw it all over.
>
> [Why?]
>
> I decided to stay here. It's difficult for me to explain that decision. I'd started to go to college, I could see life being reborn all around me. That might seem strange to people who don't remember those times, it might sound a bit grandiloquent, but I was carried away by the enthusiasm of the times. I didn't know anything about what was already going wrong at that stage, I was completely unaware of all that. I only knew that Nazism was over. Everything apart from that, which was in some kind of opposition to it, was good. And that's why I decided not to go. I wanted to start life on my own feet, from the beginning. (Marek, Interview 37)

For some people, the impulse to rebuild the country was linked with ideological motivations. Some of the people I interviewed had already been Communist activists before the war. For that reason, they had been despised, persecuted and imprisoned. For them, the postwar changes in the Polish political system were a victory for what they considered the correct ideology. There was also the chance of building a new and just world of equal human beings, a world without racial hatred and antisemitism.

> A cousin from Belgium came to take me and the child to live with them. But I didn't want to go. I believed that what was going to come here would be something just, perhaps a kind of fulfilment of my ideals. That's what I thought, that it would all come true. And that's why I stayed. (Anna, Interview 27)

It was only when the right of the survivors to call Poland their native land was questioned that this constituted for many a powerful motivation for leaving. Their right to a native land was in my view questioned by postwar acts of antisemitism, by pogroms, murders, and refusal to return to survivors property which they had left in safe keeping. Behaviour of this kind, one of the causes of which was undoubtedly wartime demoralization and impunity, could be called the 'Polish guilt' towards the survivors. After all their suffering, and after the suffering that had fallen to the lot of the Poles, they expected, I think, some kind of brotherhood and fellow feeling in suffering. They expected understanding, sympathy and respect, and not ill-treatment.

For all concentration camp prisoners and survivors of the Holocaust, a return to 'normal' life after the war was very difficult, not only in Poland. Victor Frankl writes about this (1984, pp. 101–2):

> From a psychological point of view, one could describe the feelings of the liberated prisoners as an evident depersonalization. Everything seemed unreal, extraordinary, like a dream. One couldn't yet believe it. Through those years, our dreams had too often mocked us. How many times had we dreamed of the day when we would see our friends, when we would clasp our wives to our hearts, when we'd sit down with them at the table and start to tell them everything that had happened to us over all those years; we even dreamed what the day when our meeting took place was like – the day that had become reality. … Woe to the man who discovered that the loved one, the thought of whom had been the only thing to keep him going, was not there. Woe to the man for whom the moment had come of which he had dreamed in a thousand dreams only to find that it was different, completely different, from what he had imagined. He gets on a tram, travels to that house which for years on end he has seen only through the eyes of the soul, he rings the bell, exactly as he has done in a thousand dreams. … But it is not the right person who answers it.

In Frankl's view, there are two emotions that accompany a return to a normal life: bitterness and disillusion.

> When a man of this kind came home and found that people only shrugged or produced some cheap catch phrases, he was often swept by such bitterness that he wondered why he had gone through all that suffering. If he almost never heard anything but, 'We didn't know anything about it all …', and 'We suffered, too …', he was bound to ask himself whether this was really all they had to say to him.

It is different in the case of disillusionment. In this case it is not the superficiality and emotional laziness of those close to him that so upsets him that he would like to crawl into a mouse hole and never hear or see anything any more. Now, he felt he was abandoned to fate: for many years, he had believed that he had reached the very bottom of suffering, and now he suddenly found that suffering was bottomless, that there is probably no absolute bound to suffering, that it is always possible to suffer yet more.

Let us return to the main theme of this discussion: to the reasons for remaining in Poland after the war. They included, too, hope of finding lost members of the family, and the faith that perhaps someone had survived and would turn up somewhere. It was for this reason that some prisoners released from concentration camps at once returned to Poland:

> I came back [from the camp], I came back on the first transport. Perhaps someone had survived, perhaps I'd find someone waiting. ... There was a kind of subconscious, irrational belief. This is where I'd lived, this is where I'd gone from, this is where I had to come back to. I came back on the first transport, it seemed perfectly natural. (Marek, Interview 37)

Hope of finding family and friends, even if irrational, was completely understandable and very strong. The loss of these hopes could be one of the reasons for leaving Poland later.

> I feel that I am Polish, I would never leave my country, my Warsaw, for good. I think and I feel in Polish - no one can ever take that away from me. (Ewa, Interview 17)

> But this is my country, after all. I don't know how to put it so that I don't sound pompous. I've been in France, I worked there, the people that I'm closest to in the world are there - my brother and his family. I could have stayed there - and yet I spent all the money I earned on flying back to Poland. It's an illness, I'm suffering from Polishness. (Irena, Interview 28)

> I've never hidden the fact that I'm Jewish. You have to be yourself. I can't see myself as an emigré. I've been abroad many times - in Israel, Sweden, the United States. And each time, when I thought to myself that I could soon be walking along Nowy Świat Street, I immediately wanted to come back. (Barbara, Interview 10)

The 'Polish guilt' towards the Holocaust survivors - towards people who had suffered more greatly than the Poles - lies not only in a particular kind of 'conspiracy of silence', but also in responsibility for the wrongs done to Jews in Poland after the war. Those who survived certainly did not expect to experience antisemitism again in Poland. They expected – probably naively – that the war would have wiped out old prejudices and stereotypes, and that their own suffering would have made people sensitive to other people's wrongs. They did not expect a revival of prewar antisemitism. In any case, the post-war acts of aggression against Jews were not a continuation of the pre-war antisemitism, which was largely organized and political. It would seem that postwar antisemitism was – and this in no way justifies it – a more primitive dislike of the alien, linked with hatred and the need to find a scapegoat. Polish antisemitism was not discredited by collaboration with the Germans (as had been the case, for example, in France), for there had been no collaboration of this kind at a national level in Poland.

The American historian Michael Steinlauf (1993) believes that postwar Polish antisemitism was an expression of a Polish sense of guilt which was not entirely conscious. He claims that the fact that Poles had come into possession of ex-Jewish property could not have failed to leave marks on the Polish mentality. All the more so in that many of the people whose standard of living had improved through the taking over of houses, workshops, tools and materials belonging to Jews had before the war been antisemites. They had not aimed to kill the Jews, but had opted for some other kind of 'solution of the Jewish question', through, for example, emigration. They had wanted the Jews to disappear, and that is exactly what had happened. Moreover, 'the fate of the Jews had proved economically profitable for the Poles'.

Calel Perechodnik wrote in his memoirs (1993, p. 29):

> Now Poles more and more often visit the ghetto. They mean to buy all kinds of things for practically nothing, since – as they explain – 'when they re-settle you, you'll have to leave it behind anyway'. Our concierge, a woman who was more or less brought up with my wife, has made appearances at our place, too. But not in the least to assure us that we can count on her if we need help. Since, as she gives us clearly to understand, we're already living corpses as far as she's concerned, then who would be worthy to inherit the things we leave behind, especially the bed linen? Who but she, who has been known [to] us for so many years, and is so fond of us?

And when the Jews were deported from the Otwock ghetto, Perechodnik noted

> The Poles jumped over the fence, broke in the doors with axes, and took everything that they could get hold of. Sometimes the looters came across the bodies of Jews who'd been killed, but it made no difference – they quarrelled and fought over the still warm bodies, grabbing a pillow or a suit from each other. ... After all, the Poles have clear consciences. They probably justify themselves in the depths of their souls as follows: 'We didn't kill them, and anyway, if we don't take it, then the Krauts will' (1993 p. 64).

Kazimierz Wyka noticed as early as 1945 the moral and psychological dilemma linked with having come into possession of ex-Jewish property. He wrote (1984, p. 157):

> From beneath the sword of the German executioner, carrying out a crime unprecedented in human history, the Polish shopkeeper pulled out the key to the till of his Jewish competitor, and thought that he had behaved entirely morally. The Germans committed the crime and took the blame; we took the keys and the cash-box.

Nor, in Steinlauf's view, could witnessing the Holocaust from beginning to end fail to affect the Poles. They were in a difficult situation, since after all they had committed no crime and broken no law for which they could be punished or could make amends. This muddled and delicate moral problem was insoluble and was therefore pushed to the back of the collective consciousness, and also – in line with the rules of psychology – replaced by enmity and dislike of Jews. Steinlauf (1993) claims that postwar aggression towards the Jews was an explosion of a sense of guilt directed against those who might point a finger of accusation at the Poles.

The Polish-Jewish problems of the war years became a taboo subject, were passed over in silence, although they undoubtedly influenced, and continue today to influence, the Polish mentality. In a certain sense, the Poles are therefore also victims of the Holocaust. What I have called 'the Polish guilt' is described in much stronger terms by Steinlauf, who says that the Holocaust is a serious illness of the Polish people.

Changing names

> Don't skip and hop, name of David.
> You're a name that condemns to defeat,
> not given to anyone, homeless,
> too heavy to bear in this country.
> Give your son a Slavic name,
> for here we count the hairs on your head,
> here we tell good from evil,
> by names and the cut of your eyelids.
>
> Wisława Szymborska, *Jeszcze (Still)*

Many Jews who stayed in Poland after the war retained the 'Aryan'-sounding surnames that they had used during the occupation. Why? Some say that they did not think about it particularly – they had simply got used to the names they had used through the previous few years.

> I simply didn't think about it. I was left with those false papers in which I'd entered my name. I'd written under the name of Krystyna Żywulska, I'd written that book that I'd wanted to write as a Pole from the Pawiak prison. At that time I was still, above everything else, a Pole from the Pawiak. If I'd suddenly changed my name, it would have been an alien name. (Conversation with Krystyna Żywulska)

Others thought that because the continuity of the existence of family and tradition had been broken, there was no real sense in sticking to their old name.

> There's no point in going back to old names, because no one from those days is still alive. If I'd gone back to my previous name, when I'd nobody in the world, everyone would have asked who on earth that was. (Iza, Interview 32)

> I thought at that time that since anyway there was nobody really close to me, it was of no significance. My brother was in France, and his daughter didn't even know that her family was Jewish. I wanted to get away from the whole business. I wanted to forget about it. (Irena, Interview 28)

There were also people who wanted to eliminate the traces of their wartime experiences and therefore changed their names:

> There was, I'm sure an involuntary reaction in all this … a reaction of cutting off from everything that had happened, and emphasizing the

beginning of something afresh. And as well there was some wish not to stand out. Since I was to live in Polish society, as a Pole, I ought not to be different. (Rysiek, Interview 11)

One of the women I interviewed felt guilty about changing her name. Even years later, she treated the change as a rejection of her parents, as 'being ashamed' of them. The long years of denying her identity and her origins, of not using her family name, had brought her a feeling of guilt and shame:

> The fact that I'm talking to you about these matters is a form of redemption. After all, in a sense, I rejected them (my parents). Because for a certain time I tried – that is, I didn't try to hide it, I just didn't bring the subject up, I couldn't talk about my parents easily. It was something in me, and I feel guilty to the present day. What right had I to try for so many years to wipe it out of my memory? (Irena, Interview 28)

The majority of people I talked to had not changed their surnames after the war. Just as it was a natural reaction to stay in Poland after the war, it was also quite obvious to them that they should keep their own name, or go back to it (if someone had had false papers during the war).

> During the occupation, I had an identity card in the name of Stanisława Królikowska from Krasiłowsk. I went back to my own name when I left the Central Committee and went to work at the Radio. Somebody asked me once why I'd done it. After all, a lot of people kept the documents they'd used during the occupation. I replied, 'So that I won't have to punch someone's nose one day'. That was a bit arrogant, but true. (Helena, Interview 30)

> It didn't even enter my head that I might change my name. A lot of people did, of course – mostly they kept the names they'd used during the occupation. There was a lot of discussion about it, and on the whole you were encouraged to change. This was all of no interest to me. In that respect, I had things easy. That wasn't what I went through it all for – to have to change my name. I didn't make a big thing about my background, but I didn't hide it, either. Up to today, I make a habit of making things easier for people – I tell them myself, for example, that I was in the ghetto. (Jerzy, Interview 35)

One has to remember the specifics of the situation in Poland connected with changes in the political system. As we know, so-called 'ideological factors' often argued, encouraged or demanded that people of Jewish origin should change their names. This applied mainly to those who were linked with Communism, and to the greatest extent to those returning to Poland from the Soviet Union. One of the women I interviewed mentioned this in the context of postwar antisemitism in Poland:

> It seems to me that postwar antisemitism in Poland was reinforced by the terrible policy of the Central Committee which insisted that Jews should change their names, and eliminate all traces of their past. This confirmed that there was something wrong with being a Jew. And after all, there were people who had hidden Jews during the occupation as a method of fighting against the enemy (I'm talking about people who did it from conviction, and not those who did it for money), a form of resistance against the Germans. Post-war party policy placed them in a curious situation. People coming back from the Soviet Union were also in a difficult position. They had to change their names overnight; we at least had had time to get used to our new names during the occupation. (Irena, Interview 28)

Those who had been ordered by the party to change their names were in 1968 accused by that same party of fraud and of disguising their origins ...

1968 experiences

> Barely a quarter of a century had passed since the gas chambers and concentration camps, since Auschwitz, Treblinka and Majdanek, where six million Jews were victims of premeditated murder. And suddenly in Poland, in that same country whose earth is covered with the mass graves of European Jewry, antisemitism appeared again – as one of the main themes of political life: ignoring common sense.
>
> Paul Lendvai, *Antysemityzm bez Żydów*
> (*Antisemitism without Jews*)

For many of the survivors, the organized political antisemitism of 1968 was one of the most shattering experiences since the end of the war; for many of them it became the ultimate motivation for leaving the country. A great deal has already been written and said about the events of March 1968, and I do not intend to become involved in analysis of the causes and well-known consequences. I would however like to draw attention to the significance – very largely symbolic – of the events for the Jews who had survived the war in Poland and continued to live in the country. For them, the 1968 antisemitic campaign meant a summoning back of their dramatic wartime experiences. It led to recollections that were not necessarily conscious and activated painful memories. The survivors again began to be afraid.

> The legacy of the war is fear. I was afraid again in 1968. I'm afraid of situations where I begin to be a marked man for some reason – for political reasons or because of my origins. When the people around me begin to take notice of me, then I begin to be afraid. (Tomasz, Interview 31)

> Friends of mine, who had gone away for a few months in 1968, had left their little daughter with me to look after. At that time, we didn't have piped water at home, and so I went to the corner of the street to get water. And there they were already criticizing the Jews. I went home thinking that I ought to hide little Lucy somewhere, in case they came. And then I fell to thinking that I had no safe house anywhere where I could place her. (Barbara, Interview 10)

For the majority of those among the people I interviewed who were linked with Communist ideology, the use of racial hatred for political purposes constituted the final defeat of that ideology and caused them to leave the Communist Party. One of them put it like this:

> I left the party in 1968. What put me off was the fact that the party had entirely broken away from any kind of ideology. It had already been clear for a long time that the point would come when I had to break with it. I wrote a fairly long letter at that point about my quarter-century of party membership – and I said goodbye to it. There was a terrible campaign at that time against the intelligentsia; a lot of my friends left the country – that really upset me, although I didn't suffer any unpleasantness myself – the purges came mainly in the humanities. (Ryszard, Interview 34)

The antisemitism of 1968 should be placed in the category of 'Polish guilt'. Although it is obvious that it was being used as a tool in the political struggle, nonetheless, the ease with which the Poles allowed themselves to be provoked into employing antisemitism is compromising for them (for us). This is not what the Holocaust survivors expected in their native land. One of the people I interviewed said in reply to the question of whether he thought life owed him something after the war:

Do I think that something is owing to me after those nightmare years? Well, the very least is that everywhere in the world, and certainly in Poland, antisemitism should be condemned. That doesn't mean that it's the only evil, but its effects are sufficiently well-documented for it to be condemned and banned. And in addition, I'd like the condemnation to be sincere and that radical measures should be taken to ensure that it is not tolerated. I'd like the world to pay its debts effectively – and it has no small debts – to those who survived and those who died. For the latter, if I might introduce a note of pathos, this would mean a kind of posthumous victory. The fact that this victory has lamentably not proved final is a kind of profanation of the heritage of the Holocaust. Faith has been shaken that the slogan 'Remembering for the future' would mobilize the world to accomplish something more than just advancing martyrology from the *Vae Victis* to the *Gloria Victis* stage. And the hope that the world would determinedly and consistently work towards implementing the appeal of 'Never again' has also faded. For the truth is that over a period of almost half a century one has been effectively stripped of this hope and faith – and not only in Poland by Kielce, 1968, and for example the atmosphere of the 1991 election campaign – but everywhere in the world: Biafra, the fate of the Kurds or the Gulags. (Jerzy, Interview 35)

For many survivors, the dramatic experiences of 1968 deepened the feeling of loneliness. I have written earlier of the existential loneliness that they experienced. In addition to the psychological dimension, this had a dimension in time, the dynamics of which was to a large extent dependent on external events. This loneliness was often experienced during the war, experienced painfully when living under cover on 'the Aryan side'; later it was experienced during the difficulties linked with a return to normality after the war. And the feeling became stronger for many survivors in connection with the antisemitic campaign of 1968.

I think that the worst period was that period after 1968. That was a time of such terrible loneliness, wasn't it, when everyone close had emigrated. (Adina, Interview 13)

Very, very close friends emigrated, and so you could say that the margins [of loneliness] widened. We keep up contact, but it's different when they were close at hand from when they are far away. … You felt orphaned yet again. … And loneliness. … It seems to me that everyone is lonely. (Ewa, Interview 17)

For the survivors, 1968 was a repeat experience of destiny. It showed that the Jews are always cannon fodder. It was like being branded again, having yellow patches sewn on. (Irena, Interview 28)

The demons of the past were called up again, many people were again afraid that the next stage might be the ghetto or the gas chamber. The experiences of 1968, which brought back what they had been through during the war, evoked in the survivors feelings of bitterness and disillusion as they recalled the spiritual suffering that they entailed. Victor Frankl (1984, p. 102) wrote:

All of us in the camp knew, and kept repeating to one another, that no happiness in the world could provide compensation for the suffering that we had been through. And anyway, we didn't in fact think of happiness. What kept us going, what made sense of our suffering, of our sacrifice and slow death, was not happiness. But even so, we were not prepared for unhappiness. The disillusion that many prisoners found in their new freedom constituted a blow that people recovered from only with the greatest difficulty.

The antisemitism of 1968 also brought consequences for families that had survived the Holocaust. In many cases, it was only as a result of these events that children found out about the wartime experiences of their parents, and often only then discovered what their origins were. I will write later about survivors' families, but now I would like to present a third reservation about the picture of a survivor built up in the Polish and international literature.

Non-differentiation of wartime experiences

> I remembered the Campo dei Fiori
> In Warsaw by a roundabout,
> On a fine spring evening,
> To the sound of lively music.
> Gunfire behind the ghetto wall
> Drowned the lively tune
> And the happy couples floated away
> High into the fine sky.
>
> Czesław Miłosz, *Campo di Fiori*

The third reservation deals with lack of differentiation among wartime experiences. A general label of KZ-syndrome, or post-camp asthenia, is pinned onto such wildly different experiences as: the ghetto, living under cover on 'the Aryan side', and concentration camps – which also varied from one to another. Polish research did not deal at all with ghetto experiences, and interest was taken only in concentration camp prisoners. Were there any Jews among them? Did their pre-camp experiences have any effect on their survival in the camp and its consequences? We do not know.

In research conducted elsewhere in the world, it is also true that wartime experiences are not differentiated. There, everyone investigated is a 'Holocaust survivor'. The variety of their experiences seems to be of no significance. What were they doing before they found themselves in a camp? After all, someone who was captured 'from freedom' lived through the experience in an entirely different way from someone who was previously in the ghetto and/or living under cover on 'the Aryan side'. How can one possibly reduce such varied experiences to the same thing! Let us remind ourselves (I have already written about it in the first chapter) of the differences between the ghetto and the concentration camp.

– Differences of time and space: in the ghetto, people had possession of their own time; in the camp this was no longer the case. Whatever they were like, in the ghetto they had their own 'homes', not only in the physical sense, but above all in the psychological: they had a place of refuge, they had their privacy. They still had friends and acquaintances, the possibility of deciding how and with whom they wanted to spend their time. You could at least get up in the morning when you wanted, and get washed without dozens of other people being around. Although restrictions on space were present, they were not so drastic as in the camps.

– Differences in the degree of terror: in the ghetto, despite everything, there was not so much direct physical violence as in the camps. The level of regulation and control of everyday life was incomparably lower. In the ghetto there was greater personal and private freedom, which does not mean that there was more inner freedom. There were people who retained that kind of freedom both in the ghetto and in the camps.

– Differences in the social structure: in the ghetto, elements of the social structure were preserved: the family, neighbours, local government representation. There was no enforced separation of the sexes, separation from one's nearest and dearest. The camp was a militarized structure, completely subservient to the orders and commands of the authorities. This structure created artificial divisions, of the kind that do not exist in society: according to sex, age, suitability for work, etc.

– Differences in possibilities of making choices: the degree of responsibility for oneself and one's family was incomparably greater in the ghetto than in the camp. It was necessary to secure food supplies, try to obtain work – there was none of that in the camps, where food was the same for all. People were much more 'equal' than in the ghetto, although, as we know their status in the camp was also very greatly differentiated – but according to different principles from those obtaining in the ghetto.

– Differences in the possibility of escaping: escaping from the ghetto, despite all the difficulties and restrictions, was easier than from the camp.

All these differences seem to indicate that the experience of the ghetto was easier than that of the camp. And yet, in my opinion, the greater degree of responsibility for oneself and others, the greater opportunity for making choices and indeed the necessity of making what were often inhuman choices, the nearness of 'the Aryan side' – meant that ghetto experiences were exceptionally dramatic, and that there was a basic difference between ghetto and camp. In the camp the possibilities of choice were a great deal more restricted; it was possible to live, as one of the men I interviewed put it, 'in the surviving phase', it was possible entirely to resign from responsibility for oneself, it was possible to be a puppet. The only opportunity for resistance belonged to the spiritual sphere: one could struggle with oneself to retain moral reactions.

In the ghetto it was different: it was not a camp, but neither was it the 'normal' world. There were greater possibilities for action, a greater necessity of taking decisions: more opportunities to make mistakes, greater responsibility.

Consequences of wartime experiences in the second generation

> The record made at the time when a man's actions point to self-respect and dignity constitutes a permanent record of undying value. ... If it is not to be an empty sign behind which there is no living authenticity – then no one can escape from responsibility for the survival of that record, for his part in the struggle against evil, in the struggle for the survival of values.
>
> Jan Strzelecki, *Próby świadectwa*
> (*Attempts at Witness*)

It would seem that one important consequence of the Holocaust was to disrupt the communication of cultural forms through breaking inter-generational continuity. In Margaret Mead's classic concept (1978b, p. 19) cultural identity can be arrived at in the post-figurative, configurative or pre-figurative model of culture. Traditionally, Jewish culture, with its multi-generational family model, and the authority accorded to parents and elders, was a post-figurative culture. The loss of older generations, one's ancestors, who could be the source of cultural messages, made it impossible to draw a feeling of cultural identity and continuity from the experience of earlier generations (the post-figurative model), while the loss of coevals and parents made it impossible to arrive at cultural identity through the configurative model.

On the other hand, the experiences of the Holocaust became an important element in post-figurative transfer, which was not only effected verbally. In the literature on the subject a great deal is written about 'inheritance' of wartime burdens, and attention is drawn to the fact that the children of Holocaust survivors require the services of psychoanalysts. This has led to many interpretations and various systems of classification of mechanisms for inter-generational communication in survivors' families.

It can happen that the parents, absorbed in their own suffering, concentrated on the past, are unable to take an interest in the life that their own children are living. It can happen that the problems of the children are made light of – since in comparison with the problems that they themselves faced during the war, the problems of their children seem entirely unimportant.

But at the same time, children are after all a symbol of the final victory over death, over Nazism, and have to replace a whole lost family. This is often linked with imposing upon them the identity of the idealized dead (they are often given the names of particular, deceased people), and with excessively high expectations. Children live with the awareness that after everything that their parents lived through, they ought to try not to cause them any trouble.

Ambivalent feelings towards their parents, blocked aggression towards them, difficulties in defining their own identity, lack of success in establishing inter-personal contacts – these are the most common reasons why the 'second generation' seek the help of psychoanalysts.

I would like to present now, in a very abbreviated form since this is not the basic theme of my study, the categorization of survivors' families proposed by Yael Danieli. After that, I will discuss my own studies of cases which indicate the problems of identity and identification with their parents among survivors' children in Poland.

As I have already noted, many survivors married people whose experiences were similar to their own. Often, after they had left Poland they found themselves in displaced persons (DP) camps, where they waited to obtain visas to go to other countries. There, they met people who had also lost their family and friends. After only a brief acquaintance, they quickly entered into second marriages, which Yael Danieli (1985, p. 34) calls 'marriages of despair'. These marriages took no account of prewar social divisions, differences of family background, education, life-styles; the force that held them together was that of traumatic wartime experiences. The new family was to compensate for the suffering they had been through and the loss of their dear ones. The children – and the first children were often born while their parents were still in the DP camp – were a miracle, a gift, a symbol of victory over death. Danieli distinguished four categories of survivors' families.

The first comprises victims' families. These are families where after the war the parents could not manage to cast off the psyche of the victim. They were permanently miserable, depressed, helpless and suspicious. They were afraid of the outside world and protected themselves against it by a close symbiosis within the family. Their reactions were sometimes exaggerated, often catastrophic, they had difficulties in taking decisions: they treated each decision as though it were a question of life or death. Families like this created a hermetic, closed system in which the parents exercised tight control over the children, were over-protective and constantly feared that something would happen to their offspring.

In families like this the children played the part of inter-mediaries both between their anxious parents and the outside world, and also within the household, between parents who complained about each other and were full of pretensions and mutual disillusion. 'Victims' families' deny the existence of psychological problems connected with wartime experiences. To admit them would be seen as a posthumous victory for Hitler.

The second category comprises fighters' families. Here, the parents usually had had a chance during the war of putting up active resistance to the Nazis: they took part in the Ghetto Uprising, fought with the partisans, etc. They do not have the mentality of the victim, and are not passive – they exhibit a strong drive for success, for building and creating; they are highly energetic. At home they are displeased by behaviour which might signify misery, inner weakness, or feeling sorry for oneself. And for this reason, in these families, too, it is not accepted that psychological problems are a result of wartime experience. Pride and inflexibility are regarded as virtues; relaxation, rest and pleasure are treated as dispensable.

'Fighters' families' do not recognize outside authority and do not like to be treated as victims. The problems of their children are sometimes underestimated and treated as unimportant; they require their children to be independent, self-sufficient, critical, entirely self-reliant. And therefore the children often have problems with inter-personal contacts, and difficulties in accepting or delegating responsibility.

The third category comprises moribund families. Here, both parents are often the only survivors among numerous brothers and sisters, cousins and relatives. They have often lost their previous marriage partners and children. Homes of this kind are dominated by an all-embracing silence and a damping down of all emotions, both pleasurable and unpleasant. The parents are unable to cope with any strong feelings, are completely concentrated on the past, and are unable to free themselves from painful memories. Before the children can understand the reasons for this behaviour on the part of their parents, they have been taught to restrict their own spontaneity and vital imagination. The children are expected to look after one another, and manage by themselves, and also to appreciate how greatly their parents – who work hard to guarantee them a good standard of living – love them. The children are also expected to look after and protect the parents who isolate themselves from the outside world.

The children are therefore caught up in hopeless attempts to please their parents and live up to their expectations. They do not feel loved and needed in their childhood; in adult life they have difficulties in emotional contacts, since what they expect above all from their partners is parental care.

The fourth category comprises successful families. These are the least uniform among the groups described. Danieli concludes that of all the types of family they are the most assimilated into American society. In these families, the parents were often teenagers during the war, and were therefore too young to make 'marriages of despair' immediately after the liberation. Quite often their partners are not people who had been through similar experiences, and there are many mixed marriages in this category. However, it is usually the survivor who assumes a dominant position in these relationships, and his/her ambitions and plans become the ambitions of the whole family. These families are concerned about their material status, and about the education and success of their children. They underestimate the psychological and emotional needs of their children, and pay most attention to their success. These families are often assimilated, they conceal the past which they want to forget. The children often find out accidentally or indirectly about their origins and background.

The taxonomy which Danieli proposes is not designed to introduce unambiguous and mutually exclusive types. The point is rather to present the differentiated possibilities of reaction and attitude to life after the experience of the Holocaust.

> The aim is to warn professionals who deal with psychic health against putting all individuals into one category and treating them as 'survivors', who are expected to exhibit only one 'survivors' syndrome'. For in reality differentiated reactions to persecution and

the experiences of the war in 'survivors' families make clear the need
to adapt therapeutic treatment to particular forms of reaction. (p. 38)

During my study, which began with conversations with children
of survivors who were living in Poland, it was difficult for me to
distinguish the types proposed by Danieli. Perhaps it was the
specific Polish situation which led to the fact that there were
more mixed marriages here. In families that I got to know, I
noted frequently the existence of a mixture of all the elements of
particular categories described by Danieli.

It would have been difficult for me to develop even a
provisional taxonomy, additionally so because I was not primarily
concerned with examining family problems, and the people I
interviewed included only four 'pairs' from the same family. It
was moreover extremely interesting to see how the reflections
and observations of parents and children from the same family
complemented one another and mutually confirmed each other. I
do not intend to write in detail about these families; that would go
beyond the scope of the present study, although in the future I
plan that it should be the subject of a separate study, or at least an
article. Here I would simply like to present, in order to indicate
the problems existing in Polish survivors' families, three case
studies of relationships between parents and children.

Three pairs of people I interviewed represent three different
cases of identification with parents and the resultant problems.
They could be called variants of 'being a Jew in Poland', since
their problems result not only from their parents' experiences,
but also from their experience of postwar antisemitism in
Poland, particularly the experience of 1968.

Case one: the Jew in hiding

Robert discovered that he was a Jew in 1968, when he was a boy
of twenty:

That's how it was: in 1968 my father told me. He was terribly afraid for
me at that time, he didn't want me to take part in any strikes at
university, or get mixed up in anything at all – in any case, I wasn't at
all likely to. [My father told me] not to go out into the street, he told
me to shave off my moustache – because it gave me, you might say, a
Semitic look. You could get a knock over the head for the way you

looked in those days. Whatever the case, I stayed at home. (Robert, Interview 7)

For Robert, a Jewish identity is imposed from without, associated with fear and shame. In the version that his father gave him - reinforced by the situational context - being a Jew involved some kind of undefined danger. His parents let him down: they brought him up as a Pole, he thought he was a Pole, and then - in a dangerous situation - it turned out that he was a Jew. Robert has not been able to come to terms with this imposed identity; he thinks that being a Jew is inferior, especially in Poland, where everyone is an antisemite:

> From the point of view of these 30-odd million people who live here, I'm an *Untermensch*. (Robert, Interview 7)

His parents cheated him and proved disloyal. Robert suffers because he does not feel that he is completely Polish, and at the same time, he does not want to be a Jew and declares that he does not feel like one. He wants to be just the same as everybody else, and tries very hard not to stand out. His wife apparently reinforces his fears and phobias, since she is - in the words of Robert's father - 'a typical Polish antisemite', and according to Robert's own account 'was terribly upset' when some busybody told her that Robert was a Jew.

Robert's links with his family are full of ambivalent feelings and suppressed aggression - he is an example of blocked communication. Robert has not talked to his parents about the past, about their wartime experiences:

> I knew that my father had been in Auschwitz, and later in a camp in Lower Silesia. ... I knew that he had studied medicine before the war - he talked quite a lot about that. (Robert, Interview 7)

Neither his mother nor father ever spoke about the ghetto, although they had both been in it.

> Since they themselves didn't talk about it, then clearly they themselves thought that ... clearly they didn't want to talk about it - why should I ask? (Robert, Interview 7)

Robert discovered what his grandfather was called and who he was only from a book written by his father and published when he was already grown up.

When the children were small 'our parents spoke to each other in French, so that we would not understand'. The parents did not give much time to their children:

> ... they were still asleep when I went out to school, the housekeeper woke us at half past six ... and got us ready for school. When we got back she let us in, sometimes I waited outside the door – I didn't have keys to the flat, so that I had to wait on the staircase. ... She gave us our dinner – I didn't eat dinner with my parents, they came back perhaps at 4 o'clock... It was only very rarely that they stayed at home. Mainly my father went out, because he loved playing cards. Mother stayed at home – she either wrote screenplays ... or went out somewhere with my father. So I mainly stayed at home with the housekeeper. (Robert, Interview 7)

They also went on holiday separately: the children to the country with the housekeeper, while the parents went somewhere by themselves.

The parents were authoritarian ('there was no discussion in our house, I had to do as I was told'), and they downplayed the needs ('I didn't really have any toys') and problems of their children.

> I didn't talk [to my parents about my problems]. I didn't have any problems at school, not so that they would want to expel me. Even if someone said something to me or hit me, I didn't tell my parents about it. (Robert, Interview 7)

Robert was convinced that the scale of his problems was not great. I think that he compared, not necessarily consciously, the decisions that he had to make in life with those which his parents had had to make ('I have never had to take any exceptionally important decisions, which would determine the fate of our home, life, or any major matters'). Compared with their decisions, each one of which was a life or death matter, his own problems might indeed seem trivial.

When I listened to Robert's account he made on me the impression of someone very lonely; I asked him how he knew that his parents loved him at all. He replied:

> They weren't specially interested in me, I mean only to the extent that they wanted me to be there. ... When I was late, there would be a terrible row, because it turned out that my father was in a dreadful state, that they were very anxious. (Robert, Interview 7)

I had the impression that the parents were unable to show the child that it was accepted, or to demonstrate positive feelings (for example, he never cuddled his parents); love was shown in the form of threats - fear of loss, anxiety that something might happen to him.

Robert believes that he must be loyal to his parents ('Whatever would happen if they found out that I'd told you things like this - my mother would be mortally offended with me'), even though he holds a great deal against them and there was a lot of aggression in what he said. He claimed directly that 'my parents are egoists', and he is enormously disappointed with them that they did not leave Poland in 1968. This theme of emigration came up many times during our three-hour long conversation and is in my view Robert's main problem in life. He said:

> I hold it against my parents. Naturally. I think that they should have left. ... After all, my life would have been entirely different. ... In '68 people who were a lot older emigrated - and they've managing somehow, nobody's dying of starvation. (Robert, Interview 7)

His parents decided not to emigrate because, in Robert's view:

> they believed in this political system. They believed everything that was written in the papers, what was said on the radio, they believed in Stalin, they believed in Bierut, they believed in Gomułka, they were euphoric every time. (Robert, Interview 7)

He himself didn't take the decision to emigrate although he had been abroad several times, and was even abroad at the time when martial law was declared. He believes that the fact that he did not emigrate was the greatest defeat of his life:

> It's too late now, they don't need people of my age in the West. I could have emigrated, but ... now it's too late, I don't know ... because of my parents? They ought to have done it earlier, 20 or 30 years ago. And now of course they won't go, and so I won't go. I don't want to leave them. ... Maybe, maybe I need them? (Robert, Interview 7)

Robert is torn between the need to win the acceptance (love) of his parents, and the need to live up to their expectations, doing what they want - and the feeling of being lost, including in his own ambivalent feelings about his parents. Robert is unhappy because of the Jewish identity that was imposed on him. Until his father's book was published he believed that no one knew about his background and he hid behind this ('in Poland I never talked about it to anyone'). Now, however:

> the situation is that I don't know whether they [the neighbours] know. I suspect that they do – after what my father wrote. ... I don't know whether I feel in this way that I've cheated them by not telling them about it. I should tell them straight out. I don't know whether I don't have the courage, or whether I don't want to tell them. (Robert, Interview 7)

I called Robert 'a Jew in hiding' because throughout our conversation his enormous emotional tension was visible, when we were speaking about his parents and particularly when we were speaking about his family background. He never once used the term 'Jew', employing various substitute phrases, generalizations, etc. I had the impression that it was a secret to which I had been admitted by accident.

Conversation with Arnold, Robert's father, made me fully aware of the drama of lack of communication in this family. Arnold came from a family of Jewish intelligentsia from Łódź. He went to a Hebrew grammar school, and his father was an eminent leader of the Jewish cultural and social movement. Arnold is very proud of his father: 'The further I get away from him in time, the more I realize how exceptional he was.' It seems all the more strange that Robert only found out from his father's book that he bears his grandfather's name.

In speaking of his relationship with his son, Arnold said:

> Do you know, I never spoke to my son about that [i.e. the family background]. I don't know why. We are both introverted. I regret that in the course of our lives – and I must point out that he has known me for a lot longer than I knew my parents – we have never had a frank conversation. (Arnold, Interview 9)

Parents who survived the Holocaust want their children to be happy more than other parents. It would seem that after all they had been through it would be enormously unfair if their children were not to be absolutely and unreservedly happy. In the same way, Robert's parents wanted their son to feel Polish, they wanted to protect him from the 'brand' of Jewishness, they wanted to protect him from knowledge of the tragedy of their own experience, they wanted him to be happy.

Case two: the Jew who accepted

From her early childhood, Małgorzata heard from her mother that her father was so irritable because he had lived through Auschwitz. He was a victim of the war and therefore everything had to be forgiven him, he had special privileges. Above all:

> he had thought up a profession for me before I was even born. All my childhood was a battle with my father. (Małgorzata, Interview 19)

Małgorzata's father had had a friend who had wanted to be a musician, and he himself had thought of the same thing in his youth. But unfortunately the friend died and the war prevented him from putting his own plans into effect. In view of this, his child was to fulfil his own unrealized desires. The father, Rysiek, told me:

> I am very fond of music although I didn't have major talent, no technique, and anyway I didn't have opportunities to study. I decided to give my daughter a chance, and when she was seven, I began to give her a musical education, she went to music school, she played the violin. (Rysiek, Interview 11)

Małgorzata rebelled against her father's plans for her life, she wanted to put her own plans into effect, but her father used sophisticated psychological blackmail against her.

> When I cried, or locked myself in the toilet, my father would say, 'You don't want to play, all right, I'll take your violin, you won't play'. He suffered badly on this account, because he'd worked it all out, exactly what was to happen. (Małgorzata, Interview 19)

Rysiek, talking about his daughter's attitude to music, said,

> It wasn't easy, you had to battle with it, because in the end she was a child, children have their ... there were no basic objections, but just normal difficulties in overcoming laziness, that's a certain effort, and so it wasn't simple, and sometimes there were even some more serious confrontations. ... (Rysiek, Interview 11)

In the end, Małgorzata gave in to her father, she became a violinist, and although she thinks 'it's a perfectly good profession', she regrets that she didn't follow her own path.

> If I had been very ambitious, or maybe some outstanding personality, maybe I would have won through it. But for an average person like me, parents ought to offer some opportunities for choice. For me, in spite

of everything, my parents were a great authority. I thought that they must be right, but it was difficult for me. (Małgorzata, Interview 19)

In her father's account, the problem sounds different:

Later, when a moment had come when it was necessary to decide whether to treat the thing professionally or not, I said, 'Now it's your business: decide'. And she went for it, it attracted her somehow, although she had a lot of problems with herself to overcome. She became a professional violinist, she plays in an orchestra. It seems to me that with time she's come round to the idea that it was the right choice, although she uses every opportunity to curse me for pushing her in that direction. (Rysiek, Interview 11)

He father was the 'principal actor' in Małgorzata's childhood. He loved her exceptionally strongly, but she felt that she could not manage to give him as much affection as he needed:

He sometimes held my hand. I was terribly embarrassed by this, and I think he was, too. This enormous desire [on his part] that there should be real feeling. When I was walking along and he was holding my hand, I simply felt that the hand was wooden – total paralysis. And that was terrible – for a father it must be the worst thing possible. (Małgorzata, Interview 19)

Małgorzata was sorry that she could not manage to respond to that enormous need on his part for affection, and she still feels guilty today. In my view, her feelings about her father are in general highly ambivalent. One of the poles of this ambivalence consists of sympathy, pity and a sense of guilt, and the other of fear:

The thing that stays with me most was my fear when my father was coming home. It was like this: when the lift was coming up for a long time – we lived on the fifth floor – that meant that it was coming to the fifth floor, and there were only two flats there. So when I felt that it had passed the fourth floor, I just sat. ... He came in, opened the door terribly noisily. ... My room was just by the front door, and so the first thing he did was open my door to check what I was doing. If he'd said, 'Małgorzata, are you there?', that would have been wonderful – but no, it was what was I doing, what had he caught me at. (Małgorzata, Interview 19)

In relation to his daughter, Rysiek exhibits a fear of losing the object of his love which is characteristic of Holocaust survivors.

His love of his child is exceptionally strong, in fact quite paralysing. The need for reciprocated affection completely choked him, and this is why he was so tense in contacts with his daughter that he could not manage to function normally, to be relaxed. His neurotic approach to Małgorzata built up the spiral of her ambivalent feelings – pity and fear.

This strangled emotional relationship with a child, who is burdened with all the emotional potential of the parents, is described in the literature as one of the possible symptoms of 'survivors' syndrome'. In the language of psychoanalysis, the child is the cathectic object for the parent who has lost all the objects of his love as a result of the war.

Rysiek did not tell Małgorzata about his wartime experiences even though she was very interested in them.

> He didn't like to talk about it – only when I was ill. When I had a high fever, I had a cold, and I asked him to sit down he told me about it, and he enjoyed it. (Małgorzata, Interview 19)

In contrast, Małgorzata's mother, who is not Jewish, and who took part in the Warsaw Uprising, talked a great deal and very willingly about the war. Małgorzata said,

> All through my childhood, I had a complex [because my mother] knows how to tell good stories about herself. I joined the girl guides and dreamed that Grey Ranks[6] would be formed, that war would break out, so that I could show what I was made of ... Mother showed me how it hit her, and I envied her that. (Małgorzata, Interview 19)

The contrast between her parents' wartime experiences was reinforced by the vision (probably not entirely consciously propagated by her mother) of her father as a victim. When she recalled her aversion to eating, and numerous family conflicts about this, Małgorzata said:

> My father eats very fast, and my mother always explained that daddy had had a bowl in Auschwitz and he'd had to eat quickly. ... What kind of explanation is that for a child? He ate quickly, my mother ate quickly, too, without Auschwitz. (Małgorzata, Interview 19)

In this family, the problem of Jewish origins is less generic of conflict than in the previous case examined. Małgorzata was told by her mother that she had a Jewish background. Despite her ambivalent feelings about her father, she identifies with him strongly in her sense of identity. 'I'm of Jewish origin [but] I've learned to treat it exactly as my father does.' She only feels that she is Jewish in situations of danger: 'it matters at times of some kind of pogrom, but when nothing's happening, I don't feel anything special'.

Her background became significant for the first time in 1968:

> They knew about it at school, ... in March Mother stressed that I was in danger. (Małgorzata, Interview 19)

Małgorzata herself did not feel any particular danger. She didn't suffer any unpleasantness apart from the fact that a friend said to her, 'Oh, you shuffle your feet, just like all Jews'. From that time on, for Małgorzata 'Jewishness was linked with shuffling your feet'. It seems to me that, like her father, Małgorzata did not want to stand out, that she had internalized his projection. Rysiek said of her:

> She has inherited the same thing from me – she doesn't want to stand out in the crowd, she likes to fit into the picture, she doesn't want to show originality, she doesn't want to be different. (Rysiek, Interview 11)

In the family pattern that I have described, there are clear analogies with the family of success that Danieli has written about. The high requirements of their children that are characteristic of these families are evident. 'Because my father loved me, and still loves me, very much, he thinks that I ought to be extra special.' These high demands are linked with an idealization of the beloved dead – a subconscious expectation that the child will replace the lost dear ones, that it will become a symbolic 'reincarnation'. In the case I have described, there may be additional significance in the fact that Małgorzata is physically very similar to her grandmother, Rysiek's mother.

Case three: the Jew who chose

Ala found out that she was Jewish from her mother when she was nine years old and they were going to a performance in the Jewish Theatre. 'We are going there because we're Jews', said her mother. This did not 'make such a big impression' on Ala – she admired her mother and very much wanted to be like her. A

Jewish identity was therefore yet another element which made possible a positive identification with her mother.

Adina did not spend a great deal of time with her children (Ala has an elder sister) – work was more important. In spite of that the children felt loved and accepted, even thought they were brought up to all practical purposes without a father. In Ala's recollections of her childhood, her mother was usually not at home when she was most needed. In one dramatic situation, when a fire broke out, 'at night, of course, mother was on duty, because when anything happened, mother was always on duty'. But that same mother, who came home immediately, went into the burning house to save a cat to which the children were very attached.

Like many Holocaust survivors, Adina played down the needs of her children. 'It's impossible that my daughter should have any difficulties', she said when she heard that something had gone wrong at school. Ala explains this in terms of her wartime experience:

> There was a distance, a perspective, she simply knows a lot more about the world and everything in life has a completely different dimension for her. She takes her own everyday affairs, and even our great tragedies, quite calmly. She says that tragedies like that will pass, while the ones she went through were final. There was always that difference in her. (Ala, Interview 15)

She also expected a great deal from her daughters. Ala felt that her mother expected:

> that I would grow into something different from other children. She expected of me – I remember how she explained it to me – she expected me to choose difficult things to do, that's what she expected of me. And she brought me up to be the kind of person who would keep on trying until I emerged from every situation in life as honestly as possible and [in a way] that was as inconvenient as possible for me. (Ala, Interview 15)

Adina also had imagined scenarios about the future of her children, but her daughter, unlike Małgorzata, described in the previous case study, did not give in to her pressure:

> There was conflict because my mother imagined, when she found out that I had some musical talent, that I would be a musician. And I didn't

want to be, it didn't attract me. She kept a terribly close eye on me ...
but in any event I got my own way: my hand was too small for me to
be a pianist, that was the clinching argument. (Ala, Interview 15)

Her mother did not want to talk about her wartime experiences
until a few years ago she published her memoirs. Her daughters
found out that she had been a doctor in the ghetto from her
friends and acquaintances.

Ala thinks that the war branded her mother irreversibly. This
was discernible sometimes in her behaviour in concrete
situations – for example, she could not sleep, she often woke
up in the night: 'I remember that someone dropped a spoon,
and mother jumped and thought it was a bombardment'. In
everyday life, her wartime experiences revealed themselves for
example in her attitude to eating:

I remember that for me there were terrible problems with eating. ...
When there were rows about it (which was not often, because my
mother didn't know that I threw the cutlets out of the window) – they
weren't about the fact that you were throwing cutlets through the
window, but it was always on the plane of – so many children in the
world are starving, and so on. (Ala, Interview 15)

Other dimensions of wartime experiences were less definable:

Mother did everything that she did with some sort of sub-text.
Afterwards, all her life she was a children's doctor, and so. ... There
was something in her which wasn't to be found in anyone else round
about. Those were her war-time experiences ... I have the impression
that she gave me – psychologically, of course – everything that she
couldn't give to those children who died, what they could never have.
(Ala, Interview 15)

Adina, talking about her work in a children's hospital after the
war, said:

I already had my own child, and I was terribly ashamed in the face of
those children, that my child had parents, had everything. (Adina,
Interview 13)

Ala felt that her mother was different, that her experiences were
'like a deep well underneath everything'. By reason of this
'secret', her loneliness was even more inaccessible, and at the
same time was intriguing and provoked love. Like her mother,
Ala feels lonely: 'I've been lonely since early childhood', she said.

Identifying with her mother was a method of arriving at her 'secret' - and it determined Ala's sense of identity and her choice of what to do in life.

I called Ala 'a Jew from choice' because her father was Polish - and so she could have chosen the Polish or Jewish tradition. Both her parents in fact took part in the Warsaw Uprising, and both of them talked about that.

Ala chose her mother's tradition, together with the suffering and loneliness that it entailed. She said of herself:

> I am a Polish Jew - that is, I am absolutely Polish, my place is in Poland, but all the same, the fate of my family was a bit different from that of Polish families, and that makes me completely different from anyone else. (Ala, Interview 15)

She accepted and came to terms with the fact that she was different - indeed, she really chose to be different (I would say that she chose this with a pride that was filled with bitterness), even though when she was a child she very much wanted to be like everyone else. She talked about her first stay in a *colonie de vacances*:

> I didn't know what was going on, but in the evening all the children knelt down by their beds and said their prayers. I don't know where I got the idea from that I was just the same as them, but from the first evening, when I saw that the other children were doing it, I started to pray along with them. I remember how I worked it so that I didn't start first or finish last - to start somewhere in the middle and end at different points, sometimes before the others, sometimes after. And that's how I prayed, moving my lips, and ending like all the other children by crossing myself. (Ala, Interview 15)

Ala chose the difficult and not particularly glamorous role of being a Polish Jew - and this is not just an empty declaration on her part: she is an actress in the Jewish Theatre. She justified her decision, internalizing (probably subconsciously) her mother's views:

> Who would be a Jew here if we had emigrated - there would be no Jews left in Poland at all ... (Ala, Interview 15)

Ala feels personally burdened by the experiences of the Holocaust, even though she did not live through it herself. This feeling has two dimensions for her. Firstly, it has deepened her loneliness:

> It affects me insofar as I don't know all those people that I would have known if they'd lived. That's what makes me very alone, for I more rarely meet people with whom I can really communicate. (Ala, Interview 15)

The second dimension of Holocaust experience results from identification with her mother, and with the strong emotions that Ala felt when she read her book:

> ... I got into mother's *Memoirs*, I got into it so deeply that I sometimes simply ... sometimes feel as though I'd been through the same thing myself. That's all that I know about it psychologically. (Ala, Interview 15)

Like her mother, Ala has not had a successful personal life. She is bringing up her child as a single parent (or, rather, together with her mother, with whom she lives). This is very interesting, since both she herself and her mother were brought up without fathers. This is therefore the third generation of women who have brought up children alone, while at the same time treating their professional work very seriously (Adina's mother, Ala's grandmother, was the headmistress of a grammar school). Ala is bitter:

> My mother taught me that every person is the author of his own fate, but I don't now entirely believe that. It doesn't apply to me. Nothing ever works out quite as I would want it to. (Ala, Interview 15)

Identification with her mother led her, in my view, to depression, a sense of existential loneliness – for those who might have been her friends are not alive, and indeed were never born. In a certain sense, Ala, like her mother, is a victim of the Holocaust – she is a brave, single, Jewish mother who still hopes that she will meet in life 'some really great and true love. Deeply mutual love and partnership and friendship.'

Notes

1. Most of this information was gathered on the basis of (mainly) American research carried out among survivors living in the USA – a fact which I consider exceptionally important.
2. For example in *Dzieci i Wychowanie* (*Children and Upbringing*), 1947, nr. 11; *Zdrowie Psychiczne* (*Psychic Health*), 1948, nr. 2-4, 1965, nr. 1; *Rocznik Psychiatryczny* (*Psychiatric Annual*) 1949, nr. 1; *Psychologia Wychowawcza* (*Educational Psychology*), 1949, nr. 2-3.

3. For example, *Kurier Codzienny* (*Daily Courier*), 1952, nr. 22; *Za Wolność i Lud* (*For Freedom and the People*), 1964, nr. 5; *Życie Warszawy* (*Warsaw Life*), 1964, nr. 71; *Trybuna Ludu* (*People's Tribune*), 1965, nr. 155.
4. Quoted from Frankl (1984, p. 14).
5. For example, there is no real equivalent in English of 'szmalcownik', greasy-palmer, and the word is often translated as 'blackmailer', which is not exactly the same. (Editor's note: wartime parlance distinguished, not always consistently, between the *szmalcownik* and the *szantażysta* (blackmailer): the former accosted his victims on the street and might be likened to an ordinary mugger, using the threat of denunciation rather than a pistol as his weapon. The latter, much more dangerous, ferreted out Jews in their hiding-places and demanded everything they had. In English writing on the subject, the Polish word *szmalcownik* has generally been adopted for both.)
6. 'Szare Szeregi', the name given to the underground wartime Boy Scout movement, which worked together with the Armia Krajowa (Home Army).

5

The Legacy of the Holocaust

> By my death, I wish to express the strongest possible protest against the passivity with which the world watches and allows the annihilation of the Jewish people.
>
> Szmul Zygielbojm's suicide letter, 11 May 1942

Chapter 4 considered the consequences of the Holocaust for the individual survivor; the present chapter will deal with its social and cultural consequences. I am aware that this is an enormous subject, which has been dealt with by historians, philosophers, writers and poets. Nor is it the main theme of my book, since I have been mainly interested in individuals. So I will limit myself to presenting the social consequences of the Holocaust as the people I interviewed saw them, and to offering certain of my own reflections at the end of the chapter.

How to tell people about it

> Everything that I say is a kind of ... echo of what I would like to say ... I can't formulate ...
>
> from a conversation with Krystyna Żywulska

> It is not clear whether those who did not themselves take part in it, and remained unaffected, ought to touch upon that suffering.
>
> George Steiner, *Language and Silence*

The experience of the Holocaust – personal, private and intimate – is exceptionally difficult to tell others about, if it is possible at all. Some survivors believe that it cannot be done: they do not want to talk about it, they do not write memoirs. Their experience will remain inaccessible to us.

Others talk about it, though they believe that no one who did not live through it will be able to understand them.

I don't know how someone reacts who has heard about it, but didn't live through it. After all none of us can enter into another person. I think that you can't describe it so that someone else can feel what it was like. ... How can you tell anyone what hunger is? Just as you can't tell anyone about physical pain. I can tell you that it's true what they say, that you can go numb from fear, that you have icy feet, but all the same you yourself don't feel it. (Adina, Interview 13)

The worst feeling that I know was that helpless rebellion that you felt then. You felt no pity; either for yourself or for others who were also being persecuted. Those feelings, those experiences can't be communicated: who could understand? It's even difficult to tell people who bathe every day what lice were like, when you lived for months in filth and slept on the ground. Of course, you have to recall, warn people, but you can't communicate it. (Edward, Interview 26)

Those who do not consider it completely hopeless, and decide to talk about their experience, are faced with the problem of how to get it across. Most of the people I interviewed agreed that it is basically possible only through literature and art.

Fortunately, there are great intellectuals, scholars, artists. Above all, history, literature and the arts in general – they immortalize the truth. Thanks to them the memory will last for ever. (Helena, Interview 30)

Yes, you can communicate everything, and it will be communicated. Some good writer who can manage to look at it from an impersonal perspective will be able to communicate it. It's still a bit too close, too little time has passed; for the time being everything is still locked in a tragic-dramatic circle. I believe that you want to understand it all. But to understand does not mean to know all the details. To understand means – it seems to me – to place it in some rational framework. And you can't do that in categories of individual experience, or in categories of the absolute. Maybe in historical categories. ... (Ryszard, Interview 34)

Some of the people that I interviewed believed that more than art was needed to make their survival comprehensible to the people they addressed. It was necessary for individual experience to be de-individualized, generalized, written into the metaphor of the human condition:

Maybe, perhaps you can communicate it, but on condition that you strip it of everything exotic. It has to be communicated as a human experience, not a Jewish one. What happened was a matter between human beings. (Irena, Interview 28)

The survivors' memories of the Holocaust, their attitudes to their own experiences, and the emotions that went with them have changed with the passage of time. Survivors who avoided talking about their experiences immediately after the war often began, years later – at peace with themselves – to write their memoirs or to talk. One of the men I interviewed spoke as follows about the dynamics of memory and the role of time:

You're in a hurry. You think that memory was strongest after the Holocaust and that later on it all started to fade and will go on fading. While in fact it's like a sine wave: at first it's an authentic, direct memory, untouched by the passage of time; then there's a period when you elevate the enormity of the genocide, extermination, above everything else that's ever happened in history; next there's a tendency to relativize, to reduce the dimensions and significance of the Holocaust, or even to deny that it happened. And by then it's a different memory, which helps you to understand how it could have happened. It's time then for symposia, publishing memoirs and first-hand accounts. But we'll still need to wait a bit before – in the second or third generation – the fine arts join the academic studies and essays on the Holocaust. It's only then that the most shocking research results, the most painful interpretations, the most powerful ideas, will get a chance to exert an effective influence on the imagination, to stretch the bounds of awareness, to mobilize active human involvement, when they get through to the guts. Sensitivity to the statistical expression of the enormity of the crime and the martyrdom of the time of the Holocaust gradually declines, is blunted. The guts are for a time stuffed with figures, they can't digest analyses. The food they want is eyewitness accounts. Finally the time comes for reliving the themes of the Holocaust through the art of the word and the visual image: through novels, plays, films, epics. Sensitivity – and memory – revive more strongly and permanently, take on a different shape, through fictional and epic depictions of the fate of individuals, groups and communities in prose, poetry and drama. This already began a long time ago, but it it will probably develop fully when a new devil appears in the world and man will be afraid and ashamed again. (Jerzy, Interview 35)

Perhaps the difficulties in communicating the experience of the Holocaust also stem to a certain extent from the fact that people are used to stories with morals.

> The end of all stories, irrespective of whether they are fairy tales or descriptions of certain events, usually have a moral, a point, a lesson, which is why the story was told and which is to be communicated to the audience, which is designed to stimulate the audience to thought. A moral of this kind only achieves its intended goal if the story, event, recounted has a beginning and an end: it is only then that you can comprehend it and evaluate it. (Schwartz 1983)

I discussed in Chapter 4 – when formulating reservations about the neglect of cultural and linguistic differences in research into Holocaust survivors – problems connected with the language of communication. Joachim Schwartz agrees with Martin Walser whom I quoted then, that it is impossible to communicate the history of the Holocaust, because the history told by the perpetrators is entirely different from that told by the victims. There are two separate, entirely different histories of the Holocaust, two different memories. The memory of the perpetrators explains, justifies, pushes aside guilt, and classifies it in the framework of primary dependencies. The memory of the victims, 'of the dead and of those who survived, is a frightened memory, helpless, screaming, accusing, which finds no justification, explanation or sense' (Schwartz, 1983).

For us here in Poland, it is clear that there is a third history and a third memory of the Holocaust: the history and memory of witnesses. Our neutral memory is a consequence of the history of our indifference.

Why they did not want to tell

> When Giordano
> Stepped onto the scaffold,
> He could not find in a human tongue
> Any one phrase
> To use to bid farewell to mankind,
> That mankind that would stay behind.
>
> Czesław Miłosz, *Campo di Fiori*

Let us now consider for a moment the motivations of people who did not want to talk about their wartime experiences. Apparently, this was directly linked with the psychological consequences of those experiences, with the difficult process of returning to normality, and with the loneliness of the survivors. It would seem that there are two basic reasons for their reluctance to talk. The first is a desire to escape from the trauma of remembering. I wrote about this when I described the desire to get back to normality as one of the reasons for staying in Poland. That need to get life back to normal as soon as possible did not of course apply only to those who stayed in Poland. All over the world immediately after the war the survivors wanted above all to live, build, set up families, and escape from their terrible memories. As one of the men I interviewed put it:

> I think I simply closed – perhaps subconsciously – the door to the past behind me. In a way it was a sort of defence mechanism. And later on, I couldn't open it again. It's another matter that I didn't particularly try to. I avoided that kind of conversation, and for many years I didn't talk about it at all. (Marek, Interview 37)

> Immediately after the war, I couldn't talk about it at all, or write about it – it would have seemed like flaunting your own and other people's suffering. I listened to other people; I began to make comparisons. You can't and shouldn't measure unhappiness … (Helena, Interview 30)

For many survivors, the past is an enormous burden. Memory is a cause of suffering. They often therefore try to escape from memories, to forget, push away, ignore or deny their own experiences.

Primo Levi links the reluctance to talk with the survivors' sense of guilt, which stems from their passivity and inability to act, and which appeared when they returned to 'normal' life.

> It was that same shame that we knew so well; the shame that came over us after the selection, and every time when we saw or experienced contempt; a shame unknown to the Germans, a shame felt by someone confronted with a crime committed by others. You felt shame then because of your own existence, because things had been irrevocably brought into the world which had nothing to do with your will, or you were too weak, or incapable of making the appropriate defence. (Levi 1966, pp. 14-15)

The shame of the prisoners, as Levi writes, could be revealed only after the liberation, when there was the possibility of reflection. They then became aware that they had not done anything, or had not done enough, to oppose the system. They began to imagine that it would have been possible for an uprising to break out in the camp, if they had worked together. They knew of cases of resistance in the camps and they now began to wonder why they had not acted in the same way. Almost all of them felt guilty that they had not helped others, when there was always someone alongside in a worse situation than their own. In the camps, however, there had been no time, or patience, or strength even to listen to others; the pre-condition for survival had been to think exclusively of yourself. Many of the former prisoners, aware that the best and bravest had died, felt that they were not true witnesses. Those who had experienced the most, who had touched the bottom, who had – in Levi's phrase – seen the Gorgon, did not return.

For the majority of prisoners, according to Levi, the hour of liberation had brought neither joy nor rejoicing. It brought only a tragic reminder of destruction, slavery and suffering. When they became human beings again, human cares and responsibility returned, with sorrow at the loss of friends or family, universal suffering everywhere in sight, their own exhaustion, which seemed terminal. As they emerged from the darkness, some suffered because of a returning awareness of their own humiliation. It was not because of their own will, cowardice or guilt that they had lived like animals for months or years, with days filled from dawn to dusk with hunger, fatigue, cold and fear, when there had been no time for reflection, thought or emotion. They had put up with dirt, mess and poverty more easily and with less suffering than would have been the case in normal life, because their moral framework had changed. In any event, everyone stole, in the kitchens, in the factories, in the camp, and whatever else was the case, it was still stealing. Some fell so low that they even stole bread from their fellow prisoners. They not only forgot their country and their culture, but also their families, their past and their future, because like animals they were imprisoned in the moment of the present (Levi 1989).

Being aware of one's own humiliation, awareness of passive participation in such enormous crimes, recovering the capacity for reflection and the unbearable pain of one's own memories were, Levi thinks, the cause of frequent suicides among former prisoners in the camps. Was it for these same reasons that he himself committed suicide in 1987, leaving as a testament his last book, *The Drowned and the Saved*?

An unwillingness to go back to the past is linked with the psychological consequences of wartime experiences which were described in the previous chapter. Dreams, repeated nightmares, fear, could all effectively block out both memory and the desire to share experiences. One of the men I interviewed said:

> I didn't like to talk about the war because until '61 I dreamed about the war every day. Every day I was running away, every day I was chasing somebody, I was in some kind of trouble. I'd graduated, I'd written a doctorate, I had a wife and children – and the war was still going on. I couldn't free myself from it – I had the longest war in the world. Wasn't it enough that I was dreaming about it – was I supposed to talk about it as well? It was only in '61 when I went to England that the war came to an end there. (Ryszard, Interview 34)

> [Do you have dreams?]

> Yes, I had a dream yesterday. ... Always that they're chasing me, that they're chasing me, that I'm standing on the edge of a cliff, that there's one behind me with a rifle, that in a minute I'll fall; luckily I wake up. Fear, fright ... dreams ... (from a conversation with Krystyna Żywulska)

It is entirely understandable that people who experience their wartime sufferings so clearly in their dreams are not inclined to talk about them in the light of day.

Another reason for unwillingness to talk about wartime experiences was fear of not being understood by the people around you. Many people who survived the camps or the ghetto did not for years want to talk about it; they chose silence, perhaps as a way of returning to the 'normal' world, as a way of coping with their own experience which was impossible to communicate to others. Jorge Semprun has written about silence as a reaction to camp experiences:

> Replying automatically to all those stupid questions – 'Were you hungry? Were you cold? Were you unhappy?' – I decided that I would not say any more about that journey [experience of a camp – B. E.],

310

that I would never again let a situation occur when I had to reply to questions concerning that journey. Admittedly, I was aware that this would not be possible for ever. But at least a long period of silence, years of silence – dear God, that was the only way somehow to sort it all out. Perhaps later, when nobody was talking about those journeys any more, then I would perhaps speak up. (Semprun 1964, pp. 111-12)

The people I interviewed also felt that the questions addressed to them were inappropriate:

I have never been very willing to talk about it. And people always insisted: 'Tell us what it was like in the ghetto', 'What was it like when you were in hiding?' And I usually replied, 'Well, it wasn't great'. When it was anything but great. But there it was, I can't stand harping on martyrdom, and I find some things intimate, in the sense that I feel a deep privacy about them. And altogether it's as though there's a customs officer standing over what I want to say, and warning me, 'Oh no, that's smuggling, you say one thing publicly and you're hiding something much more valuable'. (Jerzy, Interview 35)

They asked me about it, but I didn't want to talk about it, I don't like that period. When you talk about it, you usually talk rubbish. Always some stupid, unimportant detail takes first place, and that's turned into something. (Ryszard, Interview 34)

Clearly, the questions put to survivors were not the right ones, since some of them decided not to talk about it at all. We must come back here to the question of cultural differences resulting from wartime experiences. It would seem that things were different in Poland from the West: people were not asked about what they went through during the war because everyone had his own experiences, or picture of those experiences. Memory of the concentration camps is a cultural memory in Poland: knowledge about them is general. The need to rebuild the country, and individual, personal life, did not favour remembering the nightmares of war. One of the women I interviewed said:

In 1945, I intended to tell everything about it, to describe it. No one wanted to do that. Our ghetto and camp group tried to find support and help from the authorities in Łódź for putting up a monument to the murdered Łódź Jews. I don't know, I don't think there's a monument to the present day, and soon nobody will know that there were ever any Jews living in Łódź. And after all, they were Polish Jews – workers, poets, writers – they'd lived in Łódź for generations. (Barbara, Interview 10)

Memory of the concentration camps is part of the canon of Polish culture, but this is not true of memory of the ghetto. This absence of experiences of the ghetto from collective memory encouraged the fears of the survivors that their experiences would not be understood. Their wounds were often too deep for them to begin to compete with the Poles about who had suffered most. Rivalry about who had most victims would be out of place here. The unfortunate model of rivalry in martyrology, the politicizing of the wartime suffering of the Polish people, did not foster attempts to understand the experiences of the ghetto. One of the men I interviewed talked about the elements of rivalry about the level of sacrifice which was evident in quite contemporary debates in Poland:

> The misunderstanding about the Carmelite convent[1] stemmed from lack of imagination and respect for other people's suffering, for the values that they hold, and failure to understand that values are also in competition with each other. This leads into a trap in which the victims fight among themselves rather than with the enemy. The strength of intolerance is still absolutely enormous in the world. (Jerzy, Interview 35)

Fear of not being understood may be a fear of neglecting and depreciating wartime experiences. Krystyna Żywulska talked about her visit to Auschwitz after the war. She took her husband and mother to show them the place where she was imprisoned for more than a year:

> I decided that I would show them. ... And we went as far as Brzezinka.[2] I was almost in a fever, I showed them – this is where that little white building was, this is where so-and-so was, that's where something else was. My mother was looking at me strangely, and at a certain point my husband said, 'My dear, there's only grass here. It all exists only inside your head – there's nothing here'. And then I thought, that's right, what have I come here for. ... There was only grass there, there was some kind of museum story for tourists. ... That sickened me, day trippers with packets of sandwiches. ... (from a conversation with Krystyna Żywulska)

Fear of not being understood can take the form of fear of judgement of one's behaviour and attitudes during the war by people who did not know the conditions of those times. Many survivors are greatly afraid of passing judgement – something that is inevitable when they talk about it – on people whom they are talking about, events, other people's motivations and behaviour.

> All my resistance stems from the fact that whatever we say about those times, the people involved can't defend themselves. You know, I'm not so terribly concerned about the truth. I would prefer not to tell the truth if it was going to hurt somebody. There's something stupid in you at this point. You simply feel stupid. I survived, so what? Am I supposed to consider myself a hero? They didn't survive, and am I supposed to detract from their memory, for heaven's sake? I'd be the worst kind of swine if I did. In one of the gospels, it's said: set yourself not up to judge. Well, I have no desire to be a judge, and that's one of the reasons that I don't want to talk about it. All of those people – the brave ones and the ones who were a bit less brave – deserve a kind thought. (Ryszard, Interview 34)

The survivors fear that a change in the hierarchy of values, the wartime 'switched off morality', may be completely incomprehensible and unacceptable to those who did not live through the same experience. They are afraid of judgement being passed on their own and other people's behaviour according to the moral categories of peace-time.

Lawrence Langer, an American psychologist who deals with the Holocaust, has noted (1991, p. 80) that the victims inhabit simultaneously two worlds: that world of 'choiceless choice' and the current world of moral judgements about the past. There is tension between these two worlds, it is impossible to reconcile the two realities. Harmony between them is impossible. It is for this reason that some of the survivors live in the past, bury themselves in it and judge today's world in the moral categories of those times. Others, on the contrary, try to break away from the past and its ethical principles. Translating the moral categories of the ghetto into the language of peace-time ethics is both unrealistic and senseless.

Fear of lack of understanding on the part of people around can also take the form of fear of wartime experiences being stereotyped. I think that some survivors do not want to talk about their experiences because they believe that their audience expects of them stories of heroism and adventure. There is a certain canon of talking about the war as an adventure – a canon that has been rejected, it is true, by writers like Borowski, but which is nonetheless the dominant theme. The accounts by people from the ghetto on the whole diverge from this stereotyped vision of the war. Most of them bore no resemblance to any of the 'four tank men'.[3] Perhaps they think that the fact that they were hungry, dirty, were forced into hiding, were afraid, that they did not do any shooting, did not fight against the Germans – that all this is a story not worth telling, is not 'heroic'. They know that to be a victim is not a certification of morality, that the mere fact of survival does not make them heroes and does not always give them a monopoly on right and truth.

There are also people who are unwilling to talk about their wartime experiences because of 'fear of judgement', but in a slightly different sense. I am thinking here of the 'grey area' of those who in some way or other collaborated with the Germans. No one will admit today that he was employed in the Jewish Security Service, or that he was a *Kapo* in a camp. In the same way, no one will admit that during the war he was engaged in greasy palming, or that his prosperity or property was 'inherited' from those who were gassed.

Various forms of unwillingness to talk may also be linked with an inability to forgive. Because you are unable to forgive, you are unable to close the past, it is still a bleeding wound.

[Is it possible to forgive?]

Oh god … whom? I honestly don't know who I'm to forgive. I don't know who to address it to. Neither forgiveness, nor unforgiveness. I didn't have any general revenge apart from that brief time when I saw what they were doing by the crematorium, that's when I wrote that poem, 'March out through the gate'. When they all died, together with the children, everyone. I wrote that poem, a fairly long poem … but those SS men, when there were the trials, they behaved like … some of them couldn't forgive themselves, they beat their breasts, and others went on holding their heads up high – those were their orders! End of story. They're alien to me – what have I got in common with them?

[Is the other side necessary for forgiveness? That someone wanted you to forgive him?]

Probably, it's an individual problem … (from a conversation with Krystyna Żywulska)

The theme of forgiveness is linked with the question of revenge. I shall not discuss this problem in detail, but would like only to make a few comments on the subject. It would have seemed entirely understandable that people who had been through such cruel experiences would have wanted after the war to take revenge on the people responsible for inflicting them. Texts written in the ghetto contain many comments on revenge, and quite often predict a bloody settling of accounts with the Germans. Lejzor Czarnobroda noted in his diary (see Sakowska 1980, pp. 112–13):

> I don't believe in God, but if You do exist, Oh God, be a God of curses, if you exist – be a God of Vengeance for us!
>
> For nothing remains to us but a longing for revenge. Our thoughts, our dreams, our nourishment, our only desire and goal – is revenge. … Teach us to hate. To hate the world which brought degradation, shamed man, destroyed what is held holy, hanged, drew and quartered women and children, ordered mothers and fathers to watch the slaughter of their children, and killed mothers and fathers in front of their children. To hate a world like that should be Your religion, Your truth, You.

In one of the poems that she wrote in Auschwitz, Krystyna Żywulska (1987) predicted a bloody revenge by the victims:

> For after our pain, the mill of humiliations
> must come action, action alone.
> The time will come when for your march
> we will in charges, without charges
> heartlessly butcher, endlessly thrash,
> music – that'll play for you, too.
> You'll howl you've had enough,
> and we'll go on to spite you.
> For so many victims, so much blood
> you will pay, and you alone!
> For so much suffering, so many beatings –
> a knife in your heart and in your brain a bullet!
> For so much pain, so much complaint,
> a dagger in the breast, a bayonet in the neck.

Dreaming of vengeance was the revenge of the helpless. It was a defence of human dignity from total humiliation and collapse of the spirit. The inhabitants of the ghetto believed that their wrong would be revenged, that those who perpetrated the crimes would be punished, that they would not escape justice. They hoped that crime, and in particular a crime of that kind, would have to be punished. They hated the Germans, they wanted them to be defeated, humiliated, they wanted revenge. Many texts from the ghetto are interwoven with a desire for bloody vengeance. Some of the people I interviewed took their revenge after the war, but it was a specific kind of revenge:

> [Did you not want to take revenge after the war?]

> I did take revenge. I was an official of the District Office for Liquidation of Post-German Property in Jelenia Góra. It's true it wasn't for long, because I fought against corruption, for which I was thrown out. But the Germans called me the *Rausschmeiser*, the chucker-out. I wondered whether I'd revenged myself on them sufficiently, probably not. Later I was a witness at trials. (Józef, Interview 36)

The majority of the people I interviewed did not however think about revenge – perhaps it was a question of the passage of time. Krystyna Żywulska, the author of the poem quoted above, said in conversation with me: -

> [In your book about Auschwitz, you wrote a lot about hatred of the Germans. Has that passed?]

> I never had a real hatred of the Germans as a nation. There were only certain times. I knew that it couldn't apply to everyone, women, children – it disgusted me, I thought that it was racism *à rebours*, no. But there were times when you were so loaded with hatred, when you looked at the smoke, the crematoria, but later when you looked at it calmly, you understood that it was stupid.

> [And you didn't want to take revenge after the war?]

> No. No. How far can you go in hatred?

Years later, hatred dies out, pales, loses pace. You cannot feel such a strong emotion over a long period because it is too exhausting psychologically, too much of a drain on your energy. You cannot hate endlessly – that kind of emotion is destructive, not only for those against whom it is directed, but also for the person who feels it.

> I don't feel hatred for the Germans, I don't know how to hate. I despise them. Germans will never be my brothers again. To the

present day, I don't use German soap. I weep at the very memory of the kind of soap they produced. (Barbara, Interview 10)

The desire for revenge perhaps also disappears because the Holocaust survivors know that no revenge can put back the clock and prevent what happened from having happened, cannot bring the dead back to life. It would not therefore bring satisfaction, or even healing. This does not make despair less terrible.

I think that revenge is not possible. Revenge is an abstract concept. Who is to take revenge? How? On whom? Justice, not revenge. But can you speak about justice in this context? After all, they are completely different categories. (Marek, Interview 37)

Hatred pales, even though you cannot forget. But is forgiveness possible? This is a very difficult, individual problem, touching on the wounded spirits of the survivors. You cannot enforce anything here, forgiveness or waiving guilt is a particular process which for some is absolutely inconceivable. One of the men I interviewed talked about these problems:

Is it possible to forgive? Let's consider to what and to whom this should apply. Should it apply just to those who planned, carried out and helped the executioners in the 'Final Solution', or also to those who colluded, or were indifferent, or even jumped on the carousel? Or should it mean refraining from spreading the net of condemnation and hatred to the whole nation, both the people alive in those days and succeeding generations? Well, extending guilt over time and space has ominous traditions. The Jews had personal experience of the effects of this, since after all, the Church called them to account for nearly two thousand years for crucifying Christ, and looked to see what colour your eyes were long after the Holocaust. And so forgiveness has some logical sense, on the one hand as an inner act expressing opposition to revenge, but not giving up condemnation and demanding justice in the name of the law, and on the other hand as an act of human wisdom – dictated by conscience – to prevent guilt being extended 'in time and space'. But emotionally it isn't so simple, because it can happen that when he forgives, a man feels guilty because he no longer feels the hatred which he ought to feel, sees it as a kind of betrayal of those tortured and exterminated, somehow failing to keep faith.

Overlooking something is a synonym for forgiveness, but in my private dictionary, overlooking is something more complex, initially an inner feeling. It doesn't necessarily imply absolution, or forgetting. It can simply express understanding that to be an executioner is also a misfortune, and that an executioner who fully repents has become a different person, for after all, we know of people who have done evil and behaved criminally, but have genuinely examined their consciences, without any advantage to themselves in view, have not blamed other people, or resorted to arguments involving excuses. But continuing with this line of thought wouldn't take us very far. I've tried to forgive, but have I managed to do it? Thirty years passed before I decided to accept an invitation to give a lecture at the University of Giessen. I was supposed to talk about operations on brain tumours, but I prefaced the paper with a chat about the reason why I was inwardly incapable of travelling to Germany. (Jerzy, Interview 35)

Unwillingness to talk about wartime experiences had its own dynamics, it changed with time. Some survivors have never talked about their experiences and still do not want to do so today. Their experience is inaccessible to us. Fortunately, some, who immediately after the war and even for many years afterwards did not want to talk, have later changed their minds.

A return to the past

> My writing is full of crossings-out
> but it's better than silence!
> I correct, I cross out ...
> and still I'm sad
> because – can I cross out Treblinka, Majdanek?
>
> Halina Birenbaum, *Jedźcie do Treblinki*
> (*Ride Ye to Treblinka*)

With the passage of time, the pain of remembering is not so strong and immediate. The healing influence of time, the events of a whole postwar life, work, home, children – soothe the experiences of the past. Years later, recollections are often misty, and merciful memory selects them. Frequently, the survivors, when they look back on themselves with hindsight, cannot understand how they could withstand and survive all those terrible things. One of the men I interviewed said:

We are not today aware of how cruel it was. I lived through it, but now already I don't realize. I don't believe in it all, that it was like that, even though I saw it all myself ... (Władysław, Interview 25)

Victor Frankl (1962, p. 102) saw the role of psychological distance from his own experiences in a similar way. He wrote:

> At any event, for everyone who survived a camp there comes a moment when he looks at himself and simply cannot understand how he could bear it all. Just as the day of freedom came in his life, when everything seemed to be a wonderful dream, so will come the day when everything he experienced in the camp will seem like a bad dream. But the crowning glory of all the experiences of a man who has come home is the wonderful feeling that after everything that he has suffered, he will not have to fear anything in the world again - apart from his God.

Survivors often decide to talk about it when, despite all their efforts, they do not manage to forget. They cannot manage to cut themselves off from the experiences of the past. Many of the people that I interviewed spoke about unsuccessful attempts to forget, about the fact that their memories are too painful and that recalling brings too great suffering. The experiences that they push out of their consciousness appear most often in dreams:

> I defend myself against memories, because later I'm haunted by nightmares. (Ewa, Interview 17)

> My dear, for several decades we didn't open our mouths. What was the point of talking about it all? It didn't help me at all, and it was difficult to listen to someone else. Even so many years later, I don't like to remember, because when I read something, or watch something on television, then I have awful dreams. Who could believe it - after all those years? Even recently, I had a dream - and in the morning I was absolutely good for nothing. I dreamed that I and some other women were condemned to death in Auschwitz and the Germans wanted to kill us with an axe. Death, condemned to death - well, hard luck. But I begged them not to kill us with that axe, because it wouldn't work ... I woke up so sad ... (Barbara, Interview 10)

The survivors, who function in two worlds - one from fifty years ago, and the present day - live, according to Langer, in a permanent conflict of the past and the present. It can happen that the two worlds intermingle: some stimulus can call up an avalanche of connections and related behaviour. This takes place completely involuntarily, independently of human will:

> I was at Stutthof and I saw a strip of torn tallit on a bedstead, and I had
> an attack of fury … I couldn't control myself. Perhaps some kind of
> illness sits inside, inside a person … I don't like talking about it, I'd
> prefer not to remember, but it comes back of its own accord. There
> was a time when I kept on going to see Ford's *Ulica Graniczna*
> (Border Street).[4] I think I saw it fifteen times. I came back from the
> cinema, threw myself on my bed and cried. I couldn't control myself.
> It always wore me out, and still does. Sometimes the film plays itself
> back - during martial law, and especially the street fights and the
> police round-ups, I had the impression that I was back in the ghetto.
> (Edward, Interview 26)

The mixing of these two worlds, the world of the ghetto and the
contemporary world, must be tiring, inconvenient and must
sometimes make it difficult for the survivors to function
normally.

> Times come when I absolutely don't know why at that particular
> moment I go weak and I see Auschwitz. I can't go into a café that has
> some little lamp, high up, some kind of pale light bulb… It has an
> awful effect on me, it stops my breath. I can't understand it at all. Idiot
> - I'm sitting at a table, drinking wine in pleasant company, and
> suddenly I literally begin to choke - and I leave … (from a
> conversation with Krystyna Żywulska)

Despite the painfulness of recollection, which brought a
renewed experience of pain, many survivors decided to talk
about their experiences, or to write memoirs. What was the
catalyst for taking this decision? It would seem that the natural
dynamics of human life was of fundamental significance - the
natural tendency towards the end of life to recall the past, reflect
about oneself, to sum up one's life. Other factors, both internal
and external, also undoubtedly affected the decision to
communicate experiences. Inward factors include the process
of growing older, the need to bear witness, and attaining
psychological distance from one's own experience; external
factors include the publication of other people's memoirs, and
also a specific opportunity, that is, the presence of someone
who asks about their wartime experiences and listens carefully
to their replies.

As a result of these - and certainly many more - factors, we
have seen over the past decade a growth in the publication of
memoirs about the Holocaust. One of the women I interviewed,

who had published memoirs about the occupation forty years after the event, gave me the following reasons for writing them:

> I met with the reaction that because no one is capable of understanding it anyway, in general you ought not to talk about it. I thought the same myself for forty years, and only later understood that it's not true. Firstly, because so little has been said, mistaken stereotypes about the ghetto remain in circulation. Secondly, we can't allow people to forget.

> We have reached the point where we can write. In the first period, there was a profound feeling that nobody was interested, that there wasn't any point in talking about it, what for, and anyway you couldn't talk about it, that's how it seemed to us. Later, we found that we couldn't free ourselves of it, and we came to the point where we could talk or write. The great emotions passed, and we were left with a feeling of being alone with those experiences. We started to talk. (Adina, Interview 13)

Primo Levi (1988, p. 149) thought that people decided to talk about their experiences for a variety of reasons. One was that the war was a central experience in their lives, the most important experience, an event which for good or evil made its mark on their later existence. The second reason for going back to the past was the survivors' awareness that they had witnessed unique events, and that it was their duty to talk about them in order to warn others. The third reason for talking about the war, according to Levi (1988, p. 150), was that 'troubles are good for telling', that it was pleasant to sit in the warm, with food and wine, and remind oneself and others of exhaustion, cold and hunger. You talked then, often exaggerating, like an old soldier, about fear and courage, traps and encounters, defeats and victories. In recounting these things, you differentiated yourself from 'those others', confirmed your own membership of a community and reinforced your prestige.

An important element of my conversations with survivors was also the fact that these were elderly people talking about their youth. After all, accounts of this kind have rules of their own: youth is always a beautiful period, and is made more beautiful in the retelling. But the threat of wartime experiences destroyed any kind of beauty in the accounts of their youth given by the people I interviewed.

How can you talk about that experience, since it is so difficult to communicate? What can you do to make the Holocaust comprehensible to others? Can you transfer such intimate experience from the individual to the general level? Is it possible to make it a part of the common historical and cultural heritage?

The legacy of the Holocaust

> Only the victims, in as far as they are still alive, and those who are on the victims' side, can neither forget Auschwitz, nor manage to live on as though Auschwitz had never happened.

> Martin Walser, *Nasz Oświęcim (Our Auschwitz)*

The Holocaust is one of the most important symbols of the twentieth century. What will that symbol one day mean, what does it mean for us now? What is the legacy of the Holocaust? Have we - the witnesses - drawn any conclusions from these dramatic experiences?

The cultural heritage of the Holocaust is undoubtedly the axiological chaos it has introduced and the metaphysical anxiety felt by some. When we speak of a crisis of culture, we are speaking also, and perhaps primarily, of a certain intellectual and emotional ineptitude in the face of this event.

In reply to the question of whether the Holocaust changed anything in the world, whether it brought a reformation of human souls, the reply has to be, no. This is not so much a pessimistic as a realistic assessment. Human beings, contrary to naive visions and pious hopes, do not in the least learn from their own mistakes, nor do they become constantly better. In spite of the warnings of history and the teachings of many religions, they have not managed to date to construct ways to prevent further wars and genocide. Barely fifty years have passed since these tragic events: and over that period we have been able to observe, and constantly still observe, many mass murders and genocidal wars.

The majority of the people I interviewed thought that the Holocaust would remain in the memory of mankind as an historic event, and that - as with previous cases - people would not learn any lessons from this case of genocide.

> I'm afraid, though, that it will be like with the Inquisition in the middle ages. Do we today worry so very much about the fact that they burnt innocent people at the stake? History has its laws, it's something different from memory – the legend about the Holocaust will remain. Nothing else will remain. (Barbara, Interview 10)

> After a certain number of generations, the Holocaust will anyway become history, pre-history. For us, too, some sort of pogroms in Munich, the Crusades, even the pogroms in Russia are all pre-historic. Some people think that it's time to give up all the remembering, but I think that mankind doesn't have the right to forget. We need to remember, if only to make sure that nothing like it could ever happen again. I think that mankind has to remember, in order to know what human beings are capable of. (Adina, Interview 13)

Awareness that the Holocaust will leave behind only a legend is yet another element in the sufferings of the survivors. It is evidence that their sufferings were pointless. If what they had lived through – the loss of their families, their loved ones, the terrible spiritual, physical and moral wasteland that they experienced – could even to a minimal extent bring about an improvement in the world – then it would be easier for them to accept their own experiences. But they know that their sufferings were useless, that nothing resulted from them, that mankind will remain indifferent. The feeling of the uselessness of the great burden of suffering that fell to their lot is painful for many. But there is also a belief that the time will come when the experience of the Holocaust, lived through and thought over, will change something in man. However, perhaps it is still too early for this.

> History teaches us that experiences of this kind do not die either with the executioners or with the victims, or with the witnesses – which does not, of course mean that there is no need to make haste today if we want to hear their accounts and thoughts. In the end it's the Holocaust that will immortalize Hitler, just as the feast of Purim immortalizes Haman. But it's still far too early for the Holocaust to become the link in the chain of the historical progress of evil that will start a consistent retreat from the terrible things that are recorded in the history of mankind. I repeat: it's much too early – and that's a very optimistic statement. (Jerzy, Interview 35)

The Holocaust was an intimate experience, which can be communicated directly at the individual level, not the collective.

It was an intimate experience in the sense that it destroyed all bonds between human beings: family ties, ties of friendship and community bonds. People basically survived the Holocaust individually, and the survivors do not constitute a community. In the collective memory of society, the Holocaust will always take on a fairly superficial form, and will remain an historical event.

Culture cannot record the Holocaust as part of its code: only the individual can do that. For the manner of reacting to the event is an individual and not a collective choice. It is the individual choice of every human being how consciously and profoundly he will react to the experience of the Holocaust, whether he will choose it as part of his own heritage. Although I believe that the Poles, as the closest witnesses, have certain obligations, I still know that these events cannot be absorbed into Polish culture, and cannot be seen by Polish society as their own. There is however a movement in Polish culture which has tried to assimilate the experiences of the Holocaust - a movement associated with the names of Miłosz, Andrzejewski, Białoszewski, Grynberg, Wojdowski, Krall, Lem, Błoński and others.

A debate, for example, that took place in the columns of *Tygodnik Powszechny* in 1987 provides evidence of how difficult it is to understand and accept these timid attempts to integrate the Holocaust into Polish culture, and also that attitudes to the Holocaust are a question of individual sensitivity and personal choice. It was begun by a fine article by Jan Błoński, 'The Poor Poles Look at the Ghetto', expressing his own sense of moral obligation. Błoński (1987) postulated that 'in our attitude to the Jewish–Polish past, we should stop defending ourselves, justifying ourselves, bargaining, emphasizing what we were unable to do either during the occupation or earlier. We should stop putting the blame on political, social or economic circumstances. We should say first, "Yes, we are guilty".' After this voluntary examination of his conscience, Błoński wrote of Polish–Jewish relations during the war: 'We lost our home, and in that home the occupying power began to kill Jews. Did we help them with solidarity? How many of us decided that it was not our affair? There were also people (I am not talking about ordinary scum) who were silently pleased that Hitler had solved the Jewish "problem" for us. ... We were not even capable of greeting and respecting the survivors – what did it matter that they were embittered, crazed, perhaps troublesome? In a word, instead of bargaining and justifying ourselves, we ought first to think about ourselves, about our own sins or weaknesses. ... We often demand of the Jews (or their friends) a more careful and just judgement of our common history. But we should first admit our own guilt and ask for forgiveness.'

As we might easily imagine, such a bold statement by Błoński began a debate in the columns of *Tygodnik Powszechny* in which moral arguments were confronted by primitive xenophobic statements which belonged to a completely different code of values.

Another intellectual who publicly accepted the Holocaust as part of his spiritual heritage was Jarosław Marek Rymkiewicz. In 1988, he published a book entitled *Umschlagplatz*. Here he declared that 'living all around the only place on the planet where 310,000 people waited for death' (1988, p. 11) constitutes an intellectual and spiritual challenge for the Poles, represents a certain kind of obligation. Rymkiewicz thinks that Polish spirituality and Polish thought have not drawn conclusions from what Poles witnessed during the war, and have not addressed what happened in their country during the last war. All those who believe that the Shoah 'belongs not just to Jewish history, but also to Polish history' should think about this.

Rymkiewicz presents an artist's view of the prewar and wartime life of the Jews. He identifies with the victims to the point of loss of personal identity, to the point of wanting to change places with the little Jewish boy who stands with his hand raised on a famous photograph from the ghetto. In recreating the archaeology of the everyday, he rescues from oblivion minor details, and witnesses to the once-upon-a-time life of hundreds of thousands of people, and the emptiness that they left behind them: existential emptiness in the form of abandoned places and walls, and spiritual emptiness in the sense of some unfulfilled, unaccomplished testimony, obligations, dues. Rymkiewicz contrasts the prewar everyday of ordinary life and ordinary human affairs with war, death, the humiliation of the victims and the indifference of the witnesses, shameful haggling over post-Jewish property and disgraceful greasy palming. What has remained of that world? The

Umschlagplatz has remained – and empty spaces left by the Jews who died, empty spaces in Polish thought and spirituality. The most challenging and true of all the monuments of our times is 'the ramp and railway lines between Dzika and Stawki Streets. The path along which they walked with quilts and pillows stolen from the ghetto. The beach at Świder where people sunbathed, ate ice-cream while not very far away, their neighbours were being killed. The only memorials' (1988, p. 202).

*

Perhaps the Holocaust will remain a symbol of the twentieth century, and the Umschlagplatz a symbol of the Holocaust. But at the moment we are a long way from agreeing unambiguously on the significance of these symbols. The lack of an easily legible sign, a clear symbol, makes the cultural assimilation of the event more difficult. One of the men I interviewed spoke of the need for a clear symbol of this kind, which all could understand:

> Attitudes to the Holocaust contain an element of approach to the sacred. In some senses, it assumes a liturgy, ritual. We should be very careful, because when something is so terribly important, we mustn't allow on the one hand for it to become a routine, or on the other hand for fanaticism to creep in. There should be no place here either for superficiality or for intolerance. Neither a Holocaust Church nor Catechism should be allowed to take shape. The sacrum has to be protected both from bigotry and from indifference hidden behind a façade of apparent commitment. Everything sacred accrues myths, but don't let's allow stereotypes to develop.

> I think there ought to be something that would be a commemoration of the Holocaust. Because lasting memory, memory that lasts for centuries, means being able to remember every day, but not having to. Memorials to the past naturally have a role to play; the passer-by (and after all, the majority are passers-by) can stop by it, or pass on. They take on significance on certain particular days of commemoration. I think that remembering the Holocaust will also become some sort of very sad public day of commemoration, not just a religious or national holiday for Jews, but for the whole world.

> And so the Jewish Holocaust will enter the history, and I hope the guts, of the world. Thinking of religions, the point here is not taking over the Holocaust, not for example its Christianization, but of absorbing its meaning and exceptional nature into Christianity. In

Christianity, the symbol of Jesus is for some the *Pietà*, and for others the Cross. We're still looking for a symbol of the Holocaust. And we're looking for it in the archipelago of signs associated with the Holocaust: Auschwitz and Treblinka, the monument to the Heroes of the Ghetto and the Umschlagplatz - but also Yad Vashem. (Jerzy, Interview 35)

Much time must however pass - assuming that the point will ever in fact come - before the Holocaust can be assimilated into the culture and become part of the experience of society. For the moment, I believe that its heritage is an individual choice, is 'a pang of conscience for those involved'.

In making such a choice, and recording the Holocaust as part of one's own cultural heritage, one needs to consider how to remember the event. How is the Holocaust to be remembered if it is not to become a new moral imperative, a source of intolerance towards people who think differently, or who do not want to remember it? How can you live without annoying other people with your own memory? One of the men I interviewed talked of this:

We should not be vindictive, we should not overburden our memories with a register of the wrongs other people have done us. It's easy if we do that to lose our sense of proportion, and warp our sense of justice. Automatically calling other people to account in the name of your own personally experienced Jewish, human hell, or even in the name of the whole tortured community to which you belong is not a valid strategy. Firstly, it shows a failure to understand that hell is not a high peak, but an extensive area. Someone who was barely touched by the hell, or escaped it altogether, is still not *eo ipso* guilty, although it's a shame that sometimes he suffers from a lack of humility. Attribution of guilt can't take place in an atmosphere of moral terror on the part of the persecuted and their spokesmen; that only confuses the issue. It's like - *toutes proportions gardées* - the hungry accusing the man who has enough to eat, even though the latter hasn't done anything apart from eating enough.

Experiences linked with the Holocaust are an intimate matter. And so is my participation in the Holocaust and its problems. Maybe it's a sin, but I live as though nothing had happened to me. I don't go about waving a list of the persecutions I've experienced. It's true that what I went through at that time - as well as being a doctor - has made me sensitive to human misery, suffering and poverty. But they can't pursue me all the time – neither those things nor the Holocaust. It's important that they're recorded in my life, in my guts and body cells. You can't hang your head about the fact that you've managed to forget about the Holocaust. The memory lives on, it's printed, which doesn't mean that it can be verbalized at any moment. The traces of memory make an impact on your approach, your attitudes and behaviour, on your awareness that you shouldn't take part in creating conditions to bring new miseries, and that finally, you can't remain lukewarm. You need wisdom to adopt those attitudes. The memory of experiences helps you acquire that wisdom. But vindictiveness works against it. You could even say that the art of forgetting, which does not preclude memory, is divine. The ordering of memory consists in the art of remembering and forgetting, on the art of calling up things that are in the archive of the memory, where things that have apparently been forgotten are kept. This can work consciously, sub-consciously or accidentally. You can't live constantly oppressed by memory. That makes it impossible to go ahead, makes it impossible to lead a normal, relatively free life. Dr Rieux says in Camus' *The Plague*, that you can't just live fighting the plague. And he goes to bathe in the river. It's like someone who said that you need to be able to forget in order to play cards or enjoy an ice-cream with a girl. You have to be aware that obsessive remembering leads to fanaticism, and that all fanaticism contains something destructive. Vindictiveness leads to suspiciousness, you become 'investigative' and ask, 'How did it really come about that you survived?' or 'What was it that you really did in the ghetto?' and consider whether you should shake the hand of the person you're asking. (Jerzy, Interview 35)

Assuming that communicating the Holocaust is an individual and not a collective communication, then the question follows of whether knowledge about it will die together with the passing of the last person who survived it? I think so, that a part of the heritage, a certain kind of direct, emotional communication, will die. And at the same time, perhaps only then, when the communication ceases to be direct and becomes indirect, less emotional, more distanced and symbolic – can it be integrated into the culture.

*

At the end, we need to say a few words about the fact that some see a religious legacy in the Holocaust. I do not wish to examine in detail the exceptionally wide-ranging movement in philo-sophical and religious thought dealing with the subject of the significance of the *Shoah*. It is obvious that people have not only sought for the meaning of the Holocaust in the cultural dimension, but also in the religious or metaphysical one. For some this results from a profound conviction that the Holocaust had religious significance; for others, it stemmed from not only intellectual but also metaphysical helplessness in the face of the impossibility of finding any sense in the experience. Both of these standpoints lead to religious associations. The annihilation of the Jews is often compared with the sacrifice of Jesus. One of the men I interviewed spoke of this:

> It is difficult to speak about the meaning of the Holocaust. Well, there is a term connected with the martyrdom of Jesus: Golgotha. You could say that the Holocaust was the Jewish Golgotha. If I were an Armenian, I'd probably say that the slaughter of the Armenians by the Turks was Golgotha. But why, when I'm asked about the meaning of the Holocaust, do I compare the martyrdom of Jesus with that of the Jews? Well, that first Golgotha has a heritage of nearly two thousand years behind it and that heritage is by no means unambiguous. Admittedly, it turned something over in the history of mankind, it was the stimulus, the nucleus of some sort of moral revolution, but after all, it's well known what was done *ad maiorem Dei Christianitatis et doctrinae gloriam*,[5] and how the good has been mixed with evil for nearly twenty centuries. And so I would like to see the Holocaust as a Golgotha which has a less double-edged heritage. Maybe after a time it will prove that such terrible evil was necessary in order to bring about a real moral revolution. But the first half century after the Holocaust does not reinforce the hope that this will happen quickly, if it happens at all. All the new instalments in the serial, 'Contemporary Holocausts' don't make you optimistic, and we have another instalment coming up at the moment: I'm thinking of the drama of the Kurds, being played out in full view of the world. But it seemed that the Holocaust had opened the eyes of the world to a great deal, that it had shown that 'human beings had prepared that fate for human beings', and that varying degrees of civilizational progress only changed the way that extermination was carried out, and nothing more. We already know that nothing in the course of events can guarantee us safety for the future. We are already aware that every one of us may become a victim, but we are understanding too slowly and indistinctly the fact that we can unexpectedly and without noticing also be cast in the drama of life in a role diametrically different from that of victim. (Jerzy, Interview 35)

*

The experience of the Holocaust seems to me to lay an obligation on us all. An obligation which is paid off individually, on the basis of recognizing that particular event in the history of mankind as part of our own heritage. The symbolic, collective culture of the world community does not want to think of the heritage of the Holocaust, does not want to assimilate it and live with the awareness of obligation and guilt. This would be difficult, perhaps entirely impossible, because of all the other crimes committed at every moment at some place in the world. The earth, since it became – mainly thanks to the invention of television – a 'global village', has shrunk so greatly that the average citizen of the world, when he observes our planet filled with unhappiness and injustice, must construct for himself some kind of defence mechanism, since it would be impossible to feel sorry for everyone at once. With the shrinking of the world has come an increase in the distances between people, and a decline in sensitivity to other people's suffering.

I believe, however, that it is only a question of time before the Holocaust is entered in the lexicon of symbols of our culture, and that this will inevitably one day occur.

Notes

1. (Editor's note) A Carmelite convent was established near the Auschwitz *Stammlager* (Auschwitz I) in 1984. This led to protests from the Jewish community and in turn to an acrimonious debate within and outside Poland over the propriety of a Catholic establishment at the camp. In 1991 the convent was removed to a more distant site.
2. Birkenau (Auschwitz II).
3. Heroes of a popular 1960s television series *Four Tank Men and a Dog*, based on a novel by Janusz Przymanowski.
4. (Editor's note) Aleksander Ford's 1948 film about the Warsaw ghetto, considered one of the masterpieces of postwar Polish cinema.
5. To the greater glory of God, Christianity and [Christian] doctrine.

Bibliography

Aleksandrowicz, J. (1983) *Kartki z dziennika doktora Twardego* [*Leaves from the Diary of Dr Twardy*]. Kraków: Wydawnictwo Literackie.

Apfelbaum, E. and Fliederbaum, J. (eds) (1946) *Choroba głodowa: Badania kliniczne nad głodem wykonane w getcie warszawskim w roku 1942* [*Starvation Sickness: Clinical Research into Starvation Carried out in the Warsaw Ghetto in 1942*]. Warsaw: American Joint Distribution Committee.

Arendt, H. (1966) *Eichmann in Jerusalem*, New York: Viking Press.

Arendt, H. (1985) 'Zorganizowana wina i powszechna odpowiedzialność' ['Organized guilt and general responsibility'], *Literatura na Świecie*, vol. 6, no. 39.

Arendt, H. (1987a) *Eichmann w Jerozolimie*, Kraków: Społeczny Instytut Wydawniczy Znak.

Arendt, H. (1987b) 'Personal responsibility under dictatorship', in Król 1987.

Arendt, H. (1989a) *The Origins of Totalitarianism*, London: André Deutsch.

Arendt, H. (1989b) *Korzenie totalitaryzmu*, Warsaw: NOWA.

Baesler, E., and Burgoon, J. (1987) 'Measurement and reliability of nonverbal behaviour', *Journal of Nonverbal Behaviour*, vol. 11, no. 4.

Bar-On, D. (1989) 'Holocaust perpetrators and their children: a paradoxical morality', *Journal of Humanistic Psychology*, vol. 29, no. 4.

Barocas, H. and C. (1973) 'Manifestations of concentration camps: effects of the second generation', *American Journal of Psychiatry*, vol. 130.

Bartoszewski, W. (1982) *1859 dni Warszawy* [*1859 Days in the Life of Warsaw*], Kraków: Znak

Bartoszewski, W. and Lewinówna, Z. 1969. *Righteous among Nations: How Poles Helped the Jews, 1939–1945*, London: Earlscourt Publications Ltd.

Bauman, J. (1982) *Zima o poranku* [Winter in the Morning], Kraków.

Bauman, J. (1986) *Winter in the Morning: A Young Girl's Life in the Warsaw Ghetto and Beyond*, London: Virago.

Bauman, Z. (1989) *Modernity and the Holocaust*, Cambridge: Polity Press.

Bauman, Z. (1991) *Modernity and the Holocaust*, Oxford: Polity Press.

Bauman, Z. (1992) *Nowoczesność i Zagłada*, Warsaw: Biblioteka Kwartalnika Massada.

Bauman, Z. (1993) 'The Holocaust: Fifty Years Later', in Daniel Grinberg (ed.), *The Holocaust Fifty Years After,* Warsaw: Wydawnictwo DiG, pp. 23-33.

Berenstein, T. and Rutkowski A. (1958) 'Liczba ludności żydowskiej i obszar przez nią zamieszkiwany w Warszawie w latach okupacji hitlerowskiej' ('The size of the Jewish population and the area where it lived in Warsaw in the period of the Nazi occupation'), *Biuletyn ŻIH*, no. 26.

Berg, M. (1945) *Warsaw Ghetto: a Diary*, ed. by S.L. Schneiderman, New York: L.B. Fischer; 1983, in Polish, as *Dziennik z getta warszawskiego*, Warsaw: Czytelnik.

Bergmann, M.S. and Jucovy, M.E. (eds) (1982) *Generations of the Holocaust*, New York: Basic.

Berland, M. (1992) *Dni długie jak wieki* [*Days as Long as Ages*], Warsaw: NOWA.

Bettelheim, B. (1979) 'Postface', in Vegh 1979.

Bettelheim, B. (1986) *The Informed Heart,* Harmondsworth: Penguin.

Bettelheim, B. (1990) 'Schizofrenia jako reakcja na sytuacje skrajne' [Schizophrenia as a reaction to extreme situations], *Odra*, no. 9.

Biernacki, P., and Waldorf, D. (1981) 'Snowball sampling', *Sociological Methods and Research*, vol. 10, no. 2.

Blady-Szwajger, A. (1991) *I Remember Nothing More*, New York: Pantheon.

Błoński, J. (1987) 'Biedni Polacy patrzą na getto' ['Poor Poles look at the Ghetto'], *Tygodnik Powszechny*, no. 2.

Błoński, J. 1990. 'The Poor Poles Look at the Ghetto', in Polonsky (1990), pp. 34-58.

Borejsza, J. and Kaszyński, S. (eds) (1981) *Po upadku Trzeciej Rzeszy* [*After the Fall of the Third Reich*], Warsaw.

Borowski, T. (1979) *Wspomnienia, Wiersze, Opowiadania* [*Memoirs, Poems, Stories*], Warsaw: PIW.

Bryskier, H. (1968) 'Żydzi pod swastyką, czyli getto warszawskie' ('Jews under the swastika, or the Warsaw Ghetto'), *Biuletyn ŻIH*, no. 67.

Caillois, R. 1973. *Żywioł i ład* [*Element and Order*]; essays translated from the French by Anna Tatarkiewicz, Warsaw: PIW.

Carmil, D. and Carel, R.S. (1986) 'Emotional distress and satisfaction in life among Holocaust survivors – a community study of survivors and controls', *Psychological Medicine*, no. 16.

Czerniaków, A. (1983) *Dziennik getta warszawskiego* [*A Diary of the Warsaw Ghetto*], Warsaw: PWN.

Czerwiński, M. (1988) *Przyczynki do antropologii współczesności* [*Contributions to the Anthropology of the Contemporary*], Warsaw: PIW.

Czyżewski, M. and Rokuszewska-Pawełek, A. (1989) 'Analiza autobiografii Rudolfa Hoessa' ['An analysis of the autobiography of Rudolf Hoess'], *Kultura i Społeczeństwo*, no. 2.

Danieli, Y. (1982) 'Families and survivors of the Nazi Holocaust: some short- and long-term effects', *Stress and Anxiety*, vol. 8.

Danieli, Y. (1985) 'Odległe następstwa prześladowań hitlerowskich w rodzinach Ocalałych ofiar' ['Long-term effects of Nazi persecution on the families of surviving victims'], *Przegląd Lekarski*, no. 1.

Danieli, Y. (1989) 'Mourning in survivors and children of survivors of the Nazi Holocaust: the role of group and community modalities', in Dietrich and Shabad 1989.

Dashberg, H. (1987) 'Psychological distress of Holocaust survivors and offspring in Israel, forty years later: a review', *Israel Journal of Psychiatry Studies*, vol. 24, no. 4.

De Felice, R. (1972) *Le interpretazioni del fascismo*, Bari: Laterza.

De Felice, R. (1976) *Interpretacja faszyzmu*, Warsaw: Czytelnik.

De Felice, R. (1997) *Interpretations of Fascism*, Cambridge MA: Harvard University Press.

Delumeau, J. (c. 1978) *La peur en Occident, XIVe–XVIIIe siècles: une cite assiègée*, Paris: Fayard.

Delumeau, J. (1986) *Strach w kulturze Zachodu XIV–XVIII w.*, Warsaw: Pax.

Denzin, N. (1990) 'Reinterpretacja metody biograficznej w socjologii: znaczenie a metoda w analizie biograficznej' ['Reinterpretation of the biographical method in sociology: meaning and method in biographical analysis'], in *Metoda biograficzna w socjologii* [*The Biographical Method in Sociology*].

Dietrich, D. and Shabad, P. (eds) (c. 1989) *The Problem of Loss and Mourning: Psychoanalytic Perspectives*, Madison, CT: International Universities Press.

Dimsdale, J. (ed.) (1980) *Survivors, Victims and Perpetrators: Essays on the Nazi Holocaust*, Washington: Hemisphere Pub. Corp.

Dobroszycki, L. (ed.) (1965) *Kronika 1965. Kronika getta łódzkiego* [*The Chronicle of the Łódź Ghetto*), Łódź: Wydawnictwo Łódzkie.

Bibliography

Dobroszycki, L. (1984) *The Chronicle of the Łódź Ghetto 1941–1944* New Haven: Yale University Press.

Eco, U. (1994) *The Name of the Rose,* San Diego: Harcourt Brace.

Eitinger, L. (1980) 'The concentration camp syndrome and its late sequelae', in Dimsdale 1980.

Eliade, M. (1974) *Sacrum, mit, historia. Wybór esejów,* Warsaw: PIW.

Engelking, B. (1988) *Próba systematyzacji teorii wyjaśniających przyczyny antysemityzmu* [*An Attempt to Systematize Theories on the Causes of Antisemitism*], MA thesis, Faculty of Psychology, University of Warsaw, typescript.

Epstein, H. (1979) *Children of the Holocaust: Conversations with Sons and Daughters of Survivors,* New York: Putnam.

Frankl, V. (1962) *Psycholog w obozie koncentracyjnym* [*Ein Psycholog erlebt das Konzentrationslager*], Warsaw: Pax.

Frankl, V. (1984) *Homo patiens,* Warsaw.

Frankl, V. (1985) *Man's Search for Meaning: An Introduction to Logotherapy,* New York: Washington Square Press.

Fuks, M. (1989) *Muzyka ocalona* [*Music Rescued*], Warsaw: Wydawnictwa Radia i Telewizji.

Gampel, Y. (1988) 'Facing war, murder, torture and death in latency', *Psychoanalytic Review,* vol. 75, no. 4.

Grinberg, D. (ed.) (1993) *The Holocaust Fifty Years After: Papers from the conference organized by the Jewish Historical Institute of Warsaw March 29–31 1993,* Warsaw: Wydawnictwo DiG.

Grynberg, M. (ed.) (1988) *Pamiętniki z getta warszawskiego* (Memoirs from the Warsaw Ghetto), Warsaw: Wydawnictwo Naukowe PWN.

Gutman, Y. (1989) *The Jews of Warsaw: Ghetto, Underground, Revolt,* Bloomington IN: Indiana University Press.

Gutman, Y. (1993) *Żydzi warszawscy 1939–1943,* Warsaw.

Hall, E.T. (1966) *The Hidden Dimension,* Garden City NY: Doubleday.

Hall, E.T. (1976) *Ukryty Wymiar,* Warsawa: PIW.

Hilberg, R. (1961) *The Destruction of the European Jews,* Chicago, 3 vols.

Hilberg, R. (1985) *The Destruction of the European Jews,* New York: Holmes & Meier, 3 vols.

Höss, R. (1996) *Death Dealer: The Memoirs of the SS Kommandant at Auschwitz,* ed. by Steven Paskuly, New York: Da Capo Press.

Höss, R. (1989) *Autobiografia Rudolfa Hössa, komendanta obozu Oświęcimskiego* [*The Autobiography of Rudolf Höss, Commandant of the Auschwitz Camp*], Warsaw.

Huberband, S. (1987) *Kiddush Hashem: Jewish Religious Life in Poland During the Holocaust,* New York: Yeshiva University Press.

Ilicki, J. (1988a) *Den Föränderungs identiteten: om identitets förändringar hos den yngre generationen polska judar som invandrade till Sverige under åren 1968–1972: en rapport från forskningsprojektet 'Judisk identitet – förändringar i samband med migration* [*Changes in National Identity among the Younger Generation of Polish Jewish Emigrants to Sweden in 1968–1972: A Report from the Research Project 'Jewish Identity – Changes in Connection with Migration'*], Åbo (Turku): Skallskapet för Judaistik Forskning.

Ilicki, J. (1988b) *Zmiany tożsamości narodowej u młodej generacji polskich Żydów emigrującej do Szwecji w latach 1968-1972* [*Changes in National Identity among the Younger Generation of Polish Jewish Emigrants to Sweden in 1968–1972*], Uppsala University dissertation (typescript).

Jaffe, D.T. (1985) 'Self-renewal: personal transformation following extreme trauma', *Journal of Humanistic Psychology*, 4.

Kahana B., Harel Z., and Kahana E. (1988) *Human Adaptation to Extreme Stress: From the Holocaust to Vietnam*, New York: Plenum.

Kaplan, Ch. A. (1963, 1964) 'Księga życia: dziennik z getta warszawskiego', *Biuletyn ŻIH* vols 45/46 and 50, ed. by A. Rutkowski and A. Wein.

Kaplan, Ch. A. (1999) *Scroll of Agony: The Warsaw Diary of Chaim A. Kaplan*, ed. by A.I. Katsch, Bloomington: Indiana University Press.

Karski, J. (1944) *The Story of a Secret State*, Boston: Houghton Mifflin.

Kav-Venaki, S., and Nadler, A. (undated) 'Does the Survivor Syndrome Survive? A Study of the Second Generation of Holocaust Survivors' (typescript).

Kestenberg, J. (1972) 'Psychoanalytic contributions to the problem of children of survivors from Nazi persecutions', in *Israel Annals of Psychiatry and Related Disciplines*, 10.

Kępiński, A. (1992a) 'KZ-syndrom' ['KZ syndrome'], in Kępiński 1992b.

Kępiński, A. (1992b) *Rytm życia* [*The Rhythm of Life*], Warsaw.

Klein, H. and Last, U. (1983) 'Postawy emocjonalne potomstwa ofiar prześladowań wobec prześladowców hitlerowskich' ['Emotional attitudes of the children of victims towards the Nazi persecutors'], *Przegląd Lekarski*, no. 1.

Krall, H. (1977) *Zdążyć przed Panem Bogiem* [*To Beat God to It*], Kraków: Wydawnictwo Literackie.

Krall, H. (1986) *Shielding the Flame: An Intimate Conversation with Dr Marek Edelman, the Last Surviving Leader of the Warsaw Ghetto Uprising*, New York: Holt.

Kren, G. and Rappaport, L. (1980) *The Holocaust and the Crisis of Human Behavior*, New York. Holmes & Meier.

Król, M. (1987) 'Hannah Arendt', *Dodruk*, no. 1.

Krystal, H. (1968) *Massive Psychic Trauma*, New York: International Universities Press.

Landau, L. (1962) *Kronika lat wojny i okupacji* [*Chronicle of the Years of War and Occupation*], Warsaw: PWN, 3 vols, ed. by Zbigniew Landau and Jerzy Tomaszewski.

Langer, L. (1991) *Holocaust Testimonies: The Ruins of Memory*, New York: Yale University Press.

Last, U. (1989) 'The transgenerational impact of Holocaust trauma: current state of the evidence', *International Journal of Mental Health*, vol. 17, no. 4.

Łazowert, H. (1941) Letter to Roman Kołoniecki, dated 6.IX.1941. Manuscript in Polish Museum of Literature, shelf mark 2235, vol. 2.

Leśniak, R. 1964. ' Zmiany osobowości u byłych więźniów obozu koncentracyjnego Oświęcim-Brzezinka' ['Personality changes in former prisoners of the Auschwitz-Birkenau Concentration Camp'], *Przegląd Lekarski*, no. 1.

Levi, P. (1966) *La Trêve*, Paris.

Levi, P. (1989) *The Drowned and the Saved*, London: Abacus.

Lewandowska, S. (1982) *Polska konspiracyjna prasa informacyjno-polityczna 1939–1945* [*The Polish Underground Informational and Political Press 1939–1945*], Warsaw: Czytelnik.

Lewin, A. (1956) 'Dziennik z getta warszawskiego' (Diary of the Warsaw Ghetto), translated from the Yiddish by Adam Rutkowski, *Biuletyn ŻIH*, 1956, no. 19/20 and n.

Lewin, A. (1989) *A Cup of Tears: A Diary of the Warsaw Ghetto*, London: Fontana/Collins.

Lifton, R. (1980) 'The Concept of the Survivor', in Dimsdale 1980, pp. 117–30.

Lifton, R. (1983) *The Broken Connection*, New York: Simon & Schuster.

Lifton, R. and Olsen, E. (undated) *Ludzki wymiar kataklizmu* [*The Human Dimension of Cataclysm*], typescript.

Lis-Turlejska, M. (1992) 'Psychologiczne następstwa skrajnie streso-wych przeżyć' ['Psychological consequences of extremely stressful experiences'], *Nowiny Psychologiczne*, no. 2.

Marcus, P. and Rosenberg, A. (undated) *The Holocaust Survivors' Faith and Religious Behavior and Some Implications for Treatment* (typescript).

Marrus, M. (1993) *Holocaust: historiografia*, Warsaw: Wiedza Pows-zechna.

Marrus, M. (1989) *The Holocaust in History*, Harmondsworth: Meridian.

Matywiecki, P. (1994) *Kamień graniczny* [*Border Stone*] Warsaw: Latona.

Mead, M. (1978a) *Culture and Commitment: The New Relationships between the Generations in the 1970s*, New York: Columbia University Press.

Mead, M. (1978b) (Polish edition) *Kultura i tożsamość: studium dystansu międzypokoleniowego* [*Culture and Identity: A Study of Intergenerational Distance*], Warsaw: PWN.

Melchior, M. (1990) *Społeczna tożsamość jednostki [w świetle wywiadów z Polakami pochodzenia żydowskiego urodzonymi w latach 1944–1955]* [*Social Identity of Individuals* [*Based on Interviews with Poles of Jewish Descent Born between 1944 and 1955*]], Warsaw: Uniwersytet Warszawski, Instytut Stosowanych Nauk Społecznych.

Mokrzycki, E. (ed.) (1984) *Kryzys i schizma* [*Crisis and Schism*], Warsaw.

Nadler, A. and Ben-Shushan, D. (1989) 'Forty Year Later: Long-term Consequences of Massive Traumatization as Manifested by Holocaust Survivors from the City and the Kibbutz', *Journal of Consulting and Clinical Psychology*, vol. 57, no. 2.

Nathan, T., Eitinger, L. and Winnik H., 'A psychiatric study of survivors of the Nazi Holocaust. A study of hospitalized patients', *Israel Annals of Psychiatry and Related Disciplines*, vol. 2, no. 1.

Ossowska, M. (1966) *Podstawy nauki o moralności* [*The Foundations of Moral Philosophy*], Warsaw.

Ossowski, S. (1967) *Dzieła* [*Collected Works*], Warsaw.

Pawełczyńska, A. (1973) *Wartości a przemoc* [*Values and Violence*], Warsaw.

Perechodnik, C. (1993) *Czy ja jestem mordercą?* [*Am I a Murderer?*], Warsaw: KARTA.

Piper, F. (1992) *Ilu ludzi zginęło w KL Auschwitz?* [*How Many People Died at Auschwitz?*], Oświęcim: Wydawnictwo Państwowego Muzeum w Oświęcimiu.

Polonsky, A. (1990) *My Brother's Keeper? Recent Polish Debates on the Holocaust*, London: Routledge.

Rakoff, V., Sigal J. and Epstein N. (1967) 'Children and families of concentration camp survivors', *Canada Mental Health*, vol. 14.

Ringelblum, E. (1988a) *Kronika getta warszawskiego* [*Chronicle of the Warsaw Ghetto*], ed. by A. Eisenbach, Warsaw: Czytelnik.

Ringelblum, E. (1988b) *Stosunki polsko-żydowskie w czasie drugiej wojny światowej* [*Polish-Jewish Relations during the Second World War*], ed. by A. Eisenbach, Warsaw: Czytelnik.

Rosenman, S., 'Compassion versus contempt toward Holocaust victims. Difficulties in attaining an adaptive identity in an annihilative world', *Israel Journal of Psychiatry and Related Sciences*, vol. 19, no. 1.

Różycki, S. (1967) 'To jest getto' ['That's the Ghetto'], *Biuletyn ŻIH* no. 62.

Russell, A. (1982) 'Late psychosocial consequences of the Holocaust experience on survivor families: the second generation', *Journal of Family Psychiatry*, vol. 3, no. 3.

Rymkiewicz, J. (1988) *Umschlagplatz*, Paris: Institut Littéraire.

Sakowska, R. (1980) 'Archiwum Ringelbluma. Getto warszawskie lipiec 1942-styczeń 1943' ['The Ringelblum Archive. The Warsaw Ghetto, July 1942-January 1943'], Warsaw.

Sakowska, R. (1986) *Dwa etapy* [*Two Stages*], Wrocław: Zakład Narodowy im. Ossolińskich.

Sakowska, R. (1993) *Ludzie z dzielnicy zamkniętej* [*People from the Closed District*], Warsaw: Wydawnictwo Naukowe PWN.

Schütz A. (1984) 'Potoczna i naukowa interpretacja ludzkiego działania' ['Popular and scientific interpretations of human behaviour'] in Mokrzycki 1984.

Schütz A. (1985) 'Światły obywatel' ['The enlightened citizen'], *Literatura na świecie*, no. 2.

Schwartz, J. (1983) 'Przeżyłem Oświęcim, jak żyć teraz - kilka aspektów moralnych historiografii' ['I survived Auschwitz: how should I live now - a few moral aspects of historiography']. Paper given at the international seminar *Nazi Genocide in Poland and Europe 1939-1945* held in Warsaw, 14-17 April 1983.

Schwartz Lee, B. (1988) 'Holocaust survivors and internal strengths', *Journal of Humanistic Psychology*, vol. 28, no. 1.

Selye H. (1977) *Stres okiełznany* [*Stress Controlled*].

Semprun, J. (1964) *Le grand voyage*; Polish edition: *Wielka Podróż*, Warsaw: PIW.

Sereny, G. (1974) *Into that Darkness: An Examination of Conscience*, New York.

Sereny, G. (1994) *Into that Darkness: An Examination of Conscience*, London: Oberon.

Severino, S. (1986) 'Use of a Holocaust fantasy for the consolidation of identity', *Journal of the American Academy of Psychoanalysis*, vol. 14.

Shanan, J. 1989. 'Surviving the survivors: late personality development of Jewish Holocaust survivors', *International Journal of Mental Health*, vol. 17, no. 4.

Siciński A. (ed.) (1988) *Style życia w miastach polskich [u progu kryzysu]* [*Lifestyles in Polish Towns* [*On the Eve of the Crisis*]], Wrocław: Zakład Narodowy im. Ossolińskich..

Sigal, J. (1982) 'The nature of evidence for intergenerational effects of the Holocaust', in Bergman and Jucovy 1982.

Sigal, J. and Rakoff, V. (1971) 'A pilot study of effects on the second generation', *Canadian Psychiatric Association Journal*, vol. 16.

Solkoff, N. (1981) 'Children of survivors of the Nazi Holocaust: a critical review of the literature', *American Journal of Orthopsychiatry*, vol. 1.

Steinlauf, M. (1993) 'Reflections on the shadow of the Holocaust in post-war Poland', in Grinberg 1993, 61–72.

Strzelecki, J. (1989) *Próby świadectwa* [*Attempts at Witnessing*], Warsaw.

Szajn-Lewin, E. (1989) *W getcie warszawskim* [*In the Warsaw Ghetto*], Poznań: Wydawnictwo a5.

Szarota, T. (1978) *Okupowanej Warszawy dzień powszedni* [*Everyday Life in Occupied Warsaw*], Warsaw: Czytelnik.

Szlengel, W. (1979) *Co czytałem umarłym* [*What I Read to the Dead*], Warsaw: Państwowy Instytut Wydawniczy.

Tarkowska, E. (1987) *Czas w społeczeństwie. Problemy, tradycje, kierunki badań* [*Time in Society. Problems, Traditions, Avenues of Research*], Warsaw.

Thiele-Dohrmann, K. (1980) *Die Psychologie des Klatsches*; Polish edition, *Psychologia plotki* [*The Psychology of Rumour*], Warsaw: PIW.

Totten, S. (undated) *The Literature, Art and Film of the Holocaust* (typescript).

Tuchman, B. (1966) *The Proud Tower: A Portrait of the World before the War 1890–1914*, London: H. Hamilton.

Tuchman, B. (1987) (Polish edition) *Wyniosła wieża*, Warsaw: Czytelnik.

Vegh, C. (1979) *Je ne lui ai pas dit au revoir: les enfants des déportés parlent*, Paris: Gallimard.

Walser, M. (1981) 'Nasz Oświęcim' ['Our Auschwitz'], in Borejsza and Kaszyński 1981.

Werner, A. (1971) *Zwyczajna apokalipsa* [*An Ordinary Apocalypse*], Warsaw: Czytelnik.

Wiesel, E. (1979) *Wind of Auschwitz*, New York.

Wiesenthal, S. (1971) 'Anti-Semitism in Europe', in Zisenwine 1971.

Wiesenthal, S. (1992) *Prawo, nie zemsta* [*Justice not Vengeance*], Warsaw: Czytelnik.

Włodarek J. and Ziołkowski, M. (eds) (1990) *Metoda biograficzna w socjologii* [*The Biographical Method in Sociology*], Warsaw: PWN.

Wyka, K. 1984. *Życie na niby* [*Life by Pretence*], Kraków: Wydawnictwo Literackie.

Zakrzewska, E. (1988) 'Badanie życia codziennego' [Research into everyday life] in *Badanie i działanie [w poszukiwaniu metod organizowania środowiska wychowawczego*] [*Research and Action [In Search of Methods of Organizing the Educational Environment]*], Warsaw.

Żelichower, N. *Archiwum ŻIH*, 301/139.

Zisenwine, D. (ed.) (1971) *Sources of the Holocaust*, New York.

Żywulska, K. (1963) *Pusta woda* [*Empty Water*], Warsaw.

Żywulska, K. (1987) 'Wymarsz w pole' ['March out into the field'] in *Na mojej ziemi był Oświęcim* [*Auschwitz was on my Earth*], Oświęcim.

Index

Interviewees' names are in *italics*.

adaptation to the ghetto 134-6, 139
Adina 32, 57, 71, 100, 105, 109, 112,
115, 127, 154, 207, 219-20, 251,
261, 271, 282,
298-302, 305, 321, 323
Adorno, T.W. 219-20
affiliation, sense of 41
Ala 299-302
Alina 55-7, 135, 161-2, 168, 172,
192, 203-5
American Psychiatric
Association 244-5
Andrzej 217
Anna 31-2, 42, 45, 49, 54, 56, 95-6,
117, 124, 157-8, 202, 205-9, 247,
261-3, 273
'anticipatory compliance' 240
Antisemitic League 225
antisemitism
connection with the
Holocaust 221, 226-7
escape routes from 149
forms of 223-6
institutionalization of 223, 225
Nazi 83, 149, 218
Polish xiii, 33-7, 44, 198
postwar 264, 274-7, 280-3, 290
Apfelbaum, E. 173
Arendt, Hannah 13, 81-4, 129-30,
137-8, 199-200, 218-35 *passim*
armbands worn by Jews 21, 31, 34,
158-9, 176, 191

Armenian genocide 217, 329
Arnold 37-9, 88, 104, 113-14, 119,
142, 169, 177, 196, 206, 217-18,
227, 238-9, 272, 294
Aryan side, the, life for Jews on 23,
30, 43-50, 54-5
Ashkenazim culture xx
assimilation of Jews xiv-xv, 5, 24, 39,
194, 222
Association of Jewish Second World
War Ex-Combatants and War
Victims 4
Auschwitz 58-60, 64, 206, 208, 215,
235, 246, 253, 270, 291, 295, 297,
312, 315, 319, 322
Australia 217
authoritarian personality 219-20,
292

banality of evil 232-3, 248
Barbara 63-4, 169-70, 208, 217, 246,
249, 261, 275, 281, 311, 316-19,
323
Bauman, Janina 32, 135, 181-2
Bauman, Zygmunt 221, 228, 233-5,
239
Beaumarchais, P.-A. 126
begging 166-7, 189
behaviour patterns 47-9, 120
Berg, Mary 88, 96-7, 105, 117-18
Berland, Marian 150-3
Bettelheim, Bruno 244, 248

Białozewski, Miron 2
Białystok ghetto 114, 160–1
Biebow, Hans 38
biographical method of inquiry 7, 256
Birenbaum, Halina 318
Birkenau 59–60
bitterness 262
black market 104, 108, 141, 160
blackmail 52, 105
Blady-Szwajger, Adina 20, 29, 43
Błoński, Jan 15, 324–5
Bonitz, Bernard 252
Borowski, Tadeusz 2, 58–9, 313–14
Braff, Jankiel 236
bread 106–7, 119–20
Breitwieser, *Unterscharführer* 252
bribery 108, 144, 168, 190
Bryskier, Henryk 120, 159–62
Bund, the 141
bystander guilt 251
Bzura, Jurek 130

cafés 183–4
Caillois, Roger xii, xvii, 25
camp autism 254
Camus, Albert 328
cannibalism 111
capitalist society 217
Caritas 170, 197–8
Catholicism 46–9, 170, 194–7
Centnerszwer, M. 172–3, 203
certificates of employment 168, 193, 202–3
children
  care of 127
  of Holocaust survivors 10–11, 244, 286–302
choices, making of 85–6, 120, 130–2, 239–41
Christianity 218, 223–4, 326–9
  Catholicism 46–9, 170, 194–7
circumcision 47
collaboration with the
  Germans 188–90, 240, 266, 276, 314
colonialism 218
Communist Party 141, 170, 180, 217,
  273, 279, 281
community, feeling of 26–7, 41, 72
compensation payments to Holocaust
  survivors 4
concentration camp syndrome 244
concentration camps 23, 30, 58–62
  compared with the ghetto 284–5
  'passive' and 'active' existence
    in 63–4
concerts 181–3
conversions, religious 197–8
Croce, Benedetto 216
Crusades, the 218, 224, 323
cultural differences 195–6, 267, 311
cultural heritage of the
  Holocaust 322–30
cultural identity 286
  Jewish culture and traditions 241,
    286
cultural life in the ghetto 181–6
cultural oppression 85, 98, 120
curfew 20, 180
Czarnobroda, Lejzor 200–1, 207, 315
Czerniaków, Adam 21, 31, 111, 126,
  144, 159, 190, 207
Czerwiński, M. 124
Czyste hospital 174
Czyżewski, Marek 234–5

Danieli, Yael 249, 251, 267, 287,
  289–90, 298
de Toqueville, Alexis 222
death
  anonymity in 137–8, 248
  attitudes to 136
  fear of 245–6, 254
death camps 59, 64–5
decrees, anti-Jewish 21–2, 29, 36, 39,
  84, 140–1, 240
Delumeau, J. 224–5
denunciations 52
Denzin, Norman 7
dependence of Jews on Poles 24
deportations 125, 164, 193, 196,
  200–5
diasporists xiv–xv
Dickinson, Emily xvii–xviii

dignity   111–12, 119, 137, 315
disease   115–16, 254
Długa Street   185
doctors   118–19, 153, 156
documents of identity   46, 49
Dominik, M.   254
dreams   245–6, 310, 319
Dreyfus affair   225–6
dying   70–1, 120–2, 132
dysentery   119

Eco, Umberto   229
Edelman, Marek   27, 120, 127, 251
   see also Marek
Edward   5, 42, 72, 114, 131, 135, 150,
   160–1, 194, 208, 216, 220, 240,
   246–52 *passim*, 260, 262, 270, 272,
   305, 320
Eichmann, Adolf   230–1, 235
Eliade, Mircea   101
emigration of Jews from Poland   3,
   24, 271, 293
enlightened citizens, knowledge
   possessed by   12–13
entertainments   181–3
epidemics   116, 119
Ernest, Stefan   44, 104, 116
establishments of compulsory
   employment   164–6
ethnic separateness of the Jews   224
ethics   123–4, 234
ethno-methodology   12–13
euthanasia   177, 230–2
everyday life, sociology of   12–13
Ewa   30, 63, 206, 246, 249, 275, 282,
   319
expert knowledge   12
extermination of the Jews
   belief in   205–9
   perpetrators of   229–33, 307
   symbolism of   219
extreme experience   244–6, 249, 251

families
   in the ghetto   151, 178–80
   of Holocaust survivors   287–9
   see also children

fascism   216–17, 220, 227
fear   123–4, 128, 148–55 *passim*
   of death   245–6, 254
feast-times   xii, xvii, 25–6
Fischer, Ludwig   21
Fliederbaum, Julian   110–11, 173
food rations   20, 22, 102, 107, 190, 197
   ration cards   107, 114–15, 119–22
forced labour   31, 37, 114, 164, 200
forgiveness   314–18
France, fall of   147
Frank, Hans   199
Frankl, Victor   71, 93, 243, 264–6, 274,
   283, 319
Friedman, Philip   241
friendships   180
Fuswerk, Klima   182

Gazeta Żydowska   140
genocide, capacity for   217, 322
German history   217
German Jews   196
German patriotism   196
Gestapo   60, 67, 129
Ghetto Uprising   68, 86, 120, 150, 288
ghettos
   compared with the camps   284–5
   escape from   43–5
   purpose of   82–3
   sense of safety in   32–6
   see also Białystok ghetto; Łódź
      ghetto; Otwock ghetto; Warsaw
      ghetto
Godlewski, Father   197
Goering, Hermann   145
Goldin, Lejb   97–8, 101–2, 109–10, 113
Golgotha   329
Gomułka, Władysław   293
gossip   142
greasy-palmers   50–3, 67, 159, 314
Grossman, M.   111
guilt, sense of
   of Holocaust survivors   246–9, 272,
      308–9
   of Poles towards Holocaust
      survivors   274–7, 281
   see also 'bystander guilt'

Gutman, Israel   34-5, 91, 102, 161,
   190

Hall, Edward   85, 92
Hartheim   231
Hartl, Albert   231-2
Hassidim   194
hatred, feelings of   227, 315-17
Helena   34, 40-1, 44, 48-9, 52, 55,
   108, 116, 124-6, 136-7, 156-7,
   169, 176, 182, 193-5, 203, 238,
   257, 279, 305, 308
helping Jews, reasons for   52-4
heroism
   concept of   241
   in the ghetto   131-2
Hess, Rudolf *see* Höss, Rudolf
hiding places for Jews   49
Hilberg, Raul   230, 240-1
Hirszfeld, Ludwik   198, 272
Hitler, Adolf   30, 143, 198, 200, 205,
   207, 216, 218, 220, 249, 264, 288,
   323-4
hope   238-9
   in the ghetto   148-51, 155
   loss of   205
hospitals   118-19, 130, 156, 174-5
Höss, Rudolf   215, 229, 234-5
House Committees   180-1
human nature   59, 124, 265
humour   185-6
hunger   101-2, 105-15, 128, 143,
   152-3
hygiene in the ghetto   96

identity, deprivation of   41, 84, 137-9
Ignatius Loyola, St   235
Ilicki, Julian   10
illusion of innocence   62
inconsistencies in Nazi policies   31-3
inconsolable mourning   248-9
indifference to suffering   54, 136,
   139, 254
infallible prophecy, principle of   83
information   140-6
   unofficial   141-2
intelligentsia, Jewish   161-2, 184

interview methodology   7-9
Iraq   232
Irena   31, 46, 51-5, 117, 123, 126-8,
   133, 139, 142, 144, 162-3, 175,
   182-3, 193, 208, 218, 263, 275,
   278-80, 283, 306
Irka   93, 151
Israel   xx, 252, 268
Iza   220, 278

Jaffe, David   256
Jerzy   29, 31, 34, 50, 72, 90, 108, 119,
   121, 126, 130, 133-4, 137, 147-8,
   151-2, 156, 163, 174-5, 192-8
   passim, 202, 247, 259, 264, 279,
   282, 306, 311-12, 317-18, 323,
   327-9
Jewish culture and traditions   241, 286
Jewish Historical Institute   3
Jewish Symphony Orchestra   181-2
Józef   46-7, 60, 66, 252, 258, 316
   see also Niemczyński, Józef
Judenrat, the   90, 107, 118, 127, 140,
   144, 150, 155-66 *passim*, 170, 176,
   186, 197, 202-4, 207, 240
   attitudes towards   126
   employment with   189-90
   Statistical Office   102, 107

Kant, Immanuel   124
Kaplan, Chaim   xviii, 34-6, 39, 89, 97,
   99, 104, 143
Karski, Jan   91
Kempisty, C.   254
Kępiński, Antoni   253, 265
kiddush hashem   220
Kłodziński, Stanisław   253
knowledge, types of   12
Kociński, Pan   162
Korczak, Janusz   81, 122-3, 156-7,
   169-70, 175-6
Krall, Hanna   127
Kren, George   62
Królewska Street   195
Krupka, Chaim   180
Kurds   232, 329
KZ-syndrome   254, 284

labour camps 59-60, 166, 177, 202
Landau, Ludwik 35, 88
Langer, Lawrence 313, 319
language
 of communication 14-15, 66,
  269-70, 307
 of instruction 176
 of Nazism 139
Lateran Council (1215) 224
lawyers 161
Lazowert, Henryka 138, 166-7
learning, value placed on 171-4
Lec, Stanisław Jerzy 192
Lendvai, Paul 280
Leśniak, R. 254
Levi, Primo 2, 58-9, 66, 86, 112, 255,
 266, 269, 308-10, 321
Levinas, Emmanuel 1-2
Lewin, Abraham 97
Lewin, Szajn 179
Lifton, Robert 245-52 *passim*, 261
Łódź 88, 160, 240, 311
Łódź ghetto 37, 113, 119, 142, 156,
 169-71, 177, 186, 196
loneliness of survivors 259-61, 282,
 308
loudspeaker announcements 140-1,
 176

Małgorzata 295-9
Małkinia 209
Malme, Icchak 131
Malme Street 131
man in the street, the, knowledge
 possessed by 12-13
Mann, Golo 216
Marek 63, 250-1, 259, 273, 275, 308,
 317
 see also Edelman, Marek
Marr, Wilhelm 225
marriage 203, 287, 289-90
Marrus, Michael 232, 240-1
Marszałkowska Street 57
martyrology 2, 27, 282
 rivalry in 71-2, 312
Marysia, Miss 167
mass society 199, 231, 234

Matywiecki, Piotr 189
Mazak, Stanislaw 46
Mead, Margaret 286
medicines 117-19
Melchior, Małgorzata 10
memoirs about the Holocaust,
 publication of 320-1
menstruation 118
mental stupefaction 249-50
Merliska, Mme 149
metaphysical ignorance 258
Milejkowski, Izrael 198
Milosz, Czesław 283, 307
modernity and modernism 228
Mokotowski, Tobiasz 186-7
money, access to 187-8
money-making in the ghetto 188-9
mood of the ghetto 146-8
moral concern perspective 2-3
moral order and rational order 239,
 241
moral philosophy 123
morality in the ghetto 123-31
motherland 221, 262-3, 268, 272-4
Murawa, Jankel 111
'muslims' 110, 185, 250, 254

Nalewki Street 195
names, changing of 278-80
narrative interviews 7, 9
national identity
 Jewish 221-3
 Polish 23
native country 221, 262-3, 268,
 272-4
natural disasters 247-8
Nazism
 causes of 215-20
 language of 139
neighbours 180
news, sources of 140-7
Niederland, W.G. 244
Niemczyński, Józef 46
 see also Józef
normality in the ghetto 132-4,
 137-9, 152
norms 123, 126-8, 136

nouveaux riches 189
Nowolipki Street 90
Nowy Kurjer Warszawski 21

obedience, ideology of 235
Orthodox Jewry 194, 241
Orwid, M. 254
Ossowiecki, Stefan 149
Ossowska, Maria 123
Ossowski, Stanislaw 81, 98-9
Otto, Dr 142
Otwock ghetto 277
overcrowding in the ghetto 91-5,
    115, 147

Paris, fall of 147
passivity of Holocaust victims xvi,
    62, 220, 229, 236-40, 308
patriotism 23, 53, 196
Paulin, Szymon 182
pauperization 166, 189
Pawelczyńska, Anna 62, 134
Penson, Jakub 175
Perechodnik, Calel 187, 191, 236,
    276-7
permits to live 202
Peter of Cluny 224
pharmacies 118
Piłsudski Square 22
Pinkert, Motl 115, 120-1
pogroms 35, 205, 207, 226-9, 274,
    323
polarization of attitudes 28
police force
    actions of 90, 190, 241
    attitudes towards 124-6, 129
    employment in 161
Polish Army First Corps 40
Polish-German Reconciliation
    Foundation 4
Polish Workers' Party 33
political parties 32-3, 141
Polska Partia Robotnicza (PPR) 175
post-camp asthenia 284
post-camp debility syndrome 254
post-figurative culture 286
post-traumatic stress disorder 245

potato peel 113-14
Potworowski, Count 165
PPR (Polska Partia Robotnicza) (Polish
    Workers' Party) 33, 175
pretence, living by 69
prices 102-4
privileges 191
propaganda 32, 140
prostitution 129
proximics 91-2
Przegląd Lekarski 253
psychological attitudes 49, 62, 64
psychologism 258
Puder, Tadeusz 197
Puterman, Samuel 194

quadrangle action 204

racism 225
radios, use of 142
Rappaport, Leon 62
ration cards 107, 114-15, 119-22
rationality 134-5, 233, 239, 241
reading 185
religious affiliation 46-7, 196-8
religious holidays 201
religious significance of the
    Holocaust 328-9
resistance to the Germans xvi, 186,
    280
    see also passivity of Holocaust
        victims
restaurants 183-4
revenge 315-17
Ringelblum, Emanuel 3, 33, 89, 92,
    97, 107, 120-2, 140-1, 144-5, 149,
    183-6, 190, 197-8, 204
Robert 290-4
Rokuszewska-Pawelek, Alicja
    234-5
Różewicz, Tadeusz 146
Różycki, Stanislaw 103-4
Rubinsztajn, Mr 193-4
Rudnicki, Marek 122-3
Rumkowski, Chaim 38-9, 160, 169,
    177, 186, 240
rumour 142-6, 149, 206

Russia
  Jewish emigration to   3
  treatment of Jews in   40
  war with Germany   147-8
Rymkiewicz, Jarosław Marek   15, 325
Ryn, Z.   254
Rysiek   162-5, 172-3, 193, 247,
  278-9, 295-8
Ryszard   27, 32, 41, 88, 99-100, 109,
  112, 127, 131, 136, 139-43, 152,
  168, 173, 179-80, 185-6, 191-2,
  203-4, 216, 227-8, 233, 238, 258,
  263, 272, 281, 305, 310-13

sabotage   170
Sakowska, Ruta   141, 159, 169, 181,
  184
Scheler, Max   258
Schön, Waldemar   90
schools   170-1, 177
Schütz, Alfred   12, 101, 133-5
Schwartz, Joachim   307
Schwartz Lee, Barbara   256-7
selection
  of groups within society   237
  of individuals for
      deportation   200-4
self-help groups   63-4
Selye, Hans   153
Semprun, Jorge   58, 61, 71, 310-11
Sereny, Gitta   231
shame of the prisoner   308-9
shop work   168-9, 193, 202-3
Siciński, A.   85
Sienna Street   197
Simmel, George   1
Smocza Street   238
smuggling   108, 117, 121, 144, 152,
  158, 183, 189
snowball sampling   8
Sobibór   231
social divisions   104-5, 129, 187-95
social engineering   228
social status of Jewish
  communities   225
Society for the Protection of
  Health   156

Solkoff, Norman   255-6
spoken testimony   6-7
Stalin, Joseph   293
Stangl, Franz   231
starvation   101-6, 110-16, 164, 189,
  191
starvation sickness   110-11, 119,
  173
Stawki Street hospital   174
stealing   309
Stefan   44, 56-7, 87, 93, 107, 136,
  142-3, 160-6 *passim*, 180, 184,
  188-9, 202-3, 216, 227, 260
Steiner, George   304
Steinlauf, Michael   276-7
stereotypes   2, 23, 27, 313-14
Stok, Marek   36
stress, stages of   153
  post-traumatic stress disorder
      245
strikes   169-70, 290
Strzelecki, Jan   26-7, 253, 286
Stutthof   320
subjective differences between
  experience of Jews and
  Poles   22-5, 41, 57-8
suicide   112, 254, 304, 310
survival strategies   62-4, 160, 187,
  240
survivors of the Holocaust
  differentiation within   284-5, 290
  geographical locations during the
      war   4-5
  image of   14
  number of   3-4
  reluctance to talk about their
      experiences   308-18
  remaining in Poland after the
      war   271-5, 278, 308
survivors' syndrome   244, 297
symbolic interactionism   12
sympathy   139
Szaniawski, Jerzy   130
Szarota, Tomasz   88, 140, 148-9
Szeryński, Colonel   111, 197
Szlengel, Władysław   42-3, 70, 122,
  178, 236

Sznapman, Stanislaw   35, 147, 154-5
Szwizgold, D.   111
Szymborska, Wisława   278
Szymusik, A.   254

telephone services   31-2
theatres   181
Themerson, Stefan   182
Thiele-Dohrmann, Klaus   142, 145
time, sense of   25-6, 67-8, 97-101,
    112-13, 144
Tomasz   51, 281
Toporol society   173
totalitarianism   73, 81, 83-4, 129, 132,
    138, 199-200, 218-19, 226
trade unions   169
traditionalists in the Jewish
    community   xiv-xv
translation, problems of   xii, xvii-xviii
Treblinka   168, 208, 231, 241
tuberculosis   116, 119, 264
Tuchman, Barbara   225
Tygodnik Powzechny   324-5
typhus   115-17, 119

Umiastowski, Roman   40
Umschlagplatz, the   208, 325-7
underground newspapers   31, 141-2
undertakers   115, 121, 123, 158-9
unhealthy stabilisation   135
United States   267-8
Urman, Rywka   111

victims, survivors regarded as
    255-9, 267, 287-8, 302
voluntary organizations   164

Walser, Martin   270, 307, 322
Wannsee conference (1942)   30

Warsaw, capitulation of   20
Warsaw ghetto   22, 39, 156-7, 193,
    196, 200-1
    closure of   168, 241
    names of streets in   xviii-xix
    phases in history of   86
    population of   91
    transportations to   88-9
Warsaw Uprising   55-7, 68, 136, 238,
    297, 301
Weber, Max   3
Werner, Andrzej   2
Wiesel, Elie   249
Wilczyńska, Stefa   176
Władysław   53, 57, 100, 207, 220,
    318
Wojdowski, Bogdan   87
work activities   155-70
    forced labour   31, 37, 114, 164, 200
Wyka, Kazimierz   68-71, 123, 162,
    277

Yiddish   176, 194
Yugoslavia   232

Zajdman, Niuta   111
Zakrzewska, E.   12
Zalzwasser, Mr   173
Zamenhof, Ludwik   xix
Żelichower, Natan   94, 140, 150
Zionism   xiv-xv, 141, 149, 194
Znaniecki, Florian   7
Znicz, Michal   182
ŻOB   57
Zygielbojm, Szmul   304
Żywulska, Krystyna   45, 49, 60-1,
    120, 128-9, 152, 155, 179,
    181, 183, 257, 262-3, 278, 304,
    310-16 *passim*, 320